War and Genocide in Cuba, 1895 ★ 1898

War and Genocide

ENVISIONING CUBA

Louis A. Pérez Jr., editor

in Cuba, 1895 ★ 1898

BY JOHN LAWRENCE TONE

THE UNIVERSITY OF NORTH CAROLINA PRESS   Chapel Hill

Set in Quadraat and The Serif types
by G & S Typesetters
The paper in this book meets the guidelines for
permanence and durability of the Committee on
Production Guidelines for Book Longevity of the
Council on Library Resources.

Publication of this book was aided by a grant from
the Program for Cultural Cooperation between Spain's
Ministry of Culture and United States Universities.

Library of Congress Cataloging-in-Publication Data
Tone, John Lawrence.
    War and genocide in Cuba, 1895 –1898 / by John Lawrence
Tone.
        p. cm. — (Envisioning Cuba)
    Includes bibliographical references and index.
    ISBN-13: 978-0-8078-3006-2 (cloth : alk. paper)
    ISBN-10: 0-8078-3006-2 (cloth : alk. paper)
    1. Cuba—History—Revolution, 1895 –1898.
2. Spanish-American War, 1898.   I. Title.   II. Series.
    F1783.T66   2006
    973.8'9—dc22
                                            2005032816

cloth   10   09   08   07   06   5   4   3   2   1

for Sophia Louise Tone

Contents

Illustrations

Preface

I became interested in Cuba as an undergraduate at Columbia University. During the brief thaw in U.S.-Cuban relations under President Jimmy Carter, Manuel Moreno Fraginals came to New York and taught a course on modern Cuban history to students like me eager to get the perspective of an unabashedly Marxist scholar. The lessons Moreno Fraginals imparted never left me. Later, I completed graduate training as a European historian, specializing in modern Spain, but I always retained a fascination for Cuban history. My earlier work on Spain's uprising against Napoleon and on guerrilla warfare during the Spanish War of Independence, combined with my interest in Cuba, suggested the subject treated here: the Cuban War of Independence from Spain.

I encountered more than the usual share of obstacles in researching this book. The Spanish — who were able to keep more meticulous records than the Cuban insurgents — took their archives with them when they evacuated Cuba, so many of the best sources for the history of the Cuban War of Independence are, ironically, in Spain, rather than in Cuba. This is not in itself a disadvantage. However, the main military archive in Spain, the old Servicio Histórico Militar, sent all of the records relating to the Cuban war to be "reorganized" in the early 1990s, and, most inconveniently, they did not become available again until after 1998. This produced unexpected delays in completing my research.

Fortunately, with the help of two young men doing their obligatory military service at the archive in Segovia and using an old handwritten index, I was able to get some work done using wartime hospital records housed in the Segovia military archives. I also conducted forays into libraries and archives in Washington, D.C., Pasadena, Havana, and elsewhere. Finally, late in 1998, the indispensable military documents arrived at the military archive in Madrid, and I was able to see them during two subsequent research trips.

During my research I encountered documents that challenged some of my presuppositions about the war. This is the most exciting thing that can happen to a scholar — at least as far as his scholarship goes. And I quickly realized that the evidence I had uncovered would force me to argue for revisionist interpretations of a number of historical problems, some of them quite sensitive. In particular, I had to rethink my answer to the question: Who defeated Spain?

Usually, scholars adopt one of two quite different answers to this question. Until recently, Americans and Spaniards credited the United States with the victory in 1898, with a nod also to Spanish "decadence" as an underlying cause for Spain's defeat.[1] The role of the Cubans in their own liberation was discounted. However, the more one knows about what the Cuban insurgents did between 1895 and 1898, the more unacceptable this perspective appears. Already challenged in the 1970s by Philip Foner, this mainly American interpretation has given way in recent times to a view that pays much more attention to the "impact of Cuban participation" in the war, so that, as Louis A. Pérez has argued, a "redress" of the historiography has recently been under way.[2]

In contrast, Cubans have taken a very different view of the war. For most Cuban scholars, the insurrection was a juggernaut, the result of the previous emergence of Cuban nationalism, itself the outgrowth of economic development.[3] With the Cuban nation behind them, the insurgents could not lose, even when forced to fight with little more than machetes. They defeated Spain with no need of outside help.[4] There are many problems with this line of reasoning. It is too mechanistic, draining the brilliance and courage of the insurgents of their historical significance. It overstates the "countless thousands of casualties" inflicted by the Cuban insurgents during the war, for, as we shall see, the number of Spanish casualties in combat is both easy to count and quite small. It denies the importance of events in Spain, the weakness of the Spanish army, and even the role of disease, not to mention the role of the Americans.[5]

My research shows that neither side in this debate is entirely correct. For example, the evidence is overwhelming that the Cuban insurgency was in a nearly terminal condition by 1897 and had no chance of victory without outside help. On the other hand, that help did not come only in the form of American intervention. Political events in Spain and other factors undermined Spanish strength from the middle of 1897 onward. This helped to revive the Cuban insurrection. It also led to a series of events that culminated in the U.S. invasion that finally toppled the Spanish regime in Cuba.

This work is revisionist in many other ways as well. I do not see Spain's war effort as particularly bumbling and incompetent, though the Spanish army and navy were certainly in need of serious reform. This finding is in line with recent work that has shown Spain's economy and society to be less "decadent" than we once believed. I reject the notion that the Spanish fought the United States consciously knowing defeat was inevitable, a view that, though it never had much evidence behind it, has always proved strangely seductive to Hispanists. I present a new and more complex interpretation of reconcentration, the policy that forced half a million Cubans into fortified cities and concentration camps. I find that Weyler, the "butcher," did not invent reconcentration in 1896, nor was he alone in enforcing it. Rather, he shared blame with other Spaniards and with the Cuban insurgents themselves for this colossal tragedy.

These arguments will likely generate disagreement and debate. This is all to the good, for it is healthy for people to question received wisdom. This is what an interpretive work of history should do. It is time that Cubanists, historians of "Total War" and genocide, human rights scholars, and the public at large gave more thought to the war in which the concentration camp was invented, Cuba was born, Spain lost its empire, and American gained an overseas empire.

I am grateful to the many archivists and librarians who helped me retrieve documents and even decipher some of them. Several people reviewed and commented upon the manuscript. Louis Pérez Jr. wrote a chapter's worth of careful criticism that I am certain improved the book. Two colleagues at Georgia Tech's School of History, Technology, and Society, Jonathan Schneer and Andrea Tone, read several chapters and provided extensive comments. I profited from conversations with José Alvarez Junco, Ada Ferrer, Geoff Jensen, Edward Malefakis, John Offner, Francisco Pérez Guzmán, Pamela Radcliff, and Carlos Serrano. Charles Grench, my editor at the University of North Carolina Press, deserves an award for patience in shepherding this book through a rather drawn-out publication process. I would also like to thank the Atlanta Seminar on Comparative History and Society for allowing me to present a chapter on reconcentration, and the Society for Spanish and Portuguese Historical Studies for letting me present work on the Spanish navy and the use of the machete. Finally, I wish to thank the Georgia Tech Foundation, which generously funded my research.

1 ★ Eloy Gonzalo and the Disaster of War

In the Plaza de Cascorro, in the heart of old Madrid, stands a statue of Eloy Gonzalo. Most Spaniards today know little about Gonzalo or what he did to deserve a monument, but the generation that lived through the terrible war in Cuba from 1895 to 1898 knew him well enough. He was Spain's great, one might almost say her only, war hero. A common soldier, a man of the people, Gonzalo became in the fall of 1896 the central figure in one of the most celebrated episodes of a war that ended in humiliation for Spain, independence for Cuba, and a new age of global imperialism for the United States.

In 1896 the Spanish army posted Gonzalo to Cascorro, a dirt-poor garrison town in east central Cuba.[1] Cascorro had fewer than 700 inhabitants when Gonzalo saw it, half of its population having decamped between 1875 and 1895. The empty streets and ruinous houses gave the town a haunted quality. Its people behaved like refugees, leaving fields unplanted, not bothering to maintain their homes, and allowing the jungle to gain a purchase upon the town's suburbs.

Eastern Cuba was full of places like Cascorro. The region had spawned a ten-year-long separatist war from 1868 to 1878, in which Cuban guerrillas set out systematically to destroy commercial agriculture, a strategy that produced a ferocious and equally destructive Spanish response. The conflict, known as the Ten Years' War, devastated communities in the provinces of Santiago, Puerto Príncipe, and eastern Santa Clara, where Cascorro was situated. When the war ended, the Spanish government punished Cuba with seventeen years of malign neglect, especially in the rebellious East. By 1895, when a new generation of Cuban patriots declared their separation from Spain, beginning the final phase of the Cuban struggle for national independence, eastern Cuba had become a place of crushing poverty and endemic banditry, an even more perfect hotbed of discontent than it had been in 1868.[2]

During the Ten Years' War, the Spanish had built a fortified line, or trocha, bisecting the island between Júcaro, on the southern coast, and Morón, on the northern. A poor man's Maginot Line in the jungle, the trocha's wire entanglements, trenches, gun emplacements, and blockhouses had been designed to protect the plantations and towns of western Cuba from the insurgents in the East. The barrier had never been perfect: a Cuban force under Máximo Gómez crossed it briefly in 1875 to wreak havoc in eastern Santa Clara. But the trocha

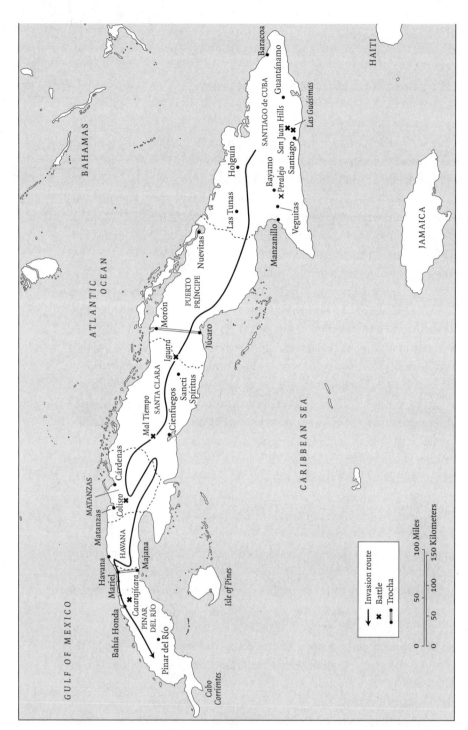

Cuba, 1895–1898

had contributed to the Spanish victory in the Ten Years' War by restricting the Cuban rebels to the underdeveloped eastern half of the island through most of the conflict.

By 1895, however, the trocha was a ruin. The jungle had reclaimed much of the line, and the Spanish scarcely guarded what remained. Along some stretches straw dummies holding sticks pointed stupidly at the jungle and dressed up in the distinctive striped cotton uniforms used by the Spanish provided the only defense. Máximo Gómez, the commander in chief of the Cuban Liberation Army, joked about the trocha with his aides. Cuban guerrillas called obscenely to the trocha's defenders during the night. And Calixto García, the grizzled veteran of the Ten Years' War given direct command of Cuban forces in the sector by Gómez, attacked Spanish positions along the line with impunity in the summer and fall of 1896. In the midst of this ruined countryside dominated by Máximo Gómez, Calixto García, and the men of the Cuban Liberation Army, Cascorro was an isolated Spanish outpost.[3]

The situation was daunting, but the garrison at Cascorro faced worse enemies than the Cuban insurgents: Mosquitoes, lice, fleas, and flies — the vectors for yellow fever, malaria, typhus, typhoid fever, and other diseases — also made the region around Cascorro their home. Indeed, the region so teemed with parasitic life that service in it even without combat constituted a mortal hazard to soldiers. Men fortunate enough to return from duty along the trocha or in one of the eastern garrisons often looked as green as the jungle, as if, through some swampy trick, the vegetation had somehow consumed them from the inside. Thousands of these cadaverous survivors never recovered their health, returning to Spain ruined men.[4]

Despite all of this, Gonzalo accepted his posting to Cascorro with equanimity, for it presented him with a chance to shed a terrible burden of dishonor. Gonzalo's whole life had been a tale of disgrace and betrayal, beginning with the circumstances of his birth. His mother, Luisa García, deposited him at the door of an orphanage hours after bringing him into the world on December 1, 1868. The note she pinned to his clothes read simply: "This boy was born at 6 A.M. He is not baptized, and we pray you will name him Eloy Gonzalo García, legitimate son of Luisa García, unwed resident of Peñafiel." Eleven days later, the orphanage turned baby Eloy over to Braulia Miguel, a woman who had lost her own child but was still lactating. For eleven years, Miguel provided sustenance and a mother's love in exchange for a monthly stipend from the orphanage, but when, by law, the money ran out, her maternal instincts did too, and she promptly kicked Eloy out of her house. In 1879 Eloy Gonzalo became one of the many poor, homeless children living in the teeming streets of Madrid.[5]

For ten years Gonzalo made his own way. Then in 1889 he enlisted in the army, a choice career for young men with no prospects. For a while Gonzalo seemed to have found a new adoptive family in which he could flourish. By July 1894 he apparently felt secure enough to ask his superiors for permission to marry. Then, suddenly, Gonzalo's life came apart. In February 1895 he caught his betrothed having sex with a young lieutenant. This new and double betrayal — by his fiancée and by an officer — was too much. Gonzalo tussled with the lieutenant and threatened to kill him. The officer filed a complaint resulting in a court martial, which found Gonzalo guilty and sentenced him to twelve years in a penitentiary in Valladolid.

Gonzalo had just begun serving time when, in August 1895, the Spanish Congress passed legislation granting clemency to convicts who agreed to fight in Cuba, much as the United States used alternative sentencing rules seventy years later to shunt convicts to the jungles of Vietnam. In November, Gonzalo invoked the new law and asked to be reassigned to Cuba so that he could, in the language he used in his petition to the minister of war, "cleanse himself shedding his blood for the nation." The usually slow government bureaucracy moved quickly to approve Gonzalo's request because the Spanish army needed every man it could get to fight the Cuban insurgents. On November 25, Gonzalo boarded a steamer leaving the port of La Coruña for Havana. There he joined the María Cristina regiment and was assigned the following year to the garrison at Cascorro, a place that seemed calculated to provide Gonzalo with the opportunity to wash away his guilt with blood — his own.

Cascorro was not defensible, and the Spanish army should not have tried to hold it. Spain's supreme commander in Cuba, Captain General Valeriano Weyler, the man the American public came to know later as "the butcher," admitted in his memoirs that Cascorro had no real importance and simply served as an easy target for the Cubans. Eventually, Weyler abandoned the place, along with other lonely and useless posts, but not before Gómez and García laid siege to it beginning on September 22, 1896.[6]

The garrison's prospects at the beginning of the combat seemed hopeless. Against the Liberation Army's 2,000 men, the Spanish had only 170. Ravaged by dysentery, malaria, typhus, yellow fever, and other illnesses, they lacked supplies and ammunition for a long fight and had no artillery to answer the three Cuban 70-millimeter guns. García offered terms of surrender, but the commander of the garrison, Captain Francisco Neila, would not hear of it. The Cubans fired 219 artillery shells upon the three little forts defending Cascorro, scoring several direct hits and killing or wounding twenty-one soldiers. The power and accuracy of the Spanish rifles kept the Cubans at bay, but long-term

prospects were not good, especially after the Cubans took a building situated only 150 feet from the main Spanish fort. Even the Cubans' antiquated Remingtons and Winchesters would be deadly accurate at such close range, so Neila had to improvise a wild plan to save the situation. He asked for a volunteer to penetrate the Cuban line and set fire to the critical building. It was a job tailor-made for a former convict in need of redemption, and Gonzalo stepped forward.

On the evening of October 5, Gonzalo approached the Cuban position alone under cover of darkness carrying a match, a tin of gasoline, and a rifle. He did not expect to live, so he had his comrades tie a long rope around his waist in order to drag his body back to the Spanish lines. As it turned out, Gonzalo set fire to the building and even stayed behind to watch his handiwork, picking off the backlit Cubans with rifle fire as they tried to douse the flames. The Cubans lost their stronghold, and Gonzalo returned unharmed. The garrison, heartened by Gonzalo's success, held out until a Spanish column under General Juan Jiménez Castellanos arrived to force García and the Cubans to lift the siege.[7]

Eloy Gonzalo's actions at Cascorro caused a sensation in Spain. The war in Cuba seemed to produce no battles of any consequence and certainly nothing to celebrate. The Cuban insurgents burned property, blew up trains, and attacked isolated outposts, and the Spanish tried, with almost no success, to hunt them down. In the midst of this lugubrious campaign, Gonzalo's heroism inspired Spaniards. Gonzalo had acted upon the Quixotic ideal of valor in the face of insurmountable odds, and he had survived and completed his mission. If Gonzalo could succeed through sheer bravado, then maybe Spain could as well, preserving Cuba even in the face of international pressure and dogged perseverance by the Cuban revolutionaries. No one seemed to notice or to care that Jiménez Castellanos had come not to reinforce Cascorro but to evacuate it.

Spaniards and Spanish expatriates around the world collected money to send to the "Hero of Cascorro," although it is not clear that any of it reached him. On April 29 a royal order granted him the Silver Cross for Military Merit and a modest lifetime pension. Gonzalo's future seemed reasonably bright. Sadly, Gonzalo had no time to enjoy his celebrity, for, like so many Spanish soldiers in Cuba, he was laid low by disease. On June 19, 1897, he died in bed from the effects of a fever of uncertain diagnosis.

His passing caused hardly a stir back home. The Spanish people had seen too much horror and death to focus on the fate of a single soldier. And the rapid pace of events in 1897 and 1898, capped by Spain's defeat at the hands of the United

Eloy Gonzalo García (left), the "Hero of Cascorro," died from disease, like so many Spanish conscripts. Courtesy Archivo Espasa, Madrid.

States in July 1898, left little time to mourn Gonzalo. Yet Spaniards did not forget Gonzalo completely. After the war ended, the army repatriated his bones, a dignity usually reserved for only the most senior officers. The order stated that "the Nation pays a debt of gratitude and admiration to Eloy Gonzalo García by bringing his remains home, symbolizing the tribute owed to all of the soldiers who gave their lives in this campaign to defend the country." For the families of the tens of thousands of men who perished in Cuba this tribute by proxy provided little comfort, but it had to suffice, for it was the only solace the penurious Spanish government could afford to give them.

On June 16, 1899, all of Madrid turned out for a funeral procession in Gonzalo's honor. Spaniards needed something to rally around as arguably the worst century in the country's history approached its end. The municipal government of Madrid understood the iconic status Gonzalo had already achieved and decided to authorize a monument. The Spanish Congress did its part by declaring the statue of Gonzalo a national landmark so that melted bronze from antique cannons could be donated for the project.

On June 5, 1902, Madrid turned out for the unveiling of the sculpture. A military band played rousing patriotic songs, and the sixteen-year-old Alfonso XIII, play-acting in the dress uniform of a captain general for one of his first official acts as king, gave a speech praising Gonzalo's sacrifice "in the holy defense of national honor."[8] The organizers of the event, with unintended irony, also requested the presence of Valeriano Weyler, the real captain general under whose leadership Gonzalo and so many other Spaniards and Cubans had lost their lives, but it is unclear whether Weyler, then secretary of war, attended the function. Perhaps he had the good taste to absent himself.

The statue dedicated that day still stands in the Plaza de Cascorro, in the center of the Rastro district, home each Sunday to the most remarkable outdoor flea market in the world. Tourists looking for bargains at the Rastro market may catch glimpses of Gonzalo as he stoically presides over the Sunday afternoon commercial chaos. But a trip to the Plaza de Cascorro at a calmer time is well worth the effort in order to contemplate without distractions this fine monument to imperial ruin and useless heroism. For the story of Eloy Gonzalo and the nature of his demise are, in fact, emblematic of the vicious and futile colonial war that Spain fought in Cuba.

The story of Gonzalo and his miserable ending serves as a promise and a warning to readers. The promise is that this account of the war in Cuba will treat the three years of warfare that preceded U.S. intervention in 1898 with the deliberation that is missing from so many histories that jump forward to the brief period of direct American involvement. Cuban insurgents fought a brilliant guerrilla campaign against Spain at the end of the nineteenth century, foreshadowing things to come in the twentieth century, when guerrilla warfare became the characteristic form of armed conflict in many colonized areas of the world. As the age of the horseman drew to a close, the Cubans created one of the best light cavalry forces ever seen. They also experimented with explosive bullets, an innovation often credited to the British military, which used dumdum bullets a few years later in the Boer War. Spain's brutal counterinsurgency was no less remarkable and fraught with tragic lessons and new departures. Most notably, Spain sought to undermine the guerrilla movement through a policy called "reconcentration," the forced relocation of the rural population to fortified cities and towns. As a result of this herding together of civilians into what the Spanish sometimes called "concentration camps," perhaps 170,000 Cubans died, one-tenth of the island's population, a proportion comparable to Russia's losses in World War II.

Historians have presented reconcentration as the evil brainchild of one man, Valeriano Weyler, but in fact it had many architects.[9] Even the Cuban insurgents had a hand in the horror, as we shall see. Cuba's insurgency and Spain's response to it are tales of woe and genocide unparalleled in the contemporary history of the Americas. The arid martial spirit that inspired both sides to sacrifice Cuban civilians in the service of abstract national goals foreshadowed greater atrocities to come in the twentieth century. Yet the story is not familiar to most readers. This is unfortunate because the military events of 1895–98 before the U.S. invasion are in many ways more paradigmatic and more interesting than the "splendid little war" that has received so much scholarly attention. In this book, I hope to rectify some of this imbalance by making clear why the Spanish-Cuban war deserves to be treated more seriously as a key episode in military history.

I also take care to tell the Spanish side of things, because, with few exceptions, histories of the Cuban war downplay Spanish affairs and make scant use of Spanish archives.[10] In much of the historical literature, Spanish actors lack depth and complexity. Spanish officers are monsters, their men, the helpless instruments of a "feudal" monarchy. This sort of caricature is taken farthest in portraits of the so-called butcher, Valeriano Weyler, who is barely recognizable as a human being in some scholarly treatments. Scholars also sometimes paint the Cuban insurgents as one-dimensional: they are heroic, friends to the poor peasants and workers castigated by the Spanish, and never lacking for patriotic zeal and energy. Using fresh sources from Spanish archives — soldiers' letters, telegrams filed away and forgotten, the logbooks of Spanish garrisons, insurgents' diaries, and Cuban correspondence — I will provide a glimpse inside the conflict as it was experienced by Cuban and Spanish soldiers and civilians, and I will try to treat Weyler and other military actors as real people rather than devils, angels, or helpless pawns.

The warning to readers is that they should expect a tragedy. The story of Eloy Gonzalo is a metaphor for the Spanish experience in Cuba. With good cause, Spaniards still refer to the war as "the disaster." Spain transported more than 190,000 men to the island, the largest army ever assembled up to that time to fight a colonial war overseas. Spain's conscripts campaigned from 1895 to 1898 against some 40,000 troops of the Cuban Liberation Army. This was a five-to-one advantage, and it doesn't even take into account several important provisos about the strength of the Cuban armed forces. First, a large proportion of the 40,000 men who signed up with the Liberation Army did so only during the last months of hostilities, after the Spanish declared a unilateral cease-fire in April 1898, thus making patriotism less risky. Second, Cuban soldiers spent more time dispersed in nonmilitary duties than they did fighting, as is always the case in guerrilla wars. As a result, the Liberation Army rarely had more than a few thousand men under arms at any given moment. Finally, the ratio of five to one does not take into account the 60,000 Cubans who served on the Spanish side in various auxiliary capacities.

Despite all of these considerations, the Spanish rarely fought battles in which they enjoyed a numerical advantage. Cuban insurgent leaders knew that there was no profit in openly facing Spanish armies, so they pursued a guerrilla campaign of hit-and-run operations aimed at property, civilians loyal to the colonial regime, and means of communication and transportation. In turn, the Spanish tried to protect loyalists and property by covering as much ground as possible. As a result, Spanish soldiers lived and fought in garrisons, detachments, and small columns, facing Cuban forces that, at any given time and place, might enjoy tactical superiority in numbers and even in firepower, as at Cascorro. Spain's problem in this regard was no different from that of any regime trying to secure territory against a well-organized and externally supplied insurrection that has the sympathy of a significant portion of civilians.

Spanish troops usually fought bravely, even when they were outnumbered. In any event, heavy fighting and losses in battle were rare. Fewer than 4,000 Spanish soldiers died in combat with the insurgents, as illustrated in Table 1, below. However, Spaniards faced another, more dangerous enemy: microbes. According to official figures, 41,288 Spanish servicemen died from dysentery, malaria, pneumonia, typhus, yellow fever, and other diseases in Cuba. Put another way, disease killed 22 percent of the military personnel sent to Cuba, accounting for 93 percent of Spanish fatalities.[11]

TABLE I. Spanish Combat Losses

Rank	Killed	Wounded
General	3	5
Colonel	2	4
Lt. colonel	9	15
Comandante	14	20
Captain	54	131
First lieutenant	46	134
Second lieutenant	97	241
Troops	3,807	10,406
Total	4,032	10,956

Source: "Ejército de Operaciones en Cuba," cable of October 22, 1898, Archivo General Militar de Madrid, Sección Capitanía General de Cuba, leg. 155.

Note: Figures include losses due to combat with American troops.

Disease caused high mortality in all armies before the advent of antibiotics and other medical advances in the twentieth century, but rarely so high as among the Spanish troops posted to Cuba, for reasons that will be discussed later. Losing over a fifth of their army to sickness with no idea how to remedy the problem — short of withdrawal — stupefied Spaniards. And for everyone who died of illness, four more were knocked out of combat by disease for some period of time. Almost no one escaped untouched. Spain's soldiers filled military hospitals to capacity throughout the war, reducing the number of effective troops in Cuba by half, sometimes by considerably more than half. Yellow fever caused especially obscene death agonies, the victims often bleeding from their noses, gums, ears, rectums, and genitals, and vomiting up a mixture of blood and tissue in a mess that looked like wet coffee grounds, all in the midst of delirious screaming that drove physicians mad. One might argue, in fact, that yellow fever, carried by the mosquito *Aëdes aegypti*, together with other diseases, defeated Spain and liberated Cuba. Accordingly, I will give attention to the issue of military sanitation, which was the deadliest problem facing the Spanish army.

Spanish troops suffered in more than just their bodies. Thousands of men returned to Spain wounded in their minds and spirits, the result of having been thrown unprepared into a kind of combat that required them to commit unspeakable acts: mistreating and murdering Cuban captives not granted the status of belligerents, brutally rounding up and relocating civilians, destroying livestock and property, and engaging in all of the other atrocious practices characteristic of modern warfare at its most squalid. In Cuba, Spaniards did and saw terrible things. Yet Spain forgot their physical and spiritual sacrifices, along with their war crimes, with an alacrity as shameful as it was understandable. Anyone able to remember the reception given to American servicemen returning from Vietnam should be able to imagine the silence, opprobrium, and collective amnesia that awaited Spanish veterans who came home after the disaster in Cuba.

The war was even more tragic for the victorious Cubans, who paid an exceedingly high price for their independence. As we shall see, as many as 170,000 civilians died in the war and the economic infrastructure of the country was destroyed. An idea of the scale of the material losses can be conveyed statistically. In the province of Matanzas, 96 percent of farms and 92 percent of sugar mills were destroyed during the war. Surveys of livestock showed that 94 percent of the horses and 97 percent of the cattle had been slaughtered. Not a single chicken or duck remained in the province, according to the same surveys.[12] Sadly, however, after all of this sacrifice, Cubans did not even control their country when the war ended. The Americans did.

Cuban revolutionaries at Baire, in eastern Cuba, proclaimed their country's independence on February 24, 1895, and they fought the Spanish for three and a half years to secure it. However, the Cuban Liberation Army found the wherewithal to face Spanish armies in open combat only on rare occasions. It was one thing to attack a garrison town like Cascorro, quite another to assemble a field army. The Cubans were too few and too poorly equipped for that, and their condition deteriorated over the course of the struggle. They fought courageously, but they could not win the war on their own, despite the conventional Cuban interpretation that claims otherwise.[13] In 1898, the United States intervened in the conflict, and ragged, undermanned units of the Cuban Liberation Army could only participate peripherally in the American naval and military defeat of the Spanish. Americans claimed the victory, and the United States doled out freedom to Cubans in "homeopathic doses" that fell far short of the egalitarian and democratic ideals for which Cubans had fought.[14]

American armed forces quickly learned to despise the Cuban insurgents, once called heroic freedom fighters, now seen as "Negro hordes" and "anarchist incendiaries" who stood in the way of America's civilizing mission. American troops disarmed these swarthy *insurrectos* and even employed for the task some of the very Spanish troops who had just been defeated, men mysteriously transformed for the occasion from barbaric "dons" into bulwarks of civilization. So it was that during the early stages of the American occupation of Cuba, cultural and racial stereotypes about Latinos and blacks reasserted themselves, and the "whiteness" of Spaniards was rediscovered. The United States secured property and returned power to Cuba's white elites, evacuating the island only in 1902, when Washington judged that free-market capitalism under white rule had been secured. The United States retained the port facility at Guantánamo, from which American troops could debouch to meet any new disturbance. And Cubans working under duress from the American occupiers wrote a constitution in which the United States possessed the right to intervene militarily in the island's affairs if anything threatened to overturn property or race relations. In short, Cuba had a republic and a form of quasi-independence, but not a revolution. That had been aborted by American meddling and the collusion of wealthy Cubans, who helped refashion the island into a neocolonial dependency of the United States. This was perhaps the greatest tragedy of all for Cuba.

There was even something about the Cuban war for Americans to regret. The old dream — at least it had been a dream — of anti-imperial republican virtue became a faint memory after 1898, as America emerged from the Spanish war in an expansionist mood. Suddenly, globes showed U.S. territory in Cuba, Puerto Rico, the Philippines, Guam, and other Pacific islands, all gained from Spain by the Treaty of Paris signed on December 10, 1898. Most Americans were proud that they had won a far-flung empire. They hardly gave any thought to the slaughter entailed by the "white man's burden" in the Philippines and elsewhere. Other Americans, a minority, were disturbed by the turn of events. They had naively believed in the Great Republic's mission to perfect its own democratic institutions and set an example for the world. Now they had to watch as that mission was subverted into something less charitable, more profitable, and seemingly permanent: the forced exportation of American values and institutions to the rest of the globe. Imperial America was not their beloved republic. That place, partly imaginary to begin with, had been decisively relegated to the past by the Spanish-American War.

The history of the Cuban war before 1898 is not familiar territory for two reasons. First, military historians like to write about big, glorious battles because they often serve as clear turning points in history, and because they can provide important lessons about human conduct and the evolution of warfare. But the war in Cuba had no great battles, especially before 1898. So scholars, above all in the United States, have tended to treat military events before American intervention in a perfunctory way.[15]

The second reason we have few military histories of the Cuban war is that most scholars tend to view the uprising of 1895 and the defeat of Spain as inevitable outcomes of underlying forces and long-term trends. Their narratives focus on the growth of Cuban nationalism, the close ties that Cuban elites forged with Americans, the weakness of Spain, and the growing economic might of the United States. They examine the way these trends led to Cuban independence, Spanish decline, and America's rise as a great power. This deterministic perspective has, in turn, made the details of the war itself seem unimportant.[16]

I reject both the proposition that great battles are the only proper focus of military history and the notion that the conflict in Cuba was inevitable and its outcome preordained. The details of combat before formal U.S. intervention on April 22, 1898, are as instructive for military history as an account of the battle of the Somme, or, most certainly, the charge of Theodore Roosevelt's Rough Riders. Also, the more one knows about the course of the war from 1895 to 1898, the more it becomes clear that there was nothing inevitable about the success of Cuban national independence or about American intervention and Spanish defeat. The military situation was fluid. The combatants were free to win or lose the war.

It is exceedingly naive, of course, to believe that people are entirely free agents of their own history. We are all hemmed in by a thousand different structures, institutions, and ideologies — our families, our socioeconomic backgrounds, our religious beliefs, our ethnic identities — that shape our freedom of choice, closing off certain avenues of activity and opening up others. In Cuba, as we shall see in the following chapter, structural economic and social problems of long duration helped generate dissatisfaction and separatist sentiment, creating the preconditions for the revolution of 1895. Likewise, long-term problems affected Spain's ability to fight a colonial war and made American intervention and victory possible. Nevertheless, Spanish defeat and Cuban independence, however desirable, were not structurally determined or inevitable.

Even the easy American victory over Spain, which, with the benefit of hindsight, seems preordained to us, did not seem so inevitable to contemporaries. Until we understand this, we miss the sense of dread and uncertainty — and false hope — people felt in 1898, and we cannot really comprehend the behavior of Spanish, Cuban, and American combatants. Until we take seriously the details of the conflict and emphasize the role of human beings in the story, the origins and outcomes of the war will remain opaque. The stern resolve of Martí, Gómez, Maceo, García, and so many other Cubans, the achievements and errors of the Spanish military establishment and especially of Weyler, the political divisions in Spain over the conduct of the war, the efforts of Cuban patriots in Tampa, New York, Key West, and elsewhere, the technical choices made by the builders of the Spanish navy, and numerous other decisions and accidents of politics and war shaped the war in Cuba and the fate of three nations. The great

English historian Edward Thompson once warned us against the enormous condescension of writing history as if it were made by impersonal forces instead of human beings using their minds and exercising their wills.[17] In the work that follows, I try to heed Thompson's warning. The result, I hope, is a fresh appreciation of the nature and importance of the Cuban War of Independence.

2 ★ The Origins of Cuban Independence

Taking a long view, the story of Cuban independence in 1898 may be said to begin with events in Great Britain and France more than a hundred years earlier. To punish Spain for supporting France in the Seven Years' War, Britain's Lord Albermarle seized Havana in 1762. The British presence in Havana was brief. It concluded with the withdrawal in January 1763 of Albermarle's forces, much reduced by yellow fever and malaria. Yet the interlude had far-reaching consequences for Cuba. The British encouraged Cubans to redirect their trade and external relations toward Great Britain, especially toward her North American colonies. This initiated a reorientation of Cuban economic, political, and cultural life away from Spain and toward the future United States. For a short time, too, the Cubans escaped onerous Spanish taxation, and this left people imagining what it might be like to escape Spanish fiscal demands permanently.

When the United States won its independence from Great Britain in 1783, American consumers of tropical products no longer had to give preferential treatment to imports from Jamaica and the other islands of the British West Indies. Americans therefore expanded the commercial contacts with Cuba that had been initiated twenty years earlier. Instantly, the United States became Cuba's best trading partner, and it became easy for Cubans to envision a more prosperous homeland unattached to Spain. Three possibilities suggested themselves: greater autonomy within the Spanish monarchy, annexation to the United States, or independence. Once these alternative futures had been imagined, they never entirely disappeared. In this way, contact with the Anglo-American world helped to give Cubans a whole new set of demands and dreams.[1]

Another fundamental shift in Cuban life occurred following the French Revolution of 1789. In 1790, slaves in the French colony of Sainte Domingue (Haiti) took Parisian radicals at their word and acted upon the ideals of liberty, equality, and fraternity by rising up against their masters. They abolished slavery, putting an end to Haiti's booming sugar economy, which had been built upon the exploitation of 200,000 blacks by a few thousand whites. The collapse of the Haitian economy caused the world price of sugar to triple in the 1790s. Cuban planters took advantage of this situation to increase their production, especially for the growing U.S. market. By the 1820s Cuba had become the world's leading source of sugar and the United States, its main trading partner, despite Spanish tariffs designed to redirect commerce toward the Mother Country. By the 1870s the island produced more than 42 percent of the world's sugar supply. Thus, as an indirect result of the Anglo-French struggle for global mastery and the twin Atlantic revolutions in British North America and France, Cuba had become an integral part of the global economy with ties to the United States. The ensuing economic transformation of Cuba was profound, and, more than any other factor, it changed the island's relationship with Spain and formed the backdrop for independence in the nineteenth century.[2]

Cuba's new status as the world's "sugar bowl" meant good times for white planters in Cuba, who exhibited a fine and pitiless entrepreneurial spirit. Cuban and Spanish businessmen participated in the transportation of over 780,000 Africans to the island between 1791 and 1867 to work as slaves in the cane fields and sugar mills, refashioning Cuba as a slave society just when slavery was coming under attack almost everywhere else.[3] Planters were also quick to grasp the importance of new technologies. They introduced steam engines into sugar mills beginning as early as 1796, at a time when steam power was still new to many industrial processes, even in Great Britain. The first railroad carried commercial traffic in 1837, just a decade after the opening up of the first railroad in England and two decades before the railroad boom in Spain. The telegraph began operation in 1851, just five years after telegraph service became available in the United States. In short, sugar barons brought hundreds of thousands of slaves and rapid economic development to Cuba, turning the island into an outpost of the world capitalist system, with roads, civic organizations, a press, and all the other social, economic, and cultural accouterments that accompany such development.[4]

When political servitude accompanies economic change and growth, it is always a recipe for trouble. White Cuban creoles may have grown fat on receipts from sugar and slavery, but they were politically impotent, a fact that became more evident with each passing year. Spain governed Cuba through captain generals, officials with near-absolute power in the island. Spain itself alternated between periods of authoritarian rule and liberal government in the nineteenth century, but it didn't seem to matter what form government took in Madrid. Spanish captain generals still gave Cubans little voice in their own affairs. This became especially striking after 1890, when Spain adopted universal manhood suffrage, making the country formally one of the most democratic in the world. However, like many constitutionally democratic regimes in the nineteenth century, the government in Madrid had a full bag of tricks designed to disenfranchise people deemed incapable of ruling themselves. In Spain, this meant the poor. In Cuba, though, it meant virtually everyone. The reformed franchise of

1890 did not extend to Cuba. Unfair electoral laws ensured that the pro-Spanish Constitutional Union Party always won Cuban elections and that candidates put up by the Liberal Autonomist Party lost, while men who actually advocated independence for the island were excluded altogether from running for office. What electoral fraud could not manage, the captain generals of Cuba did. Captain generals had almost regal powers, including the right to appoint and dismiss local governments, arrest political opponents, and censor critics, and they used these functions to keep a lid on Cuban unrest.[5] The political system in Spain may have been a caricature of parliamentary democracy, but it was still light-years ahead of what Cubans were allowed. Thus, as Spain introduced elements of liberal democratic government, it brought Cuba's subordinate status into sharper focus, serving as a terrible irritant in the colonial relationship.

If all of this was not bad enough, the culture of imperial service in Spain made things worse. The Spanish state paid colonial officials such low salaries that many turned to graft in order to make ends meet. If one was lucky enough to serve in the higher levels of administration in the Cuban colony, one could even get rich. A form of relief for impoverished aristocrats, service in Cuba became a way for the Gothic offspring of illustrious but decadent Spanish families to rebuild squandered inheritances back home.[6] Antonio María Fabié, Spain's foreign minister in 1890, recalled with disgust the men who, after only a few months of service in Cuba, returned to the Peninsula shamelessly flaunting their ill-gotten wealth. Such servants of the empire were, in the long run, some of its worst enemies because they made the essential meanness and cupidity of the colonial relationship more visible.[7]

From a Cuban perspective, perhaps the worst thing about Spanish rule was the high rate of taxation demanded by Madrid. Charges that other imperial powers bore themselves Spain laid at the feet of her Cuban colony, so that for most of the nineteenth century Cubans paid roughly twice as much in taxes per capita as Peninsular Spaniards.[8] Spain depended on tax receipts from Cuba because of her own economic difficulties. Historians have recently shown that Spain's economic performance in the nineteenth century was not as dismal as was once believed.[9] But it was not brilliant either. Maritime war with Great Britain before 1808 and Napoleon's brutal occupation of the country afterward destroyed the Spanish fleet and commerce, lives and property. The wealth of the country bled away, and subsequent Spanish governments had to make ends meet by contracting loans at usurious rates. The result was a fiscal crisis that deepened with each passing year, as state revenues went to pay interest on debt, with little left over for other uses.[10]

Making matters worse, Spain was crippled by the division of its ruling elite into two hostile camps: devotees of absolutism and liberals who wanted constitutional government. This political rift, probably deeper in Spain than in any other European country, resulted in five civil wars in the nineteenth century, most notably the First Carlist War from 1833 to 1839. In addition, Spain sustained several colonial conflicts in Africa, America, and Asia. To pay for all of these wars, Spain sold state properties, subsoil rights, monopoly concessions, and anything it could lay its hands on in order to remain solvent. It was still not enough. So Madrid raised taxes and issued more high-interest bonds, attracting into state coffers wealth that might otherwise have flowed to industry, agriculture, and consumption. This was the Spanish recipe for stagnation in an era marked in the rest of western Europe by steady growth.[11]

In this situation, Spanish politicians could not resist the temptation to adopt predatory economic and fiscal practices in their Cuban colony, despite the unrest and suffering they were sure to cause. Tax receipts from Cuba, mainly in the form of duties on imports and exports, were like a drug to which the Spanish treasury became addicted, in much the same way that shipments of silver bullion from Mexico and Peru had been habit-forming for Spanish governments in an earlier age.[12]

High tariffs and quotas on products from North America and elsewhere produced windfalls for Madrid but deformed Cuban commerce by forcing Cubans to buy goods manufactured in the Peninsula, even though these were sometimes shoddier than goods produced in America or elsewhere. On top of this, Spaniards purchased few Cuban products in return. The result was a chronic Cuban trade deficit with Spain. By 1893 Cubans bought Spanish goods valued at 24.3 million pesos but sold only 5.2 million pesos worth to Spain.[13] Such deficits were desirable from the point of view of the colonizing power, were, indeed, an essential trait of successful economic imperialism. Spain had turned Cuba into a captive market for Spanish goods. This helped Spanish producers and laborers and created a broad constituency for empire in Spain, but the colonial relationship galled Cubans, even those who harbored a lingering love for the Mother Country.[14]

The Spanish government knew that Cuban grievances were well-founded. On March 24, 1865, Antonio María Fabié, in his youth a functionary for the colonial ministry, gave a speech before the Spanish Congress in which he demonstrated a firm grasp of the Cuban situation. According to Fabié, there existed in Cuba significant numbers of nouveau riches, professionals, and intellectuals, all of whom would eventually demand a share of political power. The government had to find a way to give "due satisfaction to these political aspirations, which are legitimate and just and will in the end triumph." Unfortunately, no Spanish government ever proved willing to grant Cuba any significant measure of justice.[15]

One thing kept the lid on creole discontent. When the sugar economy took off in Cuba, population grew rapidly, and the black population grew fastest of all. White Cubans thought the island was becoming "Africanized" by the very success of the plantation economy. Racial fear, heightened by the memory of what had happened in Haiti and kept alive by frequent slave mutinies, especially the rebellion of 1843–44, induced a certain docility among whites, who saw Spain as the guarantor of the slave system and of white supremacy in Cuba. This was especially true in the West, where a large slave population worked on the great sugar plantations. As a result, when Spain lost the bulk of its American colonies in the early nineteenth century, white Cuban elites remained loyal to the Spanish crown, earning for Cuba the motto "Ever Faithful Isle."[16]

Some phrases, however, become ironic almost the moment they are uttered. As the Cuban economy matured, the creoles became more closely tied to the United States, as Louis Pérez has documented. The plantations imported their steam engines and processing equipment from the North. North American engineers and technicians arrived to run and maintain this equipment, to operate mines and foundries, and to design railroads and telegraphs. Some Cuban towns, notably Havana, Cárdenas, and Matanzas, came to have sizable communities of émigré Americans. These contacts and the growing trade with the North made American consumer products, fashions, tastes, customs, and modes of behavior visible alternatives to the culture of the Spanish colony in Cuba. American baseball replaced the bullfight as a spectacle more in line with the tastes of Cuban elites. Just as Americans came south, Cubans traveled north for a variety of purposes: education, summer holidays, and business. In America, and in contact with Americans residing in Cuba, these Cubans created a new identity for themselves. The process was disorienting, however. They came to feel like aliens in their own land. They looked at the island's provincial, stultifying, authoritarian culture, and they inevitably became critical of Spain and dangerous to Spanish rule. Indeed, separation from Spain came to seem like an absolute necessity to many of these "ever faithful" white elites.[17]

Disaffected creoles groping toward a purely Cuban identity provided critical leadership to the separatist movement, but we should be careful about pinning too much on such a small segment of society. They alone could not have carried out a successful war of liberation. For one thing, they were divided, with many of them — especially slaveholders in the West — still hoping to solve their difficulties by negotiating with Spain. Moreover, elite cultural nationalism by no means automatically translates into mass nationalism, much less into a violent armed struggle for national independence. To get to that point, a more profound, more complex, and, above all, more widespread, economic, social, and political crisis was needed.

That crisis began in eastern Cuba. The transformation of Cuba into a plantation society founded upon slavery affected western Cuba earlier and more thoroughly than it did the East, or *Oriente*. The large sugar plantations worked by slaves were located in the West. So was the bulk of the valuable tobacco production, together with most of the island's cities, roads, and commerce. In contrast, Oriente was a backwater, and, comparatively speaking, it was becoming more underdeveloped with every passing year. Dominated by rugged mountains and hills covered with dense jungle, Oriente was sparsely populated and little developed. The building of the railroads and telegraphs, for example, took place almost entirely in the West, the East remaining cut off from the most advanced parts of the island.

This uneven economic development proved crucial to the Cuban independence movement, which was always strongest in the eastern provinces of Santiago and Puerto Príncipe but weak in the West. In the West old forms of communal ownership and the customary mutual obligations between owners and tenants had disappeared by the late nineteenth century as land became a simple article of commerce under the pressure exerted by the requirements of global capitalism. The situation in the East could not have been more different. Outside of the immediate vicinity of Santiago and a few other pockets of development, capitalism in Oriente was still an exotic growth. Property was widely distributed among owner-occupiers and leaseholders. People ate locally grown food. Artisanal production remained important. Most people had neither been enslaved nor reduced to the status of wage laborer. These facts proved critical to the East's ability to mobilize for a war of liberation and to supply an insurgent army. As a general rule of historical development, communities in which small owners and tenants predominate are more adept at mobilizing for collective purposes than are places where the mass of the population has been proletarianized, that is, stripped of resources other than labor power. The great peasant revolutions of the twentieth century in Russia, eastern Europe, China, Mexico, and elsewhere bear this out. It was also borne out in Cuba, where Oriente was the soul of the rebellion against Spain.[18]

The rebellion had deep roots in social and economic conditions prevailing in eastern Cuba. While planters in the West enjoyed the good life, their brethren in the East, operating smaller, not very profitable properties, found themselves left behind in an undercapitalized sector of the economy, so their lack of a political voice came to seem like an intolerable obstacle to their prosperity. In fact, the economic troubles in eastern Cuba were in large part rooted in geographic, climatic, and other realities that had no clear political remedy, but aggrieved planters blamed the Spanish colonial political system nevertheless. A section of the eastern plantocracy "cut itself adrift" from the loyal — or at least complacent — white population and sought in the latter half of the nineteenth century to overthrow Spanish rule. It did not require a trip to Key West for such people to embrace the cause of independence. They "became Cuban" without even leaving Oriente.[19]

However, there was more even than this to Oriente's rebelliousness. While it is never possible to predict the political behavior of individuals or groups based solely on their social position, the economic and social structure of Oriente gave large numbers of people both motive and means to resist Spanish rule. The provinces of Santiago and Puerto Príncipe were considered by some contemporaries to be rural Arcadias, where peasants bartered with each other, had no truck with city folk, and practiced a "happy and perfect" subsistence agriculture. This depiction of the East glosses over the inequalities and miseries built into precapitalist societies. Yet the portrait is not entirely imagined or surreal. Peasants in eastern Cuba lived in simple houses of wood and palm fronds called bohíos, which were dispersed widely over the countryside, so that the word "neighbor" in some areas described anyone living within a few miles. It was, thought one observer, as if Orientales shunned each other's company. Under such conditions, people had to be self-reliant, providing for most of their own needs rather than relying on others to provide them in exchange for money. This self-reliance and independence from the market gave easterners an invaluable weapon against Spain: they could destroy commercial agriculture and other enterprises without damaging themselves too much.[20]

The East was Cuba's Wild West. Violent crime was a daily fact of life, as court records demonstrate.[21] Whole communities of bandits existed in the mountains, attacking the mails, tax collectors, and commerce. Communities of runaway slaves, or cimarrones, had existed in the remote Cuban interior almost from the moment the Spanish introduced slavery in the sixteenth century.[22] For a while, in the early days of the colony, cimarrones had actually outnumbered the rest of the island's population. In the nineteenth century, these runaways constituted a distinct Cuba, a Cuba Libre before the fact that was not Spanish and that stood in direct opposition to the plantation economy. In every revolutionary movement against Spain, the men and women who constituted this Cuba Libre in the interior of Oriente blended naturally into the insurgency, lending their skills and their lives to the cause of independence.

Urban elites and Spanish authorities knew very little about this world and had no ability to police it. The people of eastern Cuba "in their way of life had nothing in common with the people of Spain, because those in Spain lived in towns and hamlets, while those in Cuba were dispersed . . . over a broad expanse of territory." Exerting hegemony over such people was difficult "even in peacetime."[23] Difficult terrain and the rugged coastline added to this problem. In times of unrest, rebels and smugglers exploited this situation to land weapons and supplies on remote beaches and transport them safely into the interior. The Caribbean Sea and Gulf of Mexico isolate Cuba but also link her to the rest of the world. In effect, all of Cuba's neighbors share a long border with the island, and in the nineteenth century all of them could serve as jumping-off points for expeditionaries — called *filibusteros* — bent on arming Orientales to overthrow Spanish rule.

The weakness of commercial agriculture in the East served in another way as an inducement to rebellion. Most Orientales had little direct connection to the plantation system. Neither planters nor slaves, they belonged to a free and racially polyglot rural population devoted to ranching, craft work, subsistence agriculture, and a variety of other economic activities, of which sugar production formed only one part. Such people — especially blacks and mulattoes — were understandably less willing to give their loyalty to a government whose only purpose seemed to be the defense of slavery and the plantation system. The critique of slavery and racism and the projection of a multiracial Cuba were the work of many Cubans from all over the island, but the armed effort to produce the requisite regime change originated in Oriente, whose people dreamed of remaking the rest of the island in their own image.

In the 1860s a failed neocolonial adventure in the Dominican Republic added to Cuba's woes and helped trigger Cuba's first war of independence. It happened like this. In 1861 Haiti mounted an invasion of the Dominican Republic, and the Dominicans decided to place themselves under Spanish protection, relinquishing their independence in exchange for military help. Spain quickly neutralized the Haitian threat, but then the Dominicans decided that becoming subjects of the Spanish monarchy again was not to their liking after all. This second Dominican war went poorly for Spain because now the Spanish were not fighting an invading army but Dominican irregulars defending their home turf in a jungle war. Spanish troops fought tolerably well, but almost 8,000 perished from malaria, yellow fever, and other illnesses, and another 16,000 sick and wounded men had to be evacuated. On June 11, 1865, Spain relinquished the Dominican Republic.

The Dominican war affected Cuba profoundly in two ways. First, it taught Cubans that guerrilla tactics could be effective against Spain because malaria, yellow fever, and other diseases would do most of the dirty work. Second, the Dominican war deepened economic and fiscal problems in Cuba because Spain forced Cubans to help pay debts run up during the expensive conflict by impos-ing a tax on income and property in Cuba in 1867. It was an ill-considered novelty, difficult to bear for people already paying for imported goods priced artificially high because of Spanish tariffs. In Oriente, where the market economy was not robust and where cash was correspondingly difficult to acquire, the new tax was ruinous.

Spanish experts on tax policy predicted that it would cause trouble in the re-gion, but no one listened to them. According to one such official, trying to im-pose direct contributions on peasants who were dispersed over the countryside "in straw huts" and who had just enough money "to buy tools and animals to help them produce what they need for subsistence" was little short of insane. Many peasants practiced slash-and-burn agriculture. They cultivated little holdings for a few years until the soil became exhausted and then moved on to clear new plots from the dense, low jungle, or *manigua*, that used to cover much of the island. This made it difficult to know who owned what land and how valuable their hold-ings were. Similarly, peasants did not typically pen their animals, allowing them instead to roam half-wild to forage in the abundant greenery, and this hampered the government's ability to assign ownership and assess tax liability on livestock. Even enumerating human beings and assigning them residency for tax purposes was complicated. To make matters worse, tax officials working under the new law sometimes tried to collect for several years at once, and when the cash was not forthcoming, they seized the peasants' tools and animals. It was a practice that caused rural folk to live in constant terror, "cursing the government that placed them in such a situation of desperation, vagrancy, and crime."[24]

The situation was indeed desperate. In February 1868 a committee led by Car-los Manuel de Céspedes, a lawyer, intellectual, and not very prosperous planter from Bayamo, in eastern Cuba, opened negotiations with the Spanish regime on behalf of overtaxed Cubans. Predictably, the meetings went nowhere because the Spanish government could not afford to be magnanimous. Finally, Céspedes be-gan to speak not of negotiation but of direct resistance to Spanish depredations.

This might have gone no further, but an unexpected cataclysm in Spain al-lowed Céspedes to turn talk into action. On September 17, 1868, the city of Cádiz, which had long been a center of ultraliberal radicalism in Spain, rose up against the Bourbon regime in what Spaniards came to call "The Glorious Revolution." On September 28, the rebels, joined and led by disaffected officers from the army and navy, defeated royal forces at Alcolea. Two days later Queen Isabella fled abroad. A week after that, a provisional government led by General Juan Prím pledged to give Spain a Liberal constitution. When news of the Glorious Revolu-tion reached Cuba, Céspedes saw his chance. On October 10, from his property near Yara, outside Bayamo, Céspedes proclaimed himself in rebellion against Spain. Nothing illustrates better the close interdependence of Cuban and Spanish history in this period than the connection between the Liberal revolution in Spain and the uprising at Yara.[25]

The goals of Céspedes and his followers at the beginning of the Ten Years' War (1868–78) were not at first clear. The cry of "Viva Cuba Libre" competed with the cry of "Viva Prím" and "Viva La Constitución," a reference to the Spanish revolutionaries' promise of a Liberal constitution for Spain and her colonies. Even on the critical question of slavery Céspedes remained ambiguous, saying on the one hand that he believed everyone was created equal and on the other that emancipation would have to come gradually and include indemnification for slave owners, such as himself. Soon, however, Céspedes and the rebels realized that they needed the support of the slave population and of free blacks to have any chance of success, and this forced them to clarify their objectives after 1870: independence and emancipation. Now the movement gathered popular support as thousands of Afro-Cubans flocked to the insurrection.

The rebellion also prospered simply because Spain was in no condition to respond. The Spanish army in Cuba numbered under 14,000 men, and only 7,000 of these were really combat ready. The others were either sick or had been "farmed out" by their commanders to work on the big plantations and ranches, a foolish practice we will discuss in a later chapter.[26] The real problem, though, was that Spain was still in the midst of its own revolutionary turmoil. Following the ouster of Isabella, Spain experienced six years of progressive but weak government, punctuated by Prím's assassination and the installation of the First Republic in 1873 and ending in a civil war that almost destroyed the country. Amid this chaos, the Cuban insurgents scored important military successes that threatened Spain's hold on eastern Cuba.

Nevertheless, the rebellion remained a regional revolt that did not catch on in Cuba's rich western provinces. There are several reasons for this. The Spanish constructed a fortified line, the trocha already discussed, and, though it was far from perfect, it did help to keep the rebels from easily moving into the West. Moreover, the eastern troops lacked discipline and a national consciousness, and they refused to march west when ordered to do so. Even the inspired leadership of new military chieftains, such as Antonio Maceo, could not remedy these problems. Indeed, the rise of black officers like Maceo complicated things in one sense. Whites in western Cuba feared the insurgents in part on racial grounds, and they either refused to join the insurrection or surrendered after a short time, giving as their reason that "blacks were poised to take control" of the island.[27] The promotion of Maceo to the rank of major general, accompanied by rumors that he planned to set himself up as dictator if he should be victorious, seemed to confirm their fears. Then, too, the leaders of the revolt had no international support. Nor did they have any political experience. Above all, after 1875, when the restored Bourbon monarchy reimposed order in Spain, the Spanish army was able to turn all of its attention to Cuba. Even a second-rate standing army can defeat inexperienced insurgents who are not fighting in collusion with regular forces and who are not receiving significant outside help. General Arsenio Martínez Campos led a final offensive against the Cuban rebels, defeated them, and brought the Ten Years' War to a conclusion in 1878 with the Peace of Zanjón.

In the meantime, however, Cuba had been radically transformed by war. As already mentioned, white leaders, including slave owners like Céspedes, had embraced emancipation, freeing their own slaves, as well as any who served in the Cuban rebel army. In fact, by 1878, thousands of slaves had performed military service, and Spain could hardly negotiate an end to the conflict without recognizing the de facto freedom of these men and their families. In addition, Spain freed the few slaves who served on the Spanish side or who were born before 1810 or after 1868 and made vague promises to free everyone else when the war ended. Thus, emancipation was gradual, culminating in final legal abolition of slavery in 1886.[28]

Nevertheless, even this controlled process of abolition led to a profound crisis in Cuba, and not only because of the critical labor problems it created for the sugar industry. Hundreds of thousands of freed Afro-Cubans were able to create new lives and new identities for themselves in the two decades before 1895. Where before slaves had often been housed and policed in barracks on plantations, now at least some free black laborers lived in their own homes, away from anyone's surveillance or control. Their work on the sugar plantations was now remunerated and — miserable though the pay and the conditions of work were — wages gave them some leverage.[29] They felt their freedom and their Cubanidad for the first time as two sides of the same coin. In this sense, the Ten Years' War, although it formally ended in Spain's favor, created the conditions for a more widespread conflict in 1895, when the black population had both the wherewithal and the inclination to lend their services to an independent republic-in-arms that promised to complete the job of social and racial emancipation that had begun in 1868. Moreover, with slavery abolished, wealthy white Cubans who had viewed Spain as the guarantor of the slave system lost a powerful reason to remain loyal to the Mother Country. These facts have convinced some scholars that the entire period from 1868 to 1898 should be seen as a "thirty years' war." This usage is justified because of the many threads of causation that run from the uprising at Yara in 1868 to the uprising at Baire in 1895, when Cubans began their final push for national liberation. On the other hand, the phrase is also misleading because it tends to relegate the events of 1895–98 to outcomes determined by the earlier war and to make initiatives for peace and reform during the years from 1878 to 1895 seem foredoomed to failure. The notion of a single, thirty-year struggle also causes us to underestimate the ways in which new circumstances and new actors contributed to Cuban independence after 1895.

In fact, there were in Cuba several new forces operating in the last two decades of the nineteenth century to mobilize the generation that came of age after the Ten Years' War. First, the problem of overtaxation had become worse. Spain continued to levy high tariffs and direct taxes, heaping the cost of the Ten Years' War onto the mountain of obligations Cubans had to meet. As a result, interest payments on war debts absorbed most government spending in Cuba while very little was earmarked for infrastructure or development projects. In the seventeen years that passed between 1878 and 1895, the Spanish built no new railroad lines.[30] Roads were allowed to deteriorate. The colonial administration even discouraged the construction of schools, in the conviction that educating Cubans would only turn them into rebels — as persuasive a condemnation of Spanish rule as one could ever hope to find.[31]

One route to filthy lucre had, at least, been shut down. Slavery had always offered the greatest opportunities for corruption. The fact that slavery remained legal in Cuba until 1886, decades after international conventions prohibited the transatlantic slave trade, produced an enormous illegal slave market in Cuba. Smugglers and slave owners paid Spanish officials a high price to keep the lucrative commerce in human beings continuing, and some of the greatest fortunes in Spain and Cuba were built upon the slave trade and the corruption that accompanied it. Slavery ended in 1886, but a culture of corruption cannot be so quickly terminated. The expectation of quick riches had become ingrained in Spanish officials, who turned easily and with a ludicrous sense of entitlement to other forms of graft. Petty corruption became a way of life for state employees, who received kickbacks on all sorts of contracts and routinely skimmed government receipts, costing Cuban taxpayers untold sums of money. The Cubans who paid the bribes and who had to purchase consumer goods inflated by the added cost of "doing business" in Cuba were not blind to all of this.[32]

A different sort of crisis, born of technological innovation in the sugar industry, added to Cuba's economic woes in the late nineteenth century. Early in the century, Franz Carl Achard discovered how to extract sugar efficiently from beets, and the first sugar-beet refinery was established in Berlin. Within a few decades, sugar from beets almost completely replaced the cane variety in Europe, where the beet grows so well and where refining techniques were invented and perfected. By 1890 beet sugar accounted for 59 percent of world production. Even in Spain, despite the fact that its richest colony produced more cane sugar than any place in the world, the government encouraged farmers to grow sugar beets and placed obstacles in the way of imports of cane sugar. Once again, the nature of the colonial relationship, in which the interests of Cubans always came second, could not have been made clearer.

This shift in Europe toward the production and consumption of beet sugar undermined the long-term prospects for Cuban cane sugar. Planters knew it. Many of them were getting out of the business, selling out to large sugar concerns for cash or for annuities. Javier de Peralta, landowner and estate manager in Matanzas, connected the structural crisis caused by the Europeans' use of beet sugar to Cuba's political unrest and predicted that a new war of independence was around the corner. "The worst thing is that no one sees any remedy, because as long as the enormous plantations of sugar beets remain in Europe, it is impossible for sugar to retain value. And here, we have no other product, nor is it possible to use the land for some other crop," Peralta wrote on February 19, 1895. Five days later, the Cuban War of Independence began.[33]

Cuba's loss of the European market in the last half of the nineteenth century left the United States as its only major customer. As Cuban-American commercial ties grew closer, American businessmen invested in Cuban sugar. Some became directly involved in cane production, but it was in the refining, packaging, and marketing that American capitalists came to predominate. Techniques became more complex and capital-intensive in an effort to compete with beet sugar, and American investors, working to modernize sugar production, came to control some aspects of the industry.

This transformation of Cuban sugar in the last decades of the nineteenth century affected western Cuba differently than it affected the East, exacerbating the already profound differences between the two regions. In Oriente, the older sugar concerns collapsed or clung to a marginal existence in the face of competition from beet sugar and from the reorganized and more capital-intensive cane sugar in the West. At the same time, economic difficulties in Spain encouraged a new wave of immigrants from the Peninsula, "whitening" the population of western Cuba dramatically. As Havana grew, its hinterland experienced a significant transformation, too. Countryside previously left open or dedicated to sugar and tobacco became valuable farmland for growing potatoes, corn, and other market crops. A new class of small holders came into being with close ties to Havana and other western cities. In short, the island was fast becoming two different societies: poorer, blacker, and more rebellious in the East; richer, whiter, and more tranquil in the West. Some even expected the island to be partitioned into a black East and a white West, as the island of Hispaniola had been, into a black Haiti and a whiter Dominican Republic. Indeed, the Cuban War for Independence in 1895 can be read, at least in part, as an attempt by Cubans to halt this process.[34]

By the 1890s, Cuba, especially western Cuba, had become part of the American economic imperium. However, economic dependence on the United States became especially perilous for Cuba in the 1890s, when the world economy entered the final, deep phase of a long recession. International orders for goods of all kinds plummeted, and countries tried to protect their economies by passing stiff tariffs to exclude foreign goods from their own markets. Spain abandoned what little remained of its free-trade principles and raised duties on most imports, including American products. This turned into a disaster for Cuba when the United States responded with legislation raising tariffs on Spanish products, including Cuban tobacco and sugar. Most notable was an 1894 bill sponsored by William McKinley, Republican congressman from Ohio and future president, that raised the duty on Cuban sugar. These tariffs stripped Cuba of its American customers, who stopped smoking Cuban cigars and began to sweeten things with Hawaiian sugar preparatory to annexing that archipelago. Cuban exports of cigars and leaf to the United States fell by half in the early 1890s, and sugar exports fell by almost one-third from 1894 to 1895.[35]

The crisis that resulted in Cuba was profound. Planters cut back on production, and thousands of cane cutters, mill hands, and tobacco workers found themselves unemployed. This, in turn, affected every other sector of the Cuban economy. "Since the last months of 1894," one contemporary observed, "numerous day laborers, more than 50,000 of them, wander from town to town looking for work."[36] This was a crisis that affected the whole island. Indeed, the West, because of its dependence on world markets, felt the recession most deeply. This was one of the preconditions for the success of Cuban patriots in 1895. With plenty of desperate workers at their disposal, the insurgents had no difficulty recruiting troops, even in the traditionally more tranquil West. There is a great deal of truth, therefore, to the claim that it was U.S. tariffs in the early 1890s that made the Cuban uprising of 1895 possible.[37] As one Spaniard put it, once the McKinley bill passed, "youths, old men, women, and children cleaned off their machetes and their rusty rifles, waiting impatiently for the call to revolt."[38]

Adding to all of this misery, a series of devastating hurricanes struck Cuba in the fall of 1894. The storm of September 23–24 destroyed everything around Sagua la Grande. People fished 300 bodies from the swollen Sagua River in the following weeks. Then new storms struck Oriente and moved west, taking a track followed one year later by the Cuban insurgents. The bad weather destroyed roads, crops, workplaces, and homes. Hungry, single, unemployed cane cutters and mill hands became a vast pool of recruits for bandits and/or insurgents.[39] Bandits became bolder. One gang seized the sugar mill "Carmen" on September 30 and held it for three days. Kidnapping wealthy merchants and planters became a way of life. Bandits colluded with rebels, blending patriotism with their more mercenary demands. Highwaymen who shouted "Viva Cuba Libre" as they robbed civilians and held them for ransom became difficult to distinguish from patriots who did the same thing to raise funds for the rebellion.[40]

The telegraph carried constant reports of these tumults in the fall of 1894. As outlawry spread, the colonial government remained helpless in Havana, apparently immobilized by the poor weather.[41] In the new year, arsonists destroyed properties owned by Spaniards and Spanish supporters. On the night of January 14, 1895, 150 men invaded and sacked the town of Jibacuán. People in other towns gathered to demonstrate against a government that seemed incapable of providing them with any relief, shouting "Viva Cuba Libre" and other more menacing slogans.[42] Cuba had become a perfect hotbed of revolution.

Monitoring these events from his exile in New York City, José Martí became convinced by late 1894 that it was time to strike against the Spanish regime in Cuba. Martí had fought Spain with his pen all of his adult life. In 1868 he had embraced the ideal of Cuban independence enunciated by Céspedes at the outset of the Ten Years' War and began discussing and writing about the future of a free Cuba. In 1869 Spanish authorities discovered a compromising document written by Martí and arrested him for advocating independence during wartime. Martí was sixteen years old. The judge sentenced Martí to six years at hard labor in a prison on the outskirts of his native Havana. It was a harsh penalty for what was little more than a youthful indiscretion. On the other hand, this was José Martí, a man who at sixteen was already deadly serious.

Prison officials often farmed convicts out to work in a nearby limestone quarry, and there, under the foreman's lash, Martí's health was ruined. Mercifully, the Spanish government commuted the sentence to banishment to the Isle of Pines, off the southern coast of Cuba, and in 1871 permitted Martí to live in Spain, where he studied law. In Madrid, Martí moved in elite circles. His health recovered, he studied at the university in the morning, taught the children of wealthy patrons in the afternoons, and was a habitué of the theater in the evenings. Later, he continued his studies in Zaragoza, the capital of Aragón. There he found distraction in his first romance. Then, in 1874, his exile in Spain ended, and so did the romance, though he would always retain a special place in his heart for Zaragoza and Aragón.[1]

The fact that Spanish authorities initially handed down such a cruel penalty to Martí, only to commute it to a lenient sentence later on, requires some explanation. Madrid had a well-deserved reputation in the nineteenth century for meting out byzantine punishments to its political opponents, but in addition to being cruel, Spanish justice was remarkably capricious. Indeed, the two things — harshness and inconsistency — complement each other: weak regimes employ spasmodic exemplary violence because they cannot manage the routine enforcement of the law.

But there was more to the reversal of Martí's sentence than this. Spanish politics did not accommodate peaceful change very well, so even modest challenges to the status quo from men of standing often took the form of militancy. In

Spain the bourgeoisie — or at least part of it — was still revolutionary. Engineers, doctors, and lawyers who tried to apply basic standards in their professions found that they had to work with defective building materials, or that hygiene, equipment, and drug therapies were lacking, or that reasonably modern legal codes were violated in practice. Even some military officials felt thwarted by a lack of modern equipment. These and similar frustrating experiences turned professionals into reformers and sometimes into democrats and republicans spouting revolutionary ideas. Most of the time this was just a charade, a delicate pas de deux that young men posing as radicals danced with government officials. Everyone understood that revolutionary gestures by youths of wealth and standing were not really serious. Government officials tended to be forgiving of such transgressions, secretly admiring the youthful exuberance they indicated and interpreting such challenges to their authority as a healthy sign that the political body of Spain had some pulse. The two major monarchist parties even cultivated such men, certain that they could transform wild-eyed radicals into mature men of substance and no principles simply by bringing them into the game of national politics. This gentlemen's game even applied to Cuban revolutionaries, especially if they were white, as long as all they did was write and talk about independence. And that is all Martí had done.

In effect, Madrid mistook Martí for one of the homegrown amateurs who passed through Spanish universities and Masonic temples en route to a middle age as moderate monarchists. Martí did, indeed, join the "Harmony Lodge" of the Freemasons in Madrid and moved in high society. Radical liberalism was in vogue in Spain, which was experiencing its own revolutionary ferment. Martí found many sympathetic ears for his arguments in favor of Cuban independence.

Martí's popularity with Spanish liberals stemmed in part from an event that made it possible to paint a group of Cubans, the violent, pro-Spanish "Volunteers" in Havana, as the real villains. In 1871 a group of medical students desecrated the tomb of Gonzalo Castañón, founder of La Voz de Cuba, the Volunteer newspaper. A trial led to light sentences appropriate to the crime, but the Volunteers rioted, pressuring the Spanish authorities to retry the case. The defense attorney, a Spanish army captain named Federico Capdevila, defended his clients by demonstrating that the evidence against them was weak to nonexistent. For example, one of the students condemned to death had been in Matanzas on the day of the outrage. Beyond this, he argued that desecrating graves did not merit the capital punishment demanded by the mob of Volunteers. It was all for naught. The Volunteers — mostly Cubans born in Spain — had too much power locally. They even assaulted Capdevila during the trial and got away with it. And so the court handed down eight death sentences and prison terms for thirty others implicated in the crime. The eight died by firing squad on November 27, 1871. Martí made this cause célèbre his own and gained a wide audience with his eloquent denunciation of the Volunteers and their corruption of the judicial process.

This was something Spanish audiences enjoyed hearing. They were not to blame. It was the reactionaries in Havana who were the problem. What Spanish liberals did not know was that beneath the facade of revolutionism there lurked in Martí a real revolutionary, not an aspiring insider. Martí used the case of the student martyrs in the service of a larger agenda with which most of his readers would not have agreed. What Martí may not have realized, at least at first, was that his audience only wanted to read his words and listen to him. It amused them to experience an exciting sense of moral outrage against the dastardly Volunteers who dared assault a Spanish officer and lawyer. This did not mean that they would ever act on Martí's broader appeal for justice in Cuba.[2]

Martí completed his legal studies, while Spaniards drove their king into exile in 1873 and drafted a republican constitution for themselves. It was the most radical turn taken by Spanish politics up to that time, and Martí witnessed it all with a certain amount of delight: Perhaps the Spanish First Republic would do something for Cuba, he thought. Unfortunately, the republicans were no help to Cuba, and then they fell from power. In 1874, as the radicals bickered, a military coup brought the Bourbons back to Spain. With order restored, the Cuban insurrection faced a concerted counterattack and began its slide into defeat.

Martí left Spain in 1874 for Mexico City, where he worked as a reporter. In 1876 he met Carmen Zayas Bazán, the daughter of a wealthy Cuban exile. A year later, they were married, and when the Ten Years' War ended in 1878, the couple relocated to Havana. There, in November, Carmen gave birth to their son, José. Family responsibilities did not prevent Martí from immediately renewing his seditious activity, so Spanish authorities exiled him once again to Spain in September 1879. However, the police exercised such a lax surveillance of Martí that he quickly escaped across the Pyrenees. After a brief stay in France, Martí went to New York City, arriving on January 3, 1880. In New York Martí came into his own both as an author and as a leader of the Cuban exiles. Carmen brought little José to New York for a visit, but she could not understand her husband's deep commitment to his art and to the revolution, both of which came before family: Martí was many things, but he was not a family man. Indeed, Martí's wife soon informed him that she would be happier living under Spanish rule than living with him, and in 1881, she took her child back to Cuba.

The personal heartache of losing touch with his son inspired Martí's greatest literary work, Ismaelillo, a collection of poems published in 1882. With Ismaelillo,

Martí introduced modernism to Latin American audiences, who were still reading romantic poetry, with its strict use of meter and rhyme and its overwrought language. Martí exerted most of his energy, however, pursuing his true love — the independence of his homeland. At this stage in his life he fought for Cuba with words, but they were beautiful words, a flood of writing that made him one of the great literary figures of the nineteenth century. In a decade, he founded and edited several magazines and wrote a novel, two books of poetry, and dozens of short biographies. He wrote hundreds of articles for dozens of Spanish and English-language newspapers, such as Charles Dana's *New York Sun*. These articles were often political in nature, making the case for Cuban independence. He became so well-known, even loved, throughout Latin America, that Uruguay appointed him vice consul in 1884 and he later served as consul for Argentina and Paraguay.

Martí's position among the New York émigrés, meanwhile, suffered a serious blow. Some of his fellow exiles did not trust or even like Martí. This was especially true of the two great military chieftains Máximo Gómez and Antonio Maceo. Gómez thought Martí made a better poet than a revolutionary. He suspected that Martí was all talk and that he feared an actual war for independence, because in such a conflict he would be eclipsed by military men. Similarly, Antonio Maceo found Martí to be unlikable and unreliable, a "Machiavellian" schemer rather than a true patriot committed to armed struggle.[3] For his part, Martí suspected Gómez and Maceo of *caudillismo*, that is, the desire to set themselves up as military dictators in Cuba.[4] In 1884 Gómez and Maceo visited New York to meet with Martí and other figures within the Cuban community. Martí, accustomed to leading and dominating such situations, found that he could not. He thought Gómez particularly overbearing. He broke with the general, sending him an insulting letter that implied that Spanish rule would be preferable to a revolution in which men like Gómez held sway. Martí would not work to bring to Cuba "a regime of personal despotism, more shameful and ruinous than the political despotism" already in place. "One does not establish a people, General, the way one commands a military camp," Martí wrote. "What are we, General? The heroic and modest servants of an idea that fires our hearts, the loyal friends of an unfortunate people, or valiant military chieftains who with whip in hand and spurs on our boots prepare to take war to our people in order later to become their lords? To a war of such low origins and fearsome ends . . . I will never lend my support."[5]

Gómez did not bother to reply. But news spread quickly of Martí's break with him. The young poet had none of the prestige that attached to the general, and veterans of the Ten Years' War mounted a campaign to defend Gómez and vilify Martí. On October 20, 1884, Martí left the movement. The next few years were

José Martí forged the ideology and political organization of the Cuban independence movement but was killed in action in the early days of the War of Independence. Courtesy Library of Congress.

difficult for Martí. Cuban veterans reviled him for his lack of any military service. At one point, the insults became so demeaning that Martí challenged one of his detractors to a duel, an event that, fortunately, never came off.[6]

The rift among the leaders of the Cuban independence movement healed in the early 1890s largely through the efforts of Martí. Though the very model of the single-minded revolutionary ascetic, Martí was not a Cuban Robespierre, having none of the Incorruptible's visceral need for unanimity and taste for blood. Instead, Martí worked to unify the disparate forces that made up the exile movement and learned to live with the militarism of Maceo and Gómez. To some degree, he had no choice. He could never regain leadership of the movement so long as the allies of Gómez and Maceo maligned him as a man of words and no action.

The most important turning point in Martí's political career occurred in 1891, when he visited the vibrant Cuban communities in Tampa and Key West. In both Florida cities, Cuban entrepreneurs and tobacco workers had settled in large numbers, taking advantage of American tariffs that gave preferential treatment to Cuban leaf rolled by Americans in place of cigars imported directly from Cuba. Cigar workers in Cuba and Florida had solid radical pedigrees. Many had been shaped by the anarchist movement, which was strong in Spain and Cuba. To bring them into the fold, Martí altered his message to give more attention to the social demands of Cuban workers. Up to that point, there had always been a great deal of tension between Cuban working-class organizations and the separatists, the workers sometimes fearing the Cuban "bourgeois" revolutionaries more than they did the Spanish.[7] In contact with the exiled workers in Florida, however, Martí developed a new and appealing social agenda. Independence now came to mean agrarian reform, better wages and conditions for workers, and other concessions to the laboring people. This was the formula that finally mobilized Cuban workers — both émigrés and those still on the island — behind Martí and independence. Bringing workers into the separatist movement would prove critical to its success in the years ahead.[8]

In 1892, on a roll after his triumphs in Florida, Martí founded the Cuban Revolutionary Party (PRC) at Key West, and on March 14, 1892, he issued the first number of Patria, the newspaper that became the semiofficial organ of the revolution. Martí and the PRC called for an independent, democratic Cuba committed to racial equality and economic and political justice. The PRC gathered contributions from Cuban émigrés and used the funds to purchase arms and make other preparations for the revolution.[9] Martí's efforts may not have produced the "miracle" of the "spiritual union" of the Cuban people, as some overly optimistic historians have written, but they did apparently convince Gómez, Maceo, and other military men to drop their skepticism about the New York crowd and to work closely with Martí after 1892.[10]

Martí also understood that he needed the experience of the old veterans. In the fall of 1892 he visited Gómez in the Dominican Republic, and the two patched up relations. In 1893 he met Maceo in Costa Rica. This reconciliation among the leaders of the independence movement did not mean that all was harmony. Gómez and Maceo continued to suspect Martí's revolutionary poetics, and Martí still feared their militarism. Nevertheless, the bickering of the 1880s had been replaced by a firm working relationship.

Necessity and predestination are themes central to most people's views of history. This is certainly true when it comes to Cuban perceptions of Martí, the "apostle" of Cuban independence. Martí's early life was, according to this perspective, "a necessary stage of suffering" that gave him the strength he needed to perform the "miracle" of spiritually uniting Cubans. His years of residence in New York, like Christ's wandering in the desert and temptation by Satan, was a requisite "stage" in which "the predestined" Martí "became the living incarnation" of the "Cuban ideal." This posture as martyr and vessel of God's will was something Martí cultivated. To his oldest friend, Fermín Valdés Domínguez, he intimated that undeserved pain and suffering were "sweet," and many times he predicted his imminent death and described it as a sacrifice for the higher good. People who saw him in the last months before the Baire uprising commented on this aspect of Martí's persona. One observer "was astonished to find in him at times a Christlike silhouette. His attitudes were like those of the Sermon on the Mount."[11] The "martyrdom" of Martí, according to some of the most worshipful scholars, was no less than "the realization of his predestined role" on earth.[12]

In fact, the more one knows about the history of Cuban independence (or any history), the less predestined it seems, and the more it appears to be the work of many people exercising their minds and wills to bend capricious fate. Still, we need not accept the nonsensical, quasi-religious view of Martí as the holy vessel of history's plan to appreciate the power and influence of his intellect and organizational skill.

What marked Martí's thinking more than anything else was his conception of the nation. Most scholars today tend to view the nation as the purposeful construction of ruling elites who use nationalism to gain the consent of people opposed to them on other grounds. In this view, nationalism, especially mass nationalism, is not a fixed product of economic and social developments but an evanescent construct, rising in response to crises and elite campaigns to mobilize patriotic sentiment, dwindling away at other times, always in flux.[13] In contrast, Martí thought of nationalism as a demiurge emanating from the people themselves. Like the Italian Giuseppe Mazzini and other romantic nationalists, Martí believed that the nation existed as an intuition, an internalized sentiment, before it became an institutional reality. A more fundamental category than the individual or the state, the nation to Martí was the precondition not only for effective state formation but for individual self-realization and the collective flowering of humanity in its constituent national communities. Sharing a common language, culture, and history, Cubans had formed a nation even while subjected to Spain. In a fundamental sense, therefore, Cubans had no alternative but to be Cuban, and their struggle for independence and eventual victory were historically inevitable.

Revolutionaries faced with the prospect of years of toil and armed struggle find it useful to possess a myth telling them that God or history is on their side. Martí's romantic nationalism supplied Cubans with the necessary foundation myth that formed the bedrock of the Cuban revolutionaries' unflagging belief in the righteousness and inevitable success of their cause. In comparison, the ideal of *Cuba Española* was pale and powerless, seeming, even to many Spaniards, like nothing more than a cover for their continued exploitation of the island.[14]

In many ways, Martí's essentialist and organic view of the nation corresponded closely with nationalist ideologies emanating from Europe, and especially from Germany, in the latter half of the nineteenth century. However, Martí turned on its head a key ingredient of Germanic nationalism: the identification of the nation with racial purity. Cubans came from Africa, Europe, China, the Caribbean, Mexico, the United States, and many other places. If real nationalism were only possible in an ethnically homogeneous land, then Cuba could never be a nation. Indeed, Spaniards took comfort in the conviction that Cuba, like the United States of America, for that matter, could never form a nation because it was a collection of slaves, mongrels, and outcasts from around the world who could not possibly stand up in a fight against a real nation like Spain.

This was foolishness, of course, and Martí knew it. He denied the connection of the nation and nationalism to ethnic and racial purity. Indeed, the very concept of purity seemed like a "sin against humanity" to Martí.[15] Instead, turning the argument of the racial theorists around, he contended that racial mixing, or *mestizaje*, had created a new "anti-ethnic" people in Cuba who were naturally more modern. Moreover, his years in the United States had taught Martí many lessons, and one of them was that nationalism could trump ethnic divisions. No country had more ethnic diversity than America, and yet a mantle of national self-regard seemed somehow to keep the place together. Martí believed that fractious social and ethnic distinctions in Cuba could also be and already were being subsumed in two ways: by racial mixing and by a new, racially blind, national identity. Without any doubt, Martí's hopeful, racially inclusive conception of the nation constituted the greatest ideological strength of the revolution of 1895.[16]

Martí was a radical democrat, not a socialist. Having lived in the United States during the Gilded Age, Martí had seen unfettered capitalism at its most abusive. However, his solution to these ills was not Marxist but Jeffersonian. Martí possessed a mystic's faith in democracy, reason, and "the people." Like Rousseau and Jefferson, Martí believed in the innate goodness of common folk, the commoner the better. Cubans and Americans in general, being less corrupted than Europeans by the accretions of civilized life, were closer to a state of nature and therefore in a superior condition to govern themselves. Democracy, the realization of the general will, would be enough to ameliorate the worst excesses of the capitalist system and bring social justice and equality to Cubans without the need for socialism. Sadly, it turned out that Martí's radical democratic vision for Cuba was never realized. The requirements of a long war followed by years of American occupation and support for various forms of authoritarian rule in the twentieth century subverted genuine democratic institutions and processes. Nevertheless, Martí's radical democratic wish for Cuba served as another powerful element of the revolutionary catechism and helped to motivate the insurgents in their fight with Spain.

Another theme dear to Martí was the decadence of Spain. Although suspicious of social Darwinist conceptions of biological decline current at the time, Martí thought that a backward monarchy had corrupted and weakened the Spanish people to the point that they could barely help themselves, much less do anything for Cuba. Decadence had become so culturally ingrained in Spain as to be nearly an inherent part of the condition of being Spanish. During his years as a student in Madrid and Zaragoza, Martí watched with excitement as Spanish radicals installed a republic in 1873, inaugurating what they hoped would be a new era of progressive government and economic progress. Surely, thought Martí, the First Republic, which gave Spain one of the most democratic and liberal constitutions in the world, would grant Cuba its freedom. Unfortunately, it turned out that republicans had no interest in giving Cuba independence. Indeed, they argued that the advent of a progressive government in Spain made the independence of Cuba unnecessary. Cubans would receive their full measure of justice under the new flag of the First Republic, just like other Spaniards. And republicans made a point of hawkishly claiming that if Cubans continued to insist on more, Spanish republican armies would know how to crush them. When the First Republic collapsed, it did not perturb Martí, for he had come to realize that it made no difference to Cuba what form politics in Madrid took. Martí had become more convinced than ever that Cubans would have to fight for their independence rather than wait for a remedy from Spain.

Other leaders of Cuban independence had come to the same conclusion, which was almost unavoidable, given the deplorable state of the Mother Country in the late nineteenth century. Agricultural workers in Spain were as bad off as cane cutters and peasants in Cuba, and industrial workers in places like Bilbao and Barcelona received subsistence wages. The result in both town and country was a malnourished people with a scandalously high mortality rate and one of the slowest growing populations in Europe. Even with slow demographic growth, the lack of opportunities at home induced 1,386,000 Spaniards to emigrate between 1830 and 1900, over 400,000 of them to Cuba.[17] With so many recent immigrants from Spain, Cubans had intimate knowledge about the conditions of life there. Like the Catalonian-born José Miró, who fought beside Antonio Maceo and produced an intimate account of his actions during the war, or like José Martí, whose parents were Spanish, they had become convinced that Spain, in its poverty, could not afford to act justly toward Cuba.

It is interesting to consider this point, because, in fact, Spain did not experience any absolute decay in the nineteenth century. The economic growth and transformation characteristic of the rest of Europe affected Spain, too, and historians nowadays emphasize these positive aspects of Spain's nineteenth century as a corrective to an earlier tendency to fix only upon Spain's weaknesses. Nevertheless, Spain's slow growth rate compared to most of the rest of Europe and the Americas made the country seem backward. And in the story of Cuban independence, it was the perception of Spain as impossibly decrepit that mattered most.

Northern Europeans who traveled to Spain in the nineteenth century found Spaniards charming, colorful, uneducated, superstitious, backward, and slightly dangerous. But they also thought Spaniards vibrated with an authenticity and a life force that had been driven out of their own countrymen by the factory whistle, the clock, the schoolhouse, and the demands of the marketplace.[18] Of course, travelers see what they want and need to see. Cubans who visited Spain perceived something different: Spaniards lived in a squalid country ruled by a moribund monarchy that seemed incapable of righting its own ship of state, much less of offering any direction to its colonies. Australians and Indians could sometimes take pride in being part of the British Empire. Cubans could muster no analogous feeling toward Spain, whose people seemed to lack an aptitude for modern thinking, for science, for economic progress. Indeed, Cubans visiting or residing in Spain experienced nothing so much as a sense of satisfaction that they were Cubans rather than Peninsular Spaniards. In a moment of irony, Martí even recommended exile in Spain as the perfect antidote for anyone who might feel some lingering loyalty toward the Mother Country.[19] Salvador Cisneros Betancourt, future provisional president of the Cuban government during the War of Independence, learned "conclusively" during his time spent in Spain to "expect nothing from over there." And Juan Gualberto Gómez, one of the revolution's great ideologues, learned the depth of his Cuban identity during an interlude of banishment to Spain.[20] Another revolutionary, José María Izaguirre, after pondering the state of Spain firsthand, recalled thinking that "Chile, Argentina, Venezuela, Mexico, and even the Dominican Republic are countries that no longer trail behind the ancient Metropolis, and they certainly have more promising futures." If only Cuba could unburden itself of Spanish rule, thought Izaguirre, it, too, would enjoy a future of grandeur.[21]

In fact, Spain today is far better off than its former colonies, but in the short term, Cuban observers like Izaguirre had gotten it right. And even if they exaggerated the extent of Spain's decadence, the important point was that Cubans could easily convince themselves that they had surpassed Spain. This sense of superiority, of having a brighter future than did Spaniards, formed part of the psychological bedrock of Cuban separatism in the nineteenth century, and it helps to explain the willingness of Cubans to join the insurrection in the spring of 1895. Great hope is as important as great fear and misery in causing people to risk their lives for change. Indeed, it is often in the space that lies between the two, between actual squalor and imagined splendor, that revolutionaries are born. In 1895 many Cubans shared Martí's optimistic faith in a bright future — without Spain. Cuba was ripe for revolution.

4 ★ Emilio Calleja and the Failure of Reform

Given the troubled economic and political history of Cuba, the uprising and declaration of independence at Baire on February 24, 1895, hardly took the Spanish by surprise. Indeed, Captain General Emilio Calleja had expected something like it. For months Spanish officials abroad and in Cuba had been warning him about the likelihood of coastal landings by armed Cuban émigrés in support of a major rebellion.[1]

An event in the United States provided the clearest sign that something dramatic was afoot. On January 8, 1895, off the little Florida island of Fernandina, the U.S. Coast Guard boarded three ships contracted to transport expeditionaries and weapons to Cuba. Although a federal judge agreed with the Cubans' attorney, Horatio Rubens, and declared the seizures illegal, the expedition had been wrecked. Calleja did not know the full extent and sophistication of the Fernandina plot: The speedy yachts *Amadis*, *Lagonda*, and *Baracoa* had been contracted to take Máximo Gómez and other key exile leaders to various points along the Cuban coast, where armed parties awaited their arrival to begin the uprising. He knew enough, however, to realize that something important was about to happen.

Nevertheless, Calleja did not try to prevent or contain the uprising by taking measures that, with the benefit of hindsight, seem to us obvious and necessary. He made no special effort to watch the coast, crack down on revolutionary clubs, or detain known Cuban activists. Juan Gualberto Gómez, the man in charge of orchestrating the revolt in the region of Havana, continued to wield his eloquent pen against the Spanish regime right up to the moment he took arms against it. The newspaper *La Protesta*, connected to revolutionary leaders Enrique Collazo and José María Aguirre, published calls to rebellion in the days leading up to Baire. And men around Calleja maintained close ties with Manuel García, the famous bandit and patriot known as the King of the Cuban Countryside, who kidnapped Spaniards and pro-Spanish Cubans, collected ransom money, and turned it over to the insurgency.[2] Meanwhile, Calleja offered pardons to captured rebels and insisted that he did not need help from Madrid, despite the fact that his military forces were in terrible shape. He had fewer than 14,000 troops, and, as had been the case before the Ten Years' War, many of the men had been mustered out to work in various capacities for private individuals, so that they were not available for military duty.[3] In short, for a regime with a reputation for being brutal and depraved, the Spanish government in Havana reacted with strange languor both before and after the *Grito de Baire*. This allowed the insurgency to gain momentum, at least in the eastern half of the island.[4]

Calleja's critics attributed his inactivity to stupidity and laziness, or, even worse, to complicity with the Cuban insurgents, but these charges are not fair.[5] Spain gave its captain generals imperious authority, but Calleja had been appointed by a government in Madrid committed to compromise, limited reform, and relatively liberal, if not very democratic, government in Cuba. Calleja had neither the mandate nor the inclination to rule with an iron fist. Instead, he believed that reform was the best way to keep the separatists from gaining ground, and he continued vainly to hope that timely legislative remedies coming out of Madrid would mollify Cubans and eliminate the need for bloodshed.

Calleja was not alone in his commitment to peaceful reform as a solution to Cuba's ills. In December 1892 Calleja's friend Antonio Maura, who would become one of Spain's greatest statesmen in the twentieth century, had taken over as colonial minister in a Liberal cabinet headed by Praxedes Sagasta. On December 28, Maura rewrote Cuba's electoral laws, doubling the voting population by lowering the property qualification for voters from twenty-five pesos of taxes paid to five pesos. This was still not the universal male suffrage Spain had (on paper), but it was a significant improvement. Five months later, on June 5, 1893, Maura presented the Spanish Congress with a package of additional legislation designed to give Cubans more control over their own affairs by creating a new administrative assembly for the island and by granting municipal authorities more power and autonomy.[6] These proposed changes did not address fundamental Cuban demands for such things as lower taxes and freer trading relations, and they certainly stopped far short of granting Cuba any real independence. Nevertheless, the Maura project did promise to create a government in Havana more responsive to Cuba's needs, and Liberals hoped that this would be enough to defuse the movement for separation from Spain.[7]

At first, the reforms and projected reforms appeared to be working exactly as Maura, Calleja, and the Liberals thought they would. The expansion of the franchise in December 1892 induced thousands of Cubans who had boycotted earlier Spanish elections to cast ballots in March 1893, thereby providing a patina of legitimacy to the Spanish colonial system. The Cuban Liberal Autonomist Party seated seven representatives in the Spanish Congress, as opposed to their usual one or two. However, this was still not enough to affect the course of political debate and legislative action in Madrid. The sharing of power between Liberals and Conservatives in the Spanish government gave no scope for the

Cuban delegation to tip the balance one way or another. So the Cubans had no bargaining power and no prospect of achieving meaningful reform for the island by playing political hardball, as, for example, Parnell's Irish did in the British Parliament. Still, the seating of seven members of the Liberal Autonomist Party in 1893 gave heart to Cubans who believed that reform within the Spanish monarchy was still possible. A few months later, the mere announcement of the full Maura plan to grant Cuba greater autonomy produced massive popular demonstrations of support in the island. In a sure sign that the proposed legislation had created genuine enthusiasm, José Martí roundly condemned Maura's project as a smoke screen to divert Cubans from the path of revolution.[8] Flor Crombet, a veteran general of the Ten Years' War, thought that the Maura plan made an immediate uprising imperative, lest Spanish reforms dampen the mood of dissatisfaction in Cuba.[9] Máximo Gómez, who was in a position to know, called Maura's autonomy plan "a powerful battering ram to smash the Revolution," and he recalled 1893 as a moment of great danger, when enactment of the plan would have doomed the revolution. Indeed, a leading Cuban historian concluded that everyone in Cuba knew that "if autonomy had been implanted in time, the revolutionary movement would not have had a successful outcome; indeed, it would not have even been attempted."[10]

As it turned out, however, the Maura autonomy plan never became law because events that had nothing to do with Cuba intervened to delay consideration of the project. In September 1893 Madrid became embroiled in a colonial conflict in Melilla, one of Spain's two enclaves in Morocco. Rif tribesmen had launched a series of raids against Spanish garrisons, and on October 27 they cut to pieces a Spanish column that had been stupidly led into a narrow pass of the Atlas Mountains. The government responded by dispatching to Morocco its most famous general, Arsenio Martínez Campos, at the head of 20,000 troops.

Martínez Campos had an impressive resumé. In 1874 he had administered the coup de grâce to Spain's radical First Republic, opening the way for the return of the Bourbon monarchy. In 1878, after leading a campaign against insurgents in Cuba, he had brought an end to the Ten Years' War with the Peace of Zanjón. Martínez Campos was one of the most powerful and prestigious men in Spain. In Morocco, however, he proved to be a bungler, to the unbridled delight of Cuban separatists. In 1894 the war in Morocco degenerated into a low-level conflict with no tangible results, except to saddle Spain with the cost of equipping and feeding an army of 20,000 men that Martínez Campos did not know how to use.[11] In this situation, the distracted prime minister, Praxedes Sagasta, who had never been very interested in Cuba anyway, cut short parliamentary debate on Maura's project. Maura resigned in disgust, and nothing was done for almost a year. Finally, in late 1894, with the situation in Morocco under control, Spain's Congress of Deputies considered a legislative package of reforms for Cuba sponsored by Maura's replacement, Buenaventura Abarzuza. On March 12, 1895, the Abarzuza plan became law.

Sometimes, however, timing is everything. Had Maura's plan for Cuban autonomy been adopted in 1893, it might have changed the political situation in the island, but the almost identical Abarzuza legislation took effect sixteen days after the uprising at Baire — too late to matter very much. Even so, the Abarzuza law did create some initial confusion among the revolutionaries, who were expected to lead the uprising in the island until the great émigré leaders — Crombet, Gómez, Maceo, Martí, and the rest — could arrive. In the town of Baire itself, rebels at first raised the red and white flag of the Autonomist Party to shouts of "Long live colonial autonomy!" Only later did Jesús Rabí, Bartolomé Masó, and other Cuban leaders in the region proclaim themselves for outright independence.[12]

Indeed, Spanish reform efforts from 1892 to 1895 had instilled confusion and uncertainty in the minds of everyone. Ironically, in the long run, this played into the hands of the Cuban insurgents because Calleja was the most confused of all. Wanting to give the Abarzuza reforms adopted by his party a chance to work and reluctant to inaugurate what he hoped would be an era of more liberal government in Cuba with a bloodbath, Calleja remained stubbornly immobile after February 24. He tried to act as if nothing were amiss, for to do otherwise would have been to admit the painful truth that the time for reforms had passed. It was a costly case of self-delusion.

Revolutions are most likely to succeed when the ruling elite is weak, divided, and hesitant, a condition that can lead to a failure of nerve and morale among police and military forces who then fail to employ deadly force at some key early juncture. Something like this happened in Cuba. Pro-Spanish Cuban elites, reflecting the division in Spain between Conservatives and Liberals, had formed themselves into two hostile camps: the integristas willing to do anything to keep Cuba part of Spain and the autonomistas, with whom the Liberal Calleja sympathized and who envisioned a more flexible relationship between the colony and the Mother Country, perhaps even something along the lines of the arrangement Canada had worked out with the United Kingdom. By the time Calleja realized that this Liberal vision of a Spanish "Commonwealth" was a chimera and that he would have to declare martial law and come up with an armed response to the Grito de Baire, it was already too late. Cuban forces had consolidated their hold on parts of eastern Cuba, and by early April things had proceeded far enough that it would take a major military effort to restore peace to the island on any sort of terms acceptable to Spain. Thus, ironically, instead of derailing the revolution as Martí and Gómez feared they might, Liberal Party reforms paralyzed the captain general of Cuba at a moment when decisive action might have made a difference.

Calleja probably also underestimated the real gravity of the situation. Cuban exiles from New York to Santo Domingo plotted expeditions with some regularity, and local rebellions inside Cuba were frequent. To go back no further, on April 12, 1893, the Sartorius brothers carried out an abortive uprising near Holguín; on November 4, 1893, a conspiracy in Lajas went nowhere; and on January 25, 1895, a revolt in Ranchuelo collapsed. Rebellion and banditry had come to seem like a fact of life in Cuba, the cry of "Cuba Libre" so common as to inspire ennui. Thus, news of the activities of the émigrés and the evident heightening of tension in rural areas in January and February, which we can, with the benefit of hindsight, easily discern as forerunners of revolution, may have seemed to Calleja like nothing very extraordinary.

Other circumstances also caused Calleja to misjudge the strength of separatist sentiment. The captain general had surrounded himself with Cuban autonomists, whose dearest wish was that they could peacefully achieve an adequate degree of independence within the Spanish monarchy and thus avoid excessive bloodshed and the destruction of property. Organized in the Liberal Autonomist Party, these men assured Calleja that they could command a greater following than the separatists, and Calleja believed them. The truth is that in 1895 they may have been right. It must be remembered that the voices calling for independence were still in the minority in Cuba, while the autonomists were numerous and included some of the most wealthy and powerful men in the island. Meanwhile, Calleja ignored the brutal, though in many ways sounder, advice of the integristas calling for preemptive action against known Cuban patriots. So it was that the constant noise of advice coming from the autonomists made Calleja deaf to the sound of the approaching cataclysm.

Despite Calleja's lack of foresight, the revolutionaries suffered a series of defeats and disappointments in early 1895 that did not augur well for their future. To begin with, the disruption of the Fernandina conspiracy had been more than a minor setback. Cuban patriots opened their pockets to try to replace the financial losses, but it was not enough. Months passed before key exile leaders, such as Gómez and Maceo, could reach Cuba. In the meantime, Cuban patriots who had answered the call at Baire found themselves in a precarious position. On February 28, Spanish forces in the province of Havana captured Juan Gualberto Gómez. In Matanzas, police arrested all the key figures, including Pedro Betancourt, the designated rebel leader of the province. Manuel García, the bandit-king of the Cuban countryside, died under mysterious circumstances at about the same time. Indeed, in most areas the rebellion went nowhere, mainly because the call to revolution received no immediate, spontaneous support from the masses. The province of Puerto Príncipe, for example, remained so quiet that the Spanish waited until June to declare martial law there.

We should not be surprised at this or make too much of it. Nationalist romances habitually portray so-called people's wars as spontaneous and unanimous, and histories of the Cuban War of Independence are no exception.[13] In fact, however, there is no evidence of a widespread popular uprising in 1895. It would be more accurate to describe the insurrection as the product of intense activity by a committed revolutionary elite that had only limited support, and most of that in Oriente. Cubans were divided by class, regional identity, their association (or not) with cities and the marketplace, strategic and tactical issues, and race, as recent scholarship has amply shown.[14] Many of the combatants knew this. Luis Adolfo Miranda recalled the difficulty Gómez and Maceo had fighting against the "deeply rooted sentiment of regionalism," which made the formation of a sizable national army impossible.[15] And according to Cuban general Manuel Piedra Martel, the people desiring outright independence from Spain were always a small minority throughout the century, even at the height of the wars of independence. In all of Cuba's wars for independence, he pointed out, "the number of sons of Cuba who defended with arms the sovereignty of Spain was greater than the number who fought against it."[16] We should not expect, therefore, to see unity of purpose or action among the Cuban people in 1895.

Even the most eloquent denunciation of abuses and the most convincing program for change are not enough to make normal people kill others or risk their own violent death. It takes something else altogether more persuasive to create a widespread commitment to violence. The degrading nature of warfare itself cheapens life, gives callow boys powers exercised in normal times by mature men and women, and creates unbridgeable gulfs between people. The military men who led the Cuban revolution understood this. They knew that over time, warfare itself would serve to mobilize the Cuban people. Their job as military leaders was to remain steadfast, disrupting the daily routines of the majority with a war carried out by a committed minority. This was a better recruitment tool than appeals to nationalism and patriotism, things forged and spread to the masses during and because of the war, not before.[17]

In Santiago things went reasonably well for the revolutionaries, despite the illness and subsequent death of the province's designated military chief, Guillermo Moncada. Bartolomé Masó took over for Moncada and operated around Manzanillo. Esteban Tamayo commanded a force in Bayamo. The Sartorius brothers and the Catalonian journalist José Miró fought near Holguín. Pedro Pérez and

Quintín Bandera raised men in the areas of Guantánamo and Santiago. Joined by other veterans of the Ten Years' War and with a few hundred new recruits, these rebel leaders began guerrilla operations against isolated Spanish garrisons, Civil Guards, and towns loyal to the Spanish side.[18]

In March a dispute in Madrid between army officers and liberal journalists triggered a governmental crisis that gave the Cuban insurrection vital breathing room and new sources of support. It happened like this. On March 13, 1895, the Madrid newspaper El Resumen published an article critical of Spanish officers who were trying to avoid being sent to Cuba. Hundreds of them had, in fact, put in for early retirement when they saw that renewed warfare in Cuba would require their services.[19] But when a journalist dared to point this out, it created a furor. On the evening of March 14, some thirty rioting officers assaulted the presses of El Resumen. The next day, another newspaper, El Globo, printed an account of the attack in a barbed article sarcastically titled, "The Valiant Ones." Military men everywhere hate being the object of irony and criticism by civilians, but the Spanish military was particularly sensitive in such matters, in part because real military glory and prestige came so rarely to Spanish armed forces in the nineteenth century.[20] On March 15, 300 officers destroyed El Globo and two printing shops associated with the newspaper. When leading men in the Spanish army, including Martínez Campos, took the side of the military ruffians against the rule of law, it forced the Liberal government of Prime Minister Praxedes Sagasta to relinquish power to avoid the possibility of a military uprising.

On March 23 the Conservative statesman Antonio Cánovas del Castillo formed a government cynically pledged to defend the army's honor against "the aggression of the press." Cánovas also promised to abandon reform and negotiation in Cuba.[21] In his formal speech upon assuming office, he threw down the gauntlet to the Cuban revolutionaries, declaring that Spain would fight "to the last peseta and the last drop of blood" before relinquishing the island. In accord with this apocalyptic determination, Cánovas immediately recalled Calleja and sent Martínez Campos to Cuba. Martínez Campos left Spain on April 4 and arrived in Havana on April 16.

Martínez Campos was a moderate compared to his successor, Valeriano Weyler. Compared to Calleja, however, he was a staunch defender of the empire, and his appointment in the spring of 1895 signaled a dramatic hardening of the Spanish attitude toward Cuba. Reform was no longer an option, as Cánovas and Martínez Campos refused to consider reform until the island was first pacified. Thus, the riots of March 14–15 in Madrid and the ensuing fall of Sagasta, Calleja, and the Liberal Party ensured that Spain would only consider a military solution to the Cuban crisis. Moreover, the ministerial and administrative shuffle in Madrid took several weeks to complete, and by the time Martínez Campos was able to take over from Calleja, the hot, rainy, and unhealthy tropical summer had begun. It was no time to launch a counteroffensive.

As Martínez Campos was crossing the Atlantic, Cuba's most prestigious exiles — Gómez and Maceo — were also steaming to the island. Their arrival in the province of Santiago did more than anything else to give added impetus to the revolution.

Getting to Cuba had become difficult after the Fernandina disaster. Antonio Maceo, working with Flor Crombet and some 200 other Cuban exiles in Costa Rica, had been prepared to mount a major expedition as part of the Fernandina plan. In Costa Rica, Maceo had been the object of constant surveillance by Spanish spies, who rightly considered him the most dangerous Cuban alive. On November 10, 1894, a group of Spaniards tried to assassinate Maceo as he left a theater in San José. Maceo's friends fought the assassins off but not before Maceo suffered a gunshot wound in his back that came dangerously close to his spine. Maceo's strong constitution allowed him to recover, and the whole incident only served to make him more determined than ever to get to Cuba as soon as possible to raise the standard of rebellion.[22] However, after Fernandina, Martí had no money to give Maceo and Crombet to purchase weapons, supplies, and adequate transportation for the large enterprise they had envisioned. Feeling slighted, Maceo threatened to withdraw from the venture. Finally, though, Martí secured a $2,000 donation from the dictator of the Dominican Republic, Ulises Hereaux, and this he offered to Maceo. Still Maceo remained dissatisfied. Martí then decided to work through Flor Crombet instead. In announcing his decision, Martí could not resist scolding Maceo: "This is the time for true greatness. . . . And Flor, who has everything in hand, will arrange matters as he can." This reopened a rift between Maceo and Martí that probably never fully healed.[23]

Two thousand dollars was not enough to mount the full-scale expedition Maceo had envisioned, but under Crombet's leadership, Maceo and twenty other Cuban officers, with nine rifles and enough machetes for everyone, boarded the American commercial vessel *Adirondack* on March 25 and set out for the coast of Santiago province. A Spanish gunboat, *Conde de Venadito*, fired warning shots at the *Adirondack* as it passed through Cuban waters but did not pursue the American vessel or seek to destroy it. Even had the Spanish tried, they probably could not have caught the speedy American ship, which normally plied the waters of the Caribbean laden with bananas and other perishable fruit.

The strange thing, though, is that *Conde de Venadito* did not even try to pursue *Adirondack*. There is, however, a very logical explanation for this. The Spanish hesitated to fire directly upon or board American vessels because the least hostile action automatically produced a war furor in the United States and created pressure on the Cleveland administration to intervene in Cuba. Something like this had happened just two weeks earlier. On March 8, 1895, the American sloop *Alliance*, flying British colors as a ruse, had entered Cuban waters carrying men and munitions for the insurgents. On that occasion, too, the *Conde de Venadito* was involved. She intercepted *Alliance* and fired blank warning shots across her bow when she approached to within 1.5 miles of the coast. Then a solid warning shot was fired close to *Alliance*, and the American vessel withdrew. (*Alliance* landed the men and weapons successfully in Cuba one week later.) When news of the encounter reached the United States, the press condemned the Spanish "aggression" and generated something of a war scare. The U.S. Navy was placed on alert, and the secretary of state sent a bellicose message to Spain on March 15, denying any association of the *Alliance* with the revolutionaries and demanding that an official reprimand be given to the captain of the *Conde de Venadito*. President Grover Cleveland restored calm on the following day, but the lesson was clear: Spanish naval officers who fired upon American vessels, even those smuggling arms for the insurgents and disguised under the flags of other nations, did so at great peril, both to their own careers and to Spanish relations with the United States. This is why, some ten days later, the captain of *Conde de Venadito* did not seek to destroy or capture *Adirondack* when the vessel entered Cuban waters with Maceo, Crombet, and the others aboard.[24] The presence of the Spanish gunboat did, however, prevent Maceo's party from executing a landing. On March 29 Captain Simpson of the *Adirondack* deposited the expeditionaries on Fortune Island, in the Bahamas. He also introduced them to the local American authority, Vice Consul Farrington.

Like many Americans, Farrington was happy to work behind the scenes to subvert the Spanish colonial regime in Cuba. U.S. federal law, in compliance with international law, forbade aid to the insurgents against the recognized government of Cuba. This was the position of the Cleveland administration in 1895 and 1896 and one that McKinley initially attempted to maintain when he took office on March 4, 1897. U.S. officials tracked the activities of the émigrés, and American naval vessels stopped an occasional expedition. From a Cuban perspective, this was hostile behavior by the United States. However, seized ships and detained men were usually released quickly and Cuban agents were allowed to lobby openly in Washington and to carry out other activities in pursuit of independence. From a Spanish perspective, it looked as if the United States were flouting international law in support of revolution.

Both sides had a point. But we should remember that the U.S. federal government in the 1890s was not the monolith it is today. Federal authority was a weak thing in many state and local jurisdictions. Local police winked at the gathering on New York docks of Cuban expeditionaries, and no amount of pressure from Washington could change this behavior. Likewise, known staging areas for the insurgents in Florida and elsewhere went unguarded by local law enforcement. The Cuban exiles had for years lobbied Congress, held rallies, and issued press releases. Their cause had become popular in the United States. Americans, even employees of the federal government like Farrington, felt genuine sympathy for the Cuban rebels and a deep antipathy for Spain and all that Spain symbolized. Thus, although Cleveland himself might despise the Cuban insurgents, he could do little to impose his views on Americans outside Washington. Moreover, he had little to gain by opposing the groundswell of pro-Cuban sentiment. Indeed, the wonder is that the federal government was able to resist the pressure to aid the Cuban revolutionaries as long as it did.

On the night of March 29, 1895, Farrington, Crombet, and Maceo devised a plan to get the insurgents to their destination. Farrington lent them his own schooner, Honor, to drop them on the Cuban coast. To avoid detection in port, the Cubans posed as workers returning to a sisal farm on nearby Inagua. The only problem was finding a Bahamian crew naive enough to believe that Honor was really transporting twenty-two armed Cuban sisal workers. Eventually, Farrington found a captain and two sailors willing to make the voyage. If the crew had any doubts about their destination, they did not last long. Once aboard ship, the Cubans explained to the three seamen that they were, in fact, headed for Cuba, and gave each of them a cash bonus to compensate them for the inconvenience. On April 1 Honor landed the insurgents on Duaba Beach, near Baracoa, in eastern Cuba. However, both Honor and her captain, Solomon Key, became casualties of the landing. When the Cuban party could not make landfall in their dinghies, they forced Key to ground Honor and join them ashore, where he died, according to some accounts, from a gunshot wound inflicted accidentally by one of the Cubans as he cleaned Maceo's gun. The dead captain's portion of the bonus money was distributed among the two remaining crew members, and the expeditionaries headed inland.[25]

At first, things went badly. Within a few hours, the Spanish attacked and dispersed Maceo's group. During the next few days Spanish forces captured some of them and killed most of the rest, including Flor Crombet, a veteran of the independence struggle nearly equal in stature with Maceo himself. To avoid pursuit, the men finally separated. Maceo spent five days alone, hungry, and in hiding. At last, eighteen days after making landfall, Maceo encountered a search party that had been sent out to look for him. By then, he had contracted dysentery, which affected him throughout the first summer of the war. Still, the presence of even a sick Maceo raised everyone's spirits and lent new force to the revolution.[26]

Meanwhile, on March 25, 1895, Martí had written what would be the clarion call of the revolution. Signed jointly with Máximo Gómez and written in the general's home in Montecristi in the Dominican Republic, the *Manifesto of Montecristi* outlined the goals of the Cuban revolution. The *Manifesto* contained many of the elements of Martí's political philosophy. It announced that the time had come to overthrow the corrupt Spanish monarchy, whose promises of reform would always fall short. An independent Cuba promised a future of democracy and justice for everyone regardless of race or ethnic background. Martí proclaimed the Cuban revolutionaries' "freedom from all hatred" and "fraternal indulgence" toward Cuban neutrals. He declared his determination to respect the "honored Spaniard," to show mercy to Cuban collaborators who repented of their errors, and to be inflexible "against vice, crime, and inhumanity."[27] Sadly, under the pressure of a nasty civil and colonial war, the revolutionaries would be forced to violate some of these promises.

On April 1 Martí and Gómez sailed for the Bahamas with six other men but were abandoned there by the captain and crew of their boat. They went underground for a few days, until, on April 5, the German ship *Norstrand* took them all to Haiti, where they again hid in the home of a Cuban exile. Gómez took advantage of the detour to write one last time to his wife, enclosing a lock of his gray hair.[28] The moment of truth was fast approaching. A few days later, the revolutionaries embarked once again on *Norstrand*, and on the night of April 11, they landed in eastern Cuba near Baracoa. They completed the last leg of the journey aboard a dinghy Martí had purchased in Inagua for $100. As they pushed off from *Norstrand*, the larger vessel's wake nearly capsized them. Then, as they pulled for shore, the rough seas swept away the tiller. Finally, the storm passed, the moon emerged, and the sea-tossed men were able to land on the rocky beach of Playitas, which Máximo Gómez kissed in a dramatic gesture commemorating his return after so many years of exile.

In late April, with their most important leaders in place, forces of the Cuban Liberation Army commenced a series of offensives against small towns. On April 21 Colonel Victoriano Garzón won an important victory when he led a party against Ramón de las Yaguas, near Santiago. The Spanish garrison at Ramón de las Yaguas occupied a strong fort, which the Cubans should not have been able to take, but the Spanish commander, Lieutenant Valentin Gallego, worried about the loyalty of his own men and decided to surrender without a fight. The Cubans captured sixty-four rifles, 20,000 cartridges, and a large quantity of rations from Gallego. To complete the victory, Garzón and the Cubans burned the town utterly, and eight of the Spanish troopers joined the Cuban side, demonstrating, incidentally, that Gallego's worries about his men's loyalty had been justified.[29]

Martínez Campos had been in Cuba exactly one week when he learned about the fall of Ramón de las Yaguas, and he reacted with fury. He condemned Gallego to death by an order of May 1, 1895, and, at the same time, he enjoined Spanish troops in the island to show their mettle and to be prepared "to sacrifice the last drop of blood" for Spain.[30] Meanwhile, the small party with Gómez and Martí spent several dangerous days wandering through a countryside now swarming with Spanish troops looking for Maceo. Finally, on April 14, they met up with a group of local insurrectos. In late April they found the camp set up by Antonio Maceo's brother, José, and a few days after that, on May 5, Martí, Gómez, and Antonio Maceo met at a ruined sugar mill called La Mejorana to assess their position and to discuss a plan of action.

At first, the meeting did not go well. Maceo had not forgotten how Martí had given Flor Crombet control over their expedition from Costa Rica. He rudely interrupted Martí whenever he tried to speak. Maceo also disagreed with Gómez's determination to move immediately to an invasion of western Cuba. Maceo urged more caution, wanting to establish firm control over the East first. Maceo may also have been peeved by Gómez's decision to make a general of Martí, despite the latter's complete lack of military experience. Indeed, Maceo continued to argue that Martí should return to New York and leave the fighting to real generals. After a short initial meeting, Maceo apparently asked both Martí and Gómez to vacate his camp. It was a critical moment. Maceo commanded a much larger following, and it appeared that he had decided that he could operate without his two colleagues. Fortunately, on the following day, the three patched up most of their differences and agreed to a plan of action.[31]

Among the serious cleavages separating the three leaders of the Cuban revolution, one in particular would not go away. Gómez and Maceo, believing that victory would flow from iron military discipline rather than the spontaneous ardor of the masses, wanted to delay the democratic and social revolution until the peace and to forestall civilian meddling in the conduct of the war. In contrast, Martí thought that Cuba's best hope was a mass rising of the people, which could be accomplished by installing a civilian government and immediately instituting revolutionary social and political changes in the areas of Cuba not controlled by the Spanish.

The conflict between ideals and military necessities had faced previous revolutionary movements, and it would face others in the future. French Jacobins chose to place the ideal of liberty on hold in 1793 while they beat back the crowned heads of Europe and wiped out internal opposition, and Russian Bolsheviks after 1917 violated the limited liberal ideals they still possessed in order to fight enemies foreign and domestic. Scholars disagree about exactly how the three Cuban leaders resolved their similar conflict at Mejorana in May 1895. The proceedings were, in fact, highly secretive, and much of what went on at Mejorana has been pieced together from secondhand accounts and later correspondence. We do know that four months later, on September 13, the Cubans formed a government under the presidency of Salvador Cisneros that confirmed Máximo Gómez as commander in chief of the armed forces and Antonio Maceo as his second in command and gave them sweeping war powers.[32] The arrangement doubtless went further in the direction of autonomy for the generals than Martí would have liked. But Martí was dead by then, and it was many months before anyone dared to challenge the growing praetorianism of the revolution.

When the meeting of May 5 at Mejorana broke up, Maceo took command of most of the Cuban forces and began a campaign in Santiago, while Gómez left for the neighboring province of Puerto Príncipe to try to provide an impetus for the lagging resistance there. Gómez kept only fifty men, among them José Martí. On May 19, this small force ran into a Spanish infantry column on the road to Dos Ríos. Gómez tried to convince Martí to fall back and leave the fighting to veterans. Martí refused. Pride and the desire to show the world that he could fight Spain from the saddle as well as from behind a podium or a desk caused Martí to place himself in harm's way. He approached the Spanish position armed only with a pistol, mounted on, of all things, a white horse. He took rifle fire that wounded him mortally and knocked him to the ground, where he fell into Spanish hands. Gómez had been right. Martí made a better poet than he did a soldier.[33]

Martí's death has always had about it the odor of suicide — the white horse, the waving of the pistol, the foolhardy approach toward the Spanish lines. Indeed, like a middle-aged Werther, Martí had apparently been experiencing premonitions of his own death. He worried that he might perish obscurely and unheroically, without ever having a chance to fight in manly fashion on Cuban soil. He wrote about this theme in one of his last poems, often quoted as an indication of his state of mind just before the end.

Yo quiero salir del mundo,
por la puerta natural:
en un carro de hojas verdes,
a morir me han de llevar.

No me pongan en lo oscuro,
a morir como un traidor.
Yo soy bueno, y como bueno,
moriré de cara al sol.[34]

Martí had died in action, face to the sun, but there was nothing natural about his death or his funeral. Martínez Campos had Martí's body cleaned up and put on display before burial in Santiago, winning a public relations coup of a rather gruesome sort. At Dos Ríos the world lost a great intellect and a principled voice for democratic and egalitarian ideals, and Cuba may have lost its best chance for a liberal, democratic revolution.[35]

It took a long time for Cubans to accept Martí's death as a fact rather than a piece of Spanish propaganda. As late as June 3, the Cuban American newspaper El Porvenir ran a banner headline that read "Martí Lives!" It took several weeks more and confirmation by Gómez himself for people to believe the disastrous news.[36]

In spite of the death of Martí, the revolution prospered in the summer of 1895, at least in Oriente. Amadeo Guerra, at the head of 300 men, took control of Campechuela for two hours while its garrison was absent. At almost the same time, Esteban Tamayo occupied the undefended town of Veguitas, seizing needed weapons and supplies.[37] The most serious action occurred at the town of Jobito, about ten kilometers from Guantánamo. On May 13 Antonio Maceo, already with as many as 2,400 men, according to some sources, attacked a Spanish column of 400 infantry and 100 cavalry commanded by Colonel Juan del Bosch. Although the Cubans suffered serious losses, Maceo held the field, and Bosch died in combat. The Cuban victory of Jobito, the first real battle of the war, brought hundreds more Orientales into the revolutionary fold, making it certain that Spain would only be able to reestablish order in the East at great cost. The Spanish, along with everyone else, were about to find out how great.[38]

5 ★ Máximo Gómez and Total War

Máximo Gómez had no taste for limited war aims. After half a lifetime struggling for Cuban independence, he was determined to fight to the death, and as commander in chief of Cuban revolutionary forces, he expected everyone else to do the same. At the behest of Gómez, even the very language of compromise was proscribed. Cuban officers had orders to kill emissaries from the Spanish side who arrived speaking the honeyed language of peace through negotiation. The insurgents' penal code eventually confirmed this severe justice by declaring it treason to advocate peace on the basis of anything less than full and immediate independence.[1]

Although the rest of the world sometimes had trouble understanding this Cuban commitment to total war, it grew naturally out of the first war for independence. The Ten Years' War had ended in 1878 when Cuban leaders signed a pact with the Spanish at Zanjón. At the time, Gómez did not stand in the way of a peace accord. He knew the war had been lost and that the majority of the Cuban people wanted peace.[2] Later, however, Gómez and other stalwarts among the Cuban revolutionaries convinced themselves, against all objective evidence, that victory in the field against Spain had still been possible. The myth that Cuban traitors had snatched defeat from the jaws of victory at Zanjón served the cause of Cuban independence well because it embittered Cuban patriots and made them unwilling to negotiate or compromise in 1895. Moreover, the Convention of Zanjón had promised sweeping reforms, but the Spanish delivered very little of what they agreed to, making Cubans rightly skeptical about any peace initiatives that emanated from Spain.

The question for Gómez, therefore, was not whether to fight to the death for independence but what strategy to adopt. Gómez realized that the insurgents could not win regular battles against the larger and better-equipped Spanish army in the 1890s any more than they had been able to win such battles in the 1870s. With this in mind, Gómez called in the spring of 1895 for a strategy of guerrilla war. Cuban forces would avoid the Spanish except under very controlled circumstances and attack instead the economic resources of the island: crops, structures, and civilians.

On July 1, 1895, in the imperious language that cost him friends and has troubled his biographers, Gómez addressed the owners of plantations and ranches in Cuba. "Sugar plantations," he declared, "will cease their labors; and those that try to produce sugar will see their cane set afire and their facilities destroyed." Gómez also banned farmers from transporting and selling food, livestock, tobacco, and other basic commodities in Spanish-controlled territories, which in July 1895 still included most of Cuba. People who tried to take any prohibited products to market would be "treated as traitors and judged as such if apprehended."[3]

By destroying the Cuban economy, Gómez hoped to achieve several goals. First, eliminating commercial agriculture, especially sugar, would undercut Spanish resources. Sugar was key to Cuba and to Spain's relationship with her. Spanish shipping interests grew fat on the global trade in sugar and on transporting Spanish products to Cuba. Spanish manufacturers and farmers dumped their goods in the island and provided employment to thousands of Spanish families. Duties on exports and imports provided Madrid with the revenue it needed to govern the colony. The Spanish government could ill afford to sacrifice a penny of the revenue that came from Cuba. By destroying sugar, therefore, Gómez would make empire unprofitable to the Spanish government, to Spanish merchants, manufacturers, and laborers, and to Cuban planters aligned with Spain. As Gómez put it, the "chains of Cuba" had been "forged by her own richness." To break the chains, the wealth would have to be wiped out.[4]

Gómez also saw the destruction of capitalist agriculture as an exercise in social engineering that would produce a new, more egalitarian society in Cuba. Gómez did not direct his forces to destroy all kinds of property with equal enthusiasm. He wanted them to target big planters, manufacturers, mining operations, urban properties, and lines of communication and commerce, while protecting small farms that lay in rural regions beyond the reach of the Spanish. He knew that Spain's armed forces, in contrast, would side with big proprietors, industrialists, and the towns. By design, therefore, the war between Cubans and Spaniards contained within it a class conflict between small holders, on the one hand, and big planters and capitalists, on the other, as well as a battle between rural and urban interests. Gómez would drive Spain from the island even as he shifted the economic and social balance of power within Cuban society from the urban rich to the rural poor. Backing up Gómez, the Cuban provisional government announced that, following the declaration of peace, it would seize the big estates owned by absentees living in cities and allocate them to rural families without land. In this way, the revolution would transform the island into a Rousseauian paradise of small owners.[5]

It is worth noting that, while Gómez was committed to a radical revolution, it was quite different from the one Martí envisioned, for Gómez had embraced the ideal of equality but not the principle of democratic liberalism. Social equality would be created and directed from above by a military strongman, preferably himself. Indeed, one biographer detected in Gómez an instinctive "inclination to dictatorship."[6] As Gómez saw things, the war of liberation did not mean immediate liberty of a personal sort. Far from it. It meant iron discipline. Gómez, with his sense of Victorian prudishness, arrested citizens who dared to violate the revolution's ban on cockfights, gambling, and other forms of entertainment.[7] If something or someone did not serve the revolution, then it stood against it. This was the way Gómez's authoritarian mind worked.

An episode from the Ten Years' War illustrates this quality in Gómez. In 1872 the rebels faced a crisis. The war was not going well, and the leaders of the revolutionary government under Carlos Manuel de Céspedes felt so threatened that they proposed taking refuge in Jamaica. Hearing this, Gómez became furious. While he and his men lived in the jungle, dressed in rags, and fought endlessly, Céspedes and the well-fed civilian leaders paraded around with their ceremonial uniforms and jeweled swords, turning up their noses at the odor of real soldiers. Gómez, given to quick judgments and colorful language, could not contain himself and openly denounced the government: "Those *pendejos!* What they are is afraid! No one is leaving! Sampson will die here, along with all of the Philistines!" Gómez, in his inimitable way, had told the world that he was a modern Sampson, who would rather bring down Cuba on top of the Philistine Cuban politicians than surrender. For Gómez, the need to be obeyed came first and constituted a "spiritual necessity" that took precedence over everything else. Gómez was praetorian to the core. He mistrusted civilian politicians and their priorities, and this could not help but affect the nation that Gómez helped to "father." Equality before democracy, victory before either, was the motto written on the old caudillo's heart.[8]

Gómez also thought that burning the cane fields and tobacco plantations would attract Cuban elites in the West to join the revolution. This seems counterintuitive. Planters were reluctant to support a populist republic that so easily adopted a scorched-earth strategy and that openly promised radical land reform once the war ended. In comparison, burdensome Spanish export duties were nothing. But Gómez reasoned that economic warfare would eventually mobilize planters' support. Once the cane fields and other rural properties were wrecked, would not the planters, with nothing left to defend, cease to favor a colonial regime that had proven incapable of protecting them? It has been said that the power to destroy a thing is tantamount to its possession. If the Cuban Revolutionary Army could wipe out sugar, the planters would have to seek an accommodation with the insurgents.[9] In similar fashion, Gómez believed that ruining sugar and tobacco would cause international investors and their governments to support the revolution. Once the business community got over its shock at the scale and nature of the destruction, it would be forced to recognize that the Spanish could not protect property. When this happened, they would begin to deal with the republic-in-arms and exert pressure on Spain to give up Cuba.[10]

Gómez also hoped that a strategy of eliminating commercial agriculture would generate support among landless Cuban workers, many of them former slaves freed in 1886 but working the same cane fields and sugar mills as before. Such people eyed the big sugar estates with envy. They might be unresponsive to the finer points of nationalist and democratic ideology, but an attack on the big plantations was sure to gain their support. Moreover, if the assault on property achieved nothing else, it would force tens of thousands of these men into unemployment. This was not an unintended side effect of Gómez's strategy of total war but rather its centerpiece. Labor produced wealth, life, and order. To work was to act as a prop to the colonial regime and an enemy to the revolution. "Work means peace," proclaimed Gómez, so it followed that "in Cuba we must not permit working."[11] Burning the cane and tobacco fields and destroying the refineries would force men into idleness and give them no choice but to fall into the arms of the insurrection. This "forced strike," as one Cuban general put it, "gave a terrible aspect" to the whole war, but it was the best recruitment tool that Gómez had, better by far than any abstract appeal to the nation, democracy, equality, or humanity. In the end, the hard lessons Gómez taught using fire and dynamite mobilized Cubans as much as, and probably more than, the beautiful ideals of Martí.[12]

Gómez realized that the Liberation Army could not clothe, feed, and protect, much less arm, tens of thousands of cane cutters and other workers and their families who would be left destitute by the collapse of the economy. They could not all join the insurrection. Most of them would flee into towns and cities, where they would become the problem of the Spanish regime, or they would emigrate, or they would starve. In the summer of 1895, many of the country folk around Manzanillo and other towns in Oriente fled into the not very welcoming arms of the Spanish simply because they had no choice.[13] This was the informal beginning of reconcentration, a program later formalized by the Spanish, by which civilians were relocated to fortified towns and camps. Reconcentration will be examined at length in a later chapter. For now, it is enough to note that, by the time reconcentration ended, the human cost turned out to be greater than anyone could have imagined. But it is also important to recognize that this cost was not entirely unforeseen. Gómez knew that the strategy of shutting down the economy would bring dislocation, desperation, emigration, and death. This is what it was designed to do. But Gómez believed that he had "only one duty: to triumph" and that, to do so, "all means" were acceptable. In a letter to a friend written early in the war, Gómez predicted that if Spain did not immediately surrender, which seemed unlikely, then "stone will not remain upon stone here." All the riches of Cuba would be lost, "drowned in blood and devoured by flames." This was a war of "extermination," he wrote, and he would not be outdone by the Spanish. Gómez anticipated that the destruction of Cuban sugar would benefit the Dominican sugar industry, and he expressed hope that Dominicans would welcome the thousands of Cubans he expected to flee the island.[14]

Gómez was willing, as military leaders must be, to wager other people's lives in order to secure victory. As it turned out, between the efforts of Gómez and the later, more systematic brutality of the Spanish response, more than 100,000 civilians perished in Cuba before it was all over. Doubtless, this was a greater sacrifice than Gómez anticipated, but, given the generalissimo's character, it seems unlikely that anything could have induced him to alter his strategy.[15]

Gómez had other, very personal reasons for embracing a scorched-earth policy. In 1895 Gómez was fifty-nine years old and had been associated with the military — usually on the losing side — for most of his life. In 1861, when the Dominican Republic invited Spanish troops into the country to resist a renewed Haitian threat, Gómez enlisted in the Spanish army and was made a captain in the cavalry, serving with distinction. Gómez continued to serve with Spain against his countrymen when they rose up in 1863 to reclaim their independence. He fought well, earning promotion from captain to commander in a famous victory over the Dominican general, Pedro Florentino.

These wars in the Dominican Republic had a profound effect on Máximo Gómez, a profound and negative effect. For siding with Spain, Gómez had to forfeit his family's property and emigrate to Cuba in 1865 when the Dominican Republic regained its independence. Although Gómez received asylum in Cuba, it was all he ever got from Spain. There were no promotions, medals, or annuities, only insults and an early retirement from the service in 1867. Gómez tried to make a living cultivating a small farm near Santiago, but he was not a very good farmer. What Gómez knew best was war, and when Cuban patriots raised the banner of rebellion in 1868, Gómez joined the rebels. The Ten Years' War rescued Gómez from obscurity even as it gave him an opportunity to pay Spain back for misusing a once-loyal soldier.

By the standards of the Cuban insurrectos in 1868, Gómez was an experienced veteran, so he was elevated to the rank of colonel even before the serious fighting began. From his service in the Dominican Republic, Gómez knew Spanish tactics, and this gave him an edge over other Cuban commanders. Almost immediately, he led his troops to victory over the Spanish at Venta del Pino, near Bayamo. In this combat, he demonstrated the battlefield acumen that would make him famous. He lured a Spanish advance guard of two companies into a narrow defile, which his men had prepared with obstacles. Firing at point-blank range from the woods on either side of the road, the Cubans wiped out the Spanish in a few minutes, charging into them with machetes to finish the job. It was over almost before the Spanish knew what was happening. Venta del Pino was a crucial strategic victory because it induced a larger Spanish force tasked with retaking the town of Bayamo to withdraw. This left Bayamo the capital of Cuba Libre for four months, giving Cubans in the area a taste of life without Spain and allowing the insurrection to grow. For engineering this victory, Gómez received the rank of general. What the Spanish had not known how to appreciate, the Cubans rewarded richly.

Gómez emerged as a general of great skill and charisma during the Ten Years' War. In 1875 he led a force that penetrated briefly into Santa Clara province in central Cuba, laying waste to the region of Sancti Spíritus, with its sugar mills and cane fields. It was as far west as the insurgents ever got. Spain, having emerged from its own revolutionary turmoil, put an end to the Cuban rebellion, and Gómez went into exile once again. For the next two decades, he worked as a day laborer in Jamaica, a general in the Honduran army, and always a conspirator against the Spanish regime in Cuba. When José Martí organized the PRC and planned a new uprising for 1895, Gómez eagerly agreed to serve as commander in chief. This would be his last chance at military glory. He was too old and had fought too many losing battles to accept from himself and from Cubans anything less than an unwavering dedication to complete victory. At the end of a long life of struggle, Gómez had his eyes on the future of Cuba, not on the present situation of Cubans. If he had to play Sampson bringing down the temple around himself, so be it.[16]

At first, there was some debate about how strictly to apply the strategy of total war advocated by Gómez. José Martí, for example, had expressed misgivings before his untimely death. Martí had argued for preserving the property of sympathetic planters, partly so that the insurgents could tax them, but also to avoid utterly alienating people whom the emerging republic would need in the coming years. Martí had also wanted to avoid the widespread suffering that would surely follow the wholesale destruction of the economy, and he worried that a scorched-earth strategy would alienate public opinion overseas. Spanish propaganda painted the Cubans as bandits and incendiaries, and Martí had loathed the idea that the revolution might lend credence to this image.[17] To this, Gómez responded that if foreign planters were worried about their property then they

Máximo Gómez fought a brilliant and ruthless insurgent campaign against the Spanish and their Cuban supporters.

should plant their sugar cane somewhere else. "Cuban blood is too valuable to spill over sugar," he wrote. The only way "to plant the triumphant flag of the Cuban Republic [was] on top of the ruins" of the plantations and sugar mills and all of the other "old things" associated with colonial Cuba.[18]

Martí was not alone in his desire to prevent the destruction of the Cuban economy. Some of the civilian politicians in the revolutionary government, men Gómez scornfully called *bobos*, or morons, advocated more lenience toward the big landlords, if only so the insurgents could collect money from them. For a while in the summer of 1895, even Maceo was issuing "permits" to the landowners in Oriente to continue their operations, a sort of organized extortion that provided the republic-in-arms with a form of taxation just when it was most needed. Bartolomé Masó, general and politician, wrote to Gómez to try to persuade him to let the economy function. Gómez became furious. Annulling the permits, he ordered all of the properties in question destroyed. He demanded the demotion of the "little chiefs" who were "more merchants than warriors" and who, in his view, compromised the war effort in Oriente by acting as parasites on the economy rather than wiping it out, as ordered.[19]

The debate on this question in the spring of 1895 reprised one Gómez had lost in the 1870s when he had pushed for a similar policy of warfare aimed at sugar plantations and other commercial properties. That time around, the planter elites and politicians who controlled the movement, wanting to avoid the destruction of property perhaps as much as they wanted independence, had vetoed Gómez's recommendations. Gómez was determined in 1895 not to let this happen again.

Following Martí's death at Dos Ríos, the opposition to Gómez's position became weaker, but there were still some hesitations. Some local chieftains continued to spare the property of planters and ranchers in exchange for war contributions. Antonio Maceo's younger brother, José, did more than anyone to establish republican control over the province of Santiago in the summer of 1895.[20] But José Maceo did not carry out Gómez's orders regarding the economy. He allowed the owners of coffee plantations to stay in business, giving them "safe conduct passes" in exchange for fees. He did the same for other property owners too. He believed that Orientales should be treated differently. They sided, for the most part, with the revolution, and he wanted to cultivate and tax them, not ruin them.

This unauthorized behavior caused some concern in the revolutionary camp. The government required José Maceo to justify his program of revolutionary taxation and to provide a list of the "donors" and fees he had collected. In one area, in particular, the younger Maceo refused to carry out Gómez's orders. He did not burn the sugar mills, feeling — like many other Cuban patriots — that this went too far. Instead, he burned only the standing cane. This, he agreed, would "not only deprive the enemy of an important source of cash . . . but in consequence of the shortage of work that would result, the day laborers . . . would come to us to offer their services" as soldiers. At the same time, it would allow the sugar industry to recover more quickly once hostilities ended.[21] Although it did not please Gómez, José Maceo continued to operate in this manner throughout the first year of the war, burning cane but not buildings. As a result, he and his subordinates collected tens of thousands of dollars and channeled the money abroad for the purchase of weapons and supplies.[22] This service proved vital, however much it angered Gómez. Cuban agents in Liége and elsewhere purchased thousands of Mausers and other weapons, as, indeed, they had been doing even before the war. Arming a nation-in-the-making took a great deal of money, more, certainly, than the tobacco workers in Tampa could provide by themselves.[23]

Eventually, the provisional government saw the wisdom of Gómez's policy and disciplined José Maceo for violating it, as we shall see. As a result, Gómez was able to carry out his scorched-earth strategy with great rigor in much of the island, and this was one of the keys to the defeat of the Spanish. The economy collapsed and with it employment. Thousands of jobless men and women joined the revolution, if not as soldiers, then in support roles. There was never any shortage of work for men and women able to repair weapons, raise crops, guard livestock, transport and care for the sick and wounded, and perform the many other tasks required to keep the Liberation Army a going concern.

The Cuban republic-in-arms obliged all Cubans to serve the revolution according to their abilities, and Gómez wanted to use the army to enforce this requirement. He denied the existence of nonbelligerents. Civilians in insurgent zones had either to fight or to work for the revolution. Residents in Spanish towns were supposed to report enemy movements and pay fees to the provisional government.[24] In a war of liberation, argued Gómez, civilians had to choose sides. To be a neutral, or a *pacífico*, was to be an enemy of the revolution and a friend of Spain.

Cuban secretary of the interior Santiago García Cañizares issued clear instructions on the subject of civilians and their obligation to work for the revolution. He directed local officials in insurgent territory to form committees of residents whose task would be to destroy property, gather up livestock, and perform other jobs useful to the revolution. People who refused to carry out these orders would be turned out of their homes. Anyone who attempted to move between Spanish territory and insurgent zones of control without a passport signed by an official of the provisional government would face retribution from Cuban forces. They could be treated to the machete or hanged in "trees of justice," often guásima trees, so that victims of the new "national ritual" were said to have been *enguasimada.*[25]

Secretary of War Carlos Roloff promulgated measures that expanded upon these orders. Roloff required civilians living near main roads or Spanish towns to remove themselves to countryside considered insurgent territory. Anyone discovered within one league of a Spanish town or fortification would be shot. This project in social engineering, this "deconcentration" of the population to rural zones, anticipated in reverse the later reconcentration decrees issued by the Spanish in 1896 and 1897. When Roloff issued these orders in the fall of 1895, they were meaningless in more than half of Cuba because the insurgency had no presence yet in the West. We might also add that the republic-in-arms did not always enforce this draconian system, even when it could. Still, for civilians in Oriente living anywhere near a town, life became immediately more complicated. They either complied and went over to the revolution or fled to Spanish towns. The middle ground had been taken away, and quite graphically, too, as the suburbs around towns became a depopulated no-man's-land between urban Cuba Española and rural Cuba Libre. Although the Spanish response to the insurgents' deconcentration order — forced reconcentration — was still in the future, the beginning of the refugee problem in towns like Santiago, Guantánamo, and Manzanillo dated from 1895, when the insurgency began to implement a policy of total war aimed at civilians who tried to remain neutral. This caused thousands of Cubans to relocate to protected towns in the fall and winter of 1895 or, alternatively, to move to territory considered part of Cuba Libre.[26]

Gómez had no patience for civilians who claimed hardship and begged to be exempted from their patriotic duties. When pacíficos hid their animals in order to coax Cuban soldiers to camp on someone else's land and slaughter someone else's livestock, Gómez declared it a capital offense, though it seems clear that such harsh penalties were not strictly imposed on offenders.[27] On November 8, 1895, Gómez wrote to Zacarías Socarráz, an official of the Cuban provisional government in Monteoscuro, to complain about the behavior of pacíficos there. "Having come to my attention that some pacíficos show themselves lax in executing the orders given them to destroy their fences and to remove themselves from enemy positions, I make it known that all who adopt this attitude will be considered traitors to the cause of independence." Government officials were required to "bring before [him] all pacíficos" who behaved in this manner. Those remaining in their homes instead of evacuating to the countryside and people who continued to trade with the Spanish were to be punished most harshly.[28]

Being brought before Gómez was a fearsome proposition, for the old caudillo had a domineering manner that even his officers found marvelous to behold. Pacíficos who came to Gómez with the intention of complaining about property damage caused by Cuban troops soon repented their decision as they suffered through sermons and angry reprimands from the old general. Bernabé Boza, an aide to Gómez, recalled such a scene: "Here, we have been listening to a whole family pitifully lamenting the death of an ox and the confiscation of honey from a hive. I don't know what these stupid peasants are thinking. It seems that they don't realize that this war is real."[29]

Given these hard dealings with civilian neutrals, it is not surprising that the insurgent government condemned to death anyone who openly collaborated with the Spanish. On October 4, 1895, Gómez ordered Cubans who worked for the Spanish in any capacity "to be judged in a summary verbal trial followed by immediate execution of the sentence." Their property passed to the provisional government, which could use or destroy it. These strict measures elicited no real controversy on the Cuban side. Gómez was in a position to found a nation, and like other revolutionaries before and since, he did not mind "breaking a few eggs in order to make an omelette." But from the egg's perspective, the omelette is a nasty confection. Most Cuban civilians did not willingly sacrifice their individual existence for the abstract promise of a future collective good. When they worked for Spain, it was usually simply to survive because Spain or pro-Spanish elites paid their wages as postal workers, firemen, militiamen, plantation workers, and so forth. Likewise, when they worked for the fledgling republic, their motive was most often survival, not the lofty ideals of nationalism. Such people betrayed the homeland (Cuba or Spain) only in the minds of committed revolutionary elites like Gómez or Spaniards like Cánovas and Martínez Campos, for whom the abstraction of the nation counted more than life itself.

The pacíficos, the men and women who tried to live their lives on the margins of Cuba's great war of redemption, constituted a serious problem for the Cuban insurgents. If Cuban civilians continued to farm and sell their produce to Spanish cities, if they harvested cane and tobacco, if they put out fires in cities and towns and policed the streets, then the revolution would fail. This was the fundamental justification for Gómez's unflinching decision to take the war to civilians. Some thought that the widespread destruction of property meted out by the Cuban armed forces would come back to haunt the revolution. Boza likened the passage of the Liberation Army through a region to the destructive arrival of a hurricane. "The ranches we pass through are flattened," and, he suggested, this would produce such terrible dearth that the future of the Cuban people was threatened. Boza's observations were prophetic. The devastation wrought by the

Liberation Army set the table for a brutal Spanish response, and Cuban civilians paid the price for all of it in 1896 and 1897.[30]

In the summer of 1895 Gómez had no power to enforce his scheme of total war in half of the island. As we have already seen, the revolution had not prospered initially in the major sugar-producing provinces of central and western Cuba. In the land of cane and tobacco, it was still business as usual. The Liberation Army had become strong in the East, but if Gómez wanted to make good on his promise to wipe out the Cuban economy and with it the Spanish regime, he would have to find a way to move his forces west into the Cuban "sugar bowl."

6 ⋆ Antonio Maceo and the Battle of Peralejo

Antonio Maceo had dreamed of war his whole life. Born in 1845 near Santiago, Maceo grew up hearing tales of his Venezuelan father's military exploits fighting for Spain in the American wars of independence. As a mulatto boy (his father was white) in a slave society, Maceo chafed under the racism and Peninsular chauvinism of the Spanish colonial regime. He resolved early in life to honor his father's martial past by fighting against the country his progenitor had defended. In this way, Maceo achieved the perfect Freudian miracle of imitating and rebelling against his father and defending his mother in one and the same act.

In 1864, Maceo joined the Masonic lodge in Santiago and entered the secret world of the Cuban revolutionaries, many of whom were Masons.[1] Masons, members of a secret society founded by Scottish stonemasons, probably in the seventeenth century, seem to us now like members of some harmless club, like Rotarians with secret handshakes. In the eighteenth and nineteenth centuries, however, the Masonic order had revolutionary aspirations and included some of the leading intellectuals and radicals in the Atlantic world. As we have already seen, Martí joined the Masonic temple in Madrid, and the lodge at Bayamo included Carlos Manuel de Céspedes and many other great Cuban patriots. Fellow Masons, including Maceo, were among the first to enlist to fight with Céspedes for Cuban independence in 1868.

Through success on the battlefield, Maceo achieved rapid promotion. By the end of October 1868, he was a sergeant. Three months later, he had become a lieutenant colonel. By the end of the war, Maceo had achieved the rank of major general, the highest position in the Cuban service. It is in the nature of revolutionary armies to move men of talent rapidly through the ranks. Such armies quickly acquire unschooled but experienced officers who can readily command the loyalty of their men. Like a new Napoleon, Maceo rose to prominence rapidly but always remained popular with the enlisted men. In part, Maceo had race on his side. In both the Ten Years' War and the War of Independence, most Cuban officers were white, while most of the troops were black. As a result, Maceo was, as an officer of color, a rarity, and he was idolized by the black troops. But Maceo's eloquence, his high sense of personal honor and dignity, and, above all, his uncanny knack for winning battles made him the idol of his white troops as well. On the other hand, white Cuban elites had their doubts and fears concerning Maceo: In the 1870s, a slander circulated that accused Maceo of being a black Bonaparte, aspiring to set up a separate Afro-Cuban state.[2]

Even more than Gómez, Maceo never accepted the defeat of 1878. His rejection of Spanish peace terms — the so-called Protest of Baraguá — was absolute. He considered the peace nothing more than a cease-fire, and some of his men followed his example. Most of them were able to wait out the next seventeen years in Cuba harboring their resentment in secret and passing it on to their children, but Maceo's notoriety and intransigence meant that he was forced to live abroad: in Jamaica, New York, Haiti, Saint Thomas, the Dominican Republic, Honduras, Panama, Peru, and Costa Rica. It was a restless exile. Pursued by Spanish agents, surviving several assassination attempts, Maceo was unable to settle down or prosper for very long. Through it all he dreamed of another chance to free his homeland.[3]

Maceo believed that Cuban armed forces had gone down to defeat in the Ten Years' War mainly because they failed to take the fighting into the western half of the island. The revolution had been strong in the provinces of Santiago and Puerto Príncipe in the 1870s, but regional jealousies and local particularism, as well as the planter elites' concern for property and their fear of the black troops that composed the majority of the patriot forces, had prevented the independence movement from gaining ground in the central and western provinces of Santa Clara, Matanzas, Havana, and Pinar del Río. The revolution languished in the East and finally ran out of resources, allowing Spain to negotiate a peace unfavorable to the Cuban side. Now, in the spring of 1895, the old pattern seemed to be reasserting itself, with the insurgency really strong only in Santiago province. This was a dangerous moment for the revolution and precisely the situation Maceo wanted to avoid, lest the fledgling Cuban republic be isolated and then buried in the East, in the same grave that held the revolution of 1868.[4]

Nevertheless, Maceo was not eager to march into the teeth of Spanish-dominated western Cuba in the summer of 1895. He argued instead for postponing grand offensive actions until the Liberation Army could build up sufficient manpower and weapons. Cuban exiles in the United States, Venezuela, and other countries bordering the Caribbean busied themselves organizing expeditions of arms and men for the insurgents, but Maceo estimated that it would take several months to acquire the men and matériel for an invasion of the West. In the meantime, the "Bronze Titan" found targets he could attack with some hope of success.

Though always popular in Oriente, Maceo did not mistake popularity for unanimous and unqualified support. He understood that civilian trust and support is won by engaging the enemy and establishing a presence capable of

Antonio Maceo was the best field general in the Cuban Liberation Army,
leading the insurgent forces to westernmost Cuba before being killed in battle.

persuading or forcing people to join the rebellion. To this end, Maceo occupied, if only briefly, municipalities loyal to Spain and made it dangerous for Spanish sympathizers to show themselves in public. The idea was not so much to do battle with the Spanish as it was to scour communities of their pro-Spanish elements and to encourage supporters of independence to commit themselves to the cause. In this way, Maceo solidified his power in Oriente. Success in these endeavors then facilitated recruitment and allowed Maceo to expand operations to include attacks on Spanish outposts, couriers, and convoys.

Something Maceo could do from the beginning was prevent Spanish garrisons from foraging for themselves. He did not need large numbers of armed men to accomplish this task. Posting a few men to watch each Spanish town, Maceo could respond quickly if any small force attempted to exit to acquire provisions. This simple procedure produced important strategic benefits. It left the Spanish with just two options for feeding their garrisons. Large garrisons could sortie in force to forage, and the Spanish routinely sent out half battalions — and sometimes whole battalions — merely to gather food, firewood, and other necessities. Of course, this diverted large numbers of men from other tasks. The second option was to resupply positions by convoy, a system used especially with small garrisons that were incapable of a sortie to acquire provisions. But this method created opportunities for ambush and sniping against slow-moving Spanish columns. Either way, the guerrilla strategy of blockading towns and disrupting commerce exploited Spanish vulnerabilities and insurgent strengths.[5]

Removing Spanish partisans from the countryside left the Spanish without the logistical support and intelligence they needed from civilians to have a chance of locating and defeating Maceo. In the summer of 1895, Maceo did not have the manpower, weaponry, or reserves of ammunition to control territory against Spanish attack. Yet he did gain the ability to command the allegiance of many Orientales, so that he could state, with some justification, that in the East "the Spaniard owns only the ground on which he stands." The claim was not entirely true — some places even in eastern Cuba remained loyal to Spain — but the phrase sounded good, and it helped to build morale. Martínez Campos, touring the East in the late spring, reported to Cánovas that the situation in the region had begun to "frighten" him. In eastern Cuba, at least, the majority of the population seemed clearly to side with the insurgency. People in Oriente "who dare to proclaim themselves" for Spain did so "only in the cities," reported the captain general.[6]

By the middle of June, Maceo had 600 armed infantry and 200 cavalry under orders in Oriente, and more joined every day. By early July, Maceo had perhaps 2,000 men, though many of them were armed only with machetes and they never assembled together at one time. Still, he had enough troops to look for a regular battle with the Spanish, and on July 14, at Peralejo, he got his chance.

On the morning of July 11, Spanish brigadier general Fidel Alonso Santocildes left the coastal town of Manzanillo with 400 men and marched inland toward Bayamo. On the way, he linked up with Martínez Campos, at the head of another 400 men, and on the following day in Veguitas, a short distance east of Manzanillo, 700 more troops joined them. In the context of the Cuban war, 1,500 men was a large force and a sign that the Spanish were itching for a major engagement.

They came to the right place. The area east of Manzanillo, in the shadow of the Sierra Maestra, had never been easy for Spanish authorities to control even in times of peace. Living in small hamlets and isolated homesteads, people around Manzanillo and Bayamo farmed just enough for their own subsistence and for local trading, had little money, avoided tax collectors, and generally saw to it that their lives intersected with Spanish institutions as little as possible.

Even the Catholic Church had few devotees in the region. In the nineteenth century, Christianity served European colonial interests worldwide by taking on some of the burdens of the imperial "civilizing mission." The Catholic Church served especially well in Spain and in much of Latin America as a mechanism for reconciling people to their subordinate station in life. In Spain, however, the church had fallen on hard times. Its enormous wealth had made it the target of periodic confiscations by Madrid, and the church became defensive and elitist. Losing ground in the Mother Country, the church became unqualified to serve as an effective tool of empire in Cuba. It could not even find enough clergymen or build enough houses of worship to keep pace with the island's demographic growth. In Oriente, where the population was thinly dispersed over the countryside and towns were exotic, many people simply resided too far away from a parish church to be able to attend even for such pivotal events as baptisms and marriages. Cubans filled the vacuum left by the church's absence with their own syncretic forms of worship, such as Santería, combining elements of African, Amerindian, and European traditions. In short, the Catholic Church had failed to turn a significant number of Cubans into Christians, much less Spanish subjects.[7]

To complicate the picture around the Manzanillo-Bayamo corridor, runaway slaves, or cimarrones, had for decades taken refuge in the area, creating communities for themselves there and maintaining an especially wary attitude toward Spanish authorities. It should come as no surprise, therefore, that the region was a hotbed of separatism in the 1860s and 1870s and remained a center of revolutionary strength in 1895. It was the heart of Cuba Libre, and Santocildes and Martínez Campos were heading right for it.

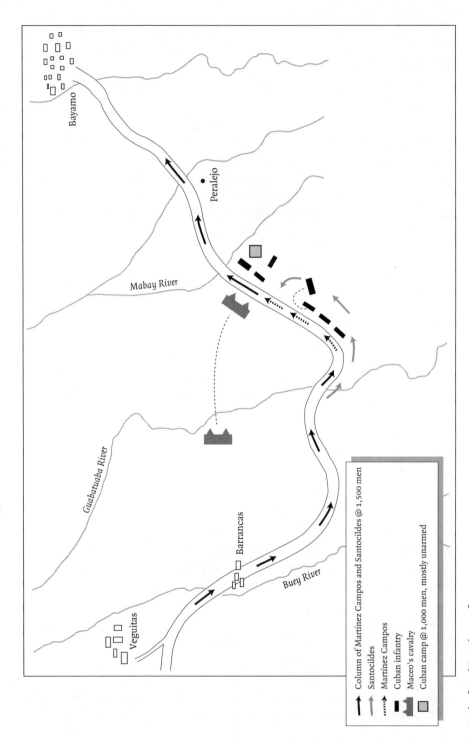

Battle of Peralejo, July 13, 1895

Bayamo

Peralejo

Mabay River

Guabatuaba River

Barrancas

Buey River

Veguitas

Column of Martínez Campos and Santocildes @ 1,500 men

Santocildes

Martínez Campos

Cuban infantry

Maceo's cavalry

Cuban camp @ 1,000 men, mostly unarmed

The Spanish soldiers stumbled with fatigue as they marched in the tropical heat on the road to Bayamo. Spain lacked an effective way to get supplies into the field — roads and railroads were primitive to nonexistent in the East — so troops had to shoulder packs heavy with ammunition and rations, turning marches into slow calvaries of pain. Heatstroke was a constant companion, prostrating otherwise healthy soldiers, turning their comrades into litter bearers, and slowing marches to crawls. Daily downpours in the summer turned roads that were little more than paths into quagmires that sucked the shoes right off men's feet. Descriptions of Spanish columns, their mountain cannon carted by struggling oxen over steep, muddy paths, remind one of images of Napoleon's Grand Army slogging through darkest Russia, or of Roman troops moving through wild Britain.

If anything, conditions were even worse in Cuba. Sometimes the Spanish had to bypass flooded roads by hacking new paths through the jungle. Then the exuberant tropical plant life clutched and tore at their uniforms, enveloping them in green and blinding them to anything that was more than a few feet away. Spanish servicemen, much like American soldiers who served in Vietnam, learned to hate the color green, which they came to associate with monotony, toil, and death, rather than life and the rejuvenation that comes with spring. Spaniards did not face Claymore mines and pangee traps, but the Cubans used dynamite, ambush, and constant sniping to make travel through the countryside a fearsome thing.[8]

Spanish soldiers could never relax. At night, Maceo's men fired at sentries, not because they expected to hit anyone — they always fired from great distances to allow for an easy getaway — but in order to keep the Spanish from enjoying uninterrupted sleep. Daylight brought heat and more marching, and the Spanish knew that their progress could be disrupted at any moment by sniper fire, which, though rarely deadly, kept them constantly alert and fearful.[9] Fear is a powerful motivator of men in combat. In the heat of battle, it can become an unbearable spiritual tension that spurs men to action. When it manifests itself this way, it is sometimes even mistaken for bravery. But constant, gnawing fear has an altogether different effect on soldiers. It tires men out in ways nothing else can. One cannot remain constantly alert to danger without suffering serious psychological and physiological consequences. In Cuba, where there were no clear battle lines and where no bivouac was safe, Spanish servicemen were always exhausted, physically, mentally, and spiritually.

On top of everything else, many of the men with Martínez Campos and Santocildes marched shaking and dripping with fever. It was the height of summer, when tropical diseases like malaria and yellow fever were most likely to strike. Gómez liked to quip that his best generals were June, July, and August, when the climate and the deadly mosquito immobilized more Spaniards than the insurgents ever could. In 1897 Ronald Ross, a British physician working in India, discovered the malaria parasite in the gut of the *anopheles* mosquito. Three years later, a Cuban physician named Carlos Finlay, completing research begun twenty years earlier, helped Walter Reed and his Yellow Fever Commission prove that the *Aëdes aegypti* mosquito was the vector for yellow fever. But no one (except Finlay and his close collaborator, Claudio Delgado) understood any of this in 1895. Regulations required Spanish troops to sleep in tents, to prevent "night airs" from disabling them. In fact, however, most camped under the open sky whenever they could. Even Weyler himself ignored the rule against sleeping in the open when on campaign: A sentry once kicked Weyler awake and began to scold him about violating sleeping regulations before realizing he was lecturing the commander in chief.[10] The deadly results of sleeping uncovered were simply not clear, and the temptation to catch any night breeze that might provide some relief from the heat was too great. Some of the men carried mosquito netting for comfort's sake, but it quickly rotted away, like everything else left outdoors in Cuba, and Spanish troops used it neglectfully, not realizing that it could save their lives. On the night of July 12, 1895, as the soldiers under Santocildes and Martínez Campos gathered at Veguitas, a plague of mosquitoes hovered over the camp, stealing the lifeblood of the Spanish troops and leaving behind an army of diseased men.

The mission of this army was not entirely clear. The men had orders to escort a supply convoy from Veguitas to Bayamo. But Santocildes and Martínez Campos also appear to have had something more dramatic in mind. Like all Spanish officers, they itched for a decisive battle. Their military training had prepared them to fight the battle of Sedán, preferably in the role of the Prussians, and they hoped to force such an encounter upon the Cubans.[11] But Cuba was not the northern European plain, the Spanish were not the Prussians, and the Cubans were not the demoralized French troops who fought so poorly in 1870 in defense of the farcical Second Empire. Cuban officers had not learned how to fight by studying textbooks on the subject of warfare or dreaming about reenacting Jena and Austerlitz. Their teacher had been experience. Cuban officers had become hardened veterans of jungle combat during the Ten Years' War. They knew that a Cuban Sedán could only play into the hands of the Spanish, so they sniped and ambushed and, above all, evaded Spanish regulars. This frustrated Spanish officers and turned them into gamblers willing to take great risks with their men in order to lure the elusive Cubans into making a stand.

In the summer of 1895, Cuban troops had little difficulty eluding the Spanish when it served their purpose. Not only did they have a better knowledge of the countryside, they also had the support of most of the rural population in areas such as Manzanillo. The aid of civilians, whether gained and maintained through persuasion or force, is always a necessary condition of successful guerrilla warfare against superior regular forces. Insurgents disappear into the civilian population between engagements, obviating, at least some of the time, the need for the organized provision of food, medicine, rest, and the other things an army must have between battles. In addition, unless an occupier is willing to annihilate or relocate noncombatants, insurgents will always enjoy a kind of invisibility because separating combatants from neutrals is almost impossible in a guerrilla war.

Civilian support also gives insurgent armies access to good military intelligence. In Cuba, especially in eastern Cuba, officers of the Liberation Army had a reputation for knowing every Spanish move ahead of time. Benigno Souza put biblical sounding poetry into Máximo Gómez's mouth when he characterized the generalissimo's almost occult powers of divination: "I know where the sucking insect lays its egg in Cuba. I know where the fat bull is and where the best water is. I know the hour when the Spaniard is wakeful and the hour when he sleeps most deeply. I divine his moments of fear, and then I am courageous and daring. And I quickly recognize when he is fearless, and then I prudently let him pass, so that he expends his bravery in a vacuum." [12]

The Cubans always seemed to know the composition and itinerary of every relief column, allowing them to set up roadblocks and ambushes. Manuel Corral recalled that in preparing one relief column the scheme was discussed so openly that "four days before we set our plans in motion, a peasant gave me a detailed account of them, something that leads me to suppose that our plans also reached the ears of the enemy." [13] The Spanish soon realized that anything they said in front of Cubans employed as grooms, valets, waiters, and the like would reach enemy ears. With every Cuban a potential spy, the Spanish began to leak disinformation and to plan their stratagems in whispers. The occupation became furtive in the presence of the occupied, a reminder to Cuban civilians, if one was needed, that the Spanish saw them as different and unreliable, as subjects — or even objects — instead of citizens.

It did not help the Spanish that they had no cavalry. Cuba produced many fine horses, but ranchers allowed them to roam and forage freely, rounding them up when necessary. [14] This made it difficult for the Spanish to requisition them. By the time they tried, it was too late. The insurgents had captured them all, and Spain, by then known more for the quality of its pack mules than its horses, could not acquire and transport enough horses from the Peninsula to make a difference. As a result, Spanish armies marched blindly, even in open country, unable to screen their advance or flanks with adequate cavalry or to scout ahead in order to locate the enemy. Nor could they pursue retreating Cuban troops if a battle developed favorably for the Spanish. The fact that the Spanish had few cavalry units was no small advantage for the Cubans. In military affairs, perhaps more than in any other field of human endeavor, apparently small matters can be decisive. Such was the case with the Liberation Army's successful monopoly of horses. Had the Spanish possessed an equal number of horses, the war might have gone differently.[15]

Already by July 1895 Spanish officers had grown tired of groping blindly after the elusive Cubans and had begun to play a dangerous game. In order to encourage the Cubans to stand their ground, officers sent out small forces — as small as they dared — and divided larger forces into separate columns hoping to create the appearance of vulnerability in order to tempt their enemy into a frontal battle. This is apparently what Santocildes planned to do.[16] Half of Maceo's 2,000 men had no weapons other than machetes, but the Spanish did not know that. Indeed, Santocildes thought Maceo had thousands more men than he really did. Nevertheless, the Spanish general, with the arrogance characteristic of Spanish officers, was certain that he could beat Maceo in an open fight. On the eve of battle, Santocildes explained his thinking in a letter to his superior, who had questioned his enthusiasm and ability. He faced superior enemy forces and lacked adequate ammunition, supplies, and staff officers, Santocildes wrote, but he would head out in search of Maceo anyway: "You will see that I am not one for passive warfare but know how to do my duty and then do it."[17] Early on the morning of July 13, Martínez Campos left Veguitas with one-third of the men and took the road to Bayamo. Santocildes marched the remaining men down a parallel route, but one not too distant, so that the two columns could join forces when they found Maceo. It promised to be "a splendid occasion to see up close the bravery of the enemy."[18]

Maceo had full intelligence of Spanish numbers, weapons, and plans. Even towns that supported the Spanish regime had Cuban spies. In Cuban strongholds like Veguitas, they were everywhere. On July 14, at one A.M., Maceo took his men to a place called Peralejo, on the road to Bayamo, and there he waited. It was hilly country, and the Cuban infantry occupied positions in heights beside the road, taking advantage of the cover provided by trees, rocks, and a fence that lined both sides of the route Spanish troops would have to take. Maceo's surprise was incomplete, however, because the Spanish also had informants. In his report of the battle to Bartolomé Masó on July 14, Maceo wrote that a Spanish spy had revealed his position, preventing him from annihilating the column. Indeed, the Spanish commanders seemed to expect an attack more or less where it occurred, a detail that, if true, only makes their lack of preparation all the more perplexing.[19]

At about ten A.M. the Cubans fired the opening shots of the battle, and Santocildes rushed to rejoin Martínez Campos. Cuban troops fired individually, aiming at their targets, taking advantage of the accuracy of their rifles to wreak havoc among their enemies. The Spanish, on the other hand, formed defensive lines and fired volleys, as they had been trained to do. It is said that at the beginning of a war, officers fight with the strategies and tactics of the previous war. Spanish officers in Cuba, though, fought using methods from an even more distant past: They employed tactics perfected during the Napoleonic era and pounded into their heads by conservative military instructors. In the eighty years that separated Waterloo from Peralejo, weapons had become more powerful and accurate, making the tactic of the massed infantry volley and bayonet charge unsuitable for the modern battlefield. The U.S. Civil War had proved this. Men armed with rifles and hunkered down in trenches and behind barriers wiped out infantry and even cavalry advancing in massed formation. But Spanish officers had observed the U.S. Civil War without really learning from it. Surely, they thought, a conflict in the wilds of the New World among undisciplined frontiersmen could not possibly teach them anything useful. As a result, exemplary disasters like Pickett's charge at Gettysburg produced no changes in the way Spaniards prepared for combat. Officers tried to fight in Cuba as they had fought a century before. Indeed, the square, used since the Renaissance by Swiss pikemen, remained their textbook response to any threat from enemy cavalry. And the Spaniards fired in volleys, as if they were using muskets, rather than according to the discretion of the troops, which is a method more suited to the rifle. These tactical problems haunted the Spanish throughout the war, and we will have more to say about them later.[20]

In one sense, the square adopted by the Spanish at Peralejo worked: it served to neutralize Maceo's superiority in horses. The Cuban cavalry charged, their machetes raised high, but volleys of rifle fire prevented them from ever reaching the Spanish lines. In another sense, however, Spanish defensive tactics played into the hands of the Cubans. The threat of Maceo's cavalry encouraged the Spanish to close up into tight formations. Fighting in this way, however, the Spanish became exceedingly vulnerable to aimed Cuban rifle fire. A Cuban officer later recalled the scene and the tactics at Peralejo: "Our infantry, from the hills in which they sheltered, picked off the Spanish in their files, while the menace of a charge from the nearby cavalry obliged the Spanish to remain in closed formation, which made it easier to score more hits on them."[21] In short, the Cubans employed superior tactics at Peralejo, using their rifles to fight in a modern, open formation, while the Spanish fought as if on a Napoleonic battlefield. This, rather than weight of numbers, surprise, morale, ideological conviction, or anything else, proved to be the decisive factor in determining the way the battle of Peralejo developed.

The Cubans, as always, were low on ammunition, but in this fight so were the Spanish. In fact, the Spanish ran out of cartridges first. The lack of horses once again haunted them, as each soldier had been forced to carry his own cartridges, with no reserve. This meant each man had only a few extra rounds, severely limiting the Spanish ability to maintain a long firefight. Firing volleys at individual enemy targets hidden in the brush did not help to conserve ammunition either. Toward the end of the battle, Spanish troops stood in formation with fixed bayonets, passively receiving Cuban rifle fire, which mercifully became sporadic as the Cubans also ran low on ammunition. Finally, some intrepid Spanish troopers dashed from their lines to pilfer ammunition from dead Cuban troops, probably cavalrymen who had perished during their machete charges at the beginning of the battle. After reloading with "shiny and new" Cuban cartridges fresh from U.S. suppliers, the Spanish continued their march into Bayamo, with the Cubans who still had ammunition taking potshots at them the whole way.[22]

The Spanish lost twenty-eight killed and ninety-eight wounded at Peralejo. In the context of the Cuban war, characterized by numerous small battles with low casualties, it was a disaster. Maceo lost 118 men between killed and wounded, almost as many as the Spanish. Nevertheless, it was a clear Cuban victory. The Spanish had abandoned the field under fire, something that rarely happened during the war, and they left behind some of the provisions they were transporting to Bayamo, providing the Cubans with a trophy of the victory. Moreover, the Cubans had killed Santocildes, though Maceo did not realize it at the time. Santocildes had exhibited his Quixotic sense of honor by remaining mounted during the fight. Cuban troopers easily spotted him, especially since the Spanish had so few mounts to begin with, and someone shot Santocildes out of his saddle. After the fight, Maceo wanted to engage the enemy again, but he soon discovered that his men had only enough ammunition left for about ten minutes of fighting, leaving him with no choice but to withdraw from the area and regroup. For his part, Martínez Campos remained in Bayamo licking his wounds.

Maceo's defeat of the Spanish at Peralejo boosted Cuban morale. For many of Maceo's men who had missed the little battle of Jobito, Peralejo was their first taste of serious combat. Burning property, enforcing revolutionary justice among Cuban neutrals and collaborators, and ambushing scouting parties was one thing, but Peralejo had been a real battle. In the aftermath, Maceo was palpably excited and eager to fight the Spanish again.[23] Peralejo was the first great turning point of the war. Cuban recruitment picked up, and Gómez and Maceo began to gather the strength they would need to break out of Oriente province three months later.[24]

While Maceo consolidated his hold on Santiago, Gómez campaigned just to the west, in Puerto Príncipe. After Dos Ríos, Gómez had been left with only twenty-five men, and even these few had to be cajoled into remaining with the colors. Fortunately, an independent guerrilla force of 200 men from Las Tunas joined Gómez and crossed with him into Puerto Príncipe on June 5.

Benigno Souza optimistically wrote that "all the youth" of Puerto Príncipe "rose up in unanimous ardor" when the old caudillo called them to arms. In fact, the reality is more complex. Local leaders let Gómez know that they did not want war in Puerto Príncipe, and they expressed irritation that a "foreigner" from the Dominican Republic dared to force war on them. Gómez responded by declaring that he would bring war to them regardless, and he recruited some 200 young men in Puerto Príncipe in the space of a few weeks. It was hardly a unanimous rising of the province, but it did give Gómez the numbers to undertake a campaign of surprise attacks against Spanish garrisons and towns. Cubans know this as the "circular campaign," because Gómez, constantly on the move, circled about the province always a step ahead of the Spanish defenders.[1]

On June 17 Gómez achieved his greatest success when he burned the undefended town of Altagracia, just northeast of the provincial capital. A few days later he forced small garrisons at El Mulato and San Gerónimo to surrender. Wherever he went, Gómez requisitioned horses, which Puerto Príncipe produced in abundance, further consolidating the Liberation Army's advantage over the Spanish in cavalry. Baffled and humiliated by Gómez, Martínez Campos asked to be relieved of command, a request the Spanish government denied.

Gómez's successes in Puerto Príncipe and Maceo's more dramatic victories in Santiago allowed the insurgents to recruit several thousand men in the summer of 1895. The problem was arming them, clothing them, and getting them cartridges. The civil arm of the revolution in districts under insurgent control included a system of prefects who were supposed to keep supplies flowing to the army. They performed heroic service, but the job was really beyond their power. Gómez and other officers complained constantly that the prefectures were not working, even in eastern Cuba, where they had been more fully implanted. As Gómez wrote to Minister of War Rafael Portuondo, "[I]t is impossible to obtain the resources an army needs, above all here in Camagüey (Puerto Príncipe), where a considerable number of saddles are needed for the cavalry." The work-shops run by the prefects even failed to supply him with shoes, he added. As a result, the men were soon reduced to going barefoot, dressing in rags, and using broken equipment.[2]

The fundamental problem for the patriots was their inability to hold towns against Spanish attack. Las Tunas was the one town of any size taken by the Liberation Army during the war. Seized by Calixto García in the summer of 1897, Las Tunas was burned and abandoned after a few days because García could not defend the place. With no ability to command centers of population and no raw materials necessary to manufacture rifles, cartridges, uniforms, medicines, and other supplies, the Cuban armed forces had to rely on what they could capture from the Spanish and, more fundamentally, on what expeditionaries brought into Cuba from abroad.[3]

Cuban émigrés, especially those based in the United States, sent dozens of so-called filibustering expeditions to Cuba from 1895 to 1898. One contemporary identified sixty-three expeditions that departed from U.S. waters alone, without counting those leaving from other countries.[4] The "filibusters" went in steamships, private schooners, yachts, and smaller craft. As one combatant put it, "[T]he Cubans would hire an oyster shell, if they thought they could send a rifle to Cuba in it."[5]

Spain's consular officials and other agents resident in the usual jumping-off points for the filibusters tried to keep Havana informed about the expeditions, but their efforts had little impact. Reading the correspondence of these agents from Santiago, Veracruz, Kingston, Santo Domingo, Key West, Tampa, Savannah, New York, and other ports frequented by the Cubans, one is left with the impression that Spanish espionage was amateurish.[6] The problem was often the same. They were informed about the activities of the Cuban émigrés, but they had no ability to use the intelligence. They passed information to the authorities, but relying on local police to enforce laws against gunrunning was futile. Many officials were sympathetic to the Cubans. Others were just uninterested in adding to their workload. They obstructed the Spanish with red tape, tipped off Cuban émigrés, and took their time about pursuing known revolutionaries. On the occasions when local law enforcement made arrests, sympathetic or bored judges let the suspects off with fines and released weapons caches back to the Cubans.

American president Grover Cleveland had no love for the Cuban revolutionaries, whom he once characterized as "the most barbarous and inhuman assassins in the world."[7] His administration officially opposed the rebellion and ordered Treasury officials and Coast Guard boats to be on the alert for Cuban filibusters. This led to bitter words by Cuban patriots, who felt the United States had allowed itself to become "Spain's guardian."[8] In fact, however, Cleveland really made only a token effort, and some Cuban officials understood this. The provisional government's representative to the United States, Tomás Estrada Palma, in a letter of August 1895 to Antonio Maceo, noted that despite some obstruction from Washington, "the United States is with us." It was just a matter of time, he predicted, before the American administration recognized Cuban belligerence and began to provide official support. Indeed, Cleveland eventually proclaimed the U.S. government "neutral" in the conflict, thus granting the rebels a level of legitimacy just short of belligerent status. As we shall see, Cleveland's successor, William McKinley, though also uncomfortable with the populist nature of the Cuban revolution, made every effort to press Spain to relinquish its hold on Cuba and did little to interdict supplies coming from the United States.[9]

It would probably have made little difference had Cleveland and McKinley been more resolute in their opposition to the Cuban rebels because, in some ways, it did not matter what attitude the U.S. federal government took. The power of Washington to enforce its will was not very impressive in the late nineteenth century, especially in the post-Reconstruction South, which happened to be the greatest center of Cuban émigré activity. The Spanish ambassador to the United States, Enrique Dupuy de Lôme, realized this. "The government promises to stop departure [of filibusters]," Dupuy wrote to his bosses in Madrid in telegraphic staccato, "but I believe our vigilance necessary because local American authorities don't obey orders from superiors" in Washington.[10] The same lack of central authority also characterized Mexico, Costa Rica, and other countries that harbored Cuban émigrés. In Venezuela and Colombia, Cubans even achieved a friendly symbiosis with local rebels opposed to rulers in Caracas and Bogotá, giving them a free hand to organize.[11]

Once an expedition entered Cuban waters, the Spanish navy was not much of a bother. Guarding Cuba's 2,000 miles of coastline would have been a challenge to the British Royal Navy, the best in the world. The Spanish, who had few decent gunboats, found the job impossible. One scholar has asserted that the Spanish navy had "complete control" of Cuban waters, so that the arrival of supply boats was always "perilous and uncertain."[12] Peril and uncertainty there were, but not because of the Spanish navy. The cañoneros and torpederos Spain had on hand to watch the coast were small, slow, and in various states of disrepair.[13] The Cubans had little trouble avoiding them. Typical was the experience of the expedition led by Colonel Fernando Méndez. Méndez ran into one of Spain's coastal vessels, but the Cubans were in the fast John Smith and easily outran the Spanish to make landfall on the coast near Havana.[14]

Spain's own military was partly to blame for the decrepit state of Cuba's coastal defenses. Army officers retained a great deal of power in Spanish politics, for reasons we will examine shortly. Reformers who dared to suggest that more of the defense budget should go to the navy or to the colonies risked being branded as traitors and finding their political careers cut short. As a result, nothing was ever done to build or maintain naval forces to protect Cuba. New ships remained unfinished in boatyards in Spain. Those already stationed in Cuba deteriorated, to the point that some were removed to dry dock, where repairs were planned but never completed. Such gunboats issued out in search of Cuban vessels only in their captains' dreams.

None of this should be taken to suggest that émigrés had an easy time getting to Cuba. They faced many personal hardships and performed marvelous acts of heroism to make the voyage. José Rutea took an especially arduous route home. Rutea's story forces us to look ahead several months to 1896, but readers should find the detour worthwhile, for it provides some insight into the commitment and tragic fate of some of the Cuban patriots living abroad.[15]

Rutea had been in Spain when war broke out in 1895. He went to Paris in December, where he found shelter with the organization established by the Puerto Rican expatriate Ramón Betances. After playing tourist for a few weeks, visiting the Eiffel Tower and other famous sights, he took a steamer to New York City. Rutea spent the next three weeks in the home of Roberto Todd, another Puerto Rican patriot living in Manhattan. By day, Rutea toured New York. He recalled especially the Statue of Liberty, the surprising commercial traffic, the elevated trains, the Brooklyn Bridge, and other products of what he called "yankee eccentricity." In the middle of January a letter arrived from Calixto García telling Rutea to stay at Todd's house from four to nine P.M. every night, packed, and ready to travel. It was time to go to Cuba.

On the evening of January 25, one of García's agents called on Rutea at eight P.M. to guide him to a mysterious rendezvous at 124th Street on the Upper East Side of Manhattan. Men from all over the city traveled to the spot. Ramiro Cabrera had advance warning and decided to stop for a big feed at the famous Delmonico's, a favorite meeting spot for Cubans, where he devoured steak and quaffed champagne as if it were a last meal. Rutea's preparation was less satisfying. His notice was a knock on his host's door and a train ride north, where he joined some 130 men furtively milling about in a fenced vacant lot used to store monumental marble slabs and blocks. It was a distinguished company. Among them were Calixto García, Juan Ruz, Avelino Rozas, Miguel Betancourt, José Cebreco, and "various doctors, lawyers, engineers, pharmacists, doctors of philosophy and letters, and a large group of students." The solemnity of the occasion, the presence of funereal marble slabs everywhere, and the freezing wind from the East River imposed a stillness and silence on them all. They blew into their hands and stamped their feet to stay warm as they waited for their transportation to arrive.

The group boarded a launch just after ten P.M. Rutea noted that a New York police officer watched the whole thing, but, "knowing who we were, he was not alarmed by our departure and wished us good luck." This sort of response, or lack of response, by local law enforcement officials in the United States had come to be taken for granted by the Cubans. The men reached New York Harbor and transferred to the J. W. Hawkins around midnight. It was bitterly cold, and they found it difficult to sleep that night and the next. Captain Bernardo Bueno took out his flute and entertained everyone with renditions of La Marseillaise, El Rigoletto, La Traviatta, and patriotic Cuban songs, played again and again to gall two Spaniards who had joined up with the Cubans. It was lucky that they all slept little and lightly on the night of January 27 because just before one A.M. on the morning of the 28th, the J. W. Hawkins began to take on water. Worse still, the Cubans discovered that the pump was broken. The ship was going down. Unfortunately, no one had thought to pack flares to signal for help. This was, after all, supposed to be a covert mission. The seas were too rough to lower the boats. In the absolute darkness, the passengers waited with resignation for the icy water to engulf them. Calixto García tried to rally their spirits, shouting, "To die for Cuba is beautiful, sirs! Viva Cuba!" Everyone took up the cry, "Viva Cuba!"

Looking for something to do, they went below and began to haul out the coal, then the arms, ammunition, and dynamite, dumping it all into the sea in the hope of gaining a few more hours of buoyancy. When dawn broke, they were still afloat, barely. One of the Spaniards, a Galician sailor named Felix de los Ríos, climbed a mast to hang an American flag upside down as a signal for help. Soon, other craft appeared, saw the flag, and came alongside. The seas were calmer now, and the Cubans were able to lower their boats in the growing light. Rutea and most of the others made their way to the ship Helena, which moved off just before noon as the Hawkins slipped beneath the water. The expedition had been ruined by bad weather, a leaky ship, and inadequate preparation.

On February 24, Rutea again tried to ship out for Cuba. This time he took the Ninth Avenue elevated train at Twelfth Street to South Ferry, where dozens of émigrés began to gather just before eight P.M. Benjamin Guerra, the treasurer of the New York junta, met them and took them to Pier 4, where they boarded a launch that took them to a steamer anchored near the Statue of Liberty. Most of the men had already transferred aboard — only García, Ruz, and Cebreco remained aboard the launch. Suddenly both steamer and launch fled the scene at top speed. It was not fast enough. The U.S. Coast Guard had made an appearance, and everyone was arrested. The next day, however, the judge in the case released everyone, satisfied with levying a fine of $1,000 on the group. Justice in these cases was always swift and lenient. Again, the policy of the U.S. government toward the Cuban insurrection was one thing: in this case, the Coast Guard did its job. Enforcement by local officials, however, was another thing altogether, as exemplified by the behavior of the judge.

On May 9, Rutea made a third attempt. This time he took the First Avenue elevated train uptown to the Ninety-second Street ferry. There he boarded a ship with eighty-six other men, including a reporter from the *New York Herald*. Rutea had been assigned as aide to General Juan Ruz, who headed the expedition. (García and some of the others from the two earlier attempts had secured passage aboard a different ship.) After a week-long voyage, they were in Cuban waters. At dawn, on May 18, they lowered their boats near Nuevitas, on the northern coast of the province of Puerto Príncipe. Offshore reefs and sandbars forced them to unload their boats and to carry the cargo on their backs for a mile through waist-high water, pulling their lightened boats behind them, before they could reload and pull for the beach.

Usually, landfall was the most dangerous moment for an expedition. The Cubans tried to scout and prepare landing sites beforehand, employing for this purpose men in the "Inspección de Costas," a service created by Máximo Gómez in August 1895. If Spanish forces were numerous and alert, however, there was little these "coastal inspectors" could do to secure an area.[16] In this case, Rutea and his comrades met up with the insurgents quickly, and by nightfall the equipment was all on pack mules, headed inland. Now, thought Rutea, the time had finally come to join the fighting.

Rutea and the rest of Ruz's expedition soon discovered, however, that there was no fighting to be had in that part of the island. From July to September 1896, Rutea participated in two minor skirmishes when Ruz's men failed to hide in time from Spanish pursuit, but overall, things were slow. The Spanish offensive in western Cuba had begun in earnest, so the Spanish troops in Puerto Príncipe were ordered to remain on the defensive, leaving the Cubans with few targets to attack. Moreover, heat and exhaustion affected Cubans and Spaniards alike during the summer months, and both sides were essentially waiting for the fall to begin active campaigning.

When the Spanish did launch a minor offensive in October 1896, it caught Ruz — and Rutea — unprepared. The Cubans found themselves surrounded by Spanish troops under Lieutenant Colonel Francisco Aguilera, who defeated and dispersed Ruz's force at Zayas on October 7. Rutea died in the fighting, and

Aguilera forwarded his captured diary to Weyler, who read the strange, sad story, from Rutea's visit to the Eiffel Tower to the last desperate battle.

Of a total of sixty-four filibustering expeditions from the United States, the Spanish stopped two, the sea took another two, and the Americans interdicted twenty-three.[17] A 60 percent success ratio sounds good, but it must be remembered that even if all the expeditions had gotten through, supplying an army by sloop and schooner was still inherently ineffective. Periodically, when some particular expedition of men and matériel made landfall, the Liberation Army would become flush with resources. Then there followed a period of activity and recruitment. Something like this happened in the late summer of 1895. On July 25 Carlos Roloff, Serafín Sánchez, and José María Rodríguez landed with one of the largest expeditions of the war: 132 men together with weapons, medicine, and 300,000 cartridges. However, even 300,000 cartridges would not last long if used too liberally. To avoid this, Gómez ordered his men in late July 1895 to avoid fighting in the open and exposing themselves to Spanish fire. Instead, Gómez instructed his troops to "take advantage of cover," conserve ammunition, and wait for clear shots at point-blank range.[18] By exercising great discipline, Gómez's men could inflict the maximum amount of damage with the minimum of bullets. Even so, the Liberation Army quickly ran through its cartridges. This created a serious problem of morale and retention among the troops. Episodes of munitions surpluses attracted men to join the insurrection, but they deserted when ammunition gave out. Even the biggest deliveries, such as the 500 shells, 2,600 rifles, 858,000 rifle rounds, and two cannon delivered by *Dauntless* in August 1896, did not go that far, producing the characteristic flurry of activity and recruitment followed by desertion.[19] This interrelated problem of supply and discipline within the Liberation Army remained a struggle for Gómez, Maceo, and all of the Cuban commanders throughout the war.

There was also another sort of morale problem. Some of the Cubans entered service in the first place with the mistaken belief that they would not be asked to fight far from their homes and that they would be allowed to return to their loved ones to perform household duties as needed. Following engagements, even if stores of ammunition remained, units of the Liberation Army often dissolved, despite every effort by their commanders to prevent it. Troops left camp without permission or failed to return when they did have legitimate leaves from duty. They brought civilians, including wives and girlfriends, into camp without approval from superiors. They fled in the face of the enemy without warning, to reform, if at all, days or weeks later, according to rhythms that had nothing to do with military exigencies. Sometimes it was the officers themselves who were the problem. Commanders allowed men to straggle and break ranks on the march or abandoned the field themselves to pursue personal or family matters. Indiscipline characterizes irregular formations everywhere, so it is no surprise that it plagued the Liberation Army throughout the war, especially during periods when ammunition, and hence meaningful military action, was lacking. Gómez and other Cuban officers fought these tendencies, but they were part of the nature of the insurgency, and they could not be eradicated by fiat.

Indeed, there was a positive side to these disciplinary problems. Cuban troops — unlike the Spanish — could and did melt back into the civilian population between battles. This is critical to the survival of any guerrilla force. Lacking regular bases and supplies, irregular armies must rely on civilians for many things. Retaining contact with the civilian population — Mao's "congenial sea" to which any insurgency must resort for nourishment — was vital to the Cuban Liberation Army. Ironically, therefore, the unreliability and instability that Cuban commanders perceived as their army's greatest weakness may have been its greatest strength, allowing it to avoid destruction by the vastly superior Spanish.[20]

After Peralejo, the only other large-scale action of the summer came on August 31, at a place called Sao del Indio. Maceo gathered his dispersed men, over a thousand of them, and surprised a Spanish column marching out of Guantánamo. As at Peralejo, the Cubans surrounded the Spanish, who adopted a defensive square in the open, while the Cubans fired on them from behind cover. Finally, the Cubans ran out of ammunition, and on September 2, the Spanish retreated back to Guantánamo. After Sao del Indio, Gómez directed his commanders to avoid combat altogether in order to preserve ammunition, even at the price of seeing men leave the ranks. They were still in the East, near their homes, and the men could always be (and were) remobilized later. In the meantime, Gómez told his officers to let the heat of late summer work its black magic against the Spanish. "Our old general says that he doesn't want to set any more ambushes," recalled Bernabé Boza, "nor cause more casualties against [Martínez Campos] than those already inflicted by our ally General September with his downpours and mud baths." Dispersing and doing nothing cost the Cubans less than active campaigning — and damaged the Spanish almost as much.[21]

In October Gómez and Maceo met with members of the republican provisional government at Mangos de Baraguá, near Santiago, to make final preparations for the invasion of western Cuba. Maceo commanded the invasion column. Mobilizing men for a long march proved rather more difficult than anticipated, however, as Maceo's reiterated entreaties and threats to his subcommanders to rendezvous with him indicate. Some of the men who had fought at Peralejo and Sao del Indio considered their duty done, and they were not eager to march west, away from their homes. Maceo had also to combat contrary orders from General Masó, who advised men to remain in Oriente, where they could protect their families.[22] As a result of these problems, by the end of October, the invading army was still not very big, just over 1,000 men.

The job of finding and stopping Maceo while he was still mobilizing in the East fell to an infantry column under Colonel Santiago de Cevallos. During the first week of November, Cevallos marched his men out of Holguín under torrential downpours along roads so impassable that new paths had to be cut through the jungle. Still, he could not find Maceo, whose men traveled on horseback and always remained several hours ahead of the pursuit. On November 7, however, Maceo found Cevallos. The Cuban general set up ambushes every 200 yards along the road to Maraguanao, near Las Tunas. Although he only succeeded in slowing the Spanish down, wounding two soldiers and killing several horses and mules, that was all Maceo needed to do. Harassment and movement, rather than serious combat, was what Maceo wanted. His ambushes made it impossible for the Spanish to make camp, eat, rest, or escape the deluge. Several of Cevallos's men had already died from fevers en route, and more had fallen sick. The men were covered with sores produced by filth, exertion, and illness, and they had worn through their cheap shoes and uniforms in a matter of days. Footwear was a particular problem. Spain issued its soldiers a shoe with a rope sole, appropriate perhaps to the dry Spanish *meseta* but absurd in the tropics. Water wicked upward into the material, so that the soldiers suffered chronically from "immersion foot," a form of rot that can make even the act of standing up painful. The damp hemp also served as an ideal home for various parasitic insects that liked nothing better than to burrow into the flesh between a man's toes. In effect, Cevallos had a troop of sick and crippled infantry with which to chase Maceo's cavalry. It was quite pointless.

By some miracle of endurance, on the evening of November 7, the limping Spanish did finally overrun a small insurgent encampment, killing seven men before the rest got away. In their hurry, the Cubans left behind two butchered cows, which the starving Spanish devoured half-cooked. On the following day, Maceo again used ambush to delay Cevallos while he took the bulk of his forces and pushed west from Las Tunas, leaving the foot-weary Spanish column behind. Cevallos had failed completely, but he was at least able to get out of the rain and leave the pursuit of Maceo to others.[23]

Maceo crossed into Puerto Príncipe, where Gómez had previously been active. José María Rodríguez and 400 horsemen added their strength to Maceo's column. Puerto Príncipe was still mostly undeveloped in 1895, a land of dense jungle, but it was also flatter than Santiago, and Maceo's mounted column moved rapidly through the province. In a few weeks, Maceo prepared to cross the Júcaro-Morón trocha into the province of Santa Clara. Writing to his brother, José, on November 30, 1895, Maceo recalled that he "had traversed all of Camagüey [Puerto Príncipe] without firing a shot." More surprising still, he had crossed the trocha and entered Santa Clara on November 29 near the town of Ciego de Avila "without the least resistance." This was exactly the kind of war Maceo wanted.[24]

At almost the same time, Gómez crossed the trocha near its southern end, surprising and capturing forty-two Spaniards manning an outpost called "Pelayo," one of seventy-three forts along the trocha that were supposed to hem the Cubans in Oriente.[25] Entering the province of Santa Clara for the first time, Gómez incorporated the locally recruited Fourth Corps (existing mainly on paper) into his column. Maceo and Gómez reunited at La Reforma, on the western side of the trocha. Serafín Sánchez, the military chief of Santa Clara, and Carlos Roloff, the secretary of war, joined them there. The Cuban invasion column now numbered almost 2,000 men, even after leaving behind some of the cavalry from Puerto Príncipe. Almost everyone was mounted and in possession of a rifle, though they were still short of ammunition by the standards of any regular army.[26] As Gómez wrote to a friend in Santo Domingo, the army was healthy, full of spirit, and "swimming in resources."[27]

Gómez addressed the assembled troops with hard words. He promised them that victory would not be easy. "Death will open gaping holes in the ranks," he warned, but death, and even the devastation of Cuba itself, was not too high a price to pay for independence. "Soldiers!" proclaimed Gómez, "do not allow the destruction of the country to frighten you. Do not let death in battle alarm you. Be frightened, rather, at the horrible idea of Cuba's future if somehow Spain emerges victorious in this contest."[28] Maceo's instructions to the men were even more explicit. He asked his forces to "destroy, destroy, always destroy. Destroy at all hours, by day and by night. Blow up bridges. Derail trains. Burn towns and sugar mills. Level crops. To annihilate Cuba is to defeat the enemy." Maceo assured his men that they would "owe no explanation to any power for [their] conduct. Diplomacy, public opinion, and history hold no value for us. It would be foolish to seek glory on the field of battle . . . as if we were a European army." Instead, by avoiding battle and focusing on the destruction of Cuba, the Liberation Army would achieve its goal. They would turn the island into "a heap of ruins" so that Spain would see no profit in continuing the campaign. "We must burn and destroy at all costs," concluded Maceo. What they could not do with artillery and rifles, they could achieve indirectly with fire and dynamite.[29]

The apocalyptic words of Maceo and Gómez foreshadowed the extraordinary destruction they were about to bring down upon Cuba in the name of national independence. The two men shared a Sorelian view of the creative potential of violence. They thought Cuba had to be destroyed before it could be re-created and that Cubans would be morally elevated in the process. Of all the terms Cubans used to describe their war against Spain, "war of redemption" was the most hopeful sounding. It evoked the deep yearning for a national community and the aspiration to create an economically and socially egalitarian society on the ashes of the old Cuba. It also expressed the desire for racial justice, which was a fundamental issue in an island less than a decade beyond slavery. In the rhetoric of the revolution, the comradeship of arms would fuse Cubans, whatever their class, race, or national origin, into a new people. This was the "redemptive virtue of just wars" about which Martí had written.[30] Men from the city, like Serafín Espinosa y Ramos, who knew nothing of the countryside, would discover the real Cuba in the "unknown but longed for manigua."[31] Orientales would encounter westerners, and the localism that had so plagued Cuban uprisings in the past would finally be purged in the fires of national unity. Cuban soldiers, "reduced to impotence" by Spanish tutelage, would reclaim their manhood.[32] People of color, many of whom had been born into slavery, would achieve full equality with whites, as men of both races fought side by side for a freedom more complete than either could enjoy under Spain. This was the vision presented to the invasion column as it prepared to invade the West.

War, it was supposed, could even redeem common criminals, and Maceo made a point of enlisting them, for he believed that by fighting in the invasion army such men would "modify their moral condition with the rude exercise of arms." In an order of October 3, 1895, Maceo advised Lieutenant Colonel Dimas Zamora to enlist "all those individuals who are pernicious . . . because of their disordered conduct," as well as anyone who opposed enlistment. By participating in the invasion of western Cuba, such men would become upstanding citizens, whether they wanted to or not.[33] Naturally, amid all of this creative nation building, a lot of civilians would resist, and the Liberation Army would have its resolve tested.[34]

On December 3 at La Reforma, Gómez divided the Liberation Army into corps, divisions, brigades, regiments, battalions, and companies. These formal designations struck Spanish officials and many others at the time as laughable because the whole Cuban force was about the size of a single regiment in any regular army. Before it was all over, some 40,000 men would serve in some capacity in the Liberation Army. However, at no time could it muster more than a fraction of this number, and the largest concentrations never exceeded a few thousand men. Spanish officers derided the Liberation Army: Cuban generals were *cabecillas*, or little chiefs, "a handful of men without God or law" who had adopted "a life of pillage, arson, and crime." Their troops were "anarchist dynamiters," bandits, and worse.[35] In fact, the undersized Liberation Army had at its core a group of hardened soldiers led by talented officers, some of them professionals and men of standing in civilian life. And as for Gómez's reorganization of the army, even if it occurred mostly on paper, it did serve an important function, for it created a system of command and accountability that proved vital in the days to come, however small the actual numbers of men were.[36]

The Second Corps of the Liberation Army, joined by other forces, became the expeditionary or "invasion" column, commanded by Antonio Maceo and assigned to take the war into western Cuba. Maceo advanced into Santa Clara at the head of almost 1,100 armed and 500 unarmed men.[37] Gómez followed with another force intended to divert Spanish troops and keep them from concentrating entirely on Maceo. As he approached the town of Iguará, Maceo evaded a large Spanish column of some 700 men under General Alvaro Suárez Valdés and ran into a small detachment under Colonel Enrique Segura left behind to defend the fort at Iguará. Maceo wished above all for an unimpeded march westward, and most of the time over the course of the next month the Spanish granted his wish. But at Iguará, where the Cubans enjoyed overwhelming superiority, and where they still had adequate munitions, Maceo forced the issue, attacking the Spanish with great determination. In predictable fashion, Segura formed his small force into a square. This stopped the Cuban machete charge, but Maceo had his men dismount and fire from behind cover into the Spanish lines. After two hours the Spanish had to withdraw. Segura's men suffered seven killed and twenty-six wounded, and the Cubans lost thirteen dead, mostly in the initial machete attack. Maceo seized the fort at Iguará, capturing fifty-four rifles and 800 cartridges in the process, a prize that made Iguará important, however minor it was as a battle.[38]

The expeditionary column passed west, through the lovely valley of Manicaragua, in the mountains of Santa Clara. On December 11 a Spanish column attacked them at Manacal. The Cubans had seized the high ground and, as usual, dismounted to fight as infantry from behind the cover of boulders. When darkness fell, the battle ended. The Cubans had used up almost all of their ammunition, and during the next two days they "retreated" toward the West, which was, of course, where they wanted to go anyway.[39] Because they were all mounted, they moved faster than the Spanish and gave them the slip on December 14, when they descended into the plains of Cienfuegos, in Matanzas province. Everyone moved quickly and silently, feeling vulnerable in an open countryside full of Spanish troops and sympathizers. Boza recalled this critical moment: "We set off on our march westward at five A.M. Everyone was grave and serious in keeping with circumstances. We were about to enter the Territory of Cienfuegos in the region of Cane, as we used to say."[40]

Indeed, the men from Oriente, when they passed into western Cuba, entered a land so hostile and unknown to them that it might as well have been Spain. Between 1868 and 1894, 417,264 Spanish civilians had emigrated to Cuba and another 219,110 soldiers had arrived in the island, some of them to stay. Most of these recent arrivals had settled in the West, where they joined earlier waves of Spanish immigrants.[41] In places like Matanzas, Spaniards from the Peninsula probably outnumbered native-born Cubans, and even Cuban leaders realized that most of the people in the West "did not follow the principles of the revolution."[42] Some 60,000 Cubans served under Spanish colors during the war, more than fought for the revolution, and most of these men made their homes in the western provinces of Matanzas, Havana, and Pinar del Río.[43] They defended rural properties, such as the sugar mill called España, where almost 200 armed civilians turned the industrial outbuildings into Spanish fortresses. They garrisoned and policed cities and towns and joined fire brigades. They made the "land of Cane" uncongenial to Maceo and Gómez.

It was not just Spanish immigrants who fought for the ideal of Cuba Española. Thousands of men born in the island also became firefighters, police, and guerrillas. At Candelaria, the garrison included not only Basques but men of color born in Cuba who, to the puzzlement of Maceo's troops, nevertheless wore their boinas — the Basque beret that formed part of Volunteers' uniforms — with as much pride as their comrades from the Basque Country and defended the Spanish flag with as much zeal.[44] The Carreño y Fernández family, which owned several plantations and a sugar refinery near Matanzas, built eleven new stone forts and had no difficulty hiring 150 militiamen, many of them blacks from among the plantation's workforce, to defend their property.[45] In a rare admission by a Cuban officer, General Manuel Piedra Martel recalled that throughout the war, the people who supported continued Spanish rule always outnumbered the people who wanted outright independence.[46]

Outnumbering both groups were the people who simply wanted to be left alone. We should be careful about accepting General Weyler's judgments about the Cubans, but he was probably correct to insist that many Cubans "wanted nothing more than to live in peace and to work" without being molested by either side.[47] It may be that this is true of almost every war, but in Cuba it was especially true in the western provinces.

The Orientales mobilized in the Liberation Army could not fathom the westerners' lack of patriotism. Indeed, they thought them altogether incomprehensible. Westerners spoke strangely. Their houses looked different. They ate different foods. The church had a greater presence in their lives. Racial relations were more polarized, and this mattered as much as anything else in defining the way the Orientales in Maceo's army related to people in the western provinces. The Liberation Army pursued, though it never quite achieved, the ideal of racial integration in the ranks. This reflected the power of Martí's ideals, but more than that it was an expression of the fact that the men came from a region where blacks outnumbered whites and free people of color had achieved significant positions of leadership in their communities.[48] Afro-Cubans constituted a majority of the invasion column.[49] As this force moved west, it encountered a plantation society dominated by whites and built upon the labor of blacks. Spain had only abolished slavery in the 1880s, and conditions for black workers had not improved that much after emancipation. Moreover, the West had recently become "whiter," due to the massive emigration from Spain in the 1880s.[50] According to one contemporary, blacks and whites in the West maintained complete segregation "over the question of even minor differences in skin color."[51] How alien it all must have seemed to Maceo's men.

Maceo's column of Orientales did not like white westerners, and the feeling was mutual. Indeed, the expeditionary column became known both among the men who composed it and among the civilians who suffered its passing as the "invasion column" rather than the "expeditionary column." This linguistic slippage is not without meaning. In large part because the expeditionary column was mostly black, whites in the West experienced the approach of Maceo as an invasion by foreigners bent upon overturning civilization and the "natural" racial hierarchy they knew. By convention, the advance of Maceo's column has come to be called "the invasion of the West," and in this case the convention is quite apt.

An examination of regimental lists yields additional information about the men who joined the Liberation Army.[52] First, as we would expect, they were almost all from rural areas. For example, in the Palos regiment, 82 percent of the men had *campo*, or "country," listed as their occupation. In the Goicuría regiment the corresponding figure was 86 percent. Interestingly, only 16 percent of these men were landless day laborers, or *jornaleros*. The rest were small farmers, suggesting that the cadres of the insurgency were not the utterly poor and dispossessed but, rather, small property owners and leaseholders. This helps to explain aspects of their behavior, such as their sensitivity to Spanish taxes and their willingness to destroy the sugar industry, which was not their direct employer but, as many of them must have thought, a blight on the peasant economy.

Almost everyone in both regiments was under thirty, with some as young as twelve years old. And almost everyone was unmarried: 94 percent in Palos and

96 percent in Goicuría. Young bachelors always form the bulk of any army, so these numbers are only a little surprising. More interesting is that only 4 percent of the soldiers were born outside of Cuba. In this sense, the uprising was "national," with men born in Spain or in other countries almost completely absent from the lists of insurgents. Artisans, students, merchants, and other occupations were a distinct minority in the Liberation Army, although officers tended to be drawn from the merchant and professional classes. Physicians and pharmacists, for example, joined out of all proportion to their numbers in society as a whole. In Cuba — as in many developing countries — medical professionals became critics of the status quo when they discovered it to be an impediment to the efficient pursuit of their work, and many of them sympathized with and worked for the separatists. This was a good thing because these medical professionals brought valuable knowledge and equipment to the Liberation Army. Overall, the data here presented on the social background of the insurgents reinforces what we know about them from more impressionistic sources: the troops were young, single peasants of African descent born in Cuba. The officers were whites from the city.

The Liberation Army became whiter toward the end of the conflict. In late 1897, as we shall see, the Spanish government tried to mollify the United States and its own liberal critics by adopting a passive military posture that allowed the insurgency to recover and grow. It was then, as some scholars have pointed out, that whites swelled the ranks of the Liberation Army, expecting to be congratulated and promoted for their decisiveness. In fact, Máximo Gómez and other white Cuban officers did begin to promote whites over blacks and even to remove blacks, including the veteran Quintín Bandera, who had been fighting for Cuba ever since the Ten Years' War. The accession of whites to the Liberation Army in 1898 should not be allowed to mask its racial composition in 1895, however.[53]

As the Liberation Army moved west it lost hundreds of men, not to casualties but to desertion. Fifteen men deserted from under Maceo's nose in late November.[54] Bartolomé Masó's Second Corps lost 180 men in a single mass desertion at Mala Noche, resulting in Masó's "promotion" to vice president of the provisional government and his removal from military office.[55] When Maceo entered the area of Matanzas, desertion became truly "alarming," and he eventually had fifteen officers and eighty-two troops sentenced to death for desertion, though, apparently, the men were never brought to trial.[56] Soldiers always have personal reasons for deserting, but the Orientales also had regional interests that made them hesitate to continue with Maceo. Some of the men who had made up their minds to fight for their country's freedom understood that to mean fighting for

Oriente, or even more specifically, for Bayamo or Las Tunas, and as the army moved ever farther west, Maceo had to exert every ounce of his will to keep men in the ranks and ready for combat. That he succeeded in making peasants with local and particular interests into an army at all is testament to his character and skill as a leader.[57]

8 ☆ The Spanish Army

When the Cuban Liberation Army embarked upon the invasion of western Cuba in the fall of 1895, Spain had close to 96,000 troops ready to combat them. In addition, some 20,000 to 30,000 Cubans, many though not all of them Spanish-born, worked for the regime in urban militias, fire brigades, and counterinsurgent guerrilla forces. Against so many enemies, the Cuban insurgents would seem to have been hopelessly outmatched. Yet the numbers are misleading. The Spanish army was wholly inadequate to the kind of war it was asked to fight in Cuba. It was, in fact, not a suitable tool of empire.

Spanish soldiers in Cuba suffered from low morale, inadequate training, and poor leadership. Above all, they were not healthy. Between February 1895 and August 1898, just over 41,000 Spanish soldiers, 22 percent of the Spanish army in Cuba, perished from disease. By way of comparison, just over 3 percent of the American forces sent to Cuba in 1898, and just under 3 percent of Americans in Europe during World War I, died from illness. Another point of comparison is the Cuban Liberation Army, which, according to the official figures compiled by Minister of War Carlos Roloff, lost only 1,321 men to illnesses. It is important to remember, too, that for every Spanish fatality, many other men were incapacitated. The chief administrator of one of Spain's military hospitals, Angel Larra y Cerezo, estimated that half of all men sent to Cuba contracted a disease during their first two months on the island. In 1896 Spanish military hospitals admitted 232,714 cases with various illnesses. As this figure suggests, many men took to bed, were "cured," and became sick later with the same or a new illness. In November 1895, as Maceo and Gómez began their march west, close to 20,000 men, or just over 20 percent of the Spanish forces at the time, lay in hospital beds and clinics, sick with malaria, yellow fever, tuberculosis, pneumonia, dysentery, and other diseases. So it was that an army of 96,000 men in the fall of 1895 had already been reduced to no more than 76,000, and many of these men were not in fighting trim. This scandalous ratio of men out of combat due to illness remained fairly constant throughout the war. By 1898, almost every soldier in the Spanish army had spent at least some time in a sick bed.[1]

It is probably safe to say that for every Spanish soldier in a hospital or clinic, another should have been there, as thousands of troops in the field were always, in truth, too sick to be counted as effectives. Many lasted only a few weeks before they had to be shifted to the rear for clinical treatment. Typical was the case of a column of 1,377 campaigning in Pinar del Río during the spring of 1896. Though suffering only a few combat losses during that time, the column saw its numbers reduced by illness to 373 active troops. No army can sustain such high noncombat casualties for long.[2]

By January 1898, the Spanish still had 114,000 troops left in Cuba, but only 50,000 were counted as active, and most of these were in such poor shape that Spanish officials did not consider them battle ready. The men stationed in and around Santiago in 1898 to meet the threat of the American invasion were a prime example. Though not officially listed as casualties, most were feverish wrecks. Soldiers have always gathered glory to themselves by heaping praise upon the fighting quality of their defeated enemies, and the Americans at Santiago expressed the highest regard for the Spanish troops there. In the memoirs and eye-witness accounts written by Americans, the Spanish sometimes appear as formidable foes. In fact, however, the Spanish defending Santiago did not fight well and could not be relied upon for a long campaign, as we shall see. Americans faced the shell of the Spanish army by July 1898, and their easy victory at Santiago stemmed in some measure from the three previous years of suffering and death inflicted upon Spanish troops by the Cubans and, even more, by tropical diseases. When it was all over, many Spanish servicemen returned to Spain barely able to disembark from troop transports or find their way to train stations for the trip home, where loved ones pretended not to be appalled at the presence of barely recognizable living cadavers.[3]

The Spanish physician Santiago Ramón y Cajal, who won the Nobel Prize in 1906 for his work in histology and neurology, recalled his youth as a medic in Cuba during the Ten Years' War, but his memories serve as a general description of conditions during the war of 1895–98 as well. Ramón y Cajal told of camps pitched in the midst of swamps, of stagnant puddles left undisturbed near cots and hammocks, of mosquitoes everywhere. "Clouds of mosquitoes surrounded us," he wrote. "Beside the *anopheles claviger*, the usual carrier of the malaria protozoan, almost invisible lice tormented us, not to mention an army of fleas, cockroaches, and ants. A wave of parasitic life enveloped us." Ramón y Cajal went to Cuba expecting a terrestrial paradise, but, like so many Spanish soldiers after him, he left thinking of it as "uninhabitable."[4]

Army engineers built dozens of hospitals and field clinics to try to relieve the suffering of the men, but overwhelmed medics lacked adequate medicine and supplies to treat so many sick. They did not even have rational medical protocols for dealing with some illnesses, and this made treatment itself deadly. For example, doctors thought that yellow fever — the worst killer of Spanish troops — was contracted through exposure to fomites, a Latin term that medical experts the world over used to describe the blood and gore that issued from yellow fever patients in their final death agonies. In terminal cases, yellow fever victims bleed from their gums, eyes, noses, and genitals, and they vomit up a bloody mess described by clinicians as looking like wet coffee grounds, except that the "grounds" were blood and tissue acted upon by the patients' gastrointestinal juices. The Spanish called yellow fever "the black vomit" after this alarming and usually terminal manifestation of the disease. At the very end, dying patients howled and ranted and had to be strapped down to their hospital beds as blood issued from every orifice to stain bedding, walls, and floors. Doctors and orderlies took great care to prevent patients from contacting these presumably infectious fomites. Bedding was burned or buried and clinics scrubbed furiously. It was all for naught, of course, as the real culprits, mosquitoes, hovered just beyond reach until it was time to feed. In this way, men cured of dysentery or broken arms, left the hospital feeling fine, little realizing that the bothersome mosquito bites they had acquired while under treatment would result a few days later in a new, more horrible crisis. Indeed, assuming that contagion could be avoided simply by preventing physical contact with fomites, hospital officials grouped wounded and ill men together in rooms open to mosquitoes, so that Spanish clinics became foci of yellow fever, to the horror and puzzlement of medical officers.

The moment doctors declared men well, the army shuttled them back to the front, a practice that had deadly consequences, too. Recovery from certain diseases was, and still is, a complicated matter. Once a person contracts malaria, for example, recuperation is fitful and sometimes incomplete because the parasite, also transmitted by mosquitoes, can live in the human bloodstream for several years. The draining of swamps, the use of mosquito-resistant clothing, water purification techniques, the perfection of drug therapies, and the widespread use of DDT and other pesticides since World War II have made warfare in the tropics much less deadly than it once was. In the 1890s, when no one understood the role of the mosquito as the vector for disease and when pesticides, repellants, and defoliant agents were unavailable, men who had barely regained their strength found themselves reassigned to the same mosquito-infested posts where they had first fallen ill, without any apparent suspicion that they had been condemned to an almost certain relapse.[5]

One of the worst scourges of any army is typhus, carried by lice. The Spanish in Cuba were no exception. The men shaved their hair to aid in eradicating the lice, and they boiled their thin striped cotton uniforms to cleanse them. The combination of shaved heads and striped clothing made Spanish soldiers look eerily like convicts, but at least this preventive measure had some effect in reducing the incidence of typhus. In the case of other diseases, however, a lack of medical knowledge and intelligent preventive action could lead to tragic consequences. For example, it was common wisdom in the late nineteenth century among Europeans in the tropics to place the feet of beds and cots in containers of water, the idea being to discourage cockroaches and ants from crawling into the bedding. No one knew that the stagnant water bred mosquitoes and that they were a much greater threat than ants and roaches.[6]

Meanwhile, the men continued to use mosquito netting carelessly, if it was available at all. This is all exceedingly ironic because as early as 1881 the Cuban physician Carlos Finlay, working with his Spanish friend and colleague Claudio Delgado, had demonstrated that a particular mosquito, Aëdes aegypti, served as the vector for the virus that causes yellow fever, and he recommended mosquito eradication and the isolation of yellow fever patients from any contact with mosquitoes as methods certain to eliminate the disease. Had the Spanish tried Finlay's theory out, they might have saved thousands of soldiers from agony and death. In 1900 an American team under Walter Reed designed an ingenious experiment to prove Finlay's mosquito theory. The Americans, unlike the Spanish, knew how to take advantage of Finlay's insight and reaped the reward in low mortality for their own occupation troops after 1900.

Similarly, in 1897 an Indian-born British doctor, Ronald Ross, proved that another kind of mosquito carried the parasite that caused malaria, and within a few years that knowledge had been tested and incorporated into preventive practices.[7] People drained standing water, sealed drafty walls, screened windows, used mosquito netting scrupulously, and implemented other rather low-tech measures that taken together curbed the incidence of both malaria and yellow fever. Colonizing activity in the tropics suddenly became much less deadly. Now the drive by Europeans and Americans to exploit Africa, Central and South America, and South Asia went into a higher gear. However, these medical advances came too late for Spain's colonial enterprise in the Caribbean and the Philippines. Had the Spanish known the role of mosquitoes in the transmission of yellow fever and malaria even a few years earlier, their losses in Cuba and the Philippines would have been minimal, because in both cases combat with the insurgents was not very deadly. Indeed, had the Finlay and Ross breakthroughs occurred in 1890, it is not beyond the realm of the possible that Spain could have defeated the insurgents in Cuba before the United States ever had a chance to intervene, altering the process of Cuban national formation and American imperial history in unpredictable ways.

The infamously poor health of the Spanish army cannot be blamed entirely on the Cuban climate and fauna or on the primitive state of medical science. The

Spanish government and military must share responsibility. The average "Juan soldado" of the Spanish army did not receive even the minimal rations and pay to which he was entitled. Rations that were supposed to include fresh and cured meat and produce were reduced in practice to boiled rice. Conscripts drawn from the lowest stratum of Spanish society were usually not robust to begin with, and in Cuba they quickly lost whatever body fat and energy reserves they may have had. Protein was in especially short supply, but so were fresh vegetables and fruits of all kinds. Muscles wasted, and the soldiers' ability to resist disease was compromised.

High prices were to blame for the short rations. The Cuban campaign of economic destruction and embargo of Spanish-controlled towns were the main culprits, driving up the price of all comestibles, but Spanish tariff policies exacerbated the situation. Authorities in Madrid refused to rescind duties on imports of food and other necessities to Cuba, even in the face of wartime shortages and despite pleas from army officials that they do so.[8] For example, in a correspondence lasting from May to December 1895, Martínez Campos begged the colonial minister in Madrid to drop the import duty on an item as essential as steel rails, so that tracks dynamited by the insurgents could be repaired and outlying garrisons supplied by train. The reply from Madrid stated that it was "legally impossible" for the government "to concede customs privileges."[9] That was always Madrid's answer.

Spanish politicians were wedded to high tariffs for three reasons.[10] Inefficient farmers in Castile and uncompetitive business interests in Catalonia and the Basque region demanded high Cuban import duties on grains and manufactured goods produced in other countries in order to preserve their market share in Cuba. Second, the Spanish government needed the revenue it collected on Cuban imports and exports, even as both declined due to the war. Finally, Spanish officials also feared that food imported to help Cuban civilians would end up in the hands of insurgents. For all of these reasons, the government continued to raise obstacles to the free flow of goods into Cuba: By starving the Cuban population, the Spanish government really hoped to starve the insurgency.[11]

This murderous policy did make life difficult for the insurgents, but Spanish conscripts starved like everyone else. Scarcity drove up prices and made paper money almost worthless. Bank notes issued in 1896 lost 96 percent of their nominal value by 1898, if local merchants accepted them at all. Troops received this devalued pay late, up to ten months late, according to protests lodged with the Spanish Congress.[12] In addition, the army routinely kept back one-third of salaries as a "reserve fund," which no one ever saw again. As prices rose, officers also felt the pinch and began to rob their own men in order to maintain a decent standard of living for themselves. Cheated by his own government and superiors, the Spanish conscript could not afford to supplement his meager ration of daily rice or, if lucky, stew, never mind purchase extra medicines and supplies. On duty, he remained as still as possible, to husband his energies. On leave, he might wander the streets, half-starved, looking for extra work or scrounging in the dirt for cigar and cigarette butts in order to revive his flagging spirits with the tobacco that he could not afford to buy.[13] Hunger accompanied him wherever he went, affecting his morale, energy, and the ability to resist illness. Even well-fed men would not have been immune to infectious diseases in Cuba, but they might have recovered instead of perishing.

Sadly, the Spanish failed to implement preventive measures that were available. Quinine, a natural bark extract discovered by Jesuits in Peru, had long been available to fight malaria. The French had learned to refine it and had perfected its use in their African colonies, discovering that it worked best prophylactically rather than as a treatment for already ill men. The Spanish knew all of this, but they were short on supplies of the drug. It could not be distributed as a prophylactic to an army of almost 200,000 men. Instead, supplies were reserved for the already sick, who received heroic doses, often administered too late to save them. Worse still, doctors routinely misdiagnosed yellow fever in its early stages as malaria and prescribed vast doses of quinine to individuals whose digestive tracts, already under assault from yellow fever, could ill-afford the insult of quinine. So it was that medical ignorance, combined with a financially strapped Spanish government, helped to create the conditions for the terrible mortality in the Spanish colonial army.

All of this was bad enough, but Spain's military troubles in 1895 went much deeper than the neglect of the troops after they arrived in Cuba. The fact is that the Spanish army had ceased to be a high-quality fighting force decades before the uprising at Baire. Developments in the nineteenth century had turned Spanish soldiers into gendarmes, good at putting down civil disturbances but of little use in a regular campaign. To understand this transformation, it is necessary to take an excursion into Spain's nineteenth-century political history.

The contemporary era began in 1808, when Napoleon invaded Spain and wiped out her armies. Most royal officials, together with the Bourbons themselves, bowed to the emperor, but hastily improvised revolutionary armies and guerrillas fought on until the French retreated in 1814. These new armies became the de facto center of Spanish national life, and newly minted officers claimed to represent the will of the nation. It was the start of a pernicious tradition. In the years that followed, the army interpreted the "national will" on its own with alarming frequency. Spain suffered through five civil wars, as many colonial conflicts, and countless lesser disturbances between 1814 and 1895, and always the army emerged as the arbiter of Spain's fate. By the middle of the nineteenth century, the army had become less an instrument of war than a security force prepared to combat the government's internal enemies.[14]

Events from 1868 to 1875 completed this transformation. In these years, Spain experienced several regime changes, including the creation of the First Republic in 1873, as we have already seen. The republicans presided over twenty-two months of chaos. Regions declared their independence. Cities and towns styled themselves self-governing communes. Carlists fought for their vision of an ultra-Catholic Spain. Radicals founded the anarchist movement in Barcelona, and workers and peasants seized property and struck for better conditions. Cuba rebelled. In this environment, republicans who wanted to preserve Spain had to turn to the army for support. In July 1874 they suspended the constitution and declared a state of siege, giving the army a free hand. It turned out to be a kind of suicide, with the army assisting. Top military officials advocated the restoration of the Bourbon dynasty, in the person of Isabella's son, Alfonso, as the solution to Spain's problems. On December 29, 1874, Brigadier General Arsenio Martínez Campos led his men in a coup against the republic. When it became clear that no one in the army would oppose Martínez Campos, the government collapsed and the Bourbon monarchy was restored in the person of Alfonso XII.

Through all of this turmoil, the military solidified its hold on Spain. The Bourbon Restoration began with an army coup and would always remain a regime profoundly beholden to the military. The truth of this has not always been obvious. Scholars sometimes depict the period after 1874 as one of peaceful civilian rule, with the army fading into the background.[15] On the surface, this was what happened. Martínez Campos's ally Antonio Cánovas del Castillo led a broad coalition of civilians backing Alfonso. One of the most brilliant statesmen in Europe, Cánovas fashioned a new constitution that gave Spain a government in which the army's role appeared to be minimized and politics was dominated instead by two major political parties, Cánovas's own Conservatives, and the Liberals, led by Praxedes Sagasta. The two parties seemed to abide by election results and to alternate peacefully in power, forming a government or acting as the loyal opposition, depending — apparently — on the will of the electorate. This system, known as the turno pacífico, differed markedly from what Spain had possessed before, when change always seemed to come about through the overt intervention of the military. Thus, compared to the sixty years of constant military coups that preceded 1875, Spain during the Restoration seemed to have a government in which the army had ceased to be the arbiter of national politics.

In fact, however, the turno was merely a brilliant illusion, and it always required the army to make it work. The Spanish introduced universal manhood suffrage in 1890, and freedom of the press and other individual liberties had been guaranteed constitutionally. However, neither Cánovas nor Sagasta really believed in democratic politics or liberalism, and election results never truly reflected public opinion. Parliamentary systems work by allowing the party, or coalition of parties, that wins a majority of seats in an election to form a government. Elections in Spain, though, worked in just the opposite way. When the monarchy felt that the party in power had weakened, for whatever reason, it dissolved the government, placed the opposition in power, and called an election, rigged to ensure that the new party gained a majority. Based on its electoral "victory," the new party ruled for a few years, until the process was repeated in reverse. In this way, the turno provided the illusion of electoral choice and political change while actually preventing any serious challenge to the status quo.[16]

The trick worked because there were no serious political differences between the two parties. The turno functioned on a local level through political bosses called *caciques* — influential landowners, employers, and other local powers who could get out the vote of people living and dead. Many were equal-opportunity swindlers, working indistinctly for Liberals or Conservatives, as required by the situation. They made certain that election results were never surprising to either party or to the people whose interests both parties represented — aristocratic landowners, industrialists, the middle class, the church, and the army. This sort of electoral fraud was not unique to Spain. Political parties in most formally democratic countries in the late nineteenth century (and, some would say, even today) served elite interests while fixing elections to create the impression of popular participation. With the turno and *caciquismo* the Spanish simply took this political prestidigitation further than most.

The turno effectively shut the masses out of politics. It had to. Spanish working families had suffered abuse almost beyond bearing. Millions of people worked seasonal jobs in agriculture that kept them just above the subsistence threshold. Millions more worked in uncompetitive industries that provided incomes lower than any other western European nation. Between 1840 and 1880, the standard of living declined sharply in most of Spain: wages lagged behind prices, educational opportunities narrowed, dietary standards deteriorated.[17] The connection between misery and political radicalism is never straightforward. Nevertheless, for men like Cánovas and Sagasta, to allow the Spanish people to exercise their voting rights honestly was out of the question.

By the 1890s a flaw had developed with the turno: some Spaniards had figured it out, and they were not happy at being duped. What if the people boycotted elections? What if they struck for better wages and working conditions and simply ignored the major political parties? What if they began to organize parties of their own? In fact, all of these things had begun to happen in the 1880s and 1890s. The solution for the government was always the same — the army. Because the parties of the turno lacked legitimacy, and because workers, Basque and Catalan separatists, republicans, and other "internal enemies" of Spain refused to disappear, the army remained the key to the survival of the Cánovite system. Indeed, it has been argued that army officers after 1875 remained as powerful as they had ever been in Spain and preserved a sense of moral superiority over civilian politicians and officials, despite the ostensible civilian dominance of the government in the last quarter of the nineteenth century.[18]

Both Cánovas and his "rival" Sagasta recognized that the army was the bulwark of the Restoration. The constitution itself suggested that the army was a more "organic" and legitimate representative of the national interest than any government could be, something with which army officers readily agreed. Article 2 of the army's legal code declared that "the first and most important mission of the army" was to defend the nation "against internal enemies." Article 22 made the Civil Guard a branch of the regular army, further reinforcing the military's domestic mission.[19] Legislation passed in the 1880s — anticipating an infamous similar law of 1906 — gave the army the power to bring civilian critics to trial in military courts, something that civilian authorities in other western European countries did not countenance.[20]

Martínez Campos defended this extensive role for the army, declaring that the military had the right and duty to intervene in political life "whenever the state loses an exact notion of what the nation wants."[21] This broad mandate for the army originated with the man responsible for the coup that killed the First Republic in December 1874, so we should not be too shocked. It is perhaps more surprising to see that Cánovas, Spain's leading civilian authority, believed in much the same thing, particularly when it came to the army's mission of fighting against Catalan and Basque autonomists and against workers. Especially workers. In an address in the famous Ateneo political club in Madrid on November 10, 1890, Cánovas argued that the army "will be in the long term, and maybe forever, the pillar of the social order, [and] the invincible barrier to the illegal actions of workers." Indeed, the government routinely used troops to break strikes, either by directly attacking workers or by taking their place as scabs. In 1883, for example, the army farmed out 1,700 soldiers to Andalusian landowners so that they could bring in the harvest left standing by striking field hands, among the lowest paid workers in Europe at that time. In February 1888 troops put down a strike by workers at the Riotinto mines, killing twenty miners and wounding others in a savage attack. The army also intervened regularly to stop demonstrations by groups calling for regional autonomy in Catalonia and the Basque region. For example, in 1893 soldiers killed several people in San Sebastián and Vitoria in response to demonstrations calling for the reinstatement of traditional Basque privileges and liberties.[22]

Because of its use against workers, peasants, and autonomists, the army became unpopular. People looked at army officers with a mixture of fear and hatred, rarely with love and admiration. Military parades inspired no cheering. No one saluted the flag, at least not when it was carried by soldiers. It was, recalled one officer, as if the national banner for civilians were different from the one used by the military.[23] Try as it might, the army seemed unable to inspire respect. On the contrary, many Spaniards came to mock the institution.

Spain suffered, therefore, from an odd sort of militarism. In Germany, military values had spread to the masses, making Germany a danger to her neighbors. In Spain, militarism remained an elite phenomenon, not a popular one. This helped to make Spain's military really dangerous only to other Spaniards. The army became extraordinarily sensitive to criticism. Officers could not distinguish legitimate concern for military readiness from antimilitarism, which they always interpreted as an attempt to destroy Spain. Faced with such an attitude on the part of military officials, few dared openly to criticize the army, because the result could be costly. Riots of army officers against the offices and presses of newspapers critical of the military became a fixture of the Restoration. The end result was that the slightest call for military reform came to be branded as unpatriotic, and so reform became impossible. The Spanish military became good at repressing unarmed internal enemies but less useful for other purposes.

To become a tool of empire, the army needed reforming desperately. Spain had the most encephalitic military in the world, meaning it had a higher ratio of officers to soldiers than any other army. In 1895 Spain had an officer for every ten enlisted men, compared to ratios of one to twenty-four in Germany, one to twenty in France, and one to eighteen in Italy. The high number of officers kept the army expensive, even when little money got earmarked for new weapons systems, rations, equipment, and pay for the troops. Salaries for officers accounted for almost 60 percent of military expenditures during peace time, with only 9 percent going to war matériel.[24] Clearly, if the army were to be modernized, its officer corps would have to be reduced in some kind of orderly way, so that savings on salaries could be reallocated for other purposes, including the modernization of the navy, which had a minuscule budget compared to the army despite its evident importance for maintaining overseas possessions. However, this sort of reform of the military was precisely what officers would not allow. Various governments tried to take steps in this direction, most notably during the tenure of Manuel Cassola as minister of war in the late 1880s. However, the officer corps, including generals with a voice in national politics, chose to paint personnel cuts as an assault on the nation. Cassola had to step down amid mounting pressure from the army, and his plan, which would have released funds for the purchase of new weapons and other pressing needs, never came to fruition. Spain had missed its best chance to correct its military and naval defects. By 1895 the navy was twenty years out of date, and the army remained too large for its mission at the same time that it was poorly equipped and underfunded in every way except for its officers' payroll. And even here there were problems. Precisely because there were too many officers, many of the lesser officials individually received substandard pay. Some even had to work second jobs to make ends meet.

If the shortage of funds made life difficult for junior officers, it was pure misery for enlisted men. Spain had almost no purpose-built barracks and no money to build new ones. Instead, conscripts occupied abandoned monasteries and other ruins, slept together in enormous and sometimes windowless common rooms, defecated in trenches, cooked over outdoor fires, and ate squatting on the ground for lack of tables and chairs.[25] Their diet (while they were garrisoned in Spain) consisted mostly of beans and potatoes, seasoned, if the troops were lucky, with a hunk of sausage. Fresh meat was an impossible luxury most of the time. The French rationed 329 grams of meat every day to every soldier, the Portuguese, 175 grams, but the Spanish conscript received only 125 grams of meat a day. And that was regulations. What soldiers actually ate was often less and worse than what they were supposed to get. As a result of these problems, men perished from military duty at an alarming rate even in peacetime. Almost 13 percent of recruits in the 1860s died during their first year of duty, and another 25 percent died in the next four years of service. And these were men serving out their time in garrisons in Spain, not engaging in jungle warfare. For the sake of comparison, of the men on both sides who fought in the Franco-Prussian war, 18 percent died, forcing us to the depressing conclusion that assignment to a Spanish garrison in peacetime was more deadly than active combat in the French or Prussian army in 1870. When Spanish parents said goodbye to a beloved son drafted into the army, they really meant it.[26]

This neglect of the common soldier originated, at least in part, in the way Spain recruited its army. The draft, or quinta, dated in most of its fundamentals from 1837. Originally, the quinta allowed some communities to designate who their draftees would be or to buy themselves out of military contributions altogether. This resulted in a great many abuses and inequities, and as the century progressed, recruitment became more uniform and routinized. Medical examinations became standard, although a man had to be almost a corpse to merit dismissal. State recruiting commissions at least took the decision out of the hands of town councils and local caciques, so that exemption through sheer favoritism became less common.

However, the Spanish state, always desperate for revenue, allowed recruits to buy their way out of the quinta. Some critics thought that this was the root of many of Spain's military problems. Exemption cost between 1,500 and 2,000 pesetas, an amount easily raised by rich or middle-class families, whose sons, therefore, did not go to war. For the average salaried employee, making about 2,500 pesetas a year, raising 2,000 pesetas by selling assets and taking on debt, might just be possible. But the sons of the lower middle class, the workers, and the peasants had no hope of escaping conscription, other than flight, an option that surprisingly few of them took.[27] As a result, Spanish soldiers were always the poorest, most powerless people available. They were also usually appallingly young and scrawny teenagers, at a time when, due to dietary and other environmental factors, men matured physically later in life. "Unformed boys" were drafted into the army and were "obliged to make up for their lack of physical strength" by confiding in the so-called spirit of the race. Supposedly, even the poorest Spaniards, descendants of Cortes, Pizarro, and the men who conquered the New World, could call upon the native ferocity and spiritual toughness of their forebears.[28] Perhaps it was inevitable that a military lacking material resources would emphasize its spiritual strength. Unfortunately, officers seem actually to have believed their own myth that the Spanish soldier was the toughest in the world. This left them unprepared for the crude realities of making war in Cuba.[29]

Officers, usually recruited from a relatively elite segment of society, treated these poor, young men with the same offhand contempt that they had heaped upon them as civilians, ignoring their pressing needs and disdaining their company. It is not going too far to suggest that they treated their men as if they were indentured servants, farming them out to work for big landowners eager to take advantage of this cheap source of labor for the harvest or other jobs. During the 1890s as many as one-third of all soldiers were assigned as *asistentes*, working privately for officers or for people rich enough to pay officers for their troops' services.[30]

Barracks life remained terrible and pointless throughout the nineteenth century and well into the twentieth. In 1909 a sergeant in the Lérida garrison noted that the barracks lacked sinks, tables, lighting, and even beds. The beds they did have were iron cots without mattresses, which the men had to rent, being too poor to purchase them. The number of men in the barracks was too high, especially the number of sergeants and corporals, who served no purpose: "The sergeant, the corporal, and the soldier sit with their arms crossed not knowing what to do." Only the lowest man on the totem pole had tasks to perform. The others lazed about, except those farmed out to work for civilians or who undertook business ventures on their own, employing their bored comrades in private enterprises.[31]

Abuse, crumbling barracks, and poor hygiene created a vicious cycle. Rich men used every means at their disposal to avoid service, which made the army more homogeneously lower class, which allowed officers to get away with greater abuse, which in turn made it harder to recruit and retain self-respecting, able-bodied men. In such a situation, the Spanish army began to accept almost anyone into its ranks. There were men entirely unfit for military duty who took money to act as substitutes for the actual inductees. One critic of military life recalled seeing "hernieated, one-legged, one-armed, asthmatic, tubercular, and even blind" conscripts in Cuba in 1895, along with the occasional sixty-year-old recruit.[32] These were the men sent to Cuba, fed on rice, stationed in swamps, and given sandals and cotton pajamas to cover themselves. No wonder so many succumbed to disease.

The Spanish press knew about these problems, despite the attempt by officers to suppress the evidence. The largest Spanish daily, El Imparcial, organized a regular campaign criticizing the army and the government for misusing funds intended for the troops.[33] Republicans like Blasco Ibáñez attacked the system of conscription and lamented the condition of the troops. In response, the minister of war cabled General Weyler on May 1, 1897, to demand not that he take care of the troops but that he write a rebuttal to this "calumny" from the press.[34] This sort of reaction was typical for both Conservative and Liberal wartime governments, always more concerned with public perceptions than with remedying the misery of the soldiers.

A few brave souls proved willing to question the army and its failings. Efeele, the cognomen of Francisco Larrea, questioned everything about the military: the morale of conscripts forced to fight for a colony that did them little good, the ineptitude of officers trained to fight striking workers at home rather than insurgents overseas, even the reputed valor of the Spanish soldier. "The army is not accustomed to hearing such things," wrote Larrea, and it would "be much more comfortable" to imitate everyone else who made careers out of covering up the "defects of the military and the errors of its members." Larrea, however, chose to speak out. Unfortunately, he found his pseudonymous courage in 1901, too late to make any difference in Cuba.[35]

Vicente Blasco Ibáñez, the great novelist and one of the most principled republican critics of the Restoration, fought a press campaign in the 1890s that called for military reforms, including the abolition of the quinta. He argued that exemption from service for the rich was unfair and led to the abuse of enlisted men. Officers looked down their noses at the men and cared nothing for their welfare. They got away with the neglect because the poor inductees' relatives back home had no influence and no way to make their protests known. Blasco Ibáñez's watchwords became, "Everyone should go, the poor and the rich," and the even more sonorous if elliptical "everyone or no one." The slogans became a national campaign that had no effect except to add to Blasco Ibáñez's standing as one of the most principled and eloquent critics of the monarchy and military.[36]

The quinta's defenders answered unabashedly that a system in which the poor gave their blood and the rich gave their money was quite satisfactory and in keeping with the laws of nature and the marketplace, which they characteristically confounded as one and the same thing. Nevertheless, the contention that the quinta was unfair to poor people was inarguably correct. That was not what landed Blasco Ibáñez in hot water. Rather, the trouble came from his contention that an army of destitute peasants and workers commanded by hateful aristocrats could not win a war. This struck at the professional pride of military careerists, who succeeded in having Blasco Ibáñez thrown into jail.

Ironically, this aspect of his critique was not even entirely correct. There is no evidence that an army that reproduces its society's social divisions will always fight poorly. Wellington's troops, whom he called "the scum of the earth," fought like demons against Napoleon. Other similar examples could be produced as well. In fact, the practice of allowing the wealthy to buy out of service has been a common feature of conscription in any number of countries with effective militaries.

Whatever the underlying justice of Blasco Ibáñez's larger critique of the Spanish military-aristocratic complex, Spain's system of conscription was not the real problem. Even arrogance, well-heeled, may show generosity to the less fortunate. The underlying problem in Spain was that officers had no resources to give to their men. Inadequate rations, late pay, poor hygiene, and lack of proper training and equipment were systemic, and were quite enough to break the morale of both officers and troops. To these complaints we must add the heartbreaking problem in Cuba of fighting against the unseen enemy of disease and the rarely seen insurgents. Both swept men away, and it was never glorious. The astounding thing, looking back on this army, is that it fought at all.

Spanish officers suffered from defects as great as those afflicting the rank and file. Beginning in the 1870s, the Spanish army talked a good deal about updating its officer training. Like everyone else, Spain wanted to copy the Germans and to instruct officials in the many lessons learned during the last great European war between Prussia and France. In fact, however, as Jaime Vicens Vives argued long ago, officers received little preparation in technical and practical subjects. For example, geography courses focused on the classics and included no material on the colonies. Officers arriving in Cuba had a fine appreciation for Strabo and Ptolemy, but no idea about the topography, climate, economy, or culture of the island. The Cuban bush reminded them of the sea, mysterious and unknown, and they left its navigation to native Cubans hired as pilots, or *prácticos*. In their academies the officers had been "educated severely, almost like Spartans, in high spiritual ideals, in the glories of the past," rather than in useful subjects.[37]

Honor and courage are indispensable martial virtues, and their cultivation is critical to officer training, but they are no substitute for real education. In excessive doses they can even be toxic. Spanish officers, with their prickly, defensive sense of pride, tended to take daring and stupid chances on the battlefield, perhaps hoping to relive the glories of Caesar, El Cid, or Córtes that had filled their minds as cadets. Combat for some of them became a way to prove their masculinity rather than a way to inflict maximum damage on the enemy while sustaining as few losses as possible among their own troops. A young José Sanjurjo, who would become a leading right-wing general in the 1930s, remarked to a comrade at the outset of a battle at Bacunagua: "Now you will see whether I am a man or not." His doubts on the matter required him to place himself in a position — useless in the context of that battle — to have his hand shot off.[38]

At the battle of Aguacate, another Spanish officer pointlessly rode to within fifty meters of the Cuban line, merely to demonstrate his devil-may-care attitude. He stopped, took out his spyglass in order to see the Cubans better, and allowed the Cuban infantry to shoot his horse from under him. He lay trapped under the beast, but the Cubans made certain not to shoot him because they knew that honor would require his men to attempt a rescue, giving the Cubans more good targets. Two Spanish soldiers died in the meaningless exercise of rescuing their commander, but honor was served.[39]

It did not help that the Spanish army in Cuba was considered "correctional" duty for some officers guilty of affronts or failures of duty back home. These men came to Cuba intent on erasing their shame and jump-starting their careers and were not averse to seeing their men take casualties along the way.[40] They suffered from what Weyler called "stupid confidence and Quixotic pride" in their own ability, and they tried to fight a war with egos better suited to individual combat between armored knights.[41] The Cubans liked to say that the Spanish were "making war as they did in the days of Viriato [an ancient Iberian hero who fought the Romans], but without Viriato." [42] In fact, the situation was even worse than this quip implied, and the wording needs to be turned around. The Spanish tried to fight a counterguerrilla campaign using advanced weapons and a modern conscript army with officers who imitated Viriato every chance they got.

After 1898, Spanish officers blamed everyone but themselves for the Cuban disaster: Spanish politicians who conceded too much (or too little) to the Cuban rebels; Americans who cynically supported the "anarchist dynamiters" and called them freedom fighters; Cuban "savages" who didn't know enough to appreciate the benefits of Spanish civilization. In fact, Spain's failure in Cuba was political, cultural, and moral, but it was above all a failure of military organization, sanitation, and leadership, even if military officials did not like to admit it.

The commander of Spain's troubled army in Cuba, Arsenio Martínez Campos, made a better politician than he did a soldier. His greatest military achievement came when he negotiated an end to the Ten Years' War in 1878, but his real fame resulted from having spearheaded the overthrow of the Spanish First Republic in 1874. As a field general, however, he left much to be desired. Martínez Campos's inept handling of the Moroccan war in 1893 had been a warning, but Cánovas paid no heed. The prime minister owed his friend a chance to prove himself in Cuba and hoped that he would be able to use his negotiating skills in a repeat performance of 1878. What both Cánovas and Martínez Campos failed to realize was that the success of 1878 had been possible only because others, men like Valeriano Weyler, had already done the hard work of fighting the Cuban insurgents during the previous ten years. In the Ten Years' War, Spanish troops had defeated the revolutionaries militarily first, and negotiation followed. In 1895 negotiation could not have produced a victory. Only war to the knife could do that, but Martínez Campos did not have the kind of moral — or immoral — constitution required to fight that kind of war.

Instead, Martínez Campos tried to use his army as a rural constabulary. In the vain hope that he could protect property and at the same time combat the insurgents, Martínez Campos ordered his forces to occupy as much territory as possible. This seemed reasonable. The Cuban Liberation Army declared that its purpose was to destroy property, so Martínez Campos responded by trying to garrison every hamlet, sugar mill, ranch, mine, railroad station, lumber mill, and so on, in order to provide protection. He even subcontracted men to plantation owners to act as guards and workers, a hallowed practice that had the advantage of producing extra income for the subcontracting commanding officer. As a result, when Gómez and Maceo embarked on the invasion of the West, Martínez Campos had only 25,000 men for field operations. With most Spanish troops waiting passively for the war to arrive on their doorstep, the Cubans recruited freely in Oriente and prepared for the invasion of the West unimpeded. In October and November 1895, undersized columns of Spanish infantry pursued the mounted Cubans for a few days here and there, but it was hopeless. Frustrated Spanish commanders soon realized that they could never catch up to the enemy and that they lacked the numbers and the organization to work in combination with each other to force a battle.[1] All of the resources that should have been dedicated to this task had been frittered away in garrisons and detachments that stood by helplessly as the Cubans passed around and beyond them.

Martínez Campos has come under heavy and well-justified criticism for this deployment of his forces in the defense of the indefensible countryside. At the time, however, the captain general was under a great deal of pressure to protect property. The owners of plantations, municipal authorities, and other interested parties wrung their hands and begged for regular troops to help them. The presence of a garrison could prevent attacks by insurgents and give confidence to the local population that they would not be overrun. This, in turn, encouraged Cubans to join urban militias and to resist the blandishments and threats of the republic-in-arms, which had called upon Cubans to cease working and to evacuate Spanish-held towns. The garrisoning of the countryside seemed reasonable from this perspective.

Yet the typical garrison was too small to prevent the Cubans from burning the sugar cane, which was the primary strategic objective of the Liberation Army anyway. One man with a torch could start a conflagration among the cane, as many a frustrated garrison commander knew, and patrols had no way to prevent this kind of incendiarism. Nor did they have the manpower to pursue the insurgents into their strongholds. They could not even secure enough territory to obtain the resources needed for their own maintenance, much less the food and other things required by the towns and plantation workers they were supposed to defend. This meant that supply columns had constantly to be organized to maintain the garrisons, and these columns also became targets for the insurgents, who got some of their weapons and ammunition by ambushing them. Meanwhile, the undersized garrisons were able to secure urban properties and valuable plantation buildings, but against the main body of the Liberation Army, even these tasks were beyond them. While Cuban loyalists viewed the presence of regular troops as essential, garrisons really achieved very little. They might as well have been in Havana, or, more to the point, in a field army capable of giving battle to Maceo and Gómez.

The case of the Cifuentes garrison was typical. A small town in Santa Clara province, Cifuentes in the fall of 1895 had a garrison of thirty-nine men, a few Civil Guards, and two dozen local Volunteers. Yet, even with over sixty men devoted to the defense of Cifuentes, the mayor, Bernardo Carvajal, complained that the garrison was just adequate to defend its own barracks and fortifications, while the local Volunteers manning the five trenches that served as the town's perimeter did not know how to use weapons, had to spend most of their time earning a living rather than being on call for military defense, and were not really capable of any offensive action. The Civil Guards, meanwhile, did no more than patrol the railroad station. As a result, the town had no ability to project any power over the surrounding environs. Cifuentes was "subject to the whims of these bandits," as Carvajal called the insurgents. They prevented food and other goods from entering the municipality, starving the townsfolk. At the same time, the insurgents "required impossible things from the poor peasants" in the country districts around the town. They forced the peasants to cease trading with Cifuentes and made them abandon cultivated land close to the town. The garrison could not protect these rural folk, and the result was that some of them decided to join the insurrection rather than starve.[2] Gómez's strategy worked in Cifuentes as it did in much of Cuba, forcing peasants to collaborate in order to survive.[3]

The limited value of small garrisons like that at Cifuentes had become apparent to Martínez Campos, yet he remained wedded to a strategy of trying to cover many points at once. Was it mulish stubbornness? A sign that he was more comfortable in the role of policeman than field marshal? Probably it was both, but it was also the effect of all the lobbying done by Cuban elites in favor of a strategy of dispersal. Martínez Campos found it hard to ignore their cries for help. After all, they were the face of Cuba Española and indispensable to the continuation of Spanish rule in Cuba. On July 10, 1895, Vicente Yriondo wrote from Colonias to the colonel stationed in nearby Ciego de Avila to appeal for men to garrison the town. What he really wanted were regular troops to safeguard his lumber mill and the 200 men he employed as loggers and mill hands. A local party of insurgents had already disrupted logging operations, stopping the flow of timber by blocking the roads and stealing the draft animals. They had also threatened his men if they returned to work. If the army would assign troops to Colonias, Yriondo would supply the material to build forts and barracks for them. All the soldiers had to do was provide the labor for construction and, of course, defend the town, the lumber mill, and the loggers after the fortifications had been completed. Martínez Campos was persuaded. He ended up garrisoning Colonias, whose chief citizen, Yriondo, and product, lumber, were too valuable to ignore.[4]

The story of Colonias was repeated in hundreds of different locales. The biggest sugar plantation owners hired guards from among their own workers and paid city boys to act as militiamen. What they really wanted, though, were garrisons of regulars, and they used their influence to have troops assigned to them. They paid Spanish officers well for the use of their men, a practical and hallowed form of corruption that Martínez Campos encouraged as a way to make the occupation profitable to his friends.

For soldiers, being posted to defend a rural property was unpleasant, often terminal, duty. They did not appreciate being in Cuba in the first place. Ever since Columbus had landed in the Antilles, promotional literature had painted Cuba and the other islands of the Caribbean as so many perfect Edens. In fact, it was difficult for Spaniards, accustomed to seasons and a dry climate, to adjust to Cuba. Spaniards learned to hate the natural beauty of Cuba. The greenery was monotonous and the isolation of life in a rural garrison depressing. The manigua was "a barbarous place of weeds, thorns, trees, vines, roots, trunks, and dead branches, all jumbled together in nature's capricious lack of order," in the words of one Spanish veteran. "It is all so boring. Once you have seen one palm tree, you have seen them all."[5]

Units assigned to remote garrisons presented a dolorous spectacle, living in their wood and earth forts and dressed in dilapidated straw hats, rotting rope-soled sandals, and the striped cotton pajamas that passed for uniforms, made threadbare because of overuse and baggy because their wearers were so emaciated. The men assigned to the eastern trocha probably suffered the most. Not only were many of the guard posts placed in the midst of swamps, but a special exhaustion affected men who had always to be vigilant. It was "a rare night when the soldier could sleep more than 3½ hours straight, and even this he had to do with his pack on and rifle within arm's reach." The stress alone was enough to weaken a man.[6]

After the battle of Jobito, the war correspondent Ricardo Burguete joined a unit stationed in Campechuela defending a "miserable hut surrounded by stakes and wires that they called a fort." He recalled with horror meeting the garrison commander, who greeted him lethargically, his countenance permanently stamped with "an expression both earthy and green" that Burguete thought must have come from the swamps themselves. Burguete was partly right. The commander's color probably had come from the swamp, in the digestive tract of its busiest and most cheerful resident, the mosquito. Spanish garrisons like Campechuela situated near standing water were deadly, but mainly to Spaniards.[7]

Planters shunned their own properties when they were in especially dangerous areas. They preferred life in Havana and turned over day-to-day management to paid administrators. This led to the neglect of garrisons stationed in such places. Lieutenant Juan Miranda commanded a small force assigned to defend Convenio de Vergara, a property belonging to José Vergara. Miranda protested bitterly that neither Vergara nor his manager, Martín Estanga, was providing anything to the men. The barracks, he said, were old, half-ruined slave quarters. They didn't even have a good water supply. Miranda had to send men on a long trek for water, running a gauntlet of Cuban snipers, whom he compared to predators skulking about water sources waiting for thirsty prey. Rations sent to the garrison disappeared on the highway, presumably stolen by the insurgents, but who knew? The men received no mail or information from the outside world. They were not even receiving their pay from the plantation owner. All the while, the more substantial buildings they were supposed to defend had not been properly fortified, so that they felt in constant danger of being overrun.

Vergara gave reassurances of his "promise to make payment in the future, when he could" and to correct other noted deficiencies. For the present, however, he lacked funds. Surely, too, Miranda must be exaggerating, he wrote. The truth, however, was that Vergara had no idea of the conditions under which the garrison lived because he had turned management of his estate over to Martín Estanga. It was his job to care for the garrison, as Vergara pointed out. In reply, Estanga objected that he had no independent authority or funds to maintain the troops. He also accused Miranda of being overly dramatic. Miranda, meanwhile, had taken to absenting himself for weeks at a time from his dangerous and miserable command, so he also did not have the best information about the conditions under which his men were laboring. Sadly, the army, the plantation owner, the estate manager, and even the local commander turned their backs on the soldiers. The one honorable thing Miranda did was to beg Havana to abandon Convenio de Vergara, but the garrison was merely allowed to dwindle by attrition until only nine men remained by the fall of 1896, at which point the last sickly troops evacuated the place.[8]

Much the same scenario existed at Ceiba Hueca. A small coastal town near Manzanillo, Ceiba Hueca must have been one of the most unhealthy places in all of Cuba. Between early June and late August 1896, twenty-three men in a garrison of thirty-one had to be evacuated to the hospital at Manzanillo. And, according to the garrison commander, Marcelino Soler, the eight men who remained all suffered from fevers and terrible ulcers in their legs that would not heal. As a result, the garrison was in no condition to perform even the lightest of duties. Rising to stagger outside to vomit was beyond some of them. "The fevers," wrote Soler, "no matter that we break them with pills or purgatives, always come back, bringing chills and attacks of painful rheumatism." Soler suspected, "according to his little knowledge," that it had something to do with the standing water that surrounded Ceiba Hueca on two sides. To the west, only 100 meters distant, stood a sink into which all kinds of muck flowed after every rain, so that it constantly emitted an evil smell. "At times like these," concluded Soler, "I wish I had some knowledge of medical science so that I could better explain . . . how prejudicial this place is to our health." Unfortunately, nobody possessed a good understanding of the causes of tropical diseases. From Soler's description of symptoms, it is certain that his men suffered from malaria, but the discovery by

Ronald Ross of the malaria parasite in the *anopheles* mosquito was still a year away. All Soler could do was ask to be relieved and beg that no one else be reassigned to Ceiba Hueca.[9]

In fact, the divisional commander in charge of the area around Manzanillo had already asked, in a letter dated June 6, 1896, for permission to abandon Ceiba Hueca, along with several other places. One of these, known as Vicana, had once been an important town, but with the coming of the war almost all of its inhabitants had fled under pressure from the insurgents to the more defensible Media Luna, which had its own Volunteer guerrilla force of fifty men in addition to a Spanish garrison. As a result, the detachment at Vicana protected a town populated by only two individuals.

Trying to hold places like Vicana and Ceiba Hueca merely created supply problems and wasted men in useless duty. Even at full strength, their garrisons could not complete their missions, for guarding standing cane from fire and protecting the rural population was impossible for such small forces. Thus, Martínez Campos's decision to disperse his men over the countryside served no purpose, except to leave him in November 1895 with insufficient manpower to stop the advance of Gómez and Maceo and to condemn conscripts to miserable and unhealthy garrison duty.

Martinez Campos's critics also blame him for his ineffective use of the Júcaro-Morón trocha, which not only failed to stop the Cubans from moving west in 1895 but produced more casualties from illness than any other sector throughout the war. At both its northern and southern ends, the trocha ran through swamps deadly to Spanish soldiers, but the poor quality of the fortifications all along the line, before it was rebuilt in 1897, left all of the trocha's garrisons exposed to insalubrious "miasmas" and "night airs," euphemisms people used back then to describe the source of illnesses that they did not understand. Nevertheless, it is easy to see why Martínez Campos tried to defend the Júcaro-Morón line. He was a veteran of the Ten Years' War. The trocha had worked then to keep the Cubans isolated in the East. In theory, it could work again. But Martínez Campos did not realize how compromised and ruinous the fortifications had become.

Beginning in the summer of 1895, Cuban troops attacked the trocha by cutting telegraph wires, burning isolated and decrepit forts of wood chinked with mud, removing the rails and railroad ties that had once provided rapid means of transportation along the line, and taking nightly potshots at Spanish guards. The absurd Spanish line-in-the-jungle made the Cubans laugh. As late as November 1895, the Spanish had not even worked out any system for defending the line. Civilians crossed the trocha regularly in order to conduct their business. Indeed, some lived within the defensive perimeter of the trocha itself because in the years between 1878 and 1895 people had built houses, even entire towns, inside the safety of its precincts. During the first months of the war, hundreds of additional civilians had taken refuge among the troops defending the line. Under these conditions, a proper defense was impossible.

On November 7, 1895, General José Aldave, the officer in charge of defending the trocha, directed his men to demolish homes abutting or inside its defenses and to prevent Cuban civilians from crossing the line. Only civilians employed directly by the army would be allowed to enter the area. Aldave also instituted such fundamental security measures as the creation of checkpoints in order to stop and register Cubans as they approached. He put an end to the practice of allowing civilians to cross the line in large groups, and he strictly forbade night crossings of any kind.[10] It was rather late in the day, however, to establish these basic protocols. Within a few weeks, the Cuban invasion force would cross the trocha easily when it was still clearly in no condition to be defended. In retrospect, we can see that Martínez Campos would have been better off leaving the trocha unmanned and concentrating his troops in a few large field armies to hunt down and destroy, or at least disperse, the Cuban invasion column. This was exactly what his critics afterward said he should have done. At the time, though, trying to shore up the trocha seemed to be a perfectly reasonable strategy, and Martínez Campos's greatest failing may simply have been that he lacked the insight, initiative, and resources to rebuild and modernize the trocha swiftly enough to stop the invasion.

To make matters worse, Martínez Campos began moving some of his men in the wrong direction, as he chose to shift forces westward beginning in October 1895 in order to protect the western half of Santa Clara province. As a result, Gómez and Maceo found that the approaches to the trocha had been left unguarded. The only Spanish opposition in Puerto Príncipe came from small garrisons that had been left behind in the path of the advancing Liberation Army, and these merely served to give the Cubans targets they could attack with some expectation of success. Once the Cubans reached the trocha itself, they discovered that it was not a substantial obstacle, and that on the other side lay miles of undefended territory between them and Spanish forces in western Santa Clara and Matanzas. From the Cuban perspective, as they began to march westward, the Spanish seemed to be confused, vulnerable, even in retreat.

Martínez Campos recognized the problems that were created by his deployment of troops both along the trocha and in hundreds of garrisons and militias months before the Cuban invasion of the West became a reality. In a letter of July 8, 1895, to Colonial Minister Tomás Castellano, Martínez Campos admitted that the main strategic problem for Spain was the requirement to protect rural property, "which, by its very nature, by its dispersal, can never be well guarded, leaving us weak everywhere."[11] Other officers in Cuba also recognized that the assignment of so many troops to garrisons weakened them fatally.[12] Nevertheless, they believed that the quality of the Spanish soldier could make up for many other deficiencies. In the bedtime stories they told themselves, Spanish officers confused their men with the veterans of the old *tercios* that had dominated Europe in the sixteenth century and conquered half the globe. Officials liked to brag that Spanish servicemen could withstand more rigorous campaigning than the soldiers of any other nation.[13] The Spanish trooper's famous, laconic cry of "*no importa*" (it matters not) in the face of danger symbolized the physical bravery said to be typical of the Spanish soldier, indeed, of Spanish men generally. The idea of Spanish individual superiority was more than a cynical cover for collective ineptitude and lack of unit preparation. It was one of the most deeply held and cherished myths of Spanish nationalism. Rooted in a glorious military past of conquest and of resistance to oppression from Roman, Moorish, and French invaders, the myth of the Spanish male as a "natural warrior" was powerful stuff, represented in history, poetry, drama, and the education given to every officer.

What officers thought, however, was likely quite different from what the poor conscripts believed about themselves. Most could not read and probably knew very little about Spain's military traditions. Besides, no soldier would rather suffer uselessly than win without a fight. If Spanish soldiers were durable and resigned, it was not the result of centuries of military tradition or their genetic makeup, and it was certainly not their choice to be that way. Instead, poor leadership, lack of preparation, and neglect by their officers forced them to be the longest suffering troops in the world, a reputation they would just as soon not have had.

Martínez Campos was not the right man for Cuba. It wasn't just a matter of his poor strategic sense or the fact that Cubans did not trust the man who had engineered the unfulfilled Zanjón pact of 1878. Martínez Campos had no stomach for hard fighting in jungle warfare, and he never had. On March 19, 1878, toward the end of the Ten Years' War and his first term as captain general in the island, he had written to Cánovas to rail against a "war that cannot be called a war," where the enemy "go about naked or almost naked," have the "sensibility of animals," and are "accustomed to a life of savagery." Warfare in Cuba was unlike anything Martínez Campos had experienced before. It is not warfare at all, he wrote, but "a hunt in a climate that is deadly to us, in terrain that is like a desert to us, where we only exceptionally find food, while they, children of this land, find plenty to eat."[14] In 1895 Martínez Campos still did not like Cuba, and he liked even less the kind of war he was being asked to wage. Writing to Tomás Castellano, he called the Cuban insurgency unstoppable, a note of resignation that should have produced his immediate recall. Indeed, as we have already seen, Martínez Campos asked to be relieved of duty after Peralejo and was turned down.[15]

What Martínez Campos clearly perceived was that the only way to defeat the Liberation Army would be to act with the utmost rigor against civilians who supported the insurrection, but this was something he was not willing to do. On July 25, 1895, he wrote a despairing letter to Cánovas: "I cannot, as the representative of a civilized nation, be the first to give the example of cruelty and intransigence. I have to wait for them [the insurgents] to begin." The Cuban Liberation Army used every means at its disposal to force or cajole civilians into aiding the revolution and to punish those who chose the wrong side. Still, this was not enough to make Martínez Campos act with the necessary rigor. He knew intellectually what had to be done: "I could reconcentrate families from the countryside to the towns," he wrote, but this would result in "horrible misery and hunger," which he didn't think Spain would be able to relieve. "I don't believe I have what it takes," he admitted, to relocate civilians, shoot captives, take hostage the families of known insurgents, and perform all of the other distasteful duties required of a commander fighting against insurgents in a colonial war. He realized that the fate of Spain was hanging in the balance, but he said his moral beliefs took precedence over everything, even the interests of the nation. Martínez Campos had searched himself and found that he was not the right man to deliver a victory in Cuba. About that, at least, he was absolutely correct.[16]

The men in the Cuban invasion column awoke before dawn on December 15, 1895. By five A.M. they were mounted and on the move, going west again. The exhausted horses walked slowly, their heads down. A sense of dread had descended upon the men. The previous day they had left behind the mountains of Santa Clara, and now they were entering the open country around Cienfuegos, where the colonial regime was strong and Spanish loyalists abundant. As one of Gómez's aides quipped, moving west toward Matanzas province was like "crossing the Pyrenees and entering Spain."[1] The column of men from Oriente were the foreigners here, and they knew it. Gómez and Maceo planned to move as quickly as possible through the region, avoiding contact with the Spanish if they could. General Quintín Bandera and 1,000 infantry took a less exposed southerly route, so that the remaining 3,000 mounted men under Gómez, Maceo, and General Serafín Sánchez would be less encumbered. None of them had any way of knowing that by noon the Cuban cavalry would be at Mal Tiempo fighting, and winning, the most important battle of the war.

At about ten A.M., the column passed through a sugar mill and plantation named Santa Teresa. Maceo took the lead, with Gómez and Serafín Sánchez in the center, and hundreds of mules and their handlers bringing up the rear. The tiny garrison at Teresa had the sense to remain holed up in one of the mill's solid buildings, watching while the Cubans burned the cane and rounded up the livestock. Scouts brought two local boys to Gómez for interrogation. They had important news. They had seen a Spanish force of 1,500 infantry under Colonel Salvador Arizón operating in the area, apparently unaware that the bulk of the Cuban army was near. Better still, Arizón had divided his force into three columns, the better to search for the enemy. One of these, made up of some 300 men under Lieutenant Colonel Rich, had marched down the Palenque road from Mal Tiempo and was headed right for the center of the Cuban column. With this information, Gómez hurried ahead to find Maceo, and together they set a trap. The plan called for Maceo on the left flank and Gómez in the center to charge simultaneously into Rich's unsuspecting column. Counting on their vastly superior numbers and the element of surprise, they expected to overrun the Spanish infantry with a machete charge before Rich could deploy.

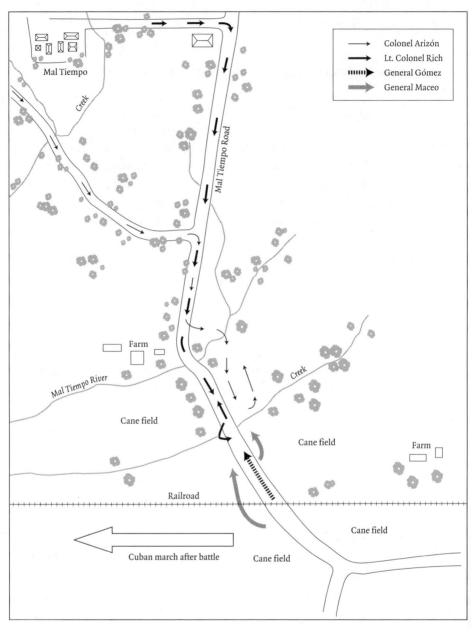

Mal Tiempo

Creek

Mal Tiempo Road

Colonel Arizón
Lt. Colonel Rich
General Gómez
General Maceo

Farm

Mal Tiempo River

Cane field

Creek

Cane field

Farm

Railroad

Cane field

Cuban march after battle

Cane field

Cane field

Battle of Mal Tiempo, December 15, 1895

In fact, the combat did not go quite as planned. Eyewitness accounts vary, but what seems to have happened was that the Cuban advance scouts, instead of waiting for the trap to spring, dismounted and began to fire into the approaching Spanish column. This eliminated the element of surprise, but with only 300 men, Rich still did not have the firepower to withstand the Cuban attack. His position along a road through woods and cane fields also meant that his men had severely limited sight lines. Even armed with repeating rifles, the thin Spanish ranks could not stop cavalry rushing suddenly from the cover of the tree line.

When Gómez and Maceo heard the sporadic firing from their vanguard, they knew that their prey had been alerted to the danger. Nevertheless, they decided to go forward with their plan. Eyewitness accounts place Gómez at the front of his men charging headlong into the Spanish. Maceo, delayed by a gully and a barbed-wire fence, arrived later and swept down upon the Spanish right flank. Theoretically, the Spanish repeating rifles should have wreaked havoc against a cavalry charge. However, for reasons we will examine below, the Spanish were terrible shots. The Cubans brushed aside their ineffective fire and got into their ranks, which they cut to pieces with machetes in fifteen minutes of hard fighting. Manuel Piedra Martel, an aide to Maceo who was wounded three times at Mal Tiempo, remembered the Spanish soldiers losing all discipline. Some threw down their weapons and ran, which only made them easier targets for Cuban cavalrymen swinging their machetes. Others cowered down in prayer, overcome with fear, and shut their eyes to the approach of their own deaths.[2] Esteban Montejo, who fought at Mal Tiempo, recalled how he and his comrades hacked to death dozens of Spanish conscripts and left piles of heads in the woods as a testament to the deadliness of the machete in close combat.[3]

Colonel Arizón showed up in the midst of this carnage with a second column of infantry to keep the catastrophe from being complete. With Arizón's help, and with the arrival on the nearby rail line of an additional relieving force, what was left of Rich's force withdrew to a better defensive position, while the Cubans held the field. The Cubans killed sixty-five Spanish soldiers at Mal Tiempo and wounded another forty, according to Colonel Arizón. According to Cuban sources, the Liberation Army captured 10,000 rounds of ammunition and numerous rifles, together with the colors and archives of the Canaries battalion, while sustaining six killed and forty-six wounded.[4]

Mal Tiempo was a clear-cut Cuban victory and a turning point in the war. It opened the way for the invasion of Matanzas, Havana, and Pinar del Río, where the Liberation Army began at last to make good on Gómez's promise to shut down Cuba's export economy by burning down everything associated with the commercial production of sugar and tobacco. Martínez Campos, who had pursued a strategy of trying to cover many points at once by dividing and subdividing his forces to protect every possible town, plantation, and sugar mill, discovered at Mal Tiempo that he had not left himself with large enough field armies to stop the fast-moving Cubans. A few days after Mal Tiempo, at a place called Coliseo, Martínez Campos led an attack upon a portion of the invasion column led by Maceo. Although Martínez Campos had the best of it that day and held the field, he lacked the resources and confidence to pursue the Cubans following the battle. A black mood of despair took control of the old general, and his removal, something he had been yearning for anyway, became certain. After the battle of Coliseo, Martínez Campos cabled Madrid: "My failure cannot be more complete. Enemy has broken through all my defensive lines. Columns lag behind. Communications cut. There are no forces between enemy and Havana." As a result of Mal Tiempo and Coliseo, Martínez Campos ended his military career in disgrace.[5]

The battle of Mal Tiempo has been the subject of intense popular interest in Cuba, and rightly so, for it was the most significant battle of the war before the American victory at Santiago in July 1898. Yet all of the attention given to Mal Tiempo has helped to perpetuate one of the most enduring myths about the Cuban war, namely, that the Cubans used machetes to defeat Spanish infantry. Indeed, it has become something of a dogma in Cuba, based on the experience of Mal Tiempo and a few other encounters, that the machete was the revolution's most fearsome weapon. Bernabé Boza, who served as an aide to Gómez, wrote in 1924 that "the historical Cuban machete" struck terror into Spaniards, who fled blindly when they heard Cuban troops cry "al machete." According to Boza, Spanish soldiers who once experienced a machete charge could never get out of their minds the horrible "chis! chas!" sound made by the machete when it severed a neck.[6] The iconic status of the machete, already apparent in Boza's use of the term "historical Cuban machete," became embedded in Cuban literature, to the point that scholars have come to consider the machete to be a kind of talisman against which even the most advanced Spanish rifles had little power.[7] Ramón Barquín, for example, described Cuban macheteros falling "like demons upon the enemy squares," which collapsed under the onslaught.[8]

American scholars have also been attracted to the machete as a historical subject. An early account in English regaled American audiences with titillating visions of machete charges in which Cubans, "screaming with the voices of a thousand hyenas," ploughed into masses of hapless Spanish infantry.[9] Philip Foner described Cubans falling "suddenly upon the enemy: their gleaming machete blades brandished on high and fierce war whoops piercing the air," a sight that in Foner's telling paralyzed even the best Spanish troopers.[10] And Joseph Smith claimed that the machete was "more deadly than the bullet of the most modern rifle."[11] In short, the machete came to serve as a shibboleth for Cuban bravery and Spanish incompetence. The implement of the cane cutter and the peasant, the machete became the ubiquitous tool of the insurgent, a fetish that seemingly had the power to ward off Spanish bullets, and the most recognizable symbol of the Cuban War of Independence as a "people's war."

Nevertheless, although the idea of whooping, machete-wielding men on horseback rolling up Spanish infantry is a compelling martial image, anyone familiar with weaponry or tactics knows that something is wrong with the picture. While it seems perfectly reasonable that the Cubans would use a machete for many purposes and that it might, under certain conditions of close combat, prove a formidable weapon, the idea that men on horseback armed with machetes could defeat infantry arrayed in formation appears doubtful, even insulting to the memory of commanders like Maceo and Gómez, who usually knew better than to send men armed with machetes charging hopelessly into a hail of fire. Indeed, there is ample evidence to show that the Cubans used machetes only in very particular circumstances, as at Mal Tiempo, and that the main battlefield weapon was the rifle, just as it was for the Spanish. An examination of the nature of combat in Cuba bears this out.

At Peralejo, at Iguará, at every important battle other than Mal Tiempo, the Cubans fought according to a set script, and the machete played a bit part. Because the Cubans usually tried to avoid battle, the Spanish constantly had to search them out, and this played into the hands of the Cubans. Relying on their network of spies, Cuban commanders could usually predict Spanish troop movements. This allowed them to adopt good defensive ground at elevated sites, river crossings, narrow roads, and paths amid dense jungle, which they prepared with barricades and trenches. The Spanish marched blindly into these traps because they had inadequate maps, little firsthand knowledge of the terrain, few supporters and spies in rural districts, and no cavalry to screen their advance. The Cubans traveled on horseback, but they did not usually fight that way. Instead, they dismounted to fire their rifles from behind cover into masses of Spanish infantry surprised in open ground. If things developed unfavorably, the insurgents had their horses ready to make a fast escape.[12]

The Cubans had developed this way of fighting during the Ten Years' War. Adolfo Jiménez Castellanos, a Spanish veteran of that war, remembered that the Cubans used horses to move rapidly across country. Once in position, though, they dismounted to ambush the Spanish. "Their main tactic," wrote Jiménez Castellanos, "was to fire from positions behind trees or broken terrain," but they "neither took the offensive in machete charges nor waited for our bayonet attacks" but preferred to fire from a distance at the formed ranks of Spanish infantry and then retreat before the Spanish could respond. These tactics explain the low casualty rate on both sides during the war.[13]

The Cubans may have first discovered this system at the battle of La Sacra on November 9, 1873.[14] A month later, Gómez used the tactic again at Palo Seco, his greatest victory of the Ten Years' War. Gómez's cavalry forced Spain's crack counterinsurgency unit, the Cazadores de Valmaseda, to form a square, following which Gómez had dismounted troops fire into the Spanish from behind a roadside fence.[15] In such scenarios, actual combat by cavalrymen armed with machetes took second place to combat with rifles. The machete-wielding cavalry had a role to play at the beginning of an engagement, charging Spanish columns, not because they expected to be able to overcome infantry armed with repeating rifles, but in order to cause the Spanish to fall back into compact formations. Once this happened, the machete became useless, but the Spanish became instantly vulnerable to aimed rifle fire from dismounted and concealed Cuban troopers.

Antonio Maceo mastered these tactics, too. On October 4, 1895, José Escudero Rico, commander of the Alcántara battalion, left Bayamo with 580 Spanish troopers and five days of rations. Escudero's purpose was to march in a broad circle through Baire, Jiguaní, and other towns around Bayamo to make the Spanish presence felt in an area where Antonio Maceo was recruiting men for the approaching invasion of the West. Maceo had thrown a trench and a barricade across the road leading into Baire, and as Escudero's column approached, the Cubans fired from behind the barricade and from concealed and elevated positions on either side of the road. The combat lasted less than one hour, and in the end the Spanish took the enemy trench by bayonet, the Cubans having had the prudence to abandon the position before any hand-to-hand fighting could take place. Advancing farther, Escudero encountered the Cuban cavalry, which charged his column of infantry several times, but not too closely, and were driven off by rifle fire before they could do any damage. Each time, Escudero's column had to stop and deploy in a defensive square, providing the Cubans with an easy target. The advance slowed to a crawl. Eventually, the Cuban forces withdrew into the mountains, pursued briefly and half-heartedly by Escudero's men. In these battles, eight Spanish soldiers took hits by rifle fire, and one died from his wounds. Six more Spaniards suffered minor contusions. No one felt the machete's edge. The Spanish column expended 4,539 rounds of ammunition, resulting in "numerous" Cuban casualties, according to Escudero, who had no way of knowing.

A brief pause is necessary here in order to say a few words about the reliability of casualty figures. It was a sore point with Spanish officers that combat was always so indecisive. "Fronts" never advanced and territory was never gained, at least not for long, so success in combat was hard to measure. This placed a premium on the "body count," just as it did in the Vietnam War, where conditions were similar in other ways as well. Above all, Spanish officers wanted to maximize their kill ratio, meaning a large number of Cubans killed compared to Spanish losses. Promotions and financial incentives were attached to high body counts and kill ratios. The details of a thousand skirmishes were published for all to see in the Boletín Oficial, published by the office of the captain general in Havana. Unfortunately, pressure to produce positive numbers turned officers into liars, reporting heavy Cuban losses based on "signs of blood" or rumors spread by noncombatants. Even worse, they sometimes calculated enemy casualties based on how many rounds they had fired at the Cubans. The logic seemed to be that expending thousands of rounds of ammunition, even when fired blindly into the jungle, had to result in someone on the other side being hit. This scandalous guessing game continued throughout the war and made Spanish estimates of Cuban losses worse than useless.[16] In fact, in the case we were just reviewing, Escudero discovered the bodies of eight Cubans when he took the enemy trench in a bayonet assault, but there is no way Escudero could have known about any other casualties on the Cuban side.

The Cubans also exaggerated Spanish losses. The insurgents could rarely approach, much less come to grips with, columns of Spanish infantry, and they almost never took Spanish positions. So their estimates of enemy losses are as unreliable as those given by the Spanish. Sometimes they reported hundreds of Spanish casualties based on the number of stretchers civilians saw in Spanish towns after a battle. Even in clear-cut victories, Cuban commanders were liable to exaggerate. After Mal Tiempo, for example, Antonio Maceo claimed that the Spanish "left 210 cadavers on the field of battle," but the real figure for Spanish losses was much lower, as we have seen.[17] As a result of this tendency by both sides to inflate enemy losses, it is imperative, whenever possible, to use Spanish sources for Spanish casualties, Cuban for Cuban, as I have tried to do throughout this work. This procedure is not perfect, of course, because each side also tended to underestimate its own losses. Nevertheless, it is likely to get us closer to the truth than any other method.

Escudero's fruitless pursuit of Maceo typified combat in Cuba. One Spanish officer recalled that he rarely ever saw the enemy, much less the business end of a machete, because the Cubans always fired potshots from behind cover and fled before the Spanish could respond.[18] These were not real battles, and there was rarely any opportunity for hand-to-hand combat with "the historical" Cuban machete. This, incidentally, helps explain why both sides suffered so few deaths in the field.[19] Gómez described these tactics of ambush and flight in his diary. Our advantage, he wrote, was that our soldiers, "always hidden behind brush and broken terrain," fired a few shots and then escaped on horseback. This was "something the Spanish could never do," not only because they were on foot but because they were always the aggressors, and in a war like that fought in Cuba "the advantage always goes to the one who waits and not to the one who advances."[20]

The Spanish did have an advantage in their choice of rifle. Spain equipped its infantry with the Mauser, the best rifle in the world at that time.[21] An elegant weapon that required less training and maintenance than earlier systems, the Mauser was a repeating rifle that fired a bullet jacketed in nickel steel, which added to its penetrating force. Frederick Funston, an American who fought with the Cubans, almost died when hit by a Mauser round, but the bullet passed cleanly through his body and a sapling before killing one of his Cuban comrades.[22] The Mauser had a range of 2,400 yards, four times greater than the effective range of the Remington, the weapon used most by the insurgents. The Mauser was less likely to be affected by moisture or dirt entering the chamber, and, because it used smokeless powder, it did not produce the clouds of dense smoke older systems did. This allowed an individual armed with a Mauser to remain concealed and to preserve a clearer field of vision.

Ironically, however, the superior Mauser was in one significant way less effective than the old Remingtons, Springfields, and Winchesters that the Cubans had. Because the Mauser fired at such a high velocity, it produced cleaner wounds, whereas older rifles often sent projectiles tumbling on an erratic and deadly course inside victims' bodies. Bernabé Boza called the Mauser a "humanitarian weapon," because it produced wounds that "either killed immediately or were quickly cured."[23] Thus, Spain's most important technological edge may not have been an edge at all. This was especially true after the Cubans began to use "explosive"—that is, dumdum—bullets, which made even old Winchesters supremely deadly. Explosive bullets had been banned by international convention, and their later use by the British in South Africa may still strike us as contemptible. But the Cubans argued that they had the right to employ any means—dynamite, fire, and explosive bullets—in order to even the playing field against an enemy that enjoyed so many material advantages.[24]

Cuban troops had a reputation for being good shots, despite their use of older weapons. They treated their rifles with great care, for they were precious to them. Officers inspected weapons every three days to make sure they were cleaned and oiled.[25] Every day the men "spent hours on end cleaning them, assembling and disassembling them, aiming them at whatever they fancy and, in short, turning the whole day into an informal sort of target practice." Gómez even thought they practiced too much and worried about accidents.[26]

Meanwhile, the Spanish, for a variety of reasons, made poor use of their Mausers. The rifle, unlike the musket, is a liberal-democratic firearm, placing a premium on the initiative and skill of the common foot soldier. Cubans seemed to adapt instinctively to the rifle. They fought in loose formation, functioning as individuals or in small groups. They used their weapons as they were meant to be used, taking careful aim and firing at their own discretion. In contrast, Spanish troops seemed always to be waiting for an order to fire. They marched and fought in closed lines and squares, as they had been drilled to do. And they fired in volleys, eliminating any advantage their more accurate Mausers may have given them.

Nevertheless, there was nothing in the Spanish "character," assuming such a thing exists, that disqualified them as marksmen. As we have already seen, the Spanish tendency to form up in defensive squares had a lot to do with the Cubans' use of their cavalry. Had the Spanish possessed a sufficient number of their own cavalry to protect their infantry, they probably would not have been so prone to adopt a defensive posture on the battlefield. Nevertheless, there was more to it than this. Closed formations, with the troops firing in volleys, helped neutralize certain problems encountered by Spanish officers.

For a variety of reasons, Spanish infantry were, in fact, notoriously bad shots. Spanish men were not familiar with firearms in general. Unlike the American male, who, through the collusion of the U.S. government, weapons manufacturers, and the National Rifle Association, embarked on a love affair with firearms in the late nineteenth century, Spanish men had little knowledge about or affection for guns.[27] The Spanish government did its best to prevent the dissemination of arms among the Spanish population, which Madrid had cause to fear in a century marked by civil war, social revolution, industrial violence, and growing regional separatism. And despite the frequency of civil wars in nineteenth-century Spain, the government was largely successful.

Even soldiers rarely took target practice with live rounds. It was not just a matter of conserving ammunition. Officers, and the Spanish state itself, simply did not trust servicemen with loaded weapons. German officers, confident that even socialist recruits loved the kaiser, trained foot soldiers for over eight hours a day and allowed them to practice with live ammunition. Other European armies followed similar regimens. In contrast, Spanish troops hardly ever practiced at all. Indeed, most never touched even unloaded weapons. The army issued rifles to conscripts only after they arrived in Cuba, and then training consisted mainly of marching around with empty weapons and standing at attention, when it occurred at all.[28] Even as they marched into possible combat situations, soldiers were told to keep their rifles unloaded until the commencement of hostilities. The concern was to prevent accidental gunshot wounds, to which junior officers in all armies, but especially conscript armies, are strangely prone. All of this meant that, although the Mauser was easier to manage than earlier rifles, soldiers often fumbled to load clips into their weapons with the thunder of hooves bearing down upon them and fired their first live rounds in actual combat. Naturally, they were not very good shots. Indeed, the decision to introduce the Mauser after the war had already begun forced veterans to switch to a new system in midcampaign and turned even experienced marksmen into novices until they became used to the new weapon. All of these defects could be corrected by deploying men in the anachronistic infantry line for offensive purposes and the square for defense. This was part of the explanation for the continued use of these tactical formations in Cuba. Spanish officers had their men form up and fire in volleys, using the Mauser as if it were a Brown Bess musket. This, they reasoned, was the only way to ensure that their men would hit anything.[29]

Against Cuban riflemen firing from the cover of woods, volleys had little impact. Indeed, volleys worked best against cavalrymen charging with machetes. Thus, it is not surprising to find that on most occasions when the Cubans committed themselves to frontal machete attacks against Spanish infantry formed into defensive squares, they suffered high casualties. At Coliseo on December 23, 1895, a week after Mal Tiempo, Spanish squares decimated three successive machete charges, allowing the Cuban cavalry to get no closer than fifty yards.[30] At Paso Real on February 1, 1896, Maceo, perhaps thinking to relive the glory of Mal Tiempo, sent 2,000 men against 900 Spanish infantry. The Spanish had settled into an excellent defensive position, though, and the Cubans suffered 262 casualties against an enemy loss of 46 men.[31] One week later, at the bridge over the Río Hondo, Maceo again sent his men charging into Spanish infantry. This time, he had little choice: the Spanish threatened to overrun the town of San Cristóbal, which Maceo wanted to hold for the revolution. In the end, the Cubans lost 100 men, as well as San Cristóbal. The new troops from Pinar del Río — where Maceo recruited in January 1896 — suffered especially severe losses. Of the fifty Pinareños ordered into the charge, twenty-five were shot from their saddles, proof of their bravery but also of the foolishness of putting too much trust in the machete.[32]

Two more examples of this futility deserve mention, one involving Gómez and the other, Maceo. On October 8, 1896, Máximo Gómez led 479 horsemen in a charge against a larger number of Spanish infantry under General Jiménez Castellanos at "el Desmayo." Frederick Funston, who was present, recalled that the Cubans lost about half of the men committed to the charge and all but 100 horses while inflicting minor damage on the Spanish infantry. Once again, Mausers proved more deadly than men armed with machetes.[33] On May 1, 1896, at the battle of Cacarajícara, which we will have occasion to examine in detail later, Maceo's troops fought from entrenched positions and inflicted heavy casualties on attacking Spanish infantry. One group of Cubans armed only with machetes played a brief role in the combat. They rode close to the Spanish infantry, waved their machetes, sustained a volley that killed some of them, and then rode away. As one Spanish veteran of the battle sourly noted, "The insurgent macheteros deported themselves heroically only when they fought milk cows and foraging parties," but "against advancing Spanish infantry, the machete was useless."[34] Of course, this was a partial assessment by a bitter enemy of Cuban liberation. For all that, it was not inaccurate. The Spanish suffered not a single machete wound at Cacarajícara.

Indeed, the more one looks closely into the actual battlefield experience during the war in Cuba, the more machete charges appear to be either terrible mistakes, tactical feints to force the Spanish into squares, or acts of desperation born of a lack of ammunition and the need to protect vulnerable supplies by slowing down advancing enemy troops. The machete charge was definitely not the tactic of first choice.

Medical evidence from Spanish battle reports and hospitals provides further evidence about the way battles were fought in Cuba. For example, as mentioned above, no Spanish troops at the battle of Cacarajícara suffered a machete wound or cut of any kind, while forty-nine were hit by rifle fire and one by shotgun pellets. A few months later, in June, at the battle at Loma del Gato, where Antonio Maceo's brother, José, lost his life, two Spanish soldiers died and thirty-four were wounded, only two of these as a result of the machete. On October 4, 1896, the Spanish lost thirty killed and eighty-four wounded, all by rifle fire, at the battle of Ceja del Negro. Explosive bullets did terrible damage to the Spanish at Ceja del Negro. The machete produced no casualties whatsoever.[35]

Published data from major hospitals during 1896 show that of 4,187 men treated for wounds, only 13 percent had suffered injuries from machetes. Rifle fire accounted for 70 percent of all wounds.[36] More detailed data from individual hospitals and clinics reinforce the published material. According to its records, the hospital of Havana took in 776 wounded soldiers in 1896. Only 15 had been stabbed or cut with machetes, while 740 men (95 percent) had been shot. Table 2 summarizes this information.

A separate account of wounds treated at several hospitals and clinics around Havana from February through June 1896 shows that 320 men were treated for

TABLE 2. Wounds Examined at the Havana Hospital in 1896

Month	Bullet	Machete	Other	Total	% Machete
January	19	3	2	24	13
February	24	1	2	27	4
March	57	4	1	62	7
April	110	1	2	113	1
May	14	0	0	14	0
June	2	0	0	2	0
July	37	2	0	39	5
August	39	1	2	42	2
September	56	0	0	56	0
October	269	1	6	276	0
November	91	2	5	98	2
December	22	0	1	23	0
Total	740	15	21	776	2

Source: Archivo General Militar, Segovia, secc. 2a, div. 4a, leg. K1.

TABLE 3. Wounds Examined at Three Hospitals in 1895

Hospital	Bullet	Machete	Other	Total	% Machete
Holguín	31	8	2	41	20
Manzanillo	76	9	10	95	9
Santiago	160	7	16	183	4
Total	267	24	28	319	8

Source: Archivo General Militar, Segovia, secc. 2a, div. 4a, leg. K1.

wounds, 286 of them caused by rifle fire, and only 13 by machete. In the month of February 1897 throughout Cuba the Spanish had 242 men wounded by rifle fire, of whom 88 died. Eight men suffered machete wounds in the same month, of whom three died. Information from fourteen additional hospitals from various parts of Cuba and covering various periods of the war indicate that 88 percent of wounds were caused by rifle fire and fewer than 7 percent by cutting instruments of any kind.[37] Detailed records for three major hospitals in Oriente during the year 1895 support the same conclusion and are presented in Table 3.

Monthly casualty reports generated by individual units confirm the information supplied by hospitals and clinics: the machete hardly came into play in combat. For example, in the month of March 1897, reports from all over Cuba showed that 496 men had been killed or wounded by rifles, and only thirty by machetes.[38]

Not recorded in the data are some of the subjective impressions about the wounds. Most of the wounds were not fatal. Indeed, most were not serious enough to result in tickets home. The machete wounds, in particular, tended to be insignificant and were sometimes even self-inflicted, for Spanish troops also carried machetes, not for combat, but for hacking paths through the jungle. Accidental cuts while performing this kind of work were fairly common. Physicians categorized most cutting and stabbing wounds as "light," usually requiring no treatment beyond a field dressing. Gunshot wounds, on the other hand, were much more likely to be listed as "grave." It also appears from the medical evidence that many of the cut and stab wounds, especially those that proved fatal, occurred after individuals were first shot, rendering them vulnerable to machete attack. In many cases, the machete must have simply provided the coup de grâce to men dying on the battlefield.

It must be said that, whenever machetes did come into play, there was always the potential for truly horrific wounds. The surgeons at the military hospital of Manzanillo saw one patient with ten machete wounds, six to the hands and forearms indicating an attempt to ward off the blows, three to the back indicating flight, and a death blow that opened up the cranium. They treated another man brought in with his hand hanging from his arm by a thin string of flesh. Another man arrived at the hospital in Sagua la Grande cut so badly that doctors had to try to stuff one of his lungs back in his chest and some of his brain back into his skull before attending to other cuts on his neck, face, and arms. Mercifully, he did not survive long. The sight of such wounds doubtless frightened new conscripts, and it may be that the terrible possibility of a machete attack demoralized Spanish troops in ways that are difficult to measure.[39] Nevertheless, all available data point in the same direction: the rifle, not the machete, was the Cubans' most important arm. Also, because the Cubans sometimes used explosive bullets, the wounds caused by Cuban rifle fire could be every bit as gruesome as those caused by machetes and generally more deadly.

How, then, does one explain Mal Tiempo? Maceo and Gómez chose to attack with machetes at Mal Tiempo for three reasons. First, Colonel Arizón created a battlefield situation that allowed the machete to be effective. As we have seen, Arizón had 1,500 troops at his disposal to face the 3,000 men of the invasion column. Yet, despite being outnumbered two to one, Arizón chose to divide his little army into three smaller columns, even in the face of a superior enemy force. Then he sent the smallest of those columns under Colonel Rich blindly forward along a path through woods that had not been reconnoitered.

These mistakes were rooted in arrogance. Spanish officers did not think that the Cubans, whom they collectively called "Pancho," could possibly stand up to Spanish soldiers.[40] This lack of respect for what another officer called the "miserable and undisciplined scum" of the Cuban Liberation Army probably contributed to Arizón's decision to fragment his column.[41] In addition, Arizón, like all Spanish officers, was exasperated with the lack of "real" combat in Cuba. The Cubans had become experts at refusing battle in order to concentrate on their real target, property. The smoke of burning cane fields, sugar mills, derailed trains, and towns told the Spanish where the Cubans were, but they could never catch up to them because the Cubans rode while the Spanish went on foot. This frustrating situation turned Spanish commanders into gamblers, willing to risk their men in the hope of luring the Cubans into frontal combat. It had caused Martínez Campos and Santocildes to take a grave risk before the battle of Peralejo, and it caused Arizón to divide his already inadequate column into three sections at Mal Tiempo. Arizón hoped the Cubans would engage one fragment of his command, giving him time to attack with the other two and force a general and decisive engagement. The first part of the ploy worked: the Cubans attacked. However, with overwhelming superiority, the Cuban machete became a deadly weapon, and the battle was over before Arizón could react.[42]

A second factor that helps to explain how the battle of Mal Tiempo developed is that the Cubans were low on ammunition, following their defense of the heights of Manacal a few days earlier. According to one source, Gómez had even considered delaying the invasion of western Cuba due to a lack of cartridges after Manacal and only lobbying by Maceo kept the invasion on course. This depiction of a cautious Gómez is difficult to credit because it seems so out of character. Still, it is safe to say that both Maceo and Gómez were concerned to avoid expending precious ammunition as they moved through the Cienfuegos district of Santa Clara. At the same time, they were well aware that behind Rich's little force, there were more than a thousand additional Spanish troops nearby. A long, stationary battle would have been foolish. These concerns help to explain Gómez's order to his scouts to avoid alerting Rich's column with rifle fire and to charge "al machete" at first contact. As we have seen, the order was disobeyed, and this may have been due to its eccentricity. All-out machete charges against Spanish infantry were just not that common.[43]

The third reason Gómez and Maceo decided to risk a machete attack was that their intelligence indicated that a part of Rich's column was made up of new conscripts who would be untrained and likely to break if faced with men on horseback waving machetes. This is precisely what happened. The main attack drove right through two companies of raw recruits, and as they turned and ran, so did some of the veterans in the Canaries battalion. Some of the men did not even have time to load their Mausers. Others loaded, but, never having drilled before with the weapons, they fired too high. The Cuban cavalry were among them with their machetes before anyone knew what was happening, and the combat was decided. At Mal Tiempo, the machete had its day, but the battle resulted from a set of errors and circumstances that would never be repeated.

In late December 1895, as news of Arizón's defeat spread, Martínez Campos continued to blunder. Even now, wedded as he was to the idea of protecting property owners, he ordered his battalion commanders to divide their forces and "to operate as individual companies protecting the sugar mills" rather than unite to face the Cuban invasion column.[44] Over the next week, Maceo and Gómez made the Spanish pay for these troop dispositions by attacking plantations and small towns, whose garrisons were too weak to mount an adequate defense. Usually, the Cubans succeeded, but not always. On December 23, Cuban cavalry encountered a Spanish force led by Martínez Campos at Coliseo. The insurgents had already engaged the garrison at Coliseo and were consequently low on ammunition again, so they decided to try another machete charge. This time, however, the Spanish infantry held their ground and inflicted terrible losses on the Cubans.[45] In Havana, people believed that finally Martínez Campos had done something to stop the invasion. In fact, the old general did nothing to follow up his advantage, and in the days following Coliseo, Martínez Campos made one of the stupidest blunders of his career.

Gómez and Maceo had withdrawn from the field, apparently licking their wounds and retreating back to the East. But it was only a ruse. And Martínez Campos fell for it. Seeing the Cubans in retreat toward Cienfuegos, Martínez Campos sent thousands of troops by train and steamship around them to block their passage back to the safe confines of Oriente. But after four days of "retreating," the Cubans turned back toward Havana. The road westward had been conveniently cleared of enemy troops by Martínez Campos himself. At Mal Tiempo, Gómez and Maceo had outfought Martínez Campos. After Coliseo they outthought him, tricking him into leaving western Cuba open to invasion.[46]

11 ★ The Invasion of the West

The war came to Sabanilla, a small town in the province of Matanzas, on January 22, 1896. Luisa, a young newlywed recently settled in Sabanilla, wrote to tell her mother the news. At 8:30 A.M. a band of insurgents rode into town shouting "Viva Cuba Libre," surprising Luisa during her morning routine. Her husband, Vijil, joined by forty other pro-Spanish Volunteers, ran to the church, which doubled as an arsenal for the town's weapons and ammunition. The insurgents saw that they could not easily take the church, so they plundered the town, "burning eleven or twelve houses" and "robbing everything they could," especially food, medicines, bedding, and clothes, which were always in short supply in the Liberation Army. Soldiers forced their way into Luisa's home, sparing her but not her possessions. When it was all over, she had only the clothes on her back and three coins she had squirreled away. They even took her sewing machine, a prize coveted by the men of the Liberation Army, who often went about dressed in rags and gunny sacks for lack of a way to fabricate new clothing or repair the old. What horrified Luisa most, though, was that about 100 blacks armed with machetes and trailing the invading force took advantage of the disorder to steal whatever they could. Some blacks from the town and nearby rural districts also joined the melee.[1]

Like many white Cubans, Luisa feared blacks, especially when they were armed with machetes. The idea of Cuba as a paradise of racial harmony was propagated by some republicans, but it was never more than a dream. The fissure that separated blacks and whites in Cuba in the nineteenth century has been probed by recent historians, and it has been found to be deeper and wider than conventional accounts of the Cuban independence movement have ever acknowledged. The "war of redemption" was supposed to bring everyone together in a harmonious national community, but it was not strong enough to do that. Racial differences and racism were the norm against which the republicans railed but could not triumph overnight.

Racism also helps to explain why it was that the people who suffered most in the combat at Sabanilla turned out to be the local black "rioters" themselves. The Liberation Army killed two pro-Spanish Volunteers and one unarmed civilian and wounded two Civil Guards. Luisa thought that the town's defenders had killed and wounded several rebels in return. What she recalled most, however, was seeing eight "local blacks" killed right in front of her house after the fighting ended. By these means, once the insurgents withdrew, whites reimposed the race relations characteristic of colonial Cuba. As must have often been the case, the Liberation Army had passed through too quickly for the health of some of its supporters and local allies, especially people of color.

In the days that followed the Cuban withdrawal, Spanish troops and engineers came to Sabanilla to build fortifications to prevent a reoccurrence of the events of January 22. Still, confidence among the white inhabitants of Sabanilla had been shattered. "Many families have fled to Matanzas," wrote Luisa. "Today the streets are deserted . . . and wherever one looks one sees only misery." The people with the means to flee to the nearest big city had done so. Only the poor remained, living in squalor, holed up behind the new fortifications, and cut off from the world. Food scarcity became an immediate problem. People who could do so fled this misery, but if they went to the city of Matanzas, as many did, it caught up with them, for Matanzas became one of the deadliest refugee centers in Cuba, as we shall see.

Luisa's experience made her afraid for her mother and family. She urged her mother not to let her younger brother wander outside in public lest one side or the other compel him to enlist. And if he did go out, Luisa advised her mother to make sure he dressed in rags and rode a nag with an old saddle, so that if stopped he could claim poverty. As in all "people's" wars, many, perhaps most, people, tried hard to stay uninvolved, as Luisa did.

Luisa felt some shame giving this advice to her family. She thought that it was her duty, and her brother's, to serve the Spanish monarchy against the rebels, whom she saw as bandits. And she was proud of her husband Vijil for his role in fighting with the Volunteers against the insurgents who came to Sabanilla. But, she warned, "anyone who lives in the countryside should avoid joining the [pro-Spanish] Volunteers, because the insurgents hate the Volunteers with a passion." Indeed, she advised that weapons and old uniforms should be hidden to avoid any implication of a connection to the Spanish regime. The Cuban Liberation Army may not have been able to hold Sabanilla for long, but it had gained permanent hold over Luisa and people like her, creating fear and dissembling among pro-Spanish elements, forcing them to lay low in an attempt to ride out the storm of war. Striking terror into the hearts of civilians is one of the fundamental objects of any guerrilla campaign, and the success of the Cuban insurgents in places like Sabanilla was an important precondition for Cuban victory.

It is hard to know how typical Luisa's case was, but the events at Sabanilla were part of a definite pattern in January 1896. On January 4, eighteen days before the assault on Sabanilla, Maceo's cavalry attacked the town of Guira de Melena, in the province of Havana, galloping up and down the deserted streets, waving their machetes, and shouting "Viva Cuba" into the silence.[2] At nearby sugar mills like Mi Rosa and San Martiro, exciting displays like this had been enough to trigger delirious celebrations. Cane cutters and mill hands, most of them Afro-Cubans, waved homemade flags, sang the Cuban anthem, and toasted the Liberation Army. Some joined the insurrection. Guira de Melena, though, was a substantial town, with a garrison of pro-Spanish Volunteers intent on defending the place. The townspeople, therefore, had to be cautious, silently counting from behind shuttered windows the number of Cuban troops invading their town versus the number of men who made up the garrison and calculating their chances if they joined one side or the other.

In fact, Gómez and Maceo had almost 4,000 men near Guira de Melena on January 4, but only a few squadrons of cavalry made the initial assault. They raced first toward the church. As in most Cuban towns, the church in Guira de Melena, built of stone and masonry, was the most substantial structure. Any defense of the town had to take place there. The local Volunteers had occupied the church, and they fired upon the Cuban cavalrymen as they rode past, wounding a lieutenant in the Third Squadron. But the Cubans kept moving. They did not want to expend precious ammunition in a siege. That would have served to immobilize them in a place vulnerable to a counterattack by regular Spanish forces, for Guira de Melena is only about twenty miles from the city of Havana in a region heavily garrisoned by the Spanish. What the Cubans wanted was food, clothing, weapons, ammunition, and additional recruits, and they wanted them quickly. So they ignored the men in the church and began a house-to-house search, flushing everyone outside, as more of Maceo's men began to enter the town.

It was at this point, standing in the streets while their homes were ransacked and the militia remained holed up in the church doing nothing to help them, that the people of Guira de Melena made their choice. Some began to sing the republican national hymn, and others began to chant "Viva Cuba Libre!" The militia in the church realized that the game was up and surrendered. Unfortunately for the people of Guira de Melena, their patriotic epiphany came too late to satisfy Maceo. His men plundered the town, with the help of some of the locals, then set it on fire, as Maceo had directed them to do to towns that put up resistance. Revolutionary laws required the death penalty for Cubans who aided Spain. The insurgents took the captured militiamen, marched them out of town, and "liberated" them later that day, though what form this liberation took is unclear.

Luisa's story about Sabanilla and the Cuban account of the attack on Guira de Melena illustrate a number of important things about the war in Cuba. Above all, they remind us to be skeptical about viewing the Cuban War of Independence as the "majoritarian" war imagined by scholars like Roig de Leuchsenring. In fact, although this is impossible to measure, it seems likely that many Cubans adopted the attitude of Luisa. It is worth remembering that 40,000 Cubans — less than 3 percent of the population of the island — actually enrolled in the Liberation Army, and many of these enlisted late in the conflict, after the Spanish had already begun to ramp down their war effort. Meanwhile, as we have already seen, at least this many Cubans (some place the figure as high as 60,000) served under Spanish colors, though this figure included men in urban militias and the like who did not see real combat. In any case, the arrival of Maceo's easterners in the West was never a simple moment of "liberation" but a complex encounter characterized by collaboration, resistance, and attempts to avoid either.

People in western Cuba responded in a variety of ways to being invaded by Orientales. In general, residents of rural areas — cane cutters, small farmers, casual laborers — were more likely to greet Cuban troops as liberators or even to join them. In contrast, city dwellers tended to see them as aliens from the East who spoke a different dialect and behaved strangely. There was also a racial divide: whites were more likely to oppose the invasion force, blacks to join it. However, the incidence of resistance and accommodation to the invasion did not obey these sociological categories in rigid fashion. Some blacks fought for Spain, some peasants fled from the insurgents, and white boys from the city went to the manigua to join the Liberation Army, looking for the adventure of a lifetime. Cubans reacted to the revolution in a fluid way, depending on local conditions, the proximity of Spanish forces, the strength of the insurgents, and other factors.

Of course, it is impossible to know how typical Luisa's experience was. Nevertheless, her story reminds us of the need to question the role assigned to Cuban women in some of the patriotic literature. According to José Miró, as Gómez gathered his forces in October and November in Oriente, women in the East greeted him with transports of joy. It was the "most beautiful period of the Revolution, the period of blind faith in victory," when all civilians seemed to support the cause with unbridled patriotism. "Everything was grand and poetic in those days," continued Miró, "because of the intervention of the woman, who, transformed by patriotic love, seemed like an emblem of glory, infusing the soldier with her passionate soul, and demonstrating her pride in the fact that it had fallen to [the men in her family] to go with the eastern caudillo to undertake the conquest of Spanish dominions in the remote West."[3] After the invasion had reached its object and Maceo had conquered much of Pinar del Río, women there also supported the revolution. Some even "took up arms and fought in pitched battles" side by side with Maceo's troops, according to one veteran.[4] American newspapers — never very attentive to the truth — even wrote of companies of Amazons assaulting the Spanish infantry lines with machetes.[5] Clearly, in this version of events, where women were joining the good fight against Spain, the Cuban nation had come of age. The power of the revolution was an emanation of a fully developed sentiment of *Cubanidad*, which was itself the product of many years of collective struggle and had come to affect the consciousness of most civilians of both sexes.[6]

Like all myths, this one has its proofs. The image of the woman-in-arms is one of the most revered of patriotic signs. According to the logic of patriotism, if women are fighting, it signifies that the war is a people's war, a national war. Therefore, patriots deploy the image of the armed woman and the hawkish woman who sends her male relatives proudly to the front as a way of bolstering their claim to speak for the people. The only problem with this sort of rhetoric in the case of the Cuban war (as in most wars) is that there is little evidence to support it. Women do not appear on Cuban military rolls, in lists of wounded or killed, or in any other documents that give us a window onto the battlefield. Cases of women, like Adela Azcuiz, who helped to doctor the men of the First Company of the Oriente Battalion, and Luz Noriega, who worked with her husband, Dr. José Hernández, were remarkable and notorious rather than typical.[7] And we do not see women flocking with their families to Cuban-held territory. Rather, the contrary is true. Most fled from the invasion column into Spanish cities. That is one of the reasons that there was such a preponderance, as we shall see, of women and children among the refugees. Most women fled the war, a not very surprising conclusion but one that needs highlighting given the emphasis in Miró, Souza, and elsewhere on the "unanimous ardor" of the Cuban people for liberation.[8]

The exceptions, by their notoriety, only serve to highlight the general truth. Paulina González was one such exception. She joined the Cuban army, becoming a lieutenant and something of a celebrity, fighting alongside her husband, Captain Rafael González, near Santa Clara. When Máximo Gómez heard of her, though, he was scandalized and issued orders to keep her and other women away from combat zones. This would not have happened if cases like that of Paulina González were really very common. Moreover, it is not at all clear that Paulina fought out of a sense of nationalism or for some more personal motive, such as remaining close to her husband.[9]

According to Cuban historian Antonio Núñez Jiménez the use of the word "cubano/a" dated from the second third of the nineteenth century.[10] The neologism described a new phenomenon, analyzed by Louis Pérez Jr. in *On Becoming*

Cuban. But the emergence of a new national identity among Cuban elites in this period is one thing, the nationalism of the masses another. For most Cubans it was the war itself—and even events after the war, such as the conflict with the United States—that sharpened their Cuban identity. We should not be surprised, therefore, to find that the Cuban "masses" were not mobilized under the banner of national freedom in 1895 and 1896.[11]

National sentiment is a slippery thing that cannot be fully captured by explanations that place too much emphasis on long-term economic and social causes. Like class, ethnicity, or any other ideological construct, nationalism is evanescent and relational, coming and going in response to immediate events and circumstances. It is not a constant companion that visits people and stays put once they become "modern" and integrated "objectively" into a national state or economy. Moreover, nationalism is in permanent competition with other identities. For example, Cubans may feel like workers, women, Hispanics, blacks, mulattoes, Caribbeans, Orientales, and Cubans all at the same time or one at a time, depending on the context in which they find themselves. A better way to understand Cuban nationalism in the nineteenth century is to see it in relation to immediate events rather than simply as a long-term, once-and-for-all product of economic, social, and political evolution over decades or centuries of time. Manuel Piedra Martel, one of the insurgent generals, got it right when he wrote, in a moment of brutal honesty, that the "national spirit of independence was never well developed in Cuba. It wasn't in 1868, and it wasn't in 1895 . . . despite the fact that some historians have tried to see an already defined separatist tendency" in the years before the uprising at Baire. "An heroic minority sustained the war of 1868 and fought for ten years amid the indifference — or even disapproval — of the immense majority of people, and the same thing happened in the war of 95."[12]

Civilians did not flock to the Liberation Army. Not at Sabanilla. Not at Guira de Melena. Not anywhere in western Cuba. The trail of smoke and ashes left behind by the invasion column as it burned down towns that resisted is proof of this. The Cuban leadership certainly realized that they would not get far relying on the spontaneous enthusiasm of Cuban civilians. According to a venerable mythology dating back at least to Machiavelli's praise of republican militias, armed citizens were supposed to be superior fighters. But Gómez and Maceo did not make this mistake. Indeed, in practice they rejected the notion that the citizen-rebel makes a better soldier. As José Miró wrote: "It has always been a grave error and the cause of not a few disasters to suppose that the insurgent, even before he knows the fundamentals of war, outperforms the regular soldier in offensive potential, as if the aptitude for war were innate to the rebel. Fortunately, the leaders [of the Cuban

Liberation Army] did not follow this theory [but] recognized the utility of military instruction and the value of discipline."[13] Gómez, Maceo, and other officers of the Cuban Liberation Army made every effort to impose discipline and training upon their men, to turn them, as much as possible, into regulars. Taking this view, the accomplishment of the revolutionary leaders comes to seem that much more impressive. A few thousand men with Gómez at their head forged Cuba, while the majority of Cubans watched passively and a significant number resisted actively.[14] The Cuban War of Independence was both a war of national liberation and a civil war about the meaning of *Cubanidad*.

During the sack of Sabanilla, Luisa witnessed a phenomenon that occurred frequently during the War of Independence. Everywhere the Liberation Army went it was trailed or joined temporarily by a large number of men, mostly Afro-Cubans, who took advantage of the war to enact a rough version of social and racial justice, or simply to get rich on plunder. These so-called *plateados* were "murderers and cutthroats of the worst order," according to an American observer friendly to the insurgents. Even Maceo hated the plateados. Perhaps especially Maceo. The plateados mocked his ideals and leadership, and even, in the eyes of some whites, discredited his race. They usually had no weapons other than machetes, making them little threat to soldiers but a scourge to unarmed civilians. In this way, the machete functioned in Cuba as it functioned in civil and ethnic wars in the twentieth century: it was the weapon of choice for attacking unarmed civilians, a brutal but absolutely necessary function of insurgent warfare. Plateados pretended to join the Liberation Army only to desert when the time came to do serious battle. This and their habit of attacking civilians seemed to hurt the cause of Cuban independence and made officials of the Liberation Army despise the plateados, who "respect neither side, but kill and rob at every opportunity."[15] From time to time, Cuban officers arrested and hanged the most notorious, but they had to walk a fine line between preserving some semblance of order within the revolution and appearing themselves to be as repressive as the Spanish. After all, plateados were addressing racial and social crimes that went back generations, and the fear they inspired could be a kind of salutary terror, making civilians less willing to defend the colonial order for fear of reprisal.

It must also be said that the difference between plateados and units of the Liberation Army was not always clear. A fragile cohesion characterized Cuban army units throughout the war. When the Spanish were campaigning hard, Cuban battalions broke apart. This occurred partly under the stress of constant fighting, but it was also by design. It is in the nature of a guerrilla campaign against a more powerful foe that companies, squadrons, and even individuals should be able to act on their own for weeks and even months at a time with little oversight. Dispersed, the guerrillas present no target for the enemy's attention. Eventually, the enemy becomes inattentive, and then the dispersed guerrillas re-form for another mission.

The trouble comes between missions. Men leave their units and do not return, or morale breaks down, and guerrillas become freebooters. In Cuba, undersized squads of one or two dozen men had to cast about for themselves for months on end, living off of the civilian population, finding missions for themselves (or not), and avoiding contact with Spanish regular forces. Inevitably, they were joined by and came to resemble plateados. Rapacious junior officers, when they learned that they would never be relieved or given adequate supplies by the provisional government, looted in order survive. With no ammunition, their only weapon was the machete, and this meant they could not engage the Spanish but only bully civilians or eliminate an occasional enemy straggler.

Isabel Rubio, a Cuban patriot living in Pinar del Río, recorded how such behavior had destroyed her friend Señora Rabasa. In a letter written on July 2, 1896, she told how the insurgents had requisitioned all of Rabasa's livestock, leaving her with one cow, but then the insurrecto Enrique Pérez came and took that, too, despite the fact that Rabasa's husband was with the Cuban army. "Afterward," Rubio reported, "the Negro, Flores, came and took her sewing machine. Now she has no alternative but to beg or cross the enemy lines to eat with the Spanish soldiers." Many people had already fled to the Spanish side out of necessity, and more would follow, she predicted, unless things changed. "We must watch closely against so many dispersed insurgents who bring nothing but damage and discredit to the cause." [16]

Unfortunately, this sort of behavior was common throughout the war. The diary and correspondence of General José Lacret are filled with complaints about dispersed units in Havana and Matanzas that "shame and sully our cause." After February 1896 the insurrection in these two provinces lost direction and began to break down. According to Lacret, some officers in Matanzas, "lacking in conscience and addicted to evil," had completely abandoned the idea of fighting the Spanish and had given themselves over entirely to "robbery and pillage." Others had set themselves up as independent operators of extortion rackets, demanding payment from planters and merchants in exchange for protection, without any intention of using the proceeds in the fight against Spain. These and other "inexplicable disorders," including the brutal treatment of poor and starving civilians, were, Lacret feared, turning people away from the idea of an independent republic. [17]

The combat diary of Antonio Gonzalez Abreu, of the Cienfuegos regiment, recorded his own unit's rough handling of civilians: "I am still in Manguito

[Matanzas], where last night, August 16, 1896, I witnessed one of the most repugnant acts of vandalism ever committed by rotten-hearted man. Commander Antonio Machado ordered the troops to burn all the houses in the hamlet of Ojo de Agua. Seeing that there was no danger [from the Spanish], he authorized them to collect shoes and clothing, but the looting spread until men and women were left completely naked." Ojo de Agua had a fort at its center, but the garrison could do nothing to protect people living on the outskirts of town, so that is where the insurgents focused their effort. That is also where most of the local supporters of the republic lived, but that fact didn't stop the pillage. "The houses in town were not burned," recalled González, "only those at some distance from the fort. These were the homes of patriots whose crops and persons served the Republic." Now, men who called themselves soldiers of the republic had destroyed them.[18]

Cuban veteran Esteban Montejo recalled one of his commanding officers, a man called Tajó, as a "thief in a liberator's clothing." Tajó devoted himself to robbery and destruction for a while, then surrendered to the Spanish in exchange for amnesty and a bounty, only to return later to the side of the insurrection when it suited him. Always, though, he devoted himself to crime. "Hell would be too good for him, but there he must be. A man who raped so many girls, who didn't leave them alone even when they were married," and who was little more than an assassin had to be in hell, according to Montejo.[19]

If the violence against noncombatants was bad, the cruelty visited upon Cubans who served the Spanish regime knew no bounds. Mail couriers and others who served in official capacities for the Spanish regime received no quarter. Here, the machete was useful. Cuban officers forced pro-Spanish Cubans to dig their own graves and had them hacked to death as they stood over or in them as a way to save ammunition.[20] Gómez, officially at least, encouraged his officers to treat captured Spanish regulars with care, hoping to encourage the Spanish to return the favor.[21] His men did not always obey his wishes in this matter, however. Quintín Bandera, who had a reputation for brutality, liked to play, quite literally, with the heads of captured Spanish troops. Bandera would ask them their names, and when they were about to answer, he would interrupt, saying, "You used to be named that," and with that, cut off their heads.[22] In general, though, Cuban turncoats received much worse treatment than the Spanish. A Chilean fighting for the republic-in-arms recalled that his regiment, even after it had dwindled by early 1898 to the size of a company and could not undertake real military action, continued assiduously to impose revolutionary justice on fellow Cubans. His unit captured seventeen Spanish sympathizers in February 1898 and, having a surplus of ammunition at the time, shot them as they stood at the edge of a mass grave that they had been forced to dig.[23] Cuban firefighters and militiamen knew very well what their fate would be if they fell into the hands of the insurgents. Gómez and Maceo had been executing Cuban "traitors" regularly since the Ten Years' War. This may seem shocking, but combatants in civil wars cannot always afford to indulge in clemency. And what, from one perspective, appears to be banditry, crime, and even terrorism is, from another perspective, a regrettable but appropriate level of violence necessary for victory.[24]

The diaries of other Cuban officers also bear witness to these practices. Baldomero Acosta, in charge of a cavalry squad of thirty men in Havana in the spring of 1896, recorded his unit's activity in a daily log. He almost never faced the Spanish but was an indefatigable hanger of spies, who seemed to be everywhere. Trials lasted a matter of minutes, followed by immediate execution, recorded by Acosta in his diary with some bland notation: "it was necessary to deprive him of life" or "hanged two spies beside road." Whenever possible, the cadavers were left at a crossroads or next to a thoroughfare as a lesson to others.[25] Months might go by without the slightest contact with Spanish regulars, especially in Havana and Matanzas, where the insurgency lost cohesion early. Yet even disorganized and weak Cuban forces remained active against collaborators, hanging, shooting, or hacking them to death in unknown numbers.[26] After the battle of Las Tunas, Calixto García's men hacked forty Cuban collaborators to death with machetes. Torture was not out of the question either. The Spanish found the body of one captured Volunteer with his nails pulled out and his fingers and toes chopped off.[27]

Naturally, pro-Spanish Cubans returned the favor when they captured insurgents. They were among the most feared and ruthless of Spain's forces, hunting down and surprising Cuban encampments and field hospitals, where not even the sick and wounded were spared. Here, too, the machete proved a useful tool for dispatching unarmed, convalescing patriots with the maximum of violence. Whole regions of Cuba were under the control not so much of the Spanish army as of pro-Spanish Cuban Volunteers. Southwestern Santa Clara province, for example, was under the dominion of a counterinsurgent guerrilla movement organized by Cubans from Cienfuegos.[28] The war diary of Manuel Arbelo reflects the reality for many Cuban patriots who fought as often against their Cuban brethren-in-arms as they did against Spanish troops.[29] These Cuban Volunteers had more at stake than Spanish conscripts, and they committed infamous atrocities against Cuban insurgents and their sympathizers.[30]

When the war ended, Máximo Gómez and the other leaders of the new republic, trying to patch up Cuba's grievous wounds, insisted that the war had brought Cubans together, but we should be careful not to take this pious wish as a statement of fact. The first chroniclers of the war were forging a nation, and it was appropriate to the task that they cover up the bitter violence that had divided Cubans.[31] Veterans of the fighting, however, knew the truth. According to Esteban Montejo, politicians who insisted after the war that everyone had been a republican at heart and a victim of Spanish tyranny were mistaken. Montejo thought that Spanish sympathizers should have been punished more and supporters of the revolution rewarded better. He also believed that the Cubans who fought for Spain should have been "exterminated" after the war.[32]

In a later chapter we will look at the exterminationist policies of Weyler and the Spanish. It must be remembered, however, that the war in Cuba was as murderous as it was, not just because of Spanish practices, but also because of the insurgency's use of violence against Cubans deemed to be insufficiently patriotic and the equivalent violence of the pro-Spanish Volunteers.

Exemplary violence was a planned and necessary component of the insurgents' strategy, and the burning of Guira de Melena and the invasion of places like Sabanilla in January 1896 had the desired effect. Many towns decided that resistance did not pay, and Maceo's Second Cavalry Division faced almost no opposition as it took possession of dozens of places in the provinces of Havana and Pinar del Río. On the morning of January 5, 100 Volunteer militiamen in Alquizar (situated only a few miles west of Guira de Melena) surrendered to Cuban forces without a fight, as the town fathers, hoping to avoid the sacking meted out to their neighbors in Guira, welcomed the Cubans on the outskirts of the municipality. That afternoon the Cuban cavalry took Ceiba del Agua, the militia having vacated the town beforehand. On January 6, Guayabal, Vereda Nueva, Hoyo Colorado, and Punta Brava fell, although, like Sabanilla, the Cubans only occupied them briefly. On January 9, it was the turn of Cabañas, which Maceo plundered, considering it a "rich prize" for his men. On January 10, a garrison of Cuban Volunteers fighting for Spain surrendered San Diego de Miñas without resistance, and on January 11, the Spanish garrison of Las Pozas fled precipitously, leaving behind 100 rifles and allowing the mayor to surrender the town peacefully in order to avoid reprisals.

During the rest of January and February it mostly went like this. Maceo's conquest of the West proceeded almost unopposed. But not always. On January 16, Maceo assaulted the provincial capital of Pinar del Río. However, this task was too much even for Maceo's united force of 1,500 men. Residents had built barricades in the streets and, together with Spanish troops and a multitude of refugees from the countryside, prepared themselves to defend the city.[33] Maceo's men surprised a mule convoy as it left town, capturing eighteen mules, two wagons, and a fancy coach after battling its small escort of regular troops.

However, Maceo lost twenty-two men even in this small encounter with regular infantry, and withdrew to a height near the road. On the following day, Maceo realized he could do nothing to take the city and left it to the Spanish and their sympathizers.

On January 22, the Cubans marched into the small town of Mantua, the westernmost municipality in Cuba. The great trek to the West had ended. In Mantua, as in so many other small towns, Maceo faced no resistance, and he occupied it for two days. By early February, as new recruits from Mantua and other parts of Pinar del Río joined up, Maceo's army swelled to 2,500 men, although almost a third were still not armed. He turned east again, marching into San Cristóbal, where the townsfolk greeted him with shouts of "Viva!" On February 14, San Antonio de las Vegas gave up peaceably. Other towns, however, began to fight back, and some switched their allegiance back to the Spanish, encouraged or forced to do so by the arrival of large numbers of Spanish troops in the province. Martínez Campos had stepped down, and his temporary replacement, General Sabas Marín proved much more energetic. On February 4, the town of Candelaria resisted with Spanish help, and Maceo was forced to withdraw, though not before burning down part of the town. Combat with Spanish regulars was still rare, but when it occurred, the results were not usually good for Maceo. At Paso Real and in the attempted defense of San Cristóbal already described, he lost over 300 men. As the number of Spanish troops grew, so did Maceo's difficulties, and he crossed back into the province of Havana, where, on February 18, the militia in the town of Jaruco made a brief stand. Maceo plundered the place and burned 131 houses.[34]

Gómez had been active himself in Havana, leading Spanish forces there on a merry chase in January and February. Now, on February 19, Gómez met with Maceo to take stock and to plan the next step. The invasion of the West had been a rousing success. Between late November and late January, the Cubans had marched the length of the island, avoiding large Spanish armies, defeating or at least fighting to a draw several smaller ones, and making their presence felt in every corner of the island. Smoke from burning cane fields and the ruins of dozens of sugar mills, bridges, and towns testified to the Liberation Army's success. Maceo's achievement, in particular, stood out as nothing short of spectacular. The American press likened Maceo's incursion into western Cuba to Sherman's march through the Deep South. In some ways, the comparison was apt. Both Sherman and Maceo targeted the economic foundations of their opponents' capacity to make war. It was warfare against civil society, and the price in civilian casualties would come later, through shortages of food, housing, means of transportation, and other basic necessities.

Maceo had overthrown colonial society in most of Pinar del Río, at least for a while. Years later, in his memoirs, Weyler would write that "Maceo destroyed in Pinar del Río whatever had existed of Spanish domination, except in the capital, changing the regime [in the province] completely."[35] Spaniards were dumbfounded. Most of Matanzas, Havana, and Pinar del Río had "no jungle, or broken terrain or anything to impede the actions of the [Spanish] soldier," yet the rebel armies remained active in these provinces throughout the winter of 1895–96 against little opposition from the Spanish.[36] Western Cuba, what the invading Orientales had referred to as "the land of cane" or simply "Spain," had been utterly devastated.

A French resident of Havana summed up the situation in western Cuba in a letter to an American friend dated February 22, 1896. Gómez and Maceo "absolutely played with the Spanish generals," and any reports of Spanish victories should be taken with a grain of salt, he wrote. "If anyone had told us four months ago that [Gómez] would be able to stop the crushing of the cane in the Province of Havana, or even in Matanzas, we would have laughed in his face. Today not a planter dares disobey his orders. They know too well what the cost would be, for he would destroy not only the cane, but their mills and machinery."[37]

All of this was about to change, however. Martínez Campos had proved that he lacked the qualities necessary to fight the kind of war being waged in Cuba. As we saw already in his letter to Cánovas in July 1895, Martínez Campos claimed that moral beliefs kept him from fighting a "dirty" war. However, his crisis of conscience did not extend so far as to prevent him from recommending a more qualified successor. Valeriano Weyler had what it took to get the job done, according to Martínez Campos. The old general had a peculiar sense of ethics: He refused to commit war atrocities but condoned their commission by Weyler. Given the obvious distaste with which Martínez Campos approached his job as captain general in wartime, it is puzzling that Cánovas waited six months to relieve him. In a charitable moment, we may like to imagine that, like Martínez Campos, perhaps Cánovas had personal reasons to delay taking the final step that would turn Cuba into a living hell. Once he made that decision, however, he, like Martínez Campos, knew exactly what to do. He called upon Weyler.[38]

In late January 1896 the Liberation Army razed towns, burned crops, and seized or slaughtered livestock in western Cuba. Thousands of civilians, perceiving the rebels as foreign invaders, fled before this onslaught. They streamed into Spanish-held towns, aided by troops who had been directed to assist them. The refugees were fearful and angry, but they were hopeful, too. It was common knowledge that Valeriano Weyler would soon take over from Martínez Campos as captain general of Cuba. Weyler's reputation for decisive action, even brutality, reassured loyalists. Weyler would kill or capture Maceo quickly, they believed, and the soldiers from Oriente would be forced to go home. Weyler would restore the social and racial hierarchy of colonial Cuba. He would be their savior.

Weyler's detractors called him other things: the quintessential Hobbesian man — nasty, brutish, and short; the sinister dwarf; the butcher. It is an ancient truth that the victors write history. Weyler was not the victor, and his name has become forever associated with all that is most vile in war. It should be stated clearly that Weyler merited most of the bad press he received. Yet, if we are to understand his behavior, we must place him in context. His life of military service, the practices of the Cuban insurgents, the international political situation, and many other things helped to shape Weyler into one of the archvillains of history.

Valeriano Weyler was born in Palma, on the island of Mallorca, on September 17, 1838. Some have said that his being an islander shaped his fate in some deep and mysterious way, shackling him to an insular destiny. Like Beatriz de Bobadilla or Columbus, Weyler became caught up in the peculiar Spanish dream shared by Cervantes's Sancho Panza: He became the governor of islands — the Canaries, the Philippines, and, finally, Cuba.

To people inclined to find necessity in history, Weyler's choice of a military career seemed inevitable as well. His father, Fernando Weyler, was a divisional general in the army medical corps, director of various military hospitals, author of numerous works on botany, geography, and medicine, and eventually the director general of Spain's army medical corps. Valeriano's mother, María Francisca Nicolau, also came from a military family. It surprised no one when Valeriano entered the Toledo military academy in 1853 at the age of fifteen.[1]

Weyler stood 4′ 10″ tall, below the already low height threshold required for military recruits. During his three years at the academy, he reached his adult stature of five feet. This was still a few millimeters too short, but no one seemed to care. In fact, the Spanish army lowered its height requirement soon thereafter, as the need to recruit troops from among the increasingly malnourished and diminutive popular classes became imperative with each new civil and colonial war during the bloody nineteenth century.[2] Despite his stature, Weyler's classmates at Toledo nicknamed him "Scipio," honoring the quality he had in common with the ancient Roman general: tireless physical strength, which Weyler retained throughout his long life. Weyler was still too young to indulge in what would become his most notorious vice, womanizing, but another of his lifelong traits, abstemiousness with alcohol, surfaced early. Later, in Cuba, while other high-ranking military officials persisted in the convenient belief that massive consumption of cold champagne would fight tropical diseases, Weyler made a show of drinking water as the troops did.[3]

The sober Weyler flourished in the Toledo academy, which was half school, half barracks, located in an ancient castle. There, he absorbed and then came to embody the values of the Spanish military, with its emphasis on discipline, routine, individual valor, and a zealous belief that the army was the one institution capable of embodying the "spirit" and collective will of Spain. Weyler excelled in the not very demanding academic portion of his training as well, graduating fourth in his class and entering the lists as a second lieutenant in 1856. From 1857 to 1862, Weyler continued his studies in the Staff Officer School, this time graduating first in his class with the rank of captain. The following year, 1863, a position became vacant in Cuba. Almost nobody of appropriate rank ever wanted to go to Cuba, where disease created new openings as fast as old ones could be filled. The island was for the young and ambitious, and Weyler took the opportunity to volunteer. The army rewarded him with a promotion to comandante (equivalent to the rank of major) and shipped him off to Havana in May 1863.[4]

Cuba was relatively placid in 1863. However, three things made it an eventful year in Weyler's life. First, he won the national lottery and used the enormous prize money to purchase a house and property back in Mallorca. Overnight he had become wealthy. Second, he contracted yellow fever in the summer, and it almost killed him before leaving him with a lifelong resistance to the disease. Third, in the fall of 1863, Weyler got his war, which was the only way for young officers to show their mettle and gain further promotions. As we have already seen, the people of the Dominican Republic, after getting the Spanish to turn back an invasion by Haiti, rose up against their neocolonial master. To fight this new war, Spain required the services of its officers and men stationed in Cuba. Weyler, just recovered from yellow fever, became staff officer under General José Gándara, commander in chief of Spanish forces in the Dominican Republic. In combats during October and November, Weyler demonstrated his ability to command in difficult situations. He won decorations for military bravery, including the army's top honor, the Cross of San Fernando. He also received promotion to lieutenant colonel in the cavalry.

The Dominican war went well for Weyler but poorly for Spain. In 1865, with the United States once again poised to enforce its will in the hemisphere, Spain relinquished the Dominican Republic. The army transferred Weyler back to Cuba, but he retained his wartime rank of lieutenant colonel, which opened up many opportunities to him and improved his pay considerably. The Dominican war was the first step in Weyler's rise to power and prestige. The contrast with the treatment accorded to Máximo Gómez, who received nothing for his labors on Spain's behalf, could not have been more stark. It was an example — a costly one as it turned out — of the way Spanish chauvinism rewarded Peninsular Spaniards and alienated men of talent who happened to be born in the colonies. Weyler remained in Cuba, with a brief interlude in Puerto Rico, until early 1868, when he returned to Spain.[5]

Weyler did not stay in Spain long. The beginning of the Ten Years' War on October 10, 1868, resulted in his being called back to Cuba. Weyler became chief of staff to General Blas Villate, Count of Valmaseda, whose column of 3,000 men Weyler reorganized and led, distinguishing himself in December during the retaking of Bayamo, which the Cuban rebels had occupied in the first days of the war. Weyler received promotion to the rank of colonel in January 1869.

Later that year, the government charged him with the task of organizing a column of Volunteers, many of them from among the fanatical pro-Spanish population of Havana. These *Cazadores de Valmaseda*, as Weyler named them in honor of his old commander, became the most feared unit in the Spanish army, fighting a brutal counterguerrilla campaign not envisioned in any Spanish military doctrine. Weyler made up the rules of engagement as he went along, and there were not many. He gave no quarter to the enemy, a word he construed broadly to include civilians in areas of combat. In fact, though not in name, Weyler had adopted a policy of establishing what the Americans in Vietnam would call "free fire zones." Civilians had to evacuate certain places. If they did not, then they were no longer civilians and became fair game for Weyler's merciless Cazadores. Thus, Weyler began his career as Spain's best and most brutal counterinsurgent. Someone once asked Weyler about the terrible acts ascribed to him and to the Cazadores in Cuba: "Is it true, my general, that your men returned from battle holding the severed heads of their enemies by the hair?" Weyler responded with a telling evasion. "What do you think war is? In war men have only one job: to kill." The legend of Weyler as a "butcher" evidently had a basis in fact.[6]

For his services, Weyler was made brigadier general in December 1872, a promotion that required him to give up command of the Cazadores. He took over a brigade operating around Puerto Príncipe and organized a mobile column that hunted down, defeated, and killed Ignacio Agramonte, one of the most famous and successful of the Cuban generals, on May 11, 1873. By then, however, the war in Cuba was becoming a secondary concern for Spaniards because Spain itself was plunged into civil war. In January 1873, Spaniards had declared a republic, provoking the ultraroyalist Carlists to rebel for the third time in fifty years.

In July Madrid recalled Weyler to help put down the Carlists. That fall Weyler led republican troops against Carlists in Valencia. However, he seemed to forget everything he had learned fighting against insurgents in the Caribbean, or perhaps, once in Spain, the Napoleonic tactics he had been taught in school reimposed themselves. Weyler sent his men charging in waves against the Carlists, who fought from behind cover and did great damage to republican forces. Indeed, the only thing that prevented Weyler's defeat was the death of the Carlist general, whose charismatic leadership had given the rebels their cohesion.[7]

Meanwhile, back in Cuba, the insurgents enjoyed a brief recovery. The Carlist threat had diverted Spanish supplies and reinforcements back to the Peninsula, and Spanish forces remaining in Cuba had to be assigned to static holding positions, where they became ineffective and vulnerable. In this new environment, the cruelty of the Cazadores received recompense. In December 1873, as Weyler fought in Valencia, Gómez destroyed most of Weyler's old command at the battle of Palo Seco, killing 507 of the 600 men in the Cazadores regiment, a death rate explicable only if Gómez took no prisoners, something he and other Cuban patriots did when they fought other Cubans.

Valencia secured, the Spanish First Republic sent Weyler to pacify Catalonia, where he became notorious for his willingness to destroy property and kill noncombatants in order to root out the Carlist rebels. Spaniards got to see up close the ruthless counterinsurgent that had been shaped in Spain's colonial wars in the Dominican Republic and Cuba, but the sight was too horrible for them. No one cared too much about this kind of war when it occurred thousands of miles from home, but butchering civilians in Catalonia was another matter. Eventually, republicans hoped to reincorporate Catalonians into the body politic, and Weyler's scorched-earth strategy promised to make that difficult. The government reprimanded Weyler for his behavior in Catalonia.

Politically, Weyler was a liberal, perhaps even a republican at heart, and his reputation suffered a serious blow when a royalist cabal, led by Martínez Campos and Cánovas del Castillo, overthrew the First Republic in December 1874. Caught unprepared, Weyler hesitated to abandon the republic and earned the mistrust of royalists as a result. He then compounded his sins by trying to defend his actions in print, a form of political intervention that the new monarchy understandably resented. The newly crowned king, Alfonso de Borbón, dismissed Weyler on August 6, 1875. Under house arrest, Weyler returned to Mallorca to escape the hurly-burly world of Madrid politics in the first year of the Bourbon Restoration.

Weyler's political mistakes were soon forgiven, however. With the country still in turmoil following the Carlist rebellion and with all of the vacancies that had resulted from the purging of republican officers, Alfonso XII needed Weyler. The king recalled him in 1876 to serve as divisional commander of forces stationed around Valencia. In 1878, at the age of thirty-nine, he became a lieutenant general, completely rehabilitated in the eyes of the Restoration monarchy. Meanwhile, the Cuban insurrection had collapsed, riven by racial, social, regional, and political differences. The Cuban leadership began peace negotiations in January 1878 with Captain General Arsenio Martínez Campos. On February 10, 1878, they signed a pact at Zanjón ending the Ten Years' War.

In the following years, Weyler served in various positions, most notably as captain general of the Philippines from 1888 to 1891, where he tested some of the policies he later put into place in Cuba. A low-level guerrilla insurgency against Spanish rule had gained momentum in the archipelago, especially on the island of Mindanao, and Weyler determined to crush it. In a four-month campaign in 1891 Weyler reestablished Spanish rule in Mindanao. Part of his strategy for victory called for the building of a military line, or trocha, to isolate the insurgents from the civilian population. The chief engineer of the Philippine trocha, José Gago, would also build trochas in Cuba. Weyler created fortified towns and villages on Mindanao, relocating civilians into them for their own protection against "pirates." This was a foretaste of the wholesale reconcentration Weyler would carry out in Cuba. Weyler came in for a good deal of criticism in Spain for his brutal behavior in the Philippines. His scheme to remove the native population from some areas and to resettle vacated enclaves with Peninsular Spaniards and Chinese immigrants seemed inhuman. But the Spanish government needed a man like Weyler for the dirty job of holding down its colonies. A career built upon combating insurgents in the tropics had shaped Weyler and his closest collaborators into something Spaniards did not like to look at but that they needed to rely upon time and again.

In the end, Weyler achieved very little of his ambitious plan in the Philippines. He discovered that some of his men had been sent to the islands for disciplinary reasons and were unreliable. The settlers and relocated Filipinos needed new bridges, roads, wells, irrigation canals, houses, and fortifications that Weyler lacked money to build. Moreover, just as he was getting started, Weyler's tenure was up. By law, the appointment to the office of captain general lasted only three years, a rule that almost ensured the incoherence of Spanish colonial policy.[8]

In November 1891, Weyler returned to Spain and relocated to Madrid, for he had been elected senator for the Balearic Islands. In 1893 the Canary Islanders made him their senator as well. But Madrid required Weyler's military talents again, this time as captain general of fractious Catalonia, where a revolutionary working class threatened direct action against the state. Weyler arrested hundreds of workers, becoming the darling of the Catalan bourgeoisie, with town after town declaring him an "adopted son." The Crown conceded him the status of "senator for life" for his role in "saving civilization" from the "barbaric" workers.[9] Weyler's repression of organized labor in Catalonia in the early 1890s made him a symbol of reactionary violence all over the world. In 1896–97 this part of Weyler's past would contribute in interesting ways to a growing sentiment around the world that Spain was unfit to rule Cuba. This is a subject we will return to in more detail in a later chapter.

Weyler was fifty-six years old and on top of the world when Cuban revolutionaries proclaimed their independence at Baire in February 1895. When it became clear by year's end that Martínez Campos could not defeat the Cubans, everyone fixed upon Weyler, the tough counterinsurgent, to replace him. In December 1895 Cánovas began negotiations with Weyler. Normally aligned with Sagasta's Liberals, Weyler hesitated to return to Cuba unless he had the Conservative government's promise of a free hand. At first Cánovas balked at this demand, but as the situation in Cuba deteriorated, he gave in, and on January 18 he called Weyler to Madrid.

On January 19, Weyler met with the cabinet to receive his instructions and to deliver an analysis of the Cuban situation to the minister of war. In this document, Weyler wrote that the key to victory would be to relocate the population. Civilians should be forced into cities and towns where they could be policed. This would allow Weyler to isolate the insurgents and at the same time bring together dispersed Spanish forces to create a few large field armies. These would be used in concert to catch and destroy the main Cuban forces. This was Weyler's recipe for victory at the time of his appointment, and he changed it not one iota after arriving in Cuba.[10]

A week after his meeting in Madrid, Weyler was in Cádiz, preparing to embark for his new command. There he met with some of the men he would take with him to Cuba, including General Juan Arolas, who had fought with Weyler in the Philippines. Weyler promised Arolas that together they would demonstrate to the world that "what we became in the Philippines will serve us well" in

Cuba and predicted that they would "teach those bandits a hard lesson."[11] Such boasts between officers are understandable, if offensive, but Weyler went too far when speaking to the press. He told one reporter that he would "end the war in little more than two years," a rash promise that showed how poorly Weyler was informed about conditions in Cuba, even after his high-level meetings in Madrid.[12]

As Weyler made last-minute arrangements for his trip to Cuba, Martínez Campos was heading for home. He landed as quietly as possible at La Coruña on February 2, 1896, but jeering mobs greeted him at every station on the train ride to Madrid, where he inspired a massive protest demonstration in the capital on February 7. A fellow officer even challenged him to a duel, which was broken up at the last minute. Martínez Campos, peacemaker at Zanjón, political insider, and the military figure most responsible for the Bourbon Restoration in 1874, had finally been destroyed by Cuba.[13]

On February 10, Weyler arrived in Havana to an enthusiastic reception the likes of which had never been seen in the city. Weyler knew better, though, than to place too much stock in the opinions of the pro-Spanish fanatics so common in the capital. En route from Spain, while in San Juan, Puerto Rico, he had received reliable and alarming intelligence from officers in Cuba. Outside of Havana and other large cities, they said, Spanish colonial society had been shattered by the Liberation Army. From one end of the island to the other, the air was filled with the smoke of burning buildings and crops. Maceo had probed the defenses of Havana itself. He had too few troops, insufficient ammunition, and no artillery, so he could not seriously threaten the city, but it had not stopped a panicky Martínez Campos from declaring martial law there on January 6. One can truthfully say that Maceo had taken war to the capital itself, if only on a psychological level. Finding Havana unassailable, Maceo had continued west to Pinar del Río, torching half of the towns there and forcing thousands to flee into Spanish cities. Gómez, meanwhile, remained in the provinces of Matanzas and Havana, blowing up trains, pillaging towns, and burning crops. Other Cuban forces dominated the central and eastern provinces, and expeditions from the United States landed unopposed in Oriente. In late March, at Baracoa, a ship landed Calixto García, who would reorder the insurgency in the East and become in the last two years of the war the most successful general the Cubans had.

Weyler confessed shock at the "extremely grave situation" he inherited. It was, he said, worse than anything he had imagined, and he knew that he needed to act quickly. As soon as he arrived in Havana, he began to impose an iron discipline on the island. On February 16, he placed under military jurisdiction civilians who "by spoken word, by means of the press, or in any other form, undermine the prestige of Spain." These actions would be judged in military courts and treated with the utmost severity.[14] On the same day, Weyler announced a three-part strategy for pacifying Cuba.[15] First, he pledged to eliminate garrisons in hundreds of indefensible plantations and hamlets in order to create large field armies capable of forcing decisive battles on the Cubans. Second, he would focus his energies and resources on one part of Cuba at a time, beginning with an assault on Maceo in Pinar del Río. Then he would move east, always driving the insurgents before him, until he could force them back across the trocha and into Oriente. The trocha would be rebuilt, and the revolution starved of resources and destroyed at leisure. Third, Weyler would relocate civilians from the countryside into towns, where they could be prevented from aiding the insurgents. Also, removing them from the countryside would eliminate the need to protect hundreds of small towns and hamlets. He called this part of his plan "reconcentration," and we will devote later chapters to the controversial subject. The rest of this chapter and the next will examine how Weyler implemented — or tried to implement — the first two parts of his plan, the reorganization of his forces and the destruction of the Liberation Army.

The first part of Weyler's strategy required that garrisons and detachments be withdrawn and consolidated. They had not been able to guard combustible cane fields and unfortified towns and hamlets. They and the convoys used to resupply them had merely provided easy targets — and sources of weapons and ammunition — to the Cuban insurgents. Weyler would reunite the troops Martínez Campos had divided, forming large mobile columns, augmented with new arrivals from Spain. The objective would no longer be the protection of property but the aggressive pursuit and destruction of the Liberation Army.[16]

This was the idea on paper. In fact, Weyler was not able to reorganize his forces as rapidly or as completely as he would have liked. Reuniting dispersed field armies required that he abandon Cubans in rural areas to their own devices, and this produced a great outcry from people loyal to Spain, who pressured Weyler, as they had pressured Martínez Campos, to protect their families, communities, and properties from the insurgents. A flood of correspondence begging that garrisons be left in place sometimes caused Weyler to do just that, against his better military judgment.[17] This helps to explain why he left Cascorro garrisoned until October and why he continued to occupy vulnerable and strategically useless places like Bayamo and Tunas in the East.

In fact, the logic of guerrilla warfare proved stronger than Weyler's aching desire to fight decisive battles with big field armies. As late as March 23, 1897, more than a year after Weyler's arrival on the scene, one could still find a small detachment under Lieutenant Santiago Sampil escorting a supervisor for a big planter back to the abandoned sugar mill Esperanza in order to retrieve personal property he had left behind. Weyler's policy was supposed to avoid actions like this, which were designed solely to aid property owners and left his soldiers vulnerable to attack even by small insurgent forces. Indeed, insurgents ambushed Sampil's seventy men, killing three, wounding five, and capturing fourteen Mausers, before evaporating.[18]

These kinds of situations were inevitable, however, given the traditions of the Spanish officer corps. Underpaid officers lower down the chain of command, like Sampil, had powerful motives to help property owners. By accepting private missions, they collected fees for themselves and their starving men. The practice was so common in Cuba that only foreigners or the profoundly naive found it remarkable. Spanish officers had always hired out their men to act as rural constables in Spain. Why should Cuba be any different? Thus, when Weyler announced his plan to withdraw garrisons from the countryside, he faced resistance from two fronts — Cubans who demanded protection and lower-echelon officers who profited by providing that protection. These were powerful constituencies, against whom Weyler could not always have his way. Significantly, Weyler's replacement in October 1897, Ramón Blanco, found that many of the forces he inherited were, in fact, still dispersed, and, like Weyler, he made it a top priority to consolidate Spanish garrisons spread too thinly to have any offensive potential. Also like Weyler, he was only partly successful.

Trying to remove protection from the tobacco and sugar plantations presented Weyler with special problems. Pinar del Río was the center of tobacco production in Cuba. Pinareños produced the most prized leaf in the world. Workers in the industry possessed a fascinating tradition of activism that directly challenged Weyler's authority. Cigars were made by hand. There was no machinery, no assembly line. The labor required skill, but it was not so absorbing that one could not simultaneously concentrate on something else. To help pass the time as they rolled cigars and performed other labors associated with their craft, workers selected one of their own as a *lector*, or reader, to impart news of the day and to introduce topics for discussion. A Spanish immigrant from Asturias, Saturnino Martínez, invented the tradition in the 1860s, at about the same time he founded La Aurora, the first workingmen's newspaper in Cuba.[19] With readers imparting the latest news and editorials from papers like La Aurora, the workplace became the site of political and moral education, the lectureship a kind of subversive pulpit. Making the parallel with church practices even more complete, on Saturdays, workers passed around a collection plate, always in support of radical causes, for, like many artisanal workers, they were politically on the Far Left. Low pay, tariffs that raised the price of Cuban cigars and gave an edge to foreign competitors, the newfangled taste for machine-rolled cigarettes: all of this threatened Cuban cigar makers. Many had become anarchists, members of a working-class movement as important in the Hispanic world and among arti-sanal workers as socialism was among industrial proletarians in other coun-tries. As anarchists, the cigar makers had an additional reason to hate Cánovas and Weyler, who together were responsible, as we shall see, for the barbaric re-pression of Spanish workers — many of them anarchists — in Barcelona and other areas of Spain. Knowing all of this, Weyler had no doubt that the workers in the Cuban tobacco industry were providing support to the insurgents. There-fore, he prohibited the commercial production of finished tobacco in order to strike out at radical laborers. This added to the seething hatred the workers felt toward Weyler.

On April 16 Weyler went even further, prohibiting the export of raw tobacco to the United States. Cuban emigrants in places like Tampa had formed impor-tant communities grounded economically in the elaboration of cigars made from Cuban leaf. These people, like their brethren in Cuba, tended to political radicalism and had their lectores and their collection plates. As we have already seen, they provided an important source of income to Martí before 1895 and to the insurgency afterward. Weyler prohibited raw tobacco exports in order to hurt Cuban American communities at places like Key West and Tampa. He hoped that by isolating the insurrection from its American sources of income and sup-plies, he could defeat the insurgents, and he reasoned that if Cuban American workers were unemployed they would not be able to contribute a portion of their income to the revolution, as they had been doing for years.[20]

The problem with Weyler's prohibition on tobacco production was that it damaged the Cuban economy more than it affected émigrés in the United States, where the business cycle had entered a robust phase after many difficult years. As for workers in Cuba, they would probably have been less trouble to Spain lis-tening to political harangues and rolling tobacco leaf than they were unem-ployed with time on their hands for arson and other subversive activities.

And what of the planters and employers in the tobacco industry? Tobacco was big business in the aggregate, but individual operations were usually small to medium in size. Planters did not usually have diversified incomes and savings to allow them to ride out tough years, and Weyler's action ruined them. Weyler's re-sponse was a shrug of the shoulders: The planters should blame the insurrection for their troubles, not the difficult but necessary steps he was forced to take in order to combat the insurgents. In hindsight, we can see that Weyler's destruc-tion of the already ailing Cuban tobacco economy made no strategic sense. It played into the hands of the revolutionaries. Planters and workers, many of them emigrants from the Canary Islands or other parts of Spain who were presumably more inclined to be loyal to the Mother Country, learned that Spanish arms could not protect them and just might assist in their destruction. At that point, they became potential recruits for the Liberation Army or, more likely, refugees in overcrowded cities. Either way, it was a situation Gómez and Maceo were glad to see, and it could have been entirely avoided, had Weyler proceeded in a different manner. That, however, was asking the impossible. His time as captain general of Catalonia, where his job was to put a stop to anarchist terrorism, had imparted to Weyler a deep loathing for the working classes, especially those influenced by anarchism. He could only envision harsh measures where anarchist workers were concerned, and consequences be damned.

Weyler faced a similar problem when it came to the sugar industry. In the winter campaign of 1895–96, the insurgents had completely destroyed about one-quarter of the sugar plantations' storage and refining facilities, but the rest had, at most, lost only their standing cane, which was easily replaced. Sugar cane is a perennial, regenerating each year from deep roots. Burning the crop, therefore, affects only one season's production. As long as the mills themselves remained standing, the reconstitution of the sugar economy would not have required much capital outlay. In the summer of 1896, the insurgents, lacking funds, promised to allow some planters loyal to the revolution to return to production in exchange for the payment of a revolutionary tax. This was a dangerous moment for Weyler. If he followed through on his promise to withdraw garrisons from the countryside, it would leave the planters with no alternative but to declare their allegiance to the revolution and pay the revolutionary tax in exchange for a license to harvest and mill their cane. The only solution was to prohibit sugar production outright. If there was no sugar to harvest, planters would not have the option of milling it and paying the insurgents their tax. They would not have to worry about it being burned by the insurgents because the Spanish would do the job for them. With these considerations in mind, Weyler shut down the sugar industry by fiat in September 1896.

Planters complained bitterly. Some even branded Weyler an enemy of property. The insurgents gloated that the Spanish had adopted the same scorched-earth policy introduced by Gómez and by doing so had helped Gómez achieve one of his dearest goals, the destruction of the sugar economy. They were right to gloat. Weyler's actions made it hard for him to pose as the defender of property and gave ammunition to those lobbying for American intervention. Even some planters, who might have been expected as a group to side with Spain, began to call for U.S. involvement.

Thus, Weyler's strategy of total war faced opposition from many quarters and was in many ways unsuccessful. He did achieve progress, however, in reorganizing his armies to give them more offensive potential. All that was required was the resolve to use these forces aggressively. Even before he arrived in the island, Weyler had replaced some of Martínez Campos's men with officers willing to "fight dirty." Under Weyler, the Spanish began to treat the Cubans as if the rules of war did not apply to them. Captives were bandits and murderers, not soldiers. Weyler had them shot. Their families were arrested, their homes and crops burned, their livestock seized or destroyed. When even Spaniards accused him of excessive cruelty, Weyler summed up his views on the matter by remarking that "one does not make war with bonbons." People who look at photographs of Weyler often notice his eyes. They seem dead, as if what lay behind them were not quite human. This might be written off as a trick of photography or an illusion born of knowing about his subsequent ruthless behavior in Cuba. Yet contemporaries remarked about it, too. Weyler's eyes frightened even his friends, who knew him as a hard man, with a reputation for cruelty. Even as he regrouped his forces, Weyler placed officers in command who were as hard as he was and willing to spare nothing in order to pacify Cuba.

Under Weyler's direction, Spanish troops began to fight in a more coordinated fashion. Morale among the troops improved overnight with the arrival of Weyler and the departure of Martínez Campos. Gómez's aide Bernabé Boza remarked in his diary on "the activity and aggression" of the Spanish from the very first day Weyler took command in Cuba.[21] On February 19, during Maceo's brief reunion with Gómez, the Spanish attacked, killing and wounding 100 and forcing the two generals to disperse their forces. On February 23, with the war exactly one year old, Maceo and Gómez split up, never to see each other again.

In March Gómez was harried out of Havana and Matanzas all the way east to Puerto Príncipe. During the retreat, his men "dying of hunger and exhaustion," Gómez suffered a serious defeat on March 9, with fighting so close to the generalissimo that he lost sixteen of his forty-man personal escort. Civilians in the areas they passed through had rallied to the Spanish cause. The tone in Boza's diary during these dark days became noticeably shrill as things fell apart. He heaped invectives on Spain and Weyler but saved his most poisonous venom for the "nauseating and cowardly" reptiles who collaborated with the Spanish. The "patriotic unity" achieved in the winter campaign of 1895–96 had been conditional, at least in part, upon the presence of victorious insurgent forces and the absence of Spanish troops.[22]

In April Gómez was back in Santa Clara. There he tried to hold firm, but his men were in no condition to put up a fight. Gómez's correspondence in the spring of 1896 gives a depressing picture of the condition of his forces. "In view

Valeriano Weyler, known by his enemies as the "butcher," organized a brutal counterinsurgency that left the Liberation Army reeling by the summer of 1897. Photograph used with permission of the Archivo Nacional de Cuba, Havana.

of the actual situation of the revolution in the western districts," he announced to Minister of War Carlos Roloff, and "attentive to the present state of the Invasion Army," which had been cut off from resupply and was "unable to undertake new actions, as it should," Gómez sent an emissary east to beg the government for resources. "Every moment is precious, and needless to say, it is necessary to take advantage of them. Without charges or complaints, I lament that the government has not sent reinforcements to the Invasion Army, abandoned to its fate and its own resources." [23]

Gómez ordered General José María ("Mayía") Rodríguez to bring the cavalry in Puerto Príncipe west to help him carry out a "second invasion," but the government gave Rodríguez a different assignment.[24] In May Gómez gave up trying to hold Santa Clara. He recrossed the Júcaro-Morón trocha, returning to the relative security of Oriente, where he could rest from the constant pursuit by the Spanish. Even there, however, the morale of the troops had suffered greatly. As many as 500 men had deserted the Liberation Army, and Gómez assigned the urgent task of dealing with this crisis to his close aide, General Serafín Sánchez.[25] Meanwhile, the military organization Gómez had given to Havana and Matanzas during his brief time there remained in place on paper, but the units he'd left behind had to disperse to avoid extermination, and their discipline and cohesion broke down.

As Gómez moved east, Maceo returned to Pinar del Río, only to find the forces he had left behind under Quintín Bandera in defeat and disarray. As the Spanish drove Bandera deeper into the mountains, they also began to rebuild the coastal towns Maceo had burned down in January and February. Bahía Honda, Bramales, Cabañas, and Cayajabos were partially reconstructed and fortified. Troops and Cuban laborers in Pinar del Río built earthworks and forts, manned by Cuban militia from the city and its hinterland.[26] The energy Weyler instilled in Spanish forces was already having an effect even before he had implemented much of his plan.[27] Most of the world knew nothing of this. The American press acted as a mouthpiece for the well-organized and skillful Cuban campaign of propaganda and reported every minor Cuban success as a great battle won. For example, on June 6, 1896, the *New York Times* reported that Maceo had attacked the western trocha with 20,000 men, plus four companies of "Amazons," women who "fought fiercely, using machetes on the Spaniards." None of this happened, of course, except in the overheated minds of the New York newsmen.[28]

One of the problems that faced Weyler was his inability to move men and matériel quickly by rail. In part the problem was structural. Cuban railroads had been designed to extract raw materials, not to facilitate long-distance travel.

Trunk lines linked mines and sugar mills to port facilities, but getting from city to city was rather more difficult. The grid was reasonably complete in the provinces of Havana and Matanzas, sketchy in Santa Clara and Pinar del Río, and primitive in Puerto Príncipe and Santiago. There was no line running west from Puerto Príncipe to Santa Clara, nor any link eastward to Santiago. Indeed, the whole of Santiago, Cuba's largest province, had only two short lines running from Guantánamo to the coast and from Santiago to nearby San Luis. The only tracks in Puerto Príncipe, aside from the military line that cut across the island from Júcaro to Morón, ran a short distance from the capital to the northern coast at Nuevitas.[29]

To further complicate things, the network, such as it was, suffered from decentralized management. Companies in one province could not ensure that coal would be available at stations in the next. That was someone else's responsibility. As a result, even trains carrying military personnel and supplies had to wait in stations for hours while the delivery of coal was negotiated with local suppliers. Sometimes, passengers and cargo had to be deboarded and moved overland to other lines that had never been joined to the grid. The phrase "you can't get there from here," humorous when spoken with a lazy New England drawl, was all too accurate a description of train travel in colonial Cuba.

Only in Havana, Matanzas, and western Santa Clara was railroad travel reasonably efficient. However, in the early spring of 1896 the insurgents blew up so much track in the West that trains crawled, by military regulations, at twelve miles per hour, so that they could stop in time to avoid obstacles such as demolished bridges and missing sections of rail. Sometimes the locomotives went even slower to allow men on horseback to scout ahead for trouble, an absurdity that brings to mind the first days of railroading in Great Britain. At other times, an "exploratory locomotive" was sent ahead with work crews to repair the tracks and troops to guard the work crews. The trains behind traveled in groups, within sight of each other, like convoys of merchant ships at sea, with the Cuban insurgents in the role of submarine wolf packs. Weyler ordered officials to keep strict accounts of train schedules, so that he could monitor the problem and speed things up, but, in fact, stopgap measures were not the answer. The only real solution was to defeat the insurgents and build more tracks, in that order.[30]

Once Weyler had reorganized his forces, he began to proceed with the second part of his strategy. Beginning in the far West, he planned to "cleanse" each Cuban province in turn, forcing the insurgents eastward, and bottling them up in Oriente. The first step was the isolation and pursuit of Antonio Maceo. To aid him in this task, he ordered work on a new military trocha running some twenty-five miles from Mariel to Majana along a north-south axis just west of Havana. This western barrier, more modern than the old Júcaro-Morón trocha, took many months to build, but even during its construction it provided a for-midable Spanish presence in Pinar del Río that hampered Maceo. Weyler placed his friend General Arolas in command of the western line with more than eleven battalions of infantry, six squadrons of cavalry, and Cuban Volunteers and guer-rillas — 15,000 men in all. The idea was to cordon off Pinar del Río with these stationary forces and at the same time throw massive reinforcements into the pursuit of Maceo. Weyler gave this last job to General Arsenio Linares, another veteran of the campaign in the Philippines. Linares organized three pursuit columns that began to inflict serious damage on Maceo. Maceo had some 4,000 men in Pinar del Río, half of them under direct command of General Quintín Bandera.[31] On March 15 a column commanded by Brigadier General Julián Suárez Inclán defeated Bandera, driving him deep into the mountains and clear-ing the northern coast. Maceo was so disgusted that he relieved Bandera, but he himself could do little against so many Spanish troops.

Towns Maceo had earlier occupied against no opposition were going over to the Spanish. Whether this happened out of conviction or fear of Spanish troops made no difference. The point was that Maceo had begun to lose his grip on Pinar del Río. His only response, since he could not really do battle with the main Spanish forces, was to punish towns that had betrayed the republican cause. On March 19, 1896, Maceo ordered Brigadier General Esteban Tamayo to "avoid be-ing attacked by the enemy" in order to escape the "disastrous consequences" of doing battle with the Spanish. Instead, Tamayo was to sack the town of Hoyo Colorado, which had earlier embraced Maceo only to return to the arms of Spain later. "I expect you to destroy [Hoyo Colorado] completely by means of fire," wrote Maceo. "Once the operation is concluded, and it must be done rapidly, re-main on the defensive and rejoin me." On March 26 Cuban cavalry did indeed in-vade Hoyo Colorado at midnight, "sacking and burning 150 houses," according to the diary kept by one of the squadron commanders. The Cubans then fled be-fore the Spanish could respond. In like fashion, Maceo's men also burned sev-eral other towns in Pinar del Río and Havana. Between the initial wave of de-struction in January and the second wave in March and April, only five significant towns in Pinar del Río, including the capital, escaped the torch, not because Maceo chose to spare them, but because Spanish troops and Cuban Volunteers succeeded in defending those few places. Maceo's campaign of destruction caused thousands of civilians to flee into the handful of intact cities, inaugurat-ing the informal phase of reconcentration in Pinar del Río that had already be-gun earlier in the rest of the island.[32]

Maceo stationed his main force in the Sierra de Rubí, in the center of Pinar del Río. There, in a mountain pass near a place called Cacarajícara, occurred one of the hardest-fought battles of the war. On the morning of April 30 Suárez Inclán and a column of 1,500 infantry left the city of Bahía Honda in search of Maceo, guided by a civilian who claimed to know the Bronze Titan's whereabouts. Just after noon, the column began to receive "a hail of lead from the jungle all around," but it continued forward nonetheless in an ordered march up the mountain road. They had found their man. Maceo had his troops "half buried in the vegetation" or hidden behind rock outcrops, so that the Spanish fire did no damage, while the bunched and exposed Spanish formation continued to suffer casualties as it advanced. In the evening, the column approached the summit at Cacarajícara and released volleys at what they thought was the main Cuban position. One Spanish veteran recalled seeing the insurgents fall "in bunches, like grain harvested by a scythe." In fact, the Cubans were carrying out a planned tactical withdrawal from the summit. As night fell, Suárez Inclán took the position, only to discover that he was on the leading edge of an area that had been prepared with an elaborate network of trenches, pits, and strong points all held by Maceo's men. The real battle still lay ahead.[33]

Maceo was unusually well prepared for combat because on April 20 a filibustering expedition landed in Pinar del Río. The *Competitor*, though later captured along with its crew, unloaded thousands of rounds of ammunition, supplies, and forty-five recruits, all gathered up by Maceo and brought to bear at Cacarajícara. One Florida man aboard the *Competitor* had come to fight the good fight hoping for a better life in Cuba. He was placed into the line at the beginning of the battle of Cacarajícara, but he died in battle a few days later. His diary, however, provides us with additional details of the combat.[34]

On the morning of May 1 Suárez Inclán ordered a bayonet assault on the Cuban trenches. His men took heavy casualties. The Cubans targeted officers, and soon sergeants were all that remained to lead the attack. Finally, the Spanish succeeded in driving off the Cubans. However, now that the Spanish had the trenches, they didn't know what to do. The position itself was useless without constant resupplying, and the Cubans had withdrawn to safety, having no intention of trying an assault against entrenched Spanish infantry. At two A.M. on May 2 Suárez Inclán broke camp and marched his column back to Bahía Honda, taking sniper fire the whole way. Suárez Inclán lost fifteen dead and seventy-two wounded in the exercise. He reported killing or wounding 400 Cubans, but, like all Spanish estimates of enemy losses, this number is far too high. The gain, if it can be called that, was that the Spanish foot soldiers, by acting as targets for Cuban fire, had caused Maceo to use up the ammunition landed by the *Competitor*. Fortunately, the approach of summer promised a respite from fighting.[35]

Maceo's position after Cacarajícara became precarious. He still won the occasional victory against town militias, but even these sorts of activities were becoming more costly, as morale among Spain's allies improved. On May 3, for example, Maceo's men tried to take Esperanza by force but only succeeded in setting part of the town on fire. Cuban Volunteers fighting with the Spanish inflicted twelve casualties on Maceo's men, who had to disperse when larger Spanish forces arrived.

The problem, in part, was that Maceo had little ammunition. The period of easy plunder, when Cuban troops armed with machetes and just a few rounds of ammunition could take over undefended towns — and their stockpiles of weapons and ammunition — had come to an end. Maceo could expect no more windfalls from that direction. At the same time, most of the expeditions from abroad made landfall in eastern and central Cuba, where the coastline was less well defended. What Maceo needed was a way to get these supplies from the East, but his link to Havana and the rest of Cuba had been severed. Although the Mariel-Majana line would not be completed until October, it already served as a formidable barrier even during its construction. A correspondent for the Times of London received special dispensation to visit and examine the line in June 1896. The southern section seemed impregnable, the center nearly so. The only weak segment was near its northern end, where it ran through rough and broken terrain and was not a continuous barrier.[36] Because of the new trocha, reinforcements and supplies Maceo repeatedly requested from the East were not arriving. Even communications were precarious. Maceo was already nearly cut off.

Gómez wrote to Maceo all summer, begging the Bronze Titan to return eastward, but these communications did not get through, as evidenced by their presence in Spanish military archives. On July 28 Gómez wrote to give Maceo painful news: his brother José had fallen in combat at Loma del Gato on July 5. At the same time, Gómez could not resist reminding Antonio Maceo of the "repeated orders I have given you to move from that side of the Mariel line" to Havana and Matanzas. Neither this message nor any of the "repeated orders" to which Gómez alluded reached Maceo. Nor did several similar messages that followed because the Spanish, daily gaining more firm control of the West, captured them all. Indeed, Maceo did not learn of his brother's death until September.[37]

Maceo's isolation in Pinar del Río was also the result of the decline of the insurgency in neighboring Havana and Matanzas. As we have already seen, Gómez had evacuated the two provinces in March, retreating to Santa Clara, then to Puerto Príncipe. He gave three reasons for his withdrawal: the Spanish were too strong; the provisional government had not sent the required reinforcements and supplies to him; and the insurgency had begun to suffer reverses even in

Puerto Príncipe and Santiago, requiring his presence there.[38] All three explanations hit the mark. The "land of cane" had turned out to be uncongenial after all. It was the heart of Cuba Española, with too many large cities and towns, too many people who supported Spain, and, above all, too many Spanish troops. The revolutionary government had done nothing to reinforce Gómez in the West, partly because it lacked resources, but also because it had its own problems in the East.

The diary of Eduardo Rosell y Malpica suggests that the forces that had remained behind in Oriente when Gómez and Maceo marched west had done little on their own other than avoid the Spanish.[39] In Puerto Príncipe enthusiasm had waned. One Cuban officer, Fermín Valdés Domínguez, claimed that the pettiness and lack of patriotism exhibited by the people of Puerto Príncipe in this period had left him feeling that the whole province should be placed "between parenthesis" in maps of Cuba.[40] The situation throughout Oriente required Gómez's presence and, he insisted, the presence of Maceo, if he could manage to get out of Pinar del Río.

The arrival of Calixto García along with much-needed supplies improved matters significantly in the East by the fall of 1896. Given command of the first three army corps stationed in Santiago and Puerto Príncipe, García provided new energy to the troops. His three "corps" really numbered only a few thousand men at most, and they were dispersed all over Oriente. Most of the time he could count on the direct command of only about 600 men. Still, García achieved prodigies with this small army, taking them on the offensive against Spanish garrisons and convoys.

In December 1896, following the offensive against Cascorro, García drove a Spanish convoy from the Cauto River back to Veguitas, its point of origin. The convoy then set out again, reinforced to a total of about 4,000 Spanish soldiers. García could not face such a force head on, but he harassed it from the flanks so severely that it had to abandon its mission and take refuge in the little hamlet of Bueicito, two leagues short of its destination, the town of Bayamo. All the while, he had detachments of special skirmishers armed with Mausers captured from the Spanish "that fired day and night" upon the garrisons at Jiguaní, Santa Rita, Guisa, Cauto Embarcadero, and Bayamo, "firing upon everything that lived," until the garrisons believed themselves "besieged by great forces" and did not dare leave their forts "even to bury the men we kill." To trick the Spaniards at Jiguaní into believing his forces were larger than they were, García had unarmed civilians, pretending to be soldiers, parade by at a safe distance but still within sight of the garrison. García had fourteen men killed and eighty-six wounded in December, but Spanish losses were at least as great, and the

Spanish towns were starving. Even the livestock died, because it could not be taken out to pasture.[41]

However, while García and Gómez were active in the East and Maceo in the far West, the insurgency in Havana, Matanzas, and Santa Clara ground to a halt. The Spanish had pacified the area around Cienfuegos, and it was now patrolled by pro-Spanish Cuban counterguerrillas.[42] The heart of the insurrection in Santa Clara was Siguanea, a place in the mountains between Cienfuegos and Sancti Spíritus. Colonel Enrique Segura led a Spanish column into the area. His mission: "the destruction of whatever he found." Segura's diary described attacks on enemy encampments and the burning of crops and food caches. The republic-in-arms had possessed a political organization in Siguanea that coordinated the production of food and clothing for the insurgency. Segura destroyed all of that and drove out the civilians who called the area home. Luis de Pando wrote to General Weyler recommending promotion for Segura and summarizing his achievement: The region had been "the secure and sacred refuge of the enemy hordes," their "place of rest on the long marches" to the West. Because of "inaccessible peaks and abysses carved by rushing rivers," Siguanea had always been an "impenetrable mystery" to Spanish forces. Segura, according to Pando, had solved the mystery, and the area would no longer serve as a conduit for insurgent forces and supplies moving from east to west.[43]

Meanwhile, the insurgency in Havana had not completely collapsed, but its nature had changed. Cuban forces had been dispersed and lacked ammunition, two things that made it impossible for them to attack any but the smallest Spanish units. Nevertheless, they continued to use the machete, the torch, and dynamite to good effect: the machete for collaborators and livestock, the torch for crops and houses, and dynamite for everything more substantial.

The commander of a company in the Calixto García regiment kept a daily record of his unit's actions from late April to late July 1896, when he and his diary were captured.[44] A typical segment of the diary in May read:

> May 14. Destroyed section of railroad track between [G]uana and Durán. Stayed night at ranch "San Francisco."
>
> May 15. At sugar mill "Merecedita" encounter with its guerrillas and those from sugar mill "San José" causing four to six enemy casualties. Stayed the night at "El Caiman."
>
> May 16. Nothing new. Stayed night at "Pimienta."
>
> May 17. Left "Pimienta" at five A.M. Destroyed railroad track between Pozo Redondo and Batabanó. Camp at nine A.M. at "Dolores" ranch near Seiba del Agua after destroying railroad track between Guira de Melena and Alquizar

and burning a house near the line. Two P.M. left for Guanajay, destroying the ranch and bridge between Gabriel and Rincón. Stayed night in Guira de Melena.

May 18. Burned hamlet "Capellanía" composed of sixty houses, some of them of solid construction. Left there at five P.M. and camped at Puerta de Guira.

The "brigade," which was about the size of an undermanned company in a regular army, studiously avoided Spanish regulars but had several battles with private forces hired by the sugar plantations. In early June, they attacked Ceiba del Agua but found it defended by an estimated 150 militia, so they set fire to fifteen or twenty houses on the outskirts of town before retreating. On June 12, they had better luck against the undefended town of Batabanó, burning down 150 houses.

Raul Martí's experience in Havana was similar. Martí commanded a squadron of forty-five men near Havana on February 16, but during the next week he lost twenty-one of them in two unexpected combats with the Spanish. Ordered on February 29 to occupy several towns near Havana, Martí found that he could not because of "heavy enemy concentrations" and the thinness of his own ranks. He was also "very short on ammunition," and most of the men who had survived the encounters with the Spanish had "dispersed," a euphemism that could mean anything from death or desertion to accidental and temporary separation. With a few loyal followers, Martí continued operations of a different sort: he set three bridges on fire and burned down a few houses and cane fields. Even this became too taxing, until finally "the tired horses and the dispersion of his men" forced him to go into hiding. He contracted yellow fever and spent several days in bed, hidden by peasants, "without knowing anything" about the whereabouts of his remaining men. "I am in bad shape," he wrote in his diary, "I can't move. I am paralyzed and without resources or aid." A Spanish patrol nearly captured him, but the peasants who had hidden him were able to boost him onto a horse and lead him into the safety of the woods.

Martí recovered, but his men did not. So many had been lost to death and desertion that Martí no longer commanded a serious fighting force. Martí's brigade belonged to the Calixto García regiment under José María Aguirre, but their numbers had eroded so dramatically that even Aguirre began to place the terms "brigade" and "regiment" in quotation marks. Nevertheless, Aguirre pursued an aggressive campaign of blowing up bridges, railroads, telegraph lines, and buildings. On the morning of April 26 insurgents exploded a bomb in the basement of the captain general's palace very near to Weyler's bedroom, but their target was already at work in his office and escaped unhurt. The Cuban reliance on dynamite in this and other attacks — especially those against passenger trains — created some bad publicity. The tactic seemed like terrorism, the sort of thing anarchists did in pursuit of their goals. Indeed, the attempted assassination of Weyler was carried out by a Cuban nationalist and two anarchists working in collaboration. The idea that they might be compared to terrorists concerned the Cuban leadership, but the world quickly forgave them. The international community seemed to accept the notion that in a people's war of liberation, unorthodox means were acceptable, even including dynamiting unsuspecting passengers on trains or attempting to assassinate Spanish leaders while they slept. After all, were not the Spanish committing greater crimes? In Spain, of course, there was no forgiveness. The insurgents became known as "anarchist dynamiters" in the press, and their use of terror seemed only to steel the resolve of Weyler and the hard-liners.

In any case, the hard-pressed insurgents of Havana had little choice in the matter. Aguirre had little ammunition in the spring of 1896, and most of his men had deserted, so he continued to contribute to Cuba's liberation with a highly effective campaign of arson and destruction. Maceo congratulated Aguirre on his creative use of dynamite and fire and encouraged him with further instructions "to destroy every building that could serve as a defensive refuge for the enemy, and every deposit of tobacco and corn you encounter in that territory."

A turning point seemed in the offing when, on July 7, 1896, at Boca Ciega beach near Havana, the yacht *Three Friends* landed some 350,000 rounds and sixty-five armed men. However, Aguirre still had trouble using the cache because he could not reunite his forces. Aguirre authorized individual officers, like Captain Jesús Planas, to recruit on their own and operate independently. Planas received what amounted to a "letter of marque" from Aguirre, giving him the right "to recruit and incorporate in his ranks any dispersed soldiers or groups" not otherwise under orders in the jurisdiction of San Antonio de los Baños. These difficulties in the province of Havana meant that Aguirre could provide no relief to Maceo nor attack the Spanish, failings that soon led to his replacement by Bruno Zayas.[45]

The dispersion of insurgent forces in Havana contributed greatly to Maceo's isolation in Pinar del Río. Arms and ammunition landed in Havana and Matanzas were supposed to be channeled through Aguirre to Maceo, but moving anything westward through Havana had become problematic. Supplies developed a tendency to melt away en route, and strong Spanish forces made any large Cuban convoy impossible. At the same time, getting across the Mariel-Majana trocha in force had also become impossible.

Raul Martí, recovered from his illness and tired of a life of flight and hiding in Havana, tried in April 1896 to cross the western trocha to join Maceo and discovered how difficult that was. Joined by several dozen men, the remnants of his "brigade," Martí made his first attempt on April 16. He was repulsed and during the retreat used up all his ammunition. On the following day he tried and failed again. "Always we encounter bullets and soldiers," wrote Martí in his diary. "I am retreating to try to cross near the south coast where they tell me it is easier." But it was not easier. At its southern end, the line went through swamps, which could be deadly to Cubans, as well as to Spaniards. Martí became bogged down, and he, along with most of his men, fell ill with malaria. Martí tried six times in April and May to get across the Mariel-Majana trocha and found himself repulsed each time with serious losses. Finally, on May 25, a Spanish force attacked him, killing four of his men and wounding thirty-one, including Martí, who was shot in the knee. Martí made no more diary entries.[46]

As bad as things were in Havana, farther east, in Matanzas, the insurgents had an even worse time. The diary of the brigade operating in Matanzas showed a few hundred men burning cane, taking potshots at passenger trains, and destroying structures in abandoned sugar mills. The high point of the summer came when they used five sticks of dynamite to blow a train off its tracks near a plantation called Crimea.[47] General José Lacret, the provincial chief, reported that his officers were deserting with their men and weapons. In June Lieutenant Colonel Pedro Miquelina used a pass issued by Lacret to go back to Santiago with fifty-three followers. The timing was unfortunate because Spain was at that moment on the offensive in the part of Matanzas where Miquelina was supposed to be stationed. The rest of his men had been left without supplies or leadership, and twenty of them decided to go over to the Spanish side, taking their horses and arms with them.

As order broke down in Matanzas, officers began to rob from the republic-in-arms, even seizing and hiding stores landed with great exertion by expeditionaries from the United States. For example, the vessel *Commodore* landed a rapid-fire cannon, 200 rifles, and 500,000 Remington cartridges in March, but most of these supplies mysteriously disappeared after they had been collected by bands of insurgents under Lacret's nominal authority. In letters to Gómez and Maceo, Lacret admitted his own culpability, for he had naively relied on the spur of patriotism without realizing that he would have to police his own officers to prevent theft. Other of Lacret's officers simply refused to do anything. Lacret tried to shame subordinates into action. In a letter of July 29, 1896, he scolded Lieutenant Colonel Aurelio Sanabria: "I am extremely surprised by your inertia. The ammunition I sent you is not for you to hold in reserve but to use against the enemy."

The problem was not just poor morale and unreliable officers. Lacret's men were dying. Brigadier Eduardo García reported that most of his men and all of the officers were sick with malaria and many had perished: "The few personnel remaining are tasked with caring for the sick. Also, you must know that we don't have a single pill of quinine to contain the terrible sickness that has become chronic among us." By August Lacret himself had no ammunition, and five of the eight cavalry squadrons in his "division" had disappeared. The remaining three were undersized. On September 10, in a letter to the provisional government's secretary of finance, Lacret wrote: "My dear friend: I write to you in a desperate situation. I have wounded and sick men and no medicine for them. I have 250 Mauser rifles, but no ammunition." Nor did he have any money to buy ammunition, because civilian officials in the province who were supposed to provide him with support had themselves gone into hiding or been arrested. "I need you to lend me 10,000 pesos." On September 21 Lacret let Maceo know that he would be in no position to join him for a winter campaign. Matanzas was lost. The insurrectionary forces had all melted away. Those who remained were "barefoot, almost naked, and sick with malaria which has reached epidemic proportions; the field hospitals are abandoned by the staff and lack medicine," because in Matanzas Cuban officials had not been able to collect taxes. A field hospital set up in January 1896 had 127 sick or wounded patients that summer but no doctor or staff because they had all abandoned their posts. A few months later, Lacret wrote to Tomás Estrada Palma, head of the Cuban delegation in New York, admitting: "I cannot militarily occupy any place at all without attracting the attention of the enemy."[48]

This state of affairs in Havana and Matanzas, which were technically under Maceo's overall command, helps us understand two things: Gómez's insistence that Maceo recross the Mariel-Majana trocha to save the situation in Havana and Matanzas, and Maceo's ignorance of these orders and of the abysmal state of things east of the trocha. Messages that did get through in the fall of 1896 came too late. The Mariel-Majana trocha had become too strong, and Maceo was no longer able to cross.[49]

Although internal correspondence reveals to us the depressing state of the insurrection in Havana and Matanzas, Aguirre and Lacret publicly presented only the rosiest news. The Cleveland administration required field reports to help clarify its Cuban policy, and Lacret and Aguirre ordered their subordinates to supply lists of men and reports of battles. When there were no men or battles to report, they required that officers supply them anyway. The Americans must not be disappointed. So they were led to believe that the insurrection remained strong in western Cuba.

In fact, Lacret had become convinced, as Weyler poured resources into the western provinces, that a Cuban victory without U.S. intervention of some sort was no longer possible. In a letter written to an American sympathizer on August 3, Lacret described the poor state of Matanzas and concluded: "Now an even greater responsibility falls to the mentor nation, the powerful and grand American nation, which perhaps with a mere raising of her eyebrow could drive from this devastated country the infernal Spanish race." Should that fail to happen, should the war go on, then "the last victorious Spanish general will rule over a heap of ruins and every Cuban will be dead."[50] Apocalyptic thinking had replaced the confidence of 1895.[51] This was a dangerous moment for the revolution. The invasion of 1895–96 had used up most of the available resources, as well as much of the initial enthusiasm. The realization was dawning that this war, like the one from 1868 to 1878, would be a war of attrition, and the worst was still to come.

13 ★ The Death of Maceo

The summer of 1896 was a trying time for Antonio Maceo. He had little ammunition left after Cacarajícara and became perforce more passive. Help arrived in the form of an expedition led by Colonel Leyte Vidal, who landed in June at Cape Corrientes, at the far southwestern tip of Cuba, with some 300,000 cartridges. However, these supplies went quickly in a series of combats in July, as Weyler gave Maceo no rest. In one of these battles, Maceo suffered a serious leg wound that incapacitated him for weeks. With ammunition low, with the rainy season at its height, and with his own health in jeopardy, Maceo ordered his forces to disperse for their own protection.

It was now that Maceo first learned of his brother's disgrace. In late 1895 and early 1896, José Maceo had commanded the province of Santiago. In late March Calixto García arrived on the scene, and the provisional government decided to place García in overall command of Cuban forces in the East, a position the Maceo brothers felt should have gone to José, who had been battling the Spanish for a year by the time García was able to land in Cuba. In effect, the younger Maceo had been "demoted" and given narrower responsibility over the district around the city of Santiago. Nevertheless, he continued to collect fees in his peculiar way, with very little of it reaching García or Gómez. Finally, Gómez had had enough. In April he ordered José Maceo to take 400 men west to fight under the command of his brother, an order later rescinded.[1] To make matters worse, Gómez accused José Maceo of hoarding ammunition and supplies. The expedition led by Rafael Portuondo Tamayo, who landed around Baracoa in the late spring, had been met by José Maceo. He used 100 mules and, he said, 3,000 soldiers and civilians to land and hide the supplies, which he seemed to feel were his to use. Gómez criticized this conduct sharply in letters that reached the elder Maceo that summer.[2]

José's loss of reputation and position put the Bronze Titan in a grim mood. To understand the full impact of his brother's disgrace, however, it is important to know something of an old dispute between García and the elder Maceo. Antonio Maceo had been one of the most successful and popular military figures of the Ten Years' War. Unlike many of the other insurgents, he had rejected the Peace of Zanjón in his "Protest of Baraguá," in which he refused to accept the half measures proffered by Martínez Campos. This principled stance made him a revered figure in his native Oriente, especially among blacks. Meanwhile, Calixto García had also fought bravely in the Ten Years' War, but he had been caught and incarcerated before it ended. He then botched a suicide attempt. He shot himself under the chin, the bullet exiting his forehead and leaving him with a distinctive scar that became, through an ironic twist of symbolism, a badge of what he had precisely not demonstrated: a determination to fight to the end. Following the peace, García emigrated to New York, where he became the chief of a network of Cuban exiles who gathered funds and plotted a new war of liberation.

In 1879, García included Maceo in these plans, leading Maceo to believe that he would be given command of a new uprising in Oriente. At the last minute, however, García removed Maceo from the project. There seems to have been an explicitly racial motive for the demotion. Maceo's staunchest supporters were blacks and mulattoes. The world over, Maceo had become identified not just as a leader of the Cuban revolution but as the leader of a "black" Cuban revolution. Sadly, this characterization, promoted by the Spanish, seemed to be accepted by at least some of the white Cuban rebels. García was white, but more to the point so were the rich patriots in New York and Jamaica who were funding the projected uprising. They asked García to replace Maceo with Gregorio Benitez, whose outstanding qualification seemed to be that he was also white. It was an example of the way race continued to divide Cubans. It was also a terrible error. The uprising in May 1879 inspired no one, and by August it was all over. The failed enterprise became known as "The Little War." [3]

Now, the same process seemed to be under way in 1896, as Maceo's younger brother, José, was forced to accept a subordinate role to García. In the long run, the decision turned out to be a good one: García was a skillful commander. Nevertheless, when Antonio Maceo heard of his brother's demotion, he interpreted it as a slap in the face. He was not happy at all with the direction being taken by the revolution and felt that, as in the past, race was fatally dividing the republic-in-arms.

While all of this was going on, Weyler's engineers completed the military line from Mariel to Majana. It was not impermeable. The line passed through swamps and broken terrain at various points, and individuals and small groups of men could sometimes get across. Crossings by large forces, however, were now out of the question. Maceo's army had been trapped, though he did not yet realize it.

Two attempts to relieve Maceo in 1896 by mounting new "invasions" of the West had come to nothing. In May Gómez had given General "Mayía" Rodríguez command of a new expeditionary column, but the provisional government diverted this force for its own purposes. [4] Then in the fall Gómez gave Mayía a new army "corps" of 300 men to try a second time. But the Spanish were equipped by the fall of 1896 to stop any renewed movement into western Cuba by the Orientales. Mayía was surprised at a ruined sugar mill called Colorado, located west of Santa Clara in an area fully controlled by Spanish forces. Mayía, among others, was wounded, and Gómez had again to call off the "second invasion."[5] Maceo would have to find a way out of Pinar del Río unaided.

As the fall campaigning season approached, Maceo still had no ammunition, and most of his men were dispersed. A constant flow of supplies reached the Cubans in the East. For example, in one week in August 1896 the *Dauntless* landed two cannon, 500 artillery shells, 2,600 rifles, and 858,000 rounds of ammunition.[6] As usual, however, none of the matériel made its way to Maceo, who needed it most. Then, on September 18, a major expedition led by General Juan Ríus Rivera landed at Cape Corrientes with long-promised supplies. With Ríus Rivera came Máximo Gómez's son, Pancho, who would become Maceo's close companion in the days ahead. The meeting was not the joyous occasion it might have been, however, because Ríus Rivera carried sad news. José Maceo had perished in combat on July 5 at Loma del Gato. It had taken almost three months for the Bronze Titan to get word of his brother's death, a measure of how isolated Maceo had become in Pinar del Río.

At least Maceo had ammunition again, including hundreds of thousands of cartridges and a pneumatic cannon, which he was eager to put to the test. The supplies arrived just in time, because Weyler was about to begin his fall offensive in Pinar. Maceo gathered some of his forces and marched eastward, intending to revive the insurrection and move against the now completed western trocha. On October 4, at a place called Ceja del Negro, in the mountains near Viñales, he met a Spanish force of 800 men under General Francisco Bernal, supplemented by 200 Cuban Volunteers from Viñales intent on stopping Maceo.

The battle of Ceja del Negro turned into one the bloodiest of the war. The fighting went as it usually did. The Cubans dug in and fought from defensive positions, aiming rifle fire at the bunched Spanish troops who advanced in column against them. Bernal's men eventually took the Cuban trenches, but only after the Cubans had withdrawn. There was no hand-to-hand combat. Cavalry did not come into play, and the Spanish suffered no wounds that day from sabers, machetes, or bayonets, though the explosive cartridges used by Cuban riflemen did cause considerable damage.

Also, as usual, the Spanish advanced against the Cubans to no purpose. Bernal took trenches he could not maintain, so he withdrew immediately, allowing Maceo to continue moving eastward. Once again, the logic of guerrilla warfare had defeated the Spanish, who suffered and died for bits of useless territory that they immediately abandoned. Bernal's only achievement, if it can be called that, was to have forced Maceo to expend 50,000 rounds of precious ammunition.

Ceja del Negro was costly to both sides. The Cubans lost 42 men killed and 185 wounded, by their own reckoning. As usual, they exaggerated Spanish losses. They claimed to have killed or wounded hundreds of Spanish, as many as 500 in the fanciful account by José Miró.[7] The real picture of Spanish losses was rather less dramatic. According to the senior physician who registered and treated the casualties, the Spanish lost thirty killed and eighty-three wounded, figures that are only slightly higher than estimates by Bernal and Weyler. Nevertheless, this was still a high price to pay, considering that nothing was gained. Moreover, sixty-three of the men wounded were listed as in grave condition, in part because the Cubans used explosive bullets, which must have been supplied by the Ríus Rivera expedition from the United States. Maceo also seems to have used the pneumatic cannon effectively at Ceja del Negro. Cubans regard the battle as a victory, in part because the Spanish were unable to stop Maceo from continuing on his way toward the Mariel-Majana line.[8]

Along the way, Maceo fought a series of small battles. His object now seemed obvious — to break out of Pinar del Río — and the Spanish were able to prepare for him. Weyler reinforced the men stationed along the western trocha, and he anchored the newly formed Division of the North in the town of Bahía Honda, on the north coast of the province. The division's seven battalions were given the job of controlling the northern littoral and seizing the mountain passes, which until then had been in Maceo's hands.

On October 21 a column under Colonel Julio Fuentes took the Cuban stronghold at Cacarajícara unopposed and spent the next few weeks digging in, building trenches, forts, a heliograph, storage facilities, and everything else the Spanish needed to hold the place. This operation gave Spain a base in the heart of what had been insurgent territory. Fanning out from Cacarajícara, the Spanish began systematically to destroy or collect crops and livestock in an attempt both to starve Maceo's men and to feed themselves and the many refugees who had fled to Cuba Española. The Spanish also discovered and seized a cache of weapons and 18,000 cartridges hastily left behind in a cave not far from Cacarajícara. All told, the Spanish captured almost 20,000 rifles from the Cubans in 1896.[9]

In late November Maceo began to spread rumors of U.S. intervention as a way of raising his troops' flagging morale. The results of the U.S. presidential election held great promise, he thought, because McKinley, who would become the sitting president in March 1897, had always been more friendly to the Cuban cause than Cleveland. Maceo told his officers that "intervention was officially a done deal" and that this would result in an end to the war "within at most three months." Maceo asked that the "good news" be spread as quickly as possible in order to encourage the long-suffering insurgent forces. They should rejoice, he said, at the proximate "definitive triumph" and fight with even greater enthusiasm "during the few days that still remain of hard combat." [10]

It should be emphasized that this position on American involvement was dramatically new for Maceo. Earlier in the year, Maceo had discounted the importance of U.S. aid and intervention, in part, no doubt, because under Cleveland there existed little chance that it would happen but also because in early 1896 it had been possible to imagine victory without external help. [11] Maceo's new attitude toward American intervention is, therefore, one more sign of how desperate the insurgents' position in Pinar del Río had become.

Meanwhile, the Spanish faced almost no opposition as they destroyed insurgent camps and field hospitals, burned isolated homes, gathered up livestock, took control of the mountain passes, and relocated civilians in Pinar del Río. The depopulation of the countryside had already been dramatic when the fall campaign began. For example, when Spanish troops entered Las Pozas in November, only three families remained. The town was a ruin, burned months earlier by Maceo. The last holdouts seemed to greet the arrival of Spanish troops as a positive event. They showed the Spanish where they had buried devotional objects and other valuables in the woods to save them from the insurgents, and they turned over an injured Spanish soldier whom they had been harboring. Then they marched off with the Spanish to what they thought was security but turned out to be a new and greater desolation: They became the latest *reconcentrados*, the last from Las Pozas.

The Spanish suffered terrible hardships during their fall offensive, but not from combat. Constant marching along muddy roads in tropical downpours and surrounded by mosquitoes inflicted severe punishment. Every convoy that brought supplies to outposts like Cacarajícara returned to Bahía Honda, Artemisa, or other bases with sick men. One whole battalion became so ill that it had to be relieved. Yellow fever raged in Bahía Honda. It affected troops and civilian refugees to such an extent that the Division of the North had to stop visiting what had been its headquarters. Maceo may have lost Pinar del Río in the fall of 1896, but it is not clear that the Spanish regained it. Instead, disease and death gripped the province at the expense of human organisms, regardless of their politics.

November brought bad news. Major General Serafín Sánchez, one of the most beloved of the Cuban generals, died in combat, hit by a Mauser round that entered his right shoulder and passed all the way through his torso to exit just above his left shoulder. "This is nothing. March on," he said, and then he died. [12]

At last Maceo became convinced that he would have to leave Pinar del Río behind and return to the East, as Gómez had been asking him to do for months. Maceo sent a few of his trusted officers, including Quintín Bandera, to Havana ahead of him in order to reactivate the insurrection there. It turned out to be an unfortunate move because it tipped off Weyler to Maceo's plan and caused the Spanish general to place troops in the area on high alert.[13]

Maceo then began to probe the Mariel-Majana line for weaknesses, but what he discovered was a barrier outfitted with electric searchlights, artillery, new fortifications, and troops stationed to create interlocking fields of fire. The new trocha seemed impenetrable. Yet cross he must, both to escape the cul-de-sac of Pinar del Río and to help Gómez in the East, where the insurrection had also fallen on hard times and where disputes between military and civilian authorities so threatened the unity of the revolution that Gómez had twice offered his resignation, an offer the provisional government wisely refused. Eventually, Maceo concluded that he would have to cross the trocha by stealth, with just a few trusted comrades.

In the end, however, Maceo did not cross the trocha at all. He found a way around it. After giving command of Pinar del Río to General Ríus Rivera, Maceo selected twenty-three men to accompany him by boat across the Bay of Mariel on the night of December 4–5. The small craft had to make four trips to transport everyone across. It stormed that night, so the Spanish gunboat that normally patrolled those waters had docked, and the crossing went without a hitch. Nevertheless, Maceo was now in an extremely vulnerable position. He had been unable to bring horses or reserves of ammunition. Spanish troops occupied the area in great numbers, and the poor state of the insurrection in Havana had made it impossible to gather much of a force to greet Maceo's arrival. Finally, some 250 Cuban troops with extra mounts did rally to Maceo, but it was not enough to overcome his pessimism, perhaps even depression, if José Miró's musings about Maceo's mood at this juncture can be trusted.

On the afternoon of December 7 the San Quintín battalion, consisting of four companies of Spanish infantry and a few dozen local guerrillas, got the drop on Maceo near the town of San Pedro. Maceo and the others mounted quickly amid the crack of rifle fire. Taken by surprise and low on ammunition, Maceo ordered a machete charge against the Spanish line, hoping by a bold counterstroke to create enough space in which to recover from the surprise or at least slip away. The result of this charge was not good for the Cubans. The men of San Quintín were veterans. They took up a position behind a fence and fired at their own discretion rather than in volleys. One of them picked out Maceo and brought him down. An aide, Alberto Nodarse, boosted the wounded Cuban commander onto a horse, but Maceo was immediately shot again, this time through the heart. Pancho Gómez came upon the scene and together with Nodarse tried to drag Maceo's body away, but now rifle fire hit Máximo Gómez's son, too, and he fell, dying, upon the lifeless body of Maceo. Nodarse, along with everyone else, had to flee as the Spanish took the field. Strangely, the Spanish troops who confiscated the belongings of the Cuban dead failed to recognize either the Bronze Titan or the son of Máximo Gómez. Their cadavers were left for the Cubans to recover later.[14]

It did not take long for news of Maceo's death to spread. In Havana, church bells rang in celebration and parishioners thanked God that the Bronze Titan's death might mean a quick end to the war. In Madrid, popular demonstrations of joy became so unruly that the police had to intervene to control the enthusiasm of the crowds.[15] The Spanish had always known that Antonio Maceo was their most dangerous enemy. Early in the war, they had sent assassins to infiltrate Maceo's forces in order to murder him.[16] Now the Spanish expected his death would cause the insurrection in western Cuba to collapse.

For the insurgency, the blow was tremendous. Maceo was the most skilled and inspirational military leader that the Cubans had. With him gone, what was left of the insurrection in western Cuba fell apart. Within a few months, General Ríus Rivera and other insurgent leaders in Pinar del Río fell into Spanish hands. In a letter written to his father, an English adventurer named James revealed much about the state of insurrectionary forces in Pinar del Río in the months after Maceo's death. James disembarked with other expeditionaries on March 23, 1897, at a point twelve miles west of the Mariel-Majana trocha. It was vital that the insurgency in Pinar receive supplies from the United States directly because contact with the East had by then become virtually impossible. James helped bring 400 boxes of ammunition ashore, along with rifles and machetes. All of it had to be done by hand, with the men wading up a creek bed of volcanic rock and over a hill covered with thorn bushes. By the end, James's "face, back, and arms were scratched and bleeding, offering an attractive field of interest to the mosquitos, which came in swarms." They finally delivered the cache to Colonel Baldomero Acosta, then headed for a rendezvous with Comandante Ignacio Morales, with whom they were to serve. Life in camp was no easier. They had little to eat apart from fruit and sweet potatoes. Insurgents came into camp alone or in small groups of "stragglers and sick men, without coats or shirts, some with only the ghost of what were once trousers, and all looking more like animals than human beings." James and the other new arrivals were shocked by the state of the Cuban troops and felt a foreboding that came from the realization that in a short time they would blend in all too well. In fact, the Spanish destroyed Acosta's force soon after James posted his letter home.[17]

In Havana and Matanzas the insurrection also became a furtive business. Matanzas was swarming with Spanish troops, and the population seemed to have turned against the revolution.[18] Most of the insurgents had already either died or gone home by the time news of Maceo's death arrived. Those who remained suffered an "absolute lack of food and supplies."[19] They went "barefoot and naked," hiding in impenetrable woods and swamps. Unable to defend the crops they cultivated for their sustenance, they starved and fell ill. "We were no longer soldiers," recalled one insurgent. "We were nothing but death in a bottle." These men longed for combat, but not for the right reason: they hoped, above all, that some of their own horses might be killed, because "without combat there is no roasted horse. Above all, we need a dozen roasted horses, with or without salt."[20] Lieutenant Colonel Benito Socorro reported that his "brigade" of seventy-seven men in Matanzas spent two months "naked and unshod," looking for equipment and arms. By midsummer 1897, the Fifth Corps, First Division, Colón Brigade boasted thirty-two "valiant" men — less than half the size of a normal company.[21]

Colonel Porfirio Díaz reported to his superior, Major General Francisco Carrillo, that the troops were in a state of "great demoralization," and he noted that "every day two or three men desert" to the Spanish. The forces that remained "suffer the greatest privations" and often went "days without eating a thing."[22] The rebels still controlled parts of the Cienaga de Zapata, an enormous swamp in the southern part of Matanzas province, where sixty-five years later the Cubans would drive out an American-backed invasion at the Bay of Pigs. But the peasants that the insurgency had relocated to the swamps lived in the most terrible squalor. They looked like "skeletons covered in yellow, dry, wrinkled skin. Others were swollen by their fevers or covered in ulcers, in which worms crawled gnawing the rot of their decomposing flesh." The insurgents throughout western Cuba began to surrender in significant numbers. And they were in no better condition than the peasants in the swamps. For clothing many had nothing but gunny sacks. They cut openings in the bottoms of the sacks to make head and arm holes, creating a rough sort of smock, but only the lucky ones had shoes and pants to complete the outfit.[23]

Farther east, in Santa Clara, the insurgency had also lost the ability to defend its cultivation zones and shut down sugar production.[24] Lieutenant Colonel José Pérez announced to Major General Carrillo that he would be unable to carry out his orders to destroy the sugar mills and fields of cane in Cienfuegos. He had no ammunition, so he could not risk engaging even the local militias paid to protect the sugar. He estimated that fourteen sugar mills were grinding cane in the district.[25]

So it was that the revolution began to recede into its heartland in Puerto Príncipe and Santiago, and even there the insurrection was experiencing difficulties. Fermín Valdés-Domínguez, who fought with Gómez in the East, recalled the dark month of February 1897 in his diary. He spent many days without food, and sometimes without water, because the Spanish patrolled the water courses. At least, he wrote, he always kept a little tobacco hidden and could retire to his hammock at night "to wait, to suffer, and to think" about what might have been had Maceo lived. At that point in the war, he recalled, everyone "placed their hope in the quick solution of all our desires thanks to American intervention." [26]

Frederick Funston, an American supporter of the Cuban cause who also fought in the East, realized by 1897 that the Cubans were near collapse. If witnessing demoralized and starving men bury their weapons and wander about in rags looking for food did not convince him, participating in a series of Cuban defeats did. In October 1896 Funston had witnessed 800 Cubans attack a smaller force of Spanish infantry at El Desmayo only to lose hundreds of men to enemy fire without inflicting any damage on the Spanish formation. And the following March 13 he watched Calixto García's army, by then the only sizable force left to the insurgents, assault a garrison at Jiguaní, only to lose 400 men without touching the Spanish at all. Funston concluded that Spain was a "plucky dame" and that only U.S. intervention could remove that "grim old mother of nations" from Cuba.[27] In the late summer of 1897 Weyler traveled all over Oriente with an escort of only 120 cavalry, something the Cubans would never have allowed a year earlier.[28]

Under these conditions, the Cubans could no longer impose their will on the economy. Trade with cities began to revive. Men placed in charge of managing livestock and horses for the Liberation Army started trading them to the Spanish, when they did not eat them out of desperation. It got to the point that the insurgents could not secure their plantations in any of the western provinces, which meant they could not eat. Even Santa Clara became a desert to them. Only Puerto Príncipe and Santiago still had some remaining cultivation zones in the service of the republic-in-arms.[29] The frustration felt by Cuban officers over this state of affairs can be seen in their insistence that new cultivation zones be created and defended and that the blockade of Spanish-held towns be enforced. In January 1897 officials in Matanzas admitted that, "despite our continuous dispositions" on the matter, "the so-called pacíficos still continue entering and leaving towns occupied by the enemy to traffic with them. What is worse, the majority carry identification papers issued by the Spanish authorities" and pay no attention to the Cuban provisional government. This "scandalous situation" required draconian justice. Civilians found with such papers would be arrested and tried. The penalty was death, and their merchandise would be distributed among the hungry troops of the Liberation Army, a final stipulation that placed a premium on discovering violators. Luckily for the violators, the insurgent forces were in no position to enforce these edicts. Cuban officers in Puerto Príncipe expressed horror that peasants were fleeing to the cities or sneaking food to family members who had remained with the Spanish. Hunger and love seemed to be trumping patriotism even in eastern Cuba.[30]

As one combatant recalled it, "the fate of the Cubans hung by a thread, a thread now within reach of Weyler's saber."[31] Gómez understood immediately upon Maceo's death that he was in a dangerous position.[32] The events of December 7, 1896, had been especially devastating for him because he had lost not only his best general but also his beloved, eldest son, Pancho. The dolorous state of the insurgency and the personal grief of Gómez help to explain the letters he directed to the American president in the spring of 1897 asking for American help. It is not clear whether Gómez desired direct American intervention at this point or not, but the letters certainly suggest a degree of desperation on Gómez's part. The "cruel and sanguinary" Weyler had destroyed western Cuba, wrote Gómez, and now he was coming to the East in order to "spread crime and desolation everywhere, assassinating noncombatants in their homes, killing children, and pursuing and raping women, after burning and leveling every house in his path." This was what Weyler called "pacification." It was to be expected from people "who expelled the Jews and the Moors, instituted the terrible inquisition, established the tribunal of blood in the Low Countries, and annihilated and exterminated the Indian population" of the Americas. Spaniards in Cuba were, if anything, worse, because they had experienced "a kind of physiological degeneration" that had caused them to "regress several centuries" in the scale of civilized behavior. Gómez admitted that for the insurgents it had now become "entirely impossible to stop these acts of vandalism." The United States, "which sustains the standard of civilization so high," would have to do something. The American people were the leaders of the Western Hemisphere and should "no longer tolerate the cold and systematic assassination" of defenseless Cubans. If America allowed the war to continue, Gómez predicted, "history would implicate her in the atrocities."[33]

Hyperbole aside, Gómez was correct. Weyler had just about finished with the West, and he was now preparing to go after Gómez in the East. And there was very little the Cubans could do about it. The insurgents in Puerto Príncipe and Santiago were becoming more isolated with each passing day as reconstruction proceeded on the eastern trocha from Júcaro to Morón. José Gago oversaw a massive effort at upgrading the old trocha, adding powerful searchlights and other modern improvements, so that "not even rats could get across it," to use the colorful expression of Máximo Gómez.[34] In public, Cuban officials heaped scorn on the trocha, but both the Júcaro-Morón line and the other defensive trochas were, in the view of a more recent assessment by a Cuban scholar, "complexly engineered defensive works, difficult to cross, despite the fact that many scholars discount their true value."[35] The redesigned eastern trocha now really fit the description given it by a Cuban officer, Manuel de la Cruz: "A colossus of iron, an obstacle at once powerful, indefinable, and strange, a pit, abyss, castle, artificial mountain of crags and artillery . . . Finisterre of Cuba Libre, written with the legendary sword of the lions of the Conquest . . . and behind it . . . stirred half of Spain, armed to the teeth."[36] The modernization of the old trocha was Weyler's penultimate task in the defeat of the insurgents. The offensive in the East was supposed to be his last.

On January 14, 1897, flush with confidence from the defeat and death of Maceo, Weyler granted an interview to a reporter for La Lucha. In response to a question about whether he had finished pacifying Pinar del Río, he replied: "Almost, almost; there only remain a few operations which I will undertake very shortly, and I count on it that in twenty days that province will be totally pacified." Weyler was never very handy when it came to press relations, as we already saw in his rash promise to journalists before departing for Cuba in February 1896 to end the war in two years. The phrase "almost pacified" was one of the most foolish things he ever uttered, and he never lived it down. Placing a twenty-day time limit on the pacification of Pinar del Río was both unnecessary and absurd: Even at their lowest point, there remained a few insurgents in Pinar who could still occasionally strike a blow. Because of his rash promise, Weyler became known forever after among his opponents as "General Almost Pacified," probably Weyler's least offensive nickname.[37]

There has been some confusion over the term "pacification" and the degree to which Weyler had really pacified western Cuba. If we define the word to mean the elimination of all resistance, then Weyler never pacified anything. Small bands of insurgents remained in western Cuba throughout the war. They did not amount to much, it is true. The Third Squadron of Raul Martí's old brigade in Havana submitted the following report on its condition on November 1, 1897: Commander Trujillo and Captain Antonio Estenoz were injured and absent while recovering. Lieutenant José Salina had joined the enemy. First Chief Domingo Molina was sick. Chief Rafael Mursuli had deserted to the enemy. Sergeant Antonio Díaz was detached. Second Sergeant Domingo Jiménez was sick. Three of the troopers were sick, and four more had deserted to the enemy.

That left on active duty Second Sergeant Rosendo García (author of the report), together with Corporal Joaquín de la Rosa and twelve troops ready for action, although two of them did not live in camp any longer, only four had horses, and they all lacked ammunition.[38]

Even a unit like this could, however, manage small acts of arson and sabotage, and it is easy to find news reports of these sorts of actions in 1897: someone detonated a stick of dynamite beneath the train track from Regla to Guanabacoa, and the towns of Güines and Bejucal near Havana experienced brief invasions by bands of insurrectos.[39] However, these were problems of public order not that different from the kinds of things Spain had encountered for decades in Cuba. The fact is that, with the death of Maceo, there were no more real battles in the West. "Almost pacified" is exactly what the West had become.

Comandante José Plasencia, given charge in April 1897 of a company that had fled Pinar del Río following Maceo's death, also faced a challenging task. The men were naked, shoeless, and had not eaten in days. "In view of the afflictions and poor condition of the forces under my command, decimated and fatigued by long marches and having gone long stretches without food[,] I determined to march off . . . to Pozo Salado" to look for livestock. The men found a yoke of oxen being used by farmers who had taken refuge in the town of Cabezas. He had been ordered not to engage the Spanish at all in order to save ammunition, but for the next month Plasencia kept his men together by raiding the cattle of Cabezas. At least they ate better than the civilians whose cattle they were robbing. By the end of May, however, the bounty had run out. Then the men ate all of their horses, and this made raiding for what livestock remained even more difficult. His men began to desert, and they couldn't be chased down for lack of mounts. In this situation, he sent a commission out to beg other units for clothing, food, and supplies. In mid-June these supplies arrived, including 169 Remingtons with cartridges. This allowed him to fight again, but an encounter with the Spanish a week later went all wrong. His force was overcome, and the straggling remnants of his company retreated into swamps along the coast. In July, back at Cabezas, he raided the town's livestock again and took two mules for food, but the cultivation zone of Cabezas was better guarded now, and a local force of Volunteers drove him off, destroyed his unit, and regained the mules. So ended Plasencia's company command.[40]

Arturo Mora at the Havana daily La Lucha, wrote to Rafael Gasset, editor of the Madrid paper El Imparcial on September 4, 1897, to report the "exhaustion of the revolution." In the province of Havana, at least, it seemed "as if the country was at complete peace."[41] The quiet around Havana made perfect sense. The Cuban forces there had been isolated for several months, unable to communicate with

Gómez, because the now-modernized Júcaro-Morón trocha had become impassible. They had no ammunition, and 50 percent of the men had malarial fevers.[42] Indeed, they became such a nonfactor that Weyler ceased to pay them any attention and turned his efforts in the summer of 1897 to the planned fall campaign in eastern Cuba.

In the spring of 1897 Gómez tried to organize one last offensive, a third "second invasion" of western Cuba to try to rescue the insurgency. He again placed Mayía Rodríguez in overall command of the enterprise, trusting that he would do better than he had done in his first two attempts. But Mayía could not muster enough men this time. By late March, the core of the invasion force numbered a mere 200 troops, only 50 of them mounted.[43] Mayía continued to advance with his small army, reaching the area of Trinidad in Santa Clara province by mid-May. However, the Spanish and their Cuban collaborators had established firm control over the area. Mayía had to hide in the mountains, where there was no food, and the men were forced to eat their own mules, making any further advance as an organized column out of the question. The demoralization of this fragment of the shattered Liberation Army was complete.[44]

One usually thinks of disease as the scourge of the Spanish army, but it also produced gaping holes in the Liberation Army. Of the Cuban soldiers who died during the war, nearly 30 percent perished from illnesses. Malaria was the worst. Forced to live in the bush and on the run, the Cubans could hardly avoid the deadly *anopheles* mosquitoes that carried the malaria parasite, even if it had crossed their minds to do so. They also lacked an adequate supply of quinine to control the illness. They suffered less than the Spanish, but their numbers to begin with were fewer, so they could not afford to lose any men. The Third Corps, stationed along the trocha, experienced the worst of it. Month after month, the corps' commanders begged for new recruits to fill vacancies, but none came, and by late 1897 the Third Corps was reduced to a handful of men.[45] When it does not kill, malaria has a way of leaving its victims weak and listless. Malaria became an epidemic in the fall of 1897.[46] In October, for example, 300 of García's men had the disease. García did not want to lose them altogether, so instead of sending them to hospitals, he kept them trailing the army. This left García extremely vulnerable. As Gómez remarked, "If the enemy comes on the attack it would be difficult [for García] to defend himself."[47]

Gómez promised to do his best to help García, but he, too, had a starving, sick mass of men. His general staff had not been immune. Gómez was so short in that department that he had to issue orders directly to his regiments and manage day-to-day operations.[48] By the spring of 1898 many units existed only on paper. Fortunately, the Spanish had decided, for political reasons that we shall examine shortly, to avoid combat in the fall of 1897. The Cubans were elated. General José María Rodríguez remarked that even in Pinar del Río, where "the enemy had been so active in the past," the Spanish were "leaving their forts and garrisons" and concentrating in the cities. Spanish columns debouched from these strong points to operate "from time to time," but they did so "with a notable lack of spirit." Rodríguez let his men rest, for they were still in no position to seek combat. He recognized that the politics that lay behind the Spanish decision to stand down might change again, and he ordered his officers to take advantage of the respite to convalesce. The men had to be got healthy and ready "in case the enemy begins a campaign" again.[49]

Civilians, as always, suffered most of all. The epidemics among the troops spread to noncombatants in both zones. Reconcentration went virtually unopposed in western Cuba in 1897, and in the late summer it was finally extended to central and eastern Cuba. The starving reconcentrados had no resistance to malaria, typhus, and dysentery. Some who had lived their whole lives in interior towns where yellow fever was absent succumbed to that disease when they were relocated to cities that had long been endemic foci of yellow fever. And because the relocated civilians were also starving, even common viruses and infections killed them. Reconcentration had entered its final, most deadly phase. This tragic story will be the subject of the next chapter.

14 ★ Reconcentration

Weyler's most controversial strategy for pacifying Cuba goes by the name of reconcentration — the forced relocation of civilians to cities and towns controlled by Spanish troops and their Cuban allies. One of the most terrible catastrophes in the history of the Americas, reconcentration turned an already cruel war into what some have termed genocide. Beginning in the spring of 1896, and picking up in 1897, Spanish troops uprooted half a million civilians and herded them into hastily built barracks, sometimes grouped into what were called "concentration camps." The army supplied rations, enough to prolong the suffering. Though scholars disagree about the number of civilians who perished due to reconcentration, over 100,000 reconcentrados certainly died, some from starvation, others in epidemics that peaked in the fall of 1897. In November 1897 the Spanish government ended reconcentration, but sickly and starving peasants could not be "deconcentrated" to a burned-out and devastated countryside by fiat. So they continued to die by the hundreds every day in cities like Matanzas, Havana, Cienfuegos, and Santa Clara. Towns passed special ordinances expanding the cemeteries. When that became impractical, the reconcentrados were interred in mass graves, and when the grave diggers and body collectors became too ill, the dead were left for dogs and birds.

Weyler's contemporaries often misunderstood reconcentration, and sometimes they printed deliberate falsehoods on the subject. This was natural. Nations and empires were at stake, and dead civilians were valuable propaganda. What this means for us is that we will have to wade through a thicket of disinformation, and we will need to bring fresh historical sources to bear on the problem, if we wish to understand reconcentration. What was it? What part did Weyler play in it? What impact did reconcentration have on civilians? This chapter will consider these questions.

Weyler issued his first reconcentration order on February 16, 1896, immediately after his arrival in Cuba. It applied only to the eastern provinces of Santiago and Puerto Príncipe, as well as to the district of Sancti Spíritus in the province of Santa Clara. On October 21, 1896, Weyler imposed reconcentration on Pinar del Río. On January 5, 1897, he extended it to Havana and Matanzas. A few weeks later, on January 30, he ordered the rest of Santa Clara reconcentrated, and on May 27, 1897, he renewed the reconcentration order for Puerto Príncipe and Santiago.[1]

The reconcentration orders gave people eight days to relocate to the nearest city or town garrisoned by the Spanish, a narrow time period that ensured non-compliance and violence. Weyler published the decrees in the *Gaceta de la Habana*, the official organ of the government, and local papers reprinted them. In a rural society still largely illiterate, the news of Weyler's order must have frequently arrived with the troops sent to enforce it, to drag people from their homes and march them into cities, past trenches and barbed wire, where they could be "protected."

Weyler mandated the creation of "cultivation zones" to be fortified and defended by Spanish troops and Cuban Volunteers and worked by the reconcentrados for their own sustenance. Crops planted outside such areas were to be destroyed. Livestock outside the cultivation zones was to be destroyed or gathered up and reconcentrated along with the people. Civilians who resisted these orders and remained in the countryside were considered to be in league with the enemy.

There were exceptions. Owners of large rural enterprises could apply for exemption. If they had clear title to their property, were paid up on their taxes, showed signs of resisting the insurgents, penned and controlled their livestock, and had resources to pay for the cost of a garrison's upkeep, they and their managers and laborers might be left alone. With this provision Weyler threw a bone to the sugar barons, big farmers, and other rural entrepreneurs who supported Spanish Cuba. The addendum reminds us that reconcentration had something about it of class warfare. It worked by design against the interests of poor peasants, many of whom did not own or lease the land they worked. Rather, they enjoyed usufruct privileges — unrecorded, customary rights — to work land they did not own in order to supplement the income they earned as laborers in the sugar industry or some other rural enterprise. This gave them a legal standing hardly greater than that of squatters. Moreover, many small proprietors owed some back taxes, which they could never hope to repay during wartime. Thus, Weyler's requirements for exemption from reconcentration — landownership and no taxes in arrears — excluded all but the rich. Weyler's chief of staff, Federico Ochando, elaborated on this aspect of the order to make sure everyone understood that "the spirit" of reconcentration "did not apply to the big agricultural and industrial establishments" but only to small "shops, ranches, and cottages" not under Spanish protection. These were the small-fry that were liable to support the insurgents whether out of choice or through coercion. They had to be removed from play.[2]

Still, we should not go too far and construe reconcentration as nothing but class war. Strategic and military interests were always paramount. Weyler did not exempt owners of big estates whose properties lay in areas that could not be secured against the insurgents, and, if military conditions allowed, the government might extend special consideration to small farmers and shopkeepers, some of whom, far from being separatists, were recent immigrants from Spain, even admirers of Weyler.[3] Their sentiments of loyalty were not necessarily in question, only their ability in practice to resist the Liberation Army and remain loyal. Some Spanish officers understood this, and they did not enforce reconcentration fully when it was a matter of rural folk in pacified zones able to remain loyal. General Agustín Luque, for example, made a point of allowing "many people to remain in their homes" as a way of affording them "the means to fight hunger."[4] Unfortunately, Luque's flexible approach was not common enough. The effect of reconcentration was generally to turn the poor into refugees, regardless of their politics.

Weyler's first decree of February 16, 1896, applying to the East was so little enforced (thus its renewal on May 27, 1897) that it is sometimes ignored in accounts of reconcentration. Yet it is an important and telling detail that Weyler issued his first reconcentration order within a week of arriving in Havana, for it reminds us that reconcentration had been in the works for some time.

Reconcentration had both long-term precedents and immediate precursors both in Cuba and around the world. Armies throughout history have relocated civilians in war zones in order to remove them from play as elements of logistical support for the enemy. Some contemporary Americans, including the naval officer and scholar French Ensor Chadwick, argued that reconcentration was unexceptional in this regard and conformed to the rules of war as everyone understood them in the 1890s.[5] In 1902 the U.S. government, after reconsidering the subject closely in light of its own war of counterinsurgency in the Philippines, concluded that Weyler's reconcentration in Cuba had not, after all, violated accepted military practices.[6] Leaving to one side what these statements indicate about the accepted rules of war, Chadwick and the U.S. government were right. Reconcentration was nothing new. The United States had practiced a form of reconcentration in its wars with Native Americans by herding them onto reservations. And Weyler, as we have already seen, had ordered the relocation of civilians in the Philippines in the period from 1888 to 1891.

The terms "concentration" and "reconcentration" were used interchangeably in Cuba, and their meaning was clear long before February 16, 1896. Indeed, one does not have to look as far afield as the United States and the Philippines for precursors to reconcentration. The same deliberate relocation of civilians had occurred right in Cuba during the Ten Years' War.[7] In that conflict, too, the insurgents targeted plantations, ranches, and farms. By 1870 they had so thoroughly disrupted agriculture and burned so many hamlets and farms in eastern Cuba that an alarming refugee problem developed there.[8] "Everyone knows," wrote the governor of Puerto Príncipe on April 26, 1870, "that the insurrectos have declared war not only against Spain but also against property, destroying everything they find in their path." As a result, a "multitude of families" from the countryside, "seeking the shelter offered by our garrisons," had taken refuge in Spanish cities and towns, where they found themselves "in the utmost state of misery" and "lacking any means of subsistence." The situation required the government to intervene creatively to rescue the refugees and restore the economy. This was something very like total war, and the captain general would have to "attend to the creation of new elements of production" with as much energy as had been devoted to the military campaign. To make this possible, authorities in eastern Cuba received approval to implement some radical measures, including the seizure of private property, especially if it remained uncultivated, in order to create cultivation zones, which were ceded temporarily to the refugees. Interestingly, even families with ties to the insurgency were to be afforded this relief. These provisions were intended to save lives, but they were also political and military expedients. The reconcentrados had to be convinced that if they remained loyal to the Spanish regime "they would not be worse off than if they remained in the mountains." Proper management of the refugee crisis, as much as military victory against the insurgents, would provide the necessary antidote to the revolution. Yet to make any of this possible, the Spanish army had to direct refugees to appropriately fortified Spanish towns with barracks and land set aside for their use. Inevitably, this introduced an element of force into the scheme.[9]

The plan of 1870 was never implemented systematically, and so its existence is little known. Weyler knew about it, however, because he alluded to it in his memoirs.[10] And we should recall where Weyler was in 1870. Fighting in Puerto Príncipe, he was in an ideal position to see reconcentration in action. Weyler drew upon this experience when he issued his reconcentration orders in 1896 and 1897. The dubious praise one sometimes sees heaped upon Weyler as "the only Spanish general in two centuries to contribute something new to military strategy" is therefore inappropriate. Reconcentration had many architects.[11]

One of these was Arsenio Martínez Campos, who used the term "reconcentration" in a letter posted in July 1895, as we have already seen. He claimed to have "higher beliefs" that prevented him from forcibly relocating the population, no matter how necessary it might be to victory, but his moral qualms did not prevent him from recommending Weyler for the dirty job. However, in a reversal of his earlier vow against making war on civilians, Martínez Campos issued direct orders to his district commanders on November 4, 1895, on the subject of reconcentration. In these directives, the captain general noted that the insurgents' practice of forcibly relocating civilians to rural districts out of the reach of Spanish protection lent "a special character" to the war by producing a much greater contrary movement: "the concentration of a portion of the peaceful inhabitants into towns" as they fled revolutionary justice. This flow of refugees into towns had produced a crisis. "It is clear," Martínez Campos continued, "that this imposes on us the burden of feeding them when they lack for resources, because we cannot abandon peaceful citizens to hunger and misery." The "unavoidable duty of humanity and of government" was to provide relief. In order to do this, the army had to make sure "that the concentrations forced [upon civilians] by the enemy take place in towns that have garrisons and are linked by rail." This, in turn, required that Spanish troops direct the refugees to the appropriate locations, and this, again, implied the use of force.

Once the reconcentrados were relocated, Martínez Campos promised that the government would help care for them, but it could not manage the herculean task alone. For one thing, it lacked the resources. For another, providing direct relief would require the use of supply convoys, and these, he warned, would become additional targets for the insurgents. Therefore, the reconcentrados would have to provide for most of their needs themselves. Martínez Campos ordered military and civilian officials to give the refugees access to "all uncultivated fields" in the vicinity of garrisoned towns, "whether belonging to the municipality or to private individuals." These would be "divided into allotments" so that they could be "worked and enjoyed by the immigrants," who were to be given tools and any other assistance they needed. Martínez Campos sent copies of this order to the War and Colonial Ministries for approval, which he received on November 29. He never carried out the plan, because he was on his way out, but it is clear that all of the elements of reconcentration were in place before Weyler had even been appointed captain general of Cuba.[12]

The refugee crisis faced by the Spanish as early as the summer of 1895 reminds us, too, that the Cuban Liberation Army had a hand in reconcentration. Cuban troops removed people who lived near Spanish towns and roads and confiscated their goods as a way to eliminate them as props to the Spanish regime. Some people cooperated with this "deconcentration" and joined the insurrection, but most sought protection with the Spanish. The scope and intensity of the refugee crisis instigated by the Liberation Army is well documented in the diaries and correspondence of both Cubans and Spaniards and needs to be taken seriously as a precursor to, and even a cause of, Weyler's reconcentration.[13]

Cuban veteran Serafín Espinosa recalled that wherever the Liberation Army went it confiscated or destroyed property so that "farmers had nothing of their own." This forced everyone, but especially women and children, to flee into cities, turning Cuba Libre into a cheerless place for the men who stayed behind, in Espinosa's estimation. At least men had the option of joining the insurrection. Women and children had little choice but to become reconcentrados.[14]

The process went furthest in Pinar del Río, where Maceo arrived in January 1896 and burned down half of the towns, as we have already seen. Juan Alvarez, one of Maceo's company commanders, recorded his impressions of the province following this orgy of destruction. Rural districts had been depopulated. Houses stood empty, crops unkempt, and livestock abandoned as peasants fled before Maceo. Alvarez spent much of his time burning houses that had been vacated in the halcyon days of the invasion in January 1896. Burning vacant houses did not seem unduly harsh. Their owners, after all, had "gone to the city with the soldiers." Sometimes, though, Alvarez targeted houses that were still occupied. For example, he burned forty homes in the suburbs of Luis Lazo, forcing the occupants to flood into the town. The boundary between insurgent Cuba and Spanish Cuba ran right through the outskirts of Luis Lazo and hundreds of other places just like it. The insurgents' objective was to turn these suburban borderlands into charred dead zones between the two alternative Cubas — urban colony and rural republic-in-arms — with no middle ground in between. When Alvarez was not burning houses, he was rounding up livestock "in order to deny resources" to the Spanish. The animals had been left behind, but their owners might return with troops to reclaim them. Better to take or even kill them than to let that happen. In this way, the first reconcentrados lost the livestock that could have fed them in their narrowed circumstances. They arrived in Spanish towns completely reliant on charity.

The same thing Alvarez reported in Pinar del Río was going on everywhere else. For example, Lieutenant Colonel Gerardo Machado devoted his cavalry squadrons to gathering livestock, "without sparing those belonging to the pacíficos," because they had been selling their animals, as well as milk, eggs, and produce, to the towns. Not even chickens and goats were spared, but everything was taken to the mountains or butchered on the spot.[15] Esteban Montejo recalled that what he did most during the war was catch and kill animals, especially pigs, in the dead of night. "We went on horseback, and on horseback we chased pigs, which were basically feral. They ranged freely, and were not fattened up. We would chase any pig we saw. For us it was a game. After the pig became tired, we would hack at its hind leg with our machetes while still mounted. The leg would fly off and the pig would not be able to run any more. We would dismount quickly and grab it by the neck. The bad part about it was that the pigs bled and screamed a lot."[16] Within no time, as visitors to Cuba observed, the countryside was barren of pigs . . . and cows, mules, horses, chickens, dogs, cats, and, finally, people.

Refugees arrived in cities not only bereft of animals but lacking seed, tools, clothing, and money. In areas where the insurgency was strong, a majority of the reconcentrados were women and children, because the men were with the insurgency or with the Spanish as Volunteers and counterguerrillas. The sexual division of labor in rural Cuba — as in many other peasant communities — had men working for wages outside the home and taking charge of tillage while women managed household animals and gardens. Destroying and confiscating livestock and homes thus separated women from their traditional means of subsistence. When women arrived in Spanish towns, local officials might give them plots of land to till, but they were unaccustomed to the plough and lacked draft animals. This produced the dolorous spectacle of women trailed by their children, all of them in rags, all of them starving, scratching the hard dirt with sharp sticks in a futile attempt to prepare the ground for planting. The situation was already so bad by January 1896 that Martínez Campos took the step of asking his officers and men to donate their labor and a portion of their pay to help these wretched women and their children. It was a hollow gesture, as almost no one volunteered for this gallant service, but it can be taken as another sign of how serious the reconcentrado problem was before Weyler's arrival on the scene.[17]

The insurgents enforced their own deconcentration of civilians throughout the conflict as a counter to Weyler's reconcentration. In the summer of 1896, Máximo Gómez could see that his prohibitions on commerce with Spanish cities were being violated when the Liberation Army did not force the issue. The worst places were Cascorro, Guaimaro, and other towns along the Júcaro-Morón trocha. "In these towns," Gómez wrote to the secretary of war, "the people eat good and abundant meat and produce from the countryside and this must be entering the towns from the surrounding areas."[18] At times, it appeared, even revolutionary officials broke the blockade, either out of sympathy with the starving people in the cities or out of a desire to profit on the high prices that could be fetched by any product that did make it to market.[19] These practices, said Gómez, had to stop. He therefore ordered that "all the families who live near the enemy towns," and who were "justifying their situation" with the excuse that they had to send food in to guarantee the survival of their relations in the town, would be removed. Units of the Liberation Army were to take them and "intern them at great distances" from their homes. To ensure "that they lose all hope of peaceful relations" with their friends and relatives in the towns, Gómez "also ordered that their houses be burned." He concluded: "It is necessary that when leaving on campaign the Spanish find nothing but a desert and complete waste around them."[20] Officers ordered their men "to persecute with the greatest severity anyone who maintains traffic and commerce" with the Spanish towns. Needless to say, these measures created the conditions for widespread starvation and misery and induced a flood of refugees into the towns.[21]

As we have seen, Gómez and Maceo never imagined that the function of the Liberation Army was to defeat Spanish armies. Rather, controlling the wealth of the countryside and blockading Spanish towns had always been their primary goal. This strategy made great sense in the context of the Cuban economy. The logistics of getting food to market in much of Cuba were complicated by the fact that broad stretches of the countryside had been dedicated to a single crop, either sugar or tobacco. This meant that local production of basic foods was often inadequate to begin with and that supplies had to be secured from relatively distant producers. As a result, cities were especially vulnerable to blockade. In the days before Weyler's arrival, the insurgents had ridden "to the very gates of Havana" to prevent food from entering the city.[22] In the city of Pinar del Río, around which the insurgents under Maceo were especially numerous, green grocers and milkmen became endangered species in the early spring of 1896. The Liberation Army hanged them, as well as any other civilians who tried to get food into the provincial capital.[23] In April 1896 Maceo ordered the destruction of all fences in Pinar del Río, hoping in this way to prevent the penning of livestock that could later be taken into the starving towns.[24] Even in late 1896 and 1897, when the Liberation Army lost the ability to do much in the strict military sense, it always retained the power to disrupt the flow of goods into Spanish towns, thus fulfilling its primary mission.

This manner of warfare made food immediately scarce, and the survival of the refugees became a serious problem. A correspondent for the *Times* of London remarked on the appalling problem of starvation in the Havana region as early as the spring of 1896, again, before the advent of official reconcentration:

Spain has another and serious danger to face in addition to the actual rebellion. The towns are crowded with refugees, a very large proportion of these being women and children. The local food supplies are nearly exhausted, and will be entirely so in a few months' time. Little or nothing is being grown to supply local needs, and the rebels do not allow any country produce to be taken to the towns for sale. The people in the towns will, therefore, be dependent on what can be purchased abroad. . . . Unless relief in some form is provided, absolute starvation will overtake a large proportion of the population before many more months are passed.[25]

But relief efforts mounted from abroad faced every sort of obstacle. For example, the British schooner J. W. Durant attempted to unload ten barrels of maize in early February 1898, but customs officials there wanted to collect a fee, so the maize sat. Fitzhugh Lee, the U.S. consul in Havana, lodged an official protest with Ramón Blanco, the man who replaced Weyler in the fall of 1897, and eventually the corn was landed.[26] Meanwhile, the Spanish Congress continued to debate the issue of what to do about relieving the hunger in Cuba. Would lowering tariffs make a difference to the really destitute? Was accepting American aid too much of a humiliation? Was it not an admission that Spain could not govern Cuba without the help of the North American colossus? Would the influx of cheap grains makes its way into the hands of the insurgents? While these interesting questions were discussed in Madrid, Cubans continued to starve as the Liberation Army's blockade of the cities tightened.

This blockade was supposed to be absolute, and Gómez became furious when exceptions were made. In practice, however, Cuban officials sometimes turned a blind eye to violators or allowed certain basic commodities, such as eggs, to get through.[27] Unit commanders, more in touch with local conditions than Gómez, allowed people "who are with us and who have families in the towns" to sneak food to their relations. With properly signed permits, they were allowed to deliver to blood relatives as much meat and vegetables "as will fit in a small saddlebag." This restriction ensured that none of the food made it to pro-Spanish elements. However, these humanitarian steps amounted in the end to mere gestures. The embargo on trade remained an absolutely essential component of Gómez's strategy if the insurgency were to have any hope of success, and we have seen that Gómez cracked down on Cuban officials and pacíficos who traded with the towns. Indeed, officially, the republic-in-arms called for the destruction of all property near towns and reiterated many times its position that the "introduction in towns of any article" of food was punishable by death. Recorded trials of desperate violators demonstrate how summary was the justice meted out to the smugglers of foodstuffs.[28] The system was harsh, but denying city folk access to food from the countryside was one of the cornerstones of the Cuban strategy.

After Weyler introduced reconcentration on a massive scale, towns developed new cultivation zones to feed the refugees, and this presented a novel challenge for the insurgency. They now had to eradicate these new plantings near the towns, and to the degree that they succeeded, they contributed to the misery and mortality of the reconcentrados. The assault on the cultivation zones served a dual purpose. First, of course, it starved the Spanish and their Cuban allies. Second, it provided the Liberation Army with much-needed food. The insurgents' civil administration, the prefects and subprefects of the republic-in-arms, did their utmost to set up their own farms to provide the Liberation Army with food. In the East, the system was reasonably successful.[29] In western Cuba, however, the Spanish and loyalist guerrillas had by 1897 destroyed the prefectures and the production of foodstuffs for the Cuban army, so that patriot troops there had to rely almost entirely on what they could rob from the cultivation zones intended for the reconcentrados.[30] Indeed, Cuban forces even began to rob their own cultivation zones. Andrés Rodríguez, an insurgent subprefect in the town of Higuanojo, wrote to Lieutenant Colonel Rafael Soriz on August 26, 1897, to complain about the behavior of Cuban troops in the area. They had been dispersed and had become mere bandits, seizing crops and livestock without permission. Rodríguez wrote: "I am taking the liberty of informing you that I believe it convenient for you to order a regular commission with energetic character to gather up individuals of the forces of General José María Rodríguez and of General Quintín Banderas who are useless in this zone and in fact prejudicial."[31]

So complete had the Cuban dependence on the reconcentrados' cultivation zones become that the American defeat of the Spaniards in 1898 constituted a serious problem for the Cuban army. As Mayía Rodríguez observed in August 1898, peace had made it impossible to feed the troops, whose "diet had up to the present depended upon the enemy cultivation zones." The suspension of hostilities "eliminated the peculiar mode the forces of our army had of attending to their subsistence" and threatened the scattered remnants of the Liberation Army with starvation.[32]

Even the First and Second Corps in Oriente, where the system of prefectures had been more solidly developed, faced this problem to a certain extent. As in the West, the reconcentrados had set up cultivation zones, and the insurgents found themselves obliged to survive by expropriating what they could from the reconcentrados. The system worked so long as hostilities continued, but when the United States forced a peace settlement, the troubles began. Major General Jesús Rabí, in command of the Second Corps around Manzanillo, complained in the late summer of 1898 that his men were going hungry, now that peace terms with Spain prevented him from robbing livestock from the townsfolk. In fact, he could not even provide an accurate enumeration of his troops, because, starved by the peace, large numbers of soldiers deserted on a daily basis.[33]

In 1897, when Weyler began to move his center of operations eastward, the insurgents stepped up their campaign to destroy towns and rural homesteads of the pacíficos that lay near centers of Spanish strength in eastern Cuba. Juan Castro, captain of a Spanish outpost at Cabaiguan, along the eastern trocha, informed his divisional commander in January 1897 that "many peaceful residents from the countryside are presenting themselves these days" seeking protection.

What should he do? he asked. The refugees were telling him "that the insurgents had taken the passes and documents they had from the Spanish identifying them as neutrals. They had told them that they had to join the rebellion and abandon their homes, and that if they did not they would be deprived of all of their property" and would find the security of their families threatened.[34] The same thing Gómez and Maceo had earlier enforced in western Cuba was beginning now in the East. Naturally, a flood of new refugees went to Cabaiguan and other towns in east central Cuba. Weyler's response was to announce his own reconcentration in the East in the spring of 1897. Now the towns of eastern Cuba became what those in the West had long been: charnel houses of starving refugees. This produced a well-justified worldwide outcry against such methods of making war, but all the blame attached to Weyler, while the Cuban insurgents' role in reconcentration went unnoticed by most of the world.

The Cuban provisional government noticed, however, and it objected to some of Gómez's stricter requirements. In the fall of 1896, Secretary of War Rafael Portuondo warned Gómez to allow food in to help the starving civilians. Gómez refused. In a letter to Portuondo dated November 21, 1896, Gómez rejected not only Portuondo's proposal but his very authority to interfere in such matters. This dispute became so serious that the provisional government forced Gómez to resign as commander in chief on December 8, 1896, when he turned authority over to Antonio Maceo. In a formal letter to his fellow cabinet members, Portuondo recommended accepting Gómez's resignation. "I understand that we must accept" Gómez's retirement, he wrote, "because there are many well-founded charges against him," as the government "knew perfectly well." Worse still, the whole country knew. The people, "vexed in their dignity," had begun "to rebel against a man they see aspiring to a dictatorship." So it had become "convenient for the health of the country to take advantage" of Gómez's offer to resign to remove him "in a gentle manner," in order "to satisfy public opinion which might otherwise demand his violent removal."[35] Gómez and the government had been at odds before, but this was the worst crisis of all. Were it not for the fact that Maceo died shortly after Gómez's resignation, it is very possible that the old caudillo would have been eased out over the issue of his treatment of civilians.

Weyler had a great deal to say on the subject of reconcentration. On December 30, 1897, after he had already been relieved of command and his name had become synonymous with genocidal cruelty, Weyler composed a defense that is worth quoting at some length:

> The orders I dictated regarding the concentration of peasants in cultivation zones should not horrify world opinion because there was nothing cruel

about them. These methods were imposed, and only in certain territories, by the necessities of war. They were designed to deprive the enemy of all kinds of services provided by peasants, sometimes voluntarily[,] other times by threats and violence. These services were extremely important to the insurgents. They included cultivating crops and caring for livestock to feed [the insurgents]; acting as local guides; supplying intelligence to direct their operations; and serving as spies to reveal [our plans].

Reconcentration was carried out in some areas in accord with my orders. . . . In other territories reconcentration resulted from the free and spontaneous movement of the rural population, fleeing the burning of their towns by the insurgents. We always aided the appallingly destitute inhabitants who took refuge in our encampments by providing food and rations [and] assisting them in their illnesses and epidemics with doctors from our battalions and hospitals. In April and May 1896, when Spanish columns entered the tobacco-growing regions of Pinar del Río for the first time, more than 15,000 souls gathered and concentrated in our coastal camps voluntarily, because the towns and hamlets of the interior had been totally destroyed by the torches of those black insurgent gangs. Whole communities of people became transformed into miserable vagabonds who wandered the countryside, leaving as evidence of their tragic passage the cadavers of children, women, and old people.[36]

No judgment is more partisan, of course, than Weyler's, and we must view anything he said or wrote about what he called Cuba's "black insurgent gangs" with skepticism. Nevertheless, in light of what we know from other sources about the precursors to reconcentration and about the participation of the insurgents in it, it is obvious that some elements of Weyler's analysis are correct. It does not mitigate his responsibility to recognize that other people were also responsible. By the time Weyler arrived in Cuba, places like Luis Lazo and its hinterland had already been transformed by war. People there had been forced to make a choice: They could head into the hills with the insurgents or flee to "Spain." Those taking the latter option had become wards of the Spanish state. This was fine with Gómez. As refugees, they helped to undermine the Spanish regime in Cuba, either by using up resources or by providing foreign journalists with the hideous spectacle of their starvation and death. In this way, dying refugees had an important part to play in national liberation. Gómez and Maceo did not make war with bonbons any more than Weyler did. Nor should we expect them to have been more humanitarian than the Spanish. That was not a fantasy in which the soldiers who fought to free Cuba from Spain could afford to indulge.

Among the several parties responsible for reconcentration were Spanish officers and troops and Cuban Volunteers fighting for the Spanish who, without prompting from Weyler, had begun to "assist" refugees fleeing into cities and towns in western Cuba in early 1896. The Spanish liked to construe this as providing "aid" and "protection" to civilians. Military telegraphs from the period contain phrases like "Sending column to protect families" and "Returned with families" or again "Returned seven night with families that we protected and nothing new to report."[37] General Alvaro Suárez Valdés wrote to Weyler to report sending a column to the area of Consolación del Sur "to help with the reconcentration of families who want to pass into that town due to having lost their homes." Suárez Valdes complained of being unable to shelter all of the peasants who wanted protection. He also lacked sufficient cavalry to pursue "the little enemy parties that continue to disturb the residents of the countryside," so more refugees were sure to be on their way. They were flooding into the city of Pinar del Río, and he could not stop the process, which threatened to make life in the provincial capital unbearable. The letter is dated March 23, 1896, seven months before Weyler imposed reconcentration on Pinar del Río.[38]

Indeed, the curious thing is that Weyler waited so long to issue a formal order of reconcentration for western Cuba. To explain this requires that we pay attention to chronology. Gómez abandoned western Cuba in May 1896, and Maceo withdrew to the mountains of Pinar del Río during the late spring and summer. During this respite, refugees began to return to their homes — to deconcentrate. Supplies that had been interdicted by the insurgents began again to trickle into the cities of the West. Moreover, neither side campaigned actively in the summer, so the situation did not call for a formal declaration of reconcentration. All of this changed as the weather improved in September 1896. On September 8, the indefatigable *Three Friends* landed an expedition in the far West, and Antonio Maceo began an offensive almost immediately. The process of rebuilding the economy came to a halt, and refugees began to arrive again in the towns. The only solution seemed to be to organize this influx of civilians and to create formal cultivation zones so that they could provide for themselves. This explains the timing of the order of October 21. Weyler promulgated the reconcentration order for Pinar del Río in response to a refugee crisis and a renewed military threat from Maceo. Now the forced relocation of civilians and the destruction of whatever they left behind began in earnest.

Within a few months, the same thing would occur in Havana, Matanzas, and

Santa Clara. In 1896 Spanish troops — again without the benefit of any formal order of reconcentration — had begun to evacuate rural districts of any inhabitants who had not already fled into cities or into rural districts under insurgent control. The Volunteer guerrilla formations aligned with Spain had come to specialize in these operations. Having cleared an area of people, they then wiped out any remaining crops and livestock, which might be used by the Liberation Army. Luis Diez del Corral reported that his Volunteer unit spent all of its time finding and destroying crops in the area around Minas Ricas, where the Liberation Army had farms. Similarly, the "principal operational object" of General Manuel Prats's forces fighting around the swampy Zapata peninsula was "to destroy the plantings of the enemy and gather up their livestock." The Volunteer formations relished these search-and-destroy missions, in part because, with the collapse of the economy, they had come to depend on the booty for their own survival.[39] In any case, these practices predated Weyler's formal reconcentration of Havana and Matanzas.

Weyler's reconcentration should be viewed, therefore, as a response both to the insurgency's practice of total war and to his army's reaction to it. The mirror image of Gómez's strategy, reconcentration was designed to deny the insurgents access to civilians and their resources by controlling or eliminating them. What it was not designed to do — though Weyler and his supporters liked to conceive of it this way — was minister to the poor refugees already displaced by Gómez and Maceo. There was absolutely nothing humanitarian about reconcentration. Even the cultivation zones clearly served the interests of Spain rather than the refugees. Each reconcentration order contained detailed instructions relating to the cultivation zones, and in these details we can see something of Weyler's mind-set. The order of January 30, 1897, which applied to Santa Clara, included the following instructions: "In each fortified town in the province a cultivation zone will be designated . . . so that current residents and recently arrived families can plant crops, excepting . . . those who have a father or husband in the insurrection." The demarcation of the cultivation zone was left to a committee, or junta, made up of the military commander of the town, the mayor, the priest, the judge, and six propertied residents. This junta was given the power to oblige people to cultivate the land assigned to them. Reconcentrados would retain usufruct rights to their assigned plots until six months after the war ended to create a cushion for them. Municipal land would be given freely. Private land would be divided up among the refugees, with compensation for the landowners provided by a tax levied on all property in the municipality. The final stipulation stated: "No taxes or any other contributions whatsoever can be levied on these reconcentrados for the use of this land while the war lasts."[40]

There are several salient points in these instructions that bear further comment. First, the denial of land and succor to families with ties to the insurgents made Weyler's reconcentration more brutal than that envisioned and partially carried out in Oriente in the 1870s. Indeed, it amounted to a death sentence for a portion of the refugees.

Second, the management of the cultivation zones was left to local elites rather than the army. This ensured that the scheme did not threaten property relations. Total war can have the effect of making belligerents, through their armies, adopt command economies subversive of private property rights. Weyler was willing to do many things and see many things sacrificed in order to keep Cuba Spanish, but he did not go so far as to nationalize production or threaten private property in any fundamental way. The purpose of the Spanish regime in Cuba was, after all, the protection of unequal property relations that had evolved out of the slave era in colonial Cuba. It is not surprising, therefore, that Weyler rated the lives of Cubans more cheaply than property.

Some aspects of the law were generous. The prohibition on charging rents, taxes, and fees for the use of the land and the extension of the land grants for six months beyond the termination of hostilities are cases in point. Unfortunately, by giving local property owners control of the process, Weyler created a situation in which the cultivation zones had no chance to succeed. Municipal officials, already overwhelmed by the influx of "voluntary" refugees, could scarcely muster any resources to build housing or provide emergency relief as envisioned by Weyler's decree. And as respectful as Weyler tried to be toward local property relations, his plan had the effect of asking propertied townsfolk to extend a helping hand to peasant refugees. In essence, one side in a military conflict was to give alms to people who were suspected, rightly or wrongly, of supporting the other side.

This took the principle of "turning the other cheek" too far for some landowners, who controlled municipal politics and had ways of resisting the decree. Troops rounded people up and marched them into cities only to find that promised barracks for the refugees had not been built. Owners of vacant lots and buildings demanded payment for giving them over to the reconcentrados. The juntas overseeing the scheme identified and set aside the most barren ground for cultivation zones. And they rarely set aside enough land. In the province of Havana, for example, Spanish officials estimated that only one-fifth of the reconcentrados were given access to land. Finally, the whole thing was implemented as if time did not matter. In fact, it ran out almost immediately. The plan required that infertile ground be prepared for cultivation by hungry people — a majority of them women and children — who had no draft animals and who needed to make the land productive overnight. Only someone like Weyler, with no knowledge of agriculture and no real interest in the fate of the reconcentrados, could have imagined that the cultivation zones had the slightest chance of success once their management was left to local elites.

A third provision of Weyler's plan allowed for a common tax on property to compensate those whose land had to be tapped for the reconcentrados. This was supposed to ensure that none of the landowners was unduly harmed by the creation of the cultivation zones. However, it also created the disgusting spectacle of rich Cubans — those with enough property in or near town to have left it uncultivated — collecting fees from other townspeople for the "service" of letting destitute refugees eke out an existence farming land that had always been (and still was) worthless wasteland.

A fourth aspect of Weyler's plan that deserves highlighting is that it forbade the owners of lands assigned for use by reconcentrados from collecting rents and use fees from their new tenants and prohibited municipalities from taxing them. This provision, positive in itself, suggests by its very enunciation that something more sinister may have been taking place. Indeed, a disturbing practice had developed during the war in which municipalities had been levying taxes on and private individuals had been collecting fees from the poor refugees. In effect, whatever property they had been able to bring with them into the cities was seized by municipal officials to compensate them for the trouble of providing relief.

There are always exceptions to any rule. Administrative records show that some municipalities created cultivation zones that worked. By the fall of 1897, a few were even producing surpluses. When the insurgents heard about a successful cultivation zone, they naturally attempted to destroy it in order to keep up the pressure of starvation in the cities. Just as the Spanish army could not protect sugar and tobacco, neither could it protect some of the cultivation zones.[41] It did not take a well-organized, large force to wipe out crops. Even the dispersed remnants of the Liberation Army that existed in the West could do the job. Thus, the diaries of Cuban officers in 1897 are filled with references to burning crops planted by the refugees.[42] Only in the largest towns with strong garrisons was there any hope of protecting the new plantings. But in such cases the crops were not always safe from Spanish troops and their allies, who "taxed" the poor reconcentrados to supply their own pressing needs.

These problems did not seem to concern Weyler very much. In fact, the cultivation zones were designed above all to save money and troops, and in this they succeeded. Weyler provided some rations to the refugees, but the mechanism of the cultivation zones placed ultimate responsibility for relief squarely with the reconcentrados, who were expected very quickly to feed themselves. This was supposed to spare the financially strapped Spanish state a new obligation and free up resources for the troops. Cultivation zones were also intended to obviate the need to supply garrison towns by convoy, thus eliminating the insurgents' favorite military target and allowing the Spanish to avoid another onerous and dangerous task.

Reconcentration was always and above all a military measure. This fact must be kept in mind. Removing civilians who might provide support and information to the Cubans was sound strategy. Following the reconcentration decree of October 21, 1896, Spanish troops conducted sweeps through Pinar del Río, removing whoever was left in the countryside to a few towns firmly under Spanish control. By then, of twenty-five municipalities in Pinar del Río, nine had been virtually erased by the insurgents. They produced refugees rather than sheltering them. Another ten were in various stages of rebuilding, and they accepted few reconcentrados. This left Artemisa, the center of operations for the forces guarding the western trocha, and Consolación del Norte and Bahía Honda, on the north coast, to receive most of the reconcentrados. They were followed by Consolación del Sur, San Cristóbal, and Mantua, in that order. The capital, Pinar del Río, though spared by the insurgents, never accepted its fair share of refugees. In any case, the success of reconcentration is one reason Maceo had to flee Pinar del Río in December 1896. The place could no longer support an army.

We will never know the exact number of Cuban civilians who died under reconcentration. At one extreme, the Spanish Liberal politician José Canalejas stated after a fact-finding mission in 1897 that 400,000 Cuban civilians had already perished and that another 200,000 would surely die before the effects of Weyler's policy could be reversed. Ramón Blanco supported Canalejas's findings, claiming that 570,000 Cubans had died in the war. In a population of just over 1.7 million people, these figures, if true, would mean that Weyler exterminated about one-third of the Cuban people, higher than the percentage of dead in Russia during World War II and a greater proportional demographic loss than in Pol Pot's Cambodia. However, the figures supplied by Canalejas and Blanco are not to be trusted. Inveterate enemies of Weyler and Cánovas, Canalejas and Blanco provided their "data" to discredit their Conservative predecessors and to solidify the Liberals' hold on power in the fall of 1897. Neither was actually in a position to have accurate information on the subject of reconcentration at the time he issued his report.[43]

American estimates also exaggerated matters for political reasons. As the American jingoes ramped up their effort to convince the American public to intervene in Cuba, Fitzhugh Lee reported that 75,000 reconcentrados had died in Havana alone and that at least 300,000 had died in the island as a whole. What greater reason to deploy American troops could there be?[44] Other American investigations produced results that echoed Lee's estimate. In 1897, President McKinley asked former congressman William J. Calhoun to look into conditions in Cuba. In June, after a three-week visit to the island in which he consulted no official sources, Calhoun issued a report that echoed Lee's: The Spanish had relocated 500,000 civilians, and 300,000 had already died. His description was stirring: "I traveled by rail from Havana to Matanzas. The countryside outside of the military posts was practically depopulated. Every house had been burned, banana trees cut down, cane fields swept by fire, and everything in the shape of food destroyed. . . . I did not see a house, man, woman or child, a horse, mule, or cow, nor even a dog. . . . The country was wrapped in the stillness of death and the silence of desolation." These words have been often quoted, with the implication that the destruction had been caused by the Spanish and that it characterized the whole island, not just the view from Calhoun's train window. Certainly, this was how Calhoun's contemporaries interpreted the matter.[45]

Calhoun's sources are not clear, but, based on his report, one could conclude that by the time reconcentration officially ended in November 1897, the number of its victims would have grown to well over 300,000, perhaps approaching the estimates given by Spanish Liberals.[46] Following his own fact-finding mission, Senator Redfield Proctor issued a report on March 17, 1898, that depicted the plight of the reconcentrados in moving terms and stated that more than 300,000 had perished, the same figure Lee and Calhoun had bandied about. It is not unknown for "fact-finding" missions to find each other and to repeat each other's conclusions instead of looking for and finding the facts. As we shall see, Proctor's report helped provide one final push for the United States to declare war, but it was based on nothing solid.[47]

Scholars often cite the findings of Canalejas, Blanco, Lee, Calhoun, and Proctor, apparently unaware of the limitations of these historical sources. As a result, extraordinarily high mortality figures, usually ranging from 300,000 to 400,000, have, by force of repetition, come to be accepted as fact by many scholars.[48] There is evidence from census data, however, that gives us cause to reject such high numbers of civilian deaths. The census of 1899, administered by American officials, revealed 1,572,797 inhabitants in Cuba, compared to a population of 1,708,687 in 1895. Simple arithmetic suggests that 135,890 more people died or left Cuba during the war than were born or entered the island. The

Cuban demographers Juan Pérez de la Riva and Blanca Morejón and the economic historian Julio Le Riverend used these census data (although they calculated the figure for Cuba's population in 1895 at 1,730,000) to arrive at a figure for population loss of 157,203. They also ascribed all of these losses to fatalities caused by reconcentration, discounting losses from war casualties, emigration, starvation and disease not directly ascribable to reconcentration, and other causes. Le Riverend, still not satisfied, "rounded" the resulting number for deaths upward again to 200,000, blaming all of these deaths on reconcentration.[49]

If one can round up, one can also round down. Some scholars, using the same census data, have argued for lowering the mortality caused by reconcentration. They note that emigration from Cuba during the war, the loss of growth due to lower immigration from Spain, and other sources of population loss must be taken into account. Taking all of these problems into account, economic historian Jordi Maluquer de Motes has suggested that between 155,000 and 170,000 Cubans died due to reconcentration. This is the most careful calculation performed to date using the census data.[50] But this figure was too high for other scholars. David Trask and Joseph Smith thought the number of fatalities should be placed closer to 100,000. Ivan Musicant thought that 95,000 civilians had died. The Cuban scholar Tiburcio Pérez Castañeda concluded in 1925 that only 90,000 civilians died in reconcentration. And, recently, Carmelo Mesa-Lago believed that 60,000 civilians perished in the war.[51]

Something is terribly wrong with a methodology that arrives at such widely varying conclusions. Fortunately, data exist in the documentation generated by the administrators in charge of reconcentration's dismantling from November 1897 to January 1898 that can be used to test the census data. On November 28 Ramón Blanco, who had just replaced Weyler as captain general of Cuba, sent a questionnaire to the provincial governors. He wanted to know: (1) How many people had been reconcentrated in the province? (2) How many men, women, and children were still reconcentrated? (3) How many had died? (4) What was the condition of the remaining reconcentrados? And (5) What steps could be taken to provide relief? Table 4 is a compilation of the data that the provincial governors sent back to Blanco. These data, though incomplete, provide fresh information to the debate on reconcentration.[52]

The governors of Puerto Príncipe and Santiago did not report the numbers of dead due to reconcentration, but they estimated that only 6,800 people had been reconcentrated in Santiago and a mere 2,245 in Puerto Príncipe. These numbers are low because the Spanish never fully implemented the reconcentration decrees in the East. Certainly, many people fled "voluntarily" to eastern towns, and they might have escaped enumeration as official reconcentrados, but the situa-

TABLE 4. Reconcentrados in Cuba

Province	Population	Reconcen-trados	%	Fatalities	%
Pinar del Río	226,692	47,000	21%	23,495	50%
Havana	—	—	—	—	—
Matanzas	273,174	99,312	36%	25,977	26%
Santa Clara	—	140,000	—	52,997	38%
Puerto Príncipe	—	2,245	—	—	—
Santiago	—	6,800	—	—	—
Total	—	295,357	—	102,469	35%

Source: Archivo General Militar de Madrid, doc. sobre Cuba, caja 61; Sección Capitanía General de Cuba, leg. 167.

tion of such people in places like Manzanillo and Santiago differed dramatically from that of their counterparts in places like Havana and Matanzas. They were never so numerous, so they were not crowded together in vast barracks, where devastating diseases like malaria, yellow fever, and typhus did their worst. In a census of 1907, children aged ten to thirteen constituted a higher percentage of the population in the two eastern provinces than in the rest of Cuba, suggesting that people got through the war years and had children in the East. Without firm data, we can only surmise based on the low number of official reconcentrados that mortality in Santiago and Puerto Príncipe would have been quite low.

The numbers for Matanzas and especially Pinar del Río are most reliable and useful because they are broken down by municipality, age, sex, and other categories of analysis. This is owing to the zeal of provincial governors Francisco de Armas and Fabio Freyre, who seem genuinely to have been moved to do whatever they could for the reconcentrados.

The worst mortality in Pinar del Río, as elsewhere, occurred after reconcentration had officially ended in November 1897. According to Freyre, the number of reconcentrados peaked at 39,495 in November. A few months later, fewer than 16,000 remained. Freyre thought the difference, 23,495, had almost all died. He reported that it was "indisputable that the great majority of [these people] have succumbed. We cannot secure any official notice of their deaths because in most cases no formalities were observed in their burial. Sometimes they were interred where they lay." The "daily number of deaths was so high" in the fall of 1897 and the "indifference" to their disappearance so complete that a precise figure for mortality could never be found. In December 1897 and January

1898, though, Freyre knew of 5,000 people interred in the cemetery. In a separate accounting, Freyre documented 47,000 reconcentrados in the province all told. This was 21 percent of the population in Pinar del Río. If we trust Freyre, and there seems to be no reason not to, then over one-fifth of the population was reconcentrated in Pinar del Río and at least 23,495 of them died.[53]

Reconcentration began later but proceeded with greater intensity in Havana. José Bruzón, governor of Havana, submitted a horrifying report on the condition of the reconcentrados there. The moats that defended the old city had become a terrible spectacle. The municipal government had given them over to the reconcentrados, and there they lived and died by the thousands, some not even buried but becoming food to glut dogs and carrion birds. As bad as things were in the capital, Bruzón knew they were much worse in other towns. In 1897 very few places had actually bothered to set up the mandated cultivation zones. Bruzón thought that only about one-fifth of the reconcentrados had access to these lands, which they cultivated practically with their bare hands, lacking tools and animals. He reckoned that "thousands" had died in every month since the beginning of reconcentration and that 75 percent of the reconcentrados had either died or returned to the countryside. We know from other sources that as many as 120,000 people in the province of Havana were reconcentrated. If the percentage that died were similar to mortality rates in Pinar, Matanzas, and Santa Clara, then it would translate to a figure of 42,000 dead. Nevertheless, because it is mere speculation, this number is not included in the table. Bruzón gave no firm data.

The data for Matanzas province is the most complete and detailed and inspires great confidence. Francisco de Armas gave a precise figure of 25,977 dead, based on the reports of local juntas charged with ministering to the reconcentrados. This number is roughly one-fourth of the nearly 100,000 people relocated to towns and cities in Matanzas.

As depressing as the numbers are for Pinar, Havana, and Matanzas, factors related to the chronology of the fighting limited mortality there. Weyler decreed reconcentration in Pinar del Río in October 1896, but it could not be enforced until later in the year, especially after the death of Antonio Maceo in December 1896. It was then, too, that he extended the system to Havana and Matanzas. Only a few months later, and certainly by the summer of 1897, insurgent forces had been routed in all three western provinces. As a result, the insurgents could not destroy all of the cultivation zones set up to feed the reconcentrados. Some towns even produced surpluses for local trade, which became possible as Spanish forces secured roads and railroads in the spring and summer of 1897. Indeed, in parts of the West, the reconcentrados were already returning to the

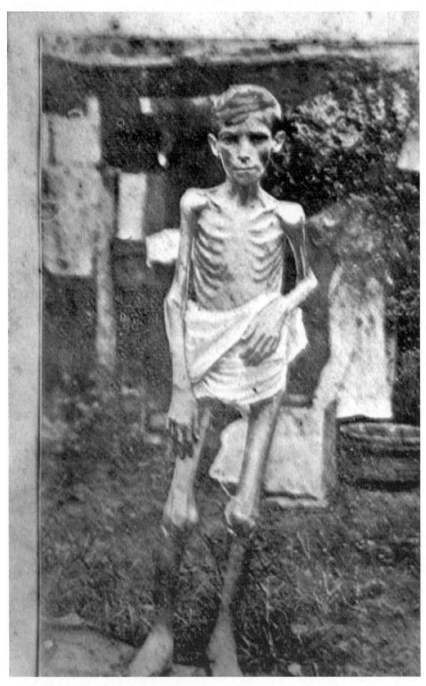

Many victims of reconcentration were children, like this boy.
Photograph used with permission of the Archivo Nacional de Cuba, Havana.

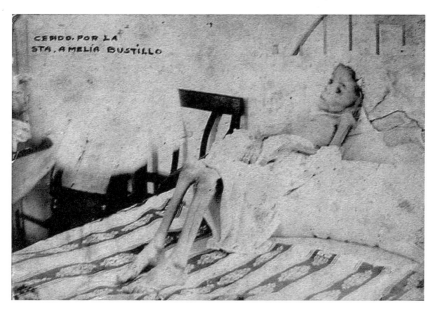

Many reconcentration victims were women, like this one, forced by the war into fortified Spanish towns and concentration camps. Photograph used with permission of the Archivo Nacional de Cuba, Havana.

countryside even before Blanco arrived in Havana in October 1897. Towns in Pinar del Río destroyed by insurgents had already been or were being rebuilt in the summer of 1897, and tobacco farms were back in normal operation in much of the province. Sugar plantations and mills in Havana and Matanzas, at least those that had not been completely demolished by the Liberation Army during the war, produced sugar again in 1897. What all of this meant was that, as bad as reconcentration was in the three westernmost provinces, the pacification of the region and the beginnings of economic recovery limited mortality to some small extent.

In the center of the island, in Santa Clara, people suffered even more than in the West. Of the 140,000 civilians who became reconcentrados, more than 52,997 of them died, according to the report of the provincial governor. This terrible mortality rate of 38 percent requires some explanation. Santa Clara became the "front line" of the war in 1897. As Spanish forces advanced eastward toward the Júcaro-Morón trocha, they carried out reconcentration behind the lines. But cultivation zones could not be set up so quickly nor defended well in a province still contested by the Cubans. In the less developed East, the insurgents controlled the situation. In the West, the Spanish did. Santa Clara occupied the

So many civilians died during reconcentration that their bodies could not be buried, as in this picture of skeletons piled high at a cemetery in Havana. Photograph used with permission of the Archivo Nacional de Cuba, Havana.

deadly zone in between, in which neither side dominated. Civilians are always the victims in such situations, and Santa Clara was no exception. For reasons we will examine in the next chapter, Weyler's Conservative backers in Spain began to lose their hold on power in August 1897, and Weyler realized that his days in Cuba were numbered. Unfortunately for the people of Santa Clara, the Spanish Liberals could not form a ministry for another two months, and in the meantime Weyler carried out reconcentration with extra rigor as he was determined to complete the pacification of the island as much as possible before he was relieved. The destruction of Santa Clara was Weyler's parting shot to Cuba.

One of the terrible ironies of reconcentration is that the worst mortality occurred after Weyler's departure, under the Liberal government charged with dismantling reconcentration. Weyler had been removed on October 9, but Ramón Blanco did not arrive in Havana until October 31. Then followed another deadly delay of two weeks before Blanco officially ordered an end to reconcentration on November 13. Blanco decreed that farmers, agricultural workers, artisans, and their families could return to their homes. Along with this measure, Blanco also redeployed Spanish troops and Cuban Volunteers to garrison dozens of previously abandoned rural properties and small towns in order to protect the reconcentrados once they returned to the countryside. Blanco believed that, with the Cuban insurrection reduced to its original strongholds in Oriente, the time had come to repopulate and rebuild rural western Cuba.

Unfortunately, returning the reconcentrados to the countryside proved to be difficult. Indeed, one year later, in October 1898, American military officials occupying Cuba complained that reconcentration was still in effect.[54] Thousands of ill and malnourished people, many of them widows and orphans, could not simply be turned out of their lodgements, however miserable they might be. They had to be cured and fed first and then reinserted gradually into whatever they could reconstruct of their previous lives. To manage this transition, Blanco ordered the creation of "protective juntas" to manage the reconcentrados. Each municipality was supposed to form a junta of local notables charged with administering emergency rations and medicines and with overseeing the construction and repair of hospitals and housing for any remaining reconcentrados who had been unable to return immediately to their former lives.

Blanco's plan to end reconcentration achieved very little at first because the "protective juntas" administering the plan had no resources. The local elites who formed the juntas, even assuming that they were willing to use their own resources to provide relief to the reconcentrados, had been tapped out during almost three years of war. Indeed, except in particular cases, the scale of the crisis precluded local solutions, and Havana had to provide the money to manage deconcentration. Letters poured in to Blanco in November complaining that people continued to die in the streets as American photographers snapped their pictures. Only a grant of money from Blanco could rectify the situation.

Finally, on November 23, Blanco got the message and ordered a credit of 100,000 pesos set aside for distribution to the provinces. Not only did the credit of 100,000 pesos come too late. Not only was the sum not nearly enough. But Blanco made it difficult to use. Juntas had to issue such detailed receipts justifying their expenses that it made helping the reconcentrados all but impossible. Finally, Blanco doled out the credit with a miserly hand, assigning portions to each province only on November 29 but holding back half of the total until December 23.

Moreover, he coupled this grant of money with a new burden: the army would cease to provide emergency rations, which had previously been the only source of food for some of the reconcentrados. In future, all relief would have to come from the juntas, drawing upon the grants allotted to them by Blanco.

One of the greatest obstacles to deconcentration continued to be the insurgents. When Blanco began to facilitate the return of peasants to the countryside it alarmed the Cubans. "Because the enemy is trying to allow the reconcentrados to leave the towns and return to the countryside," read one proclamation, the Liberation Army would have to be more strict in enforcing the "system of warfare" put in place by Gómez. Townsfolk would not be allowed to leave, unless they came all the way over to the revolutionary camp. Simply returning to their homes was not to be permitted. On the contrary, "heads of families and men over sixteen years old" would be required to plant crops in zones protected by the republic-in-arms, and if they refused, they would be "expelled" from Cuba Libre and forced back into the cities. If the Spanish would not enforce reconcentration, the insurgents would.[55]

The American press treated readers to daily fare on the subject of reconcentration. No account was too gruesome. On May 17, 1896, *New York World* correspondent James Creelman sought to slake his readers' thirst for tales of others' misery: "Blood on the roadsides, blood in the fields, blood on the doorsteps, blood, blood, blood. The old, the young, the weak, the crippled, all are butchered [by the Spanish] without mercy." Stories of Cuban slaughter comforted Americans not only by giving them solace in others' misery but also by reinforcing a familiar stereotype of the cruel, lascivious, and lazy Spaniard, historically the key antithesis to the humane, restrained, and industrious Anglo-Saxon, whose burden it was to save humanity.[56] The "black legend" of Spain, inherited from the victims of Spanish hegemony in the sixteenth and seventeenth centuries, held that Spaniards suffered from fiery temperaments, fanaticism, laziness, inconstancy, and an excess of bloodlust.[57] As the Spanish empire crumbled, Spain became the quintessential "dying nation," in Lord Salisbury's memorable phrase. She became even more capricious and dangerous, like an aging lion that has not yet admitted it is no longer the alpha male of the pride.[58] This was the Spain that undertook infant slaughter and warfare against women without a second thought. Joseph Pulitzer's *World* warned that "a new Armenia lies within eighty miles of the American coast," and the Chicago *Times-Herald* predicted that without U.S. intervention the slaughter would go on until no one was left in Cuba, because no number of civilian dead would be enough to satisfy "the thirst for blood inherent in the bull-fighting citizens of Spain."[59]

Lurid accounts of reconcentration, combined with lower newspaper prices, more photographs, and flashier typefaces, allowed Pulitzer to increase subscriptions to the World from 400,000 in 1895 to 822,804 in 1898. William Randolph Hearst employed the same techniques and stories to raise the circulation of his New York Journal even more dramatically, from 150,000 in 1896 to almost 800,000 in 1898. Major dailies in Atlanta, Boston, Chicago, New Orleans, St. Louis, San Francisco, Washington, and other American cities purchased and reprinted what the so-called yellow press in New York ran. As a result, day after day, Americans received a consistent and relentless tale of genocide in Cuba. It would have been hard to live in America and not have a very clear, though false, idea about reconcentration.

The yellow press loved to single out Weyler. He was such an easy target. An arrogant martinet, Weyler seemed to be the embodiment of the haughty Spaniard. Weyler's personality was not suited to handling questions from the press. Asked for statements and explanations, Weyler was likely to reply with brutal and hateful quips, as if to uphold his reputation for toughness and cutoff conversation. Weyler could not hide his distaste for reporters. At their best, they revealed his notorious womanizing, poked fun at his diminutive stature, or gave him nicknames like "General Almost Pacified." At their worst, they undermined the security of the Spanish state. Weyler's dislike for reporters was notorious, and we should not be surprised that the press returned his loathing in equal measure.

In fairness to the press, Weyler had made it difficult to gain anything other than a Cuban perspective on events. He attempted to create a news blackout by imposing rigid controls over telegraph communications and restricting the presence of journalists who wanted to see the war from the inside. This ensured that only the Cuban version of events reached the American public. The handful of reporters who went to Cuba to gain a firsthand experience of the war had to seek out Cuban hosts. Journalists like Grover Flint marched with Gómez, García, or Maceo, and not with the Spanish, in part because Weyler gave them no choice in the matter. And they filed stories by telegraph in Jamaica or Florida from the longhand notes they smuggled out because wiring articles directly from Cuba past Spanish censorship was impossible. What they wrote reflected their frustration with official Spain and their better treatment by the Cuban insurgents. In this way, Weyler's press controls backfired.

What American reporters wrote about reconcentration came mostly from Cuban sources. Cuban patriots were not only superb practitioners of guerrilla warfare, they were also skilled propagandists. Officials of the Cuban provisional government provided information on Spanish human rights abuses to anyone who would listen, especially to journalists. The political bias of such information was obvious, but at the time no one seemed to mind. Few American reporters understood Spanish, and even fewer wanted to go to Cuba. Given these limitations, journalists could hardly pursue leads and check facts with any rigor. Most filed whatever they were given by agents of the Cuban republic-in-arms and were content to call it journalism. Indeed, many reporters relied on briefings at the so-called Peanut Club, where Horatio Rubens, Tomás Estrada Palma, and other Cuban leaders in New York City issued daily press releases on Cuban victories and Spanish atrocities.[60]

Officials of the Cuban republic-in-arms, both in Cuba and in the United States, had grasped the crucial role that the press and world opinion would play in the outcome of the war, while Weyler and the Spanish regime clearly had not. Where the Cubans appeared solicitous and eager to talk, Weyler seemed haughty and elusive. Inevitably, Cuban perspectives came to dominate public perceptions of reconcentration around the world.

Sometimes the journalists were themselves members of the Cuban junta in New York. The *Daily Inter-Ocean* printed a piece by Salvador Cisneros-Betancourt, who asked his American audience: "Will not the continuance of [Spain's] supremacy in Cuba mean the perpetuation of medieval traditions . . . and the upholding of all that to men of the nineteenth century is debased and barbaric?"[61] Another member of the junta was given space in the *World* to describe his "impartial" account of the way Spanish troops "inhumanly hacked" Cuban patriots into pieces "in the fury of fiendish vindictiveness."[62]

Henry Sylvester Scovel had a greater impact on American public opinion than any other journalist. His most famous contributions to public discourse in the United States were the articles he published in the *World* on November 21 and 30, 1896, summarizing several months of fieldwork in Cuba. Spain's "settled purpose" in carrying out reconcentration, according to Scovel, was the "extermination of the Cuban people under the cloak of civilized warfare." Scovel captivated his audience by detailing atrocities that the Spanish "dons" committed against civilians, especially against women and children. Scovel deployed the rhetoric of human rights and the techniques of yellow journalism to enthrall readers, sell papers, and prepare public opinion in the United States for war all at the same time.[63]

Not every American journalist produced stories favorable to the Cuban cause. George Bronson Rea, after spending time with Maceo and Gómez, concluded that most of the stories of Cuban victories and Spanish atrocities had been fabricated. However, Rea's case was unusual. He worked for the *New York Herald*, one of the few papers to maintain some critical distance from official Cuban propaganda. And even the *Herald* would not print some of Rea's material because it cast doubt on so much that was exciting, horrible, and profitable. In the end, Rea had to publish his findings in a book, where it had no impact on American opinion or foreign policy.[64]

Foreign journalists, too, injected a note of skepticism and doubt about the Cuban reports. The *Times* of London had placed a man in Cuba who confessed that "[n]ewspapers in the United States publish repeatedly stories of such atrocious barbarities perpetrated under the Spanish regime, and committed by Spanish officers, that the Spaniards would be deservedly placed outside the pale of civilization if one-half of the charges formulated were true. I cannot obtain any proof to substantiate the wild talk indulged in with regard to these barbarous acts. . . . As for the charges made against General Weyler personally, they are too ridiculous to merit serious attention." The "wild talk" suggested that Spanish troops strip-searched Cuban women, raped them, killed their babies, tortured and murdered their husbands in cold blood, and shackled the survivors in dungeons and imprisoned them behind barbed wire, where food and medicine could be denied them. Weyler was supposed to be especially fond of rape and torture. Most American investigative journalists confirmed these and other practices reported to them by the Cubans. Reconcentration was mass murder on a gigantic scale carried out deliberately by the satanic Weyler and his Spanish demons.[65]

We can glimpse in detail an example of the way Cuban patriots fed American journalists doctored accounts of Spanish "atrocities" in an investigation carried out by the Spanish foreign minister into a sinister story that hit the American presses in late 1897. An American newsman reported that the commander of the garrison of Nuevitas had set himself up as a little dictator and had declared it a capital offense for anyone to leave their homes. When people left in order to procure food, he had them shot. One woman in Puerto Príncipe seemed to have been shot under such circumstances, sparking a protest by several foreign consuls in Havana and raising a scandal in Madrid. In the mind of the American public, this became twisted into the belief that no one, anywhere, at any time could step outside without risking death. The image of the Cuban people furtively going out for a breath of air, hiding around corners from Spanish sentries, was a pleasing one to the American public. These were people who clearly needed liberating. The real story, unearthed after an investigation by Foreign Minister Segismundo Moret and Ramón Blanco was less press worthy. The garrison commander in Nuevitas had declared it a capital offense for civilians to leave their homes during an attack by insurgents, a routine provision of martial law. The attack never occurred, and the penalty was never imposed. By then, however, an incredulous American public believed that the Spanish were capable of anything.[66]

In another example, Senator Roger Mills publicly accused the Spanish of capturing and murdering Antonio Maceo and Pancho Gómez, despite all evidence to the contrary. As we have seen, the two illustrious Cubans died in battle, and the Spanish soldiers present did not even recognize their bodies, leaving them behind for the Cubans to recover. Nevertheless, even after the details became known, most of the American public remained convinced that the Spanish had murdered the Bronze Titan and the young son of Máximo Gómez.[67]

Cuban patriots in New York were tireless in their efforts to persuade Americans to intervene in Cuba. In one of hundreds of examples, Ricardo Delgado wrote a long piece for the *New York World*, which served as a conduit for Cuban propaganda in the United States, on August 23, 1896. Delgado described how he narrowly escaped when one of Maceo's camps in Pinar del Río was overrun by the Spanish. He explained that even with 80,000 [sic] men under arms, the Liberation Army could not stop the Spanish from murdering civilians. He knew of at least 10,000 who had been murdered. "They have been shot down in their houses or by the roadside and their bodies left to the birds of prey." He knew personally of the assaulting of many women, "even young girls of ten, by these brutal, bloodthirsty Spanish troops." He told of how Weyler forced the wife of an insurgent to disrobe, and, how, with his riding boots still on, he mounted her, spurring her flesh as he forced her to crawl on all fours. Later he turned her and other captured Cuban women over to the common troops, who used them until they died, mutilating their bodies after death. "God forbid the continuation of the hellish atrocities that are now going on daily and hourly in Cuba. . . . Will not the people of America help us?"[68]

American officials were just as dependent on Cuban sources of information as members of the American press were. The Cuban junta in Manhattan had close ties to various figures in the government, especially Wilkensen Call and William Sulzer, House representatives from Florida and New York, and Don Cameron and Henry Cabot Lodge, senators from Pennsylvania and Massachusetts. A Cuban legation at the Raleigh Hotel in Washington had a bankroll of $1 million and exerted all of its effort to lobby Congress and the administration.[69]

One of the Cubans' most important allies was U.S. consul Fitzhugh Lee. The nephew of Robert E. Lee, a former Confederate cavalry commander, and the ex-governor of Virginia, Fitzhugh Lee was an indispensable political asset. This made his ignorance of Spain, Cuba, and the Spanish language forgivable and even useful, especially when there were so many English-speaking Cuban field officers happy to keep Lee up to date on the reconcentration problem.[70] Despising everything about Spain and Spanish culture, Lee was no friend to Weyler, who treated Lee coldly.[71] To Lee's queries about civilian suffering, Weyler responded that "everything is fair in war," a line of argument designed to anger rather than court Lee.[72] It is not surprising that Lee — and every other American in Cuba — turned exclusively to Cuban sources for intelligence about reconcentration. This ensured that Washington had the propaganda tools it needed to sell a war in Cuba to the American public.

Summing up what we know about reconcentration, the available data, summarized in Table 4 above, indicate that 295,357 Cubans were reconcentrated, not counting those in the province of Havana, which supplied no data. It is certain that if we had solid data for the province of Havana, the total number of reconcentrados would be higher. We know from the numbers on mortality in Matanzas, Las Villas, and Pinar del Río that 102,469 reconcentrados died. The governors of Havana, Puerto Príncipe, and Santiago provided no firm data. If they had — especially if the missing data for Havana were included — the total number of reconcentrados who died in Cuba might approach a figure close to the undoctored estimates based on the censuses, as well as those worked out by Jordi Maluquer de Motes, who concluded that between 155,000 and 170,000 of the reconcentrados died.

Although not quite the 300,000 or 400,000 dead of legend, the figure of 155,000 to 170,000 civilian casualties is enormous, amounting to about 10 percent of the total Cuban population of around 1,700,000. While it is true that Weyler was neither the first nor the last person to relocate civilians in wartime, and while it is true that the Cuban revolutionaries, among others, must share the blame for reconcentration and the extension of warfare to the civilian population, Weyler's enterprise was unprecedented at the time for its scale, intensity, and efficiency. In later years, Weyler and his defenders liked to point out that, with the war in Cuba barely ended, the British imposed a brutal form of reconcentration on the Boer population in the Transvaal and Free Orange State and "everyone thought it natural and did not make the least protest."[73] The same thing happened in the Philippines, where Americans herded civilians into fortified camps to choke off a movement against the American occupation, causing mortality worse than anything that had happened under the Spanish, with only a murmur of criticism. Indeed, this may help to explain why, in 1902, the U.S. Congress officially absolved Weyler of any wrongdoing, as if it were in its power to do so. We may add that in Vietnam the French had their *agrovilles* in the 1940s, which became the Americans' "strategic hamlets" in the 1960s. Many similar examples could be cited. The point is that Weyler's reconcentration formed part of a long tradition of counterinsurgency warfare, and it is incorrect to credit him with any particular military genius, even an evil one. On the other hand, the Spanish administration of Cánovas, and their servant in Cuba, Weyler, conducted a campaign of warfare against civilians in Cuba that led to the death of some 10 percent of the population. That others contributed to it and that similar examples of atrocious military practices in other countries can be cited in no way exculpates the responsibility of the Spanish regime. Sometimes "black legends" contain some truth, and when they do, they must be faced squarely.

Reconcentration worked to undermine the Cuban insurgency, but it backfired by creating an outcry in the United States against Spanish barbarism. When a state — especially a populist republic — embarks on foreign military adventures, it is essential to prepare the ground by clothing war in the language of human rights and a civilizing mission. Reconcentration gave the American jingoes the tool they needed to do this. As a result, the American public went to war in Cuba confident that its cause was righteous. Even so, American intervention was not inevitable. It required an unforeseen cataclysm in Spain to make that happen.

History sometimes turns on the unforeseeable actions of individuals. This injects a complexity into human affairs that frustrates scholars who want to reduce human experience to a predictable, manipulable, and safe social science. This complexity delights historians, however, and it serves an important function. It reminds us that we are agents of our own destiny, free to be angels or demons.

The unpredictable event that helped to produce Spain's defeat in Cuba was the assassination of Antonio Cánovas del Castillo, Spain's great Conservative statesman. In 1874 Cánovas had written the seventeen-year-old Alfonso's *Sandhurst Manifesto*, the founding document of the Bourbon Restoration in Spain. It was he who crafted the Spanish constitution and he who created the ingenious system of electoral prestidigitation known as the turno pacífico. Cánovas restored order to Spain and inaugurated the most stable parliamentary government the country had ever seen. European and American statesmen held him in high esteem. Bismarck, for example, considered Cánovas one of the few people with whom he could really have a conversation.[1]

Like Bismarck, but on a smaller stage, Cánovas used foreign adventures to bind fractious Spaniards together and solve political crises at home. In 1860, for example, he exulted over the sharp, decisive victory against Morocco, not so much because he was interested in the occupation of Tetuán, but because it generated, if only briefly, a sense of national community and mission in Spain. Cánovas opposed Spain's withdrawal from the joint Franco-Spanish attempt to seize Mexico in the 1860s, and he fought the decision to abandon the Dominican Republic in 1865, despite the fact that both the Mexicans and the Dominicans had made it quite clear that the Spanish presence would not be tolerated. On the face of it, this intransigence appears foolish: Cánovas argued that once Spain committed its armies to a foreign adventure, sounding the retreat would damage Spanish prestige so badly that it would prove more costly in the long run than investing additional resources in salvaging the situation. In a famous speech before the Spanish Congress on March 29, 1865, Cánovas expressed himself on the subject of the Dominican war: "What we cannot do is brandish our sword, wave the flag, and go into combat against a miserable army of half savages on the beaches of America, and return defeated, leaving our reputation and our glory in a shambles." That, he said, would send a signal to the world that Spain was in its death throes, and the vultures in Great Britain and America would not be long in descending on other Spanish possessions and even, perhaps, on Spain itself. Above all, he feared that any signs of weakness would encourage the Cubans to claim their independence. In this, at least, he was right.[2]

Part of Cánovas's intransigence stemmed from his metaphysical nationalism. He believed that "nations were the work of God" and not a human invention. To allow anything to threaten the power of Spain, mother of nations, would therefore be a crime against God. Ironically, although Cánovas loved Spain, he did not seem to think much of Spaniards. The Spaniard was "radically ungovernable, essentially anarchic," and needed a firm guiding hand. For this reason, the Bourbon monarchy had to be defended and preserved, for to do otherwise was to risk Spain's integrity. A check in Cuba, Morocco, or the Philippines might have dire consequences in the Peninsula, for it might encourage people in Catalonia or the Basque provinces to seek greater autonomy.

As prime minister in 1891, Cánovas gave a speech before the Congress of Deputies in which he promised that if Cuban insurrectos rose up, his government would fight "to the last man and the last peseta," a phrase that later came to describe the unbending position of the whole Spanish operation in Cuba. In opposition to the Liberal government between 1892 and 1895, Cánovas helped to scuttle Maura's reform bill, arguing that no concessions should be offered to the Cubans until they had proven their adhesion and loyalty to Spain. Given all of this, when Cánovas assumed power in the spring of 1895, it surprised nobody that he adopted a hard-line policy toward Cuba and brooked no discussion of negotiations until and unless military victory were secured. Cánovas was the power behind Weyler, and everyone knew that Cuba Española stood or fell with him.[3]

In domestic affairs, Cánovas also followed a hard-line policy of opposition to reform. He treated Basque and Catalonian nationalists who desired greater autonomy for their regions as if they were terrorists bent on destroying Spain. And he had nothing but scorn for the demands of working people. In 1883 the Liberal government uncovered an anarchist conspiracy in Andalucía, dubbed the "Black Hand," that was aimed, so said alarmists, at overthrowing Christian civilization. Cánovas drew a dubious political lesson from the Black Hand episode: Liberal tolerance of opposition elements had come dangerously close to allowing anarchists to destroy Spain. When Cánovas returned to power in 1884, no one was surprised that he cracked down on all dissent from workers and peasants.

Cánovas was an elitist at heart, with a deep mistrust of the popular classes. "I am profoundly convinced," he wrote, "that inequality comes from God, that it is part of our nature." Elites were utterly different from the masses. Their superiority manifested itself in their "actions, intelligence, and even morality." Consequently, "intelligent minorities will always govern the world, one way or another." The equation of wealth with intelligence and fitness to rule was absolute. As one of Cánovas's friends in the government summed it up in an address to the Congress, "Poverty, sirs, is a sign of stupidity." It was Cánovas's mission in domestic politics to keep poor, stupid men from ruling. God had gifted man with inequality, "the great treasure of humanity," and the state should never intervene to disrupt God's design. The difficulties that faced working people could be met by two means only: private charity and public repression. From Cánovas, quite obviously, workers could expect no help.[4] So it was that working people in Spain hated Cánovas as much as Cuban patriots did. Laborers knew him simply as "the Monster," a nickname that followed him abroad, especially among working-class audiences in Cuba.

In 1897 Cánovas's uncompromising politics in Cuba and Spain proved his undoing when an Italian anarchist named Michele Angiolillo, aided by Spanish workers and Cuban patriots, assassinated him. The forces in Spain and Cuba that had struggled for 2½ years to preserve Cuba Española went immediately on the defensive, opening the door to a revival of the Cuban independence movement and the intervention of the United States. This chapter will tell the story of Angiolillo and Cánovas and examine the political fallout from this assassination, which shaped the fate of Spain, Cuba, and the United States to an extent not often appreciated. The tale will serve to remind us that Cuban independence required the intervention of many people, and that it was not inevitable but the result, at least in part, of historical accidents.

Spain went through a difficult time in the 1890s.[5] The long world depression that began in 1872 affected Spain less than countries with more advanced capitalist economies, such as Germany. Indeed, the 1870s and 1880s were relatively prosperous years for most Spaniards. But in the early 1890s a sharp decline in prices at the end of a long deflationary cycle generated a crisis that Spaniards could not escape. Low prices caused great suffering around the world, especially among farmers and small manufacturers. As a result, some of Spain's best trading partners adopted protective tariffs to rescue their own industries and farms, and this resulted in a fall in the demand for Spanish goods. Even the things Spain produced well, like olive oil and wine, lost market share. Heavy industry, textile plants, and other manufacturing concerns, which were inefficient and uncompetitive to begin with, lost so many orders that they had to close down production and release workers.[6]

This crisis had a particularly devastating impact on industrious Catalonia. Moreover, economic troubles became political problems there, because the turno had ceased to work very well in Barcelona and other industrial cities in Catalonia. Traditional elites — the caciques who ran the game of political corruption in Spain — had no hold over the industrial workforce of Catalonia. Having developed their own rudimentary organizational life in cooperatives and other fraternal societies, workers had begun to vote and think as they pleased, not as they were instructed. A vigorous press, including papers oriented toward the Left, such as El Socialista and La Solidaridad, revealed the corruption of Spanish politics and made the hypocrisy of the whole electoral system apparent to workers, more and more of whom were becoming literate. Some concluded that they would have to look for other avenues of political expression. They rejected the system of parliamentary democracy altogether, and in the context of the desperate economic situation of the 1890s, they attempted to effect political change through direct action: striking, demonstrating, engaging in street violence.

Some of them became anarchists. Anarchism got its start as an organized movement in Spain during the chaotic years from 1868 to 1874. Because anarchism was illegal, we have no reliable membership figures. The anarchist union, the Confederación Nacional de Trabajadores (CNT), eventually became the largest organization of workers in Spain, before Franco dismantled working-class institutions in 1939. Almost immediately after its founding in 1910, the CNT had a membership of 800,000, suggesting that vast reservoirs of anarchist support existed among workers before 1910. The actual numbers of anarchists will never be known, but numbers did not matter that much anyway because anarchists did not particularly count on democratic processes that rewarded the exercise of suffrage in national elections.

What anarchists believed and what they practiced had to do, above all else, with practical and local matters. Anarchists organized unions, strikes, boycotts, and other actions to further workers' interests when no one else would or could. Unlike socialism, anarchism did not identify with the "working class" as such but with all poor working people, including agricultural laborers and peasants who owned or leased small plots of land, small artisans and shopkeepers, students, schoolteachers, and many others. These occupational groups far outnumbered the industrial workforce in Spain, because industrial capitalism had not been thoroughly implanted there. Socialism's close identification with the industrial proletariat and its relegation of artisans and peasants to the past made it seem irrelevant to many Spanish workers. Anarchism, in contrast, had a less exclusive vision, and this made it more appealing in Spain.

Even the industrial workforce in Spain looked different from its counterpart in more developed countries. Spanish workers labored in smaller shops and factories. They lived in the midst of a country still overwhelmingly rural, where personal relationships and local needs and identities still ordered their lives. These realities in Spain made it difficult for workers to organize for any national purpose. The German Socialist Party's mastery of national electoral politics in the decades before World War I had no counterpart in Spain. Thus, the emphasis placed by socialists and republicans on running candidates and contesting elections did not attract working people as much as it might have or as much as the anarchist attention to local issues did.[7]

The grand philosophical and spiritual doctrines of anarchism also attracted Spaniards in ways socialism could not. Anarchist intellectuals had a Rousseauian faith in "Natural Man." They valued and trusted the spontaneous and untutored impulses of the average person. "Authenticity" became for them a critical measure of worth. Cosmopolitan behavior might be fine for bourgeois or authoritarian socialists, but not for libertarian anarchists.

The anarchist glorification of individualism and spontaneity particularly resonated with Spaniards because these were already core Spanish values. Like the conquistadores who escaped the constraint of the state to conquer a new world, like the guerrillas who fought Napoleon, like proverbial Don Quixotes, anarchists believed in the absolute liberty and dignity of the individual and were suspicious of state-led enterprises and initiatives. Anarchists believed that no collective project for future worldly betterment could ever justify sacrificing the integrity of the individual and placing him in thrall to the state. This was not that different from the Catholic belief in the irreducible centrality of the soul in the drama of life. Anarchists despised the church, but that does not mean they were not powerfully affected, like everyone else in Spain, by the ancient Catholic culture of the country. For people who lacked the means to take collective action on a national scale and in desperate need of immediate solutions to problems of subsistence, the anarchist emphasis on the individual sounded better than the messages of self-sacrifice and slow transformation voiced by worldly middle-class reformers and socialists, and it resonated with their Catholic souls. In short, anarchism seemed tailor-made for Spaniards, and it became the most important working-class movement in Spain in the late nineteenth century.

Anarchists usually rejected parliamentary democracy. They did not run candidates for office. Often, they did not vote. In any case, they knew that the police would arrest an avowed anarchist candidate, and, come election day, the caciques would "lose" votes for politicians sympathetic to anarchist causes. So a small minority of anarchists turned to violence, in accord with their profound philosophical attachment to individual, spontaneous action. They believed in something they called "propaganda by deed." An anarchist assassinated a public figure. Then, if he was courageous enough, he waited to be arrested, tortured, tried, and executed. His purpose, during trial, was to use the courtroom as a stage, to testify publicly to the misery of the masses, and to propose anarchist remedies. Giving their bodies up for torture and execution, anarchists sought to unmask the real nature of government, to show that it was founded on force and violence rather than on the consent of the governed.

In the 1890s anarchist violence reached a new stage in a series of spectacular assassinations and bombings in Barcelona. In 1893 a young laborer named Paulino Pallás tossed a bomb at Martínez Campos as he participated in a religious procession. Pallás did not attempt to escape, seeking instead a martyr's death, which he received, though his bomb only injured Martínez Campos slightly. Moments before he died by strangulation, a more excruciating form of death than either shooting or hanging, he issued a prophetic warning: "The vengeance will be terrible."[8]

Pallás was right. A month later his friend Santiago Salvador avenged Pallás's death by throwing two bombs into a crowded theater, killing sixteen and wounding many more. Unlike Pallás, Salvador fled the scene and was not arrested until January 1894. In the meantime, however, a panicky Madrid placed Weyler in charge of Catalonia and gave him a license to hunt anarchists. He declared martial law and arrested hundreds of workers. In the dungeons of Montjuich, after suffering the most hideous tortures, several of them confessed to Salvador's crime. Even after the real author of the theater bombing was brought to justice, the earlier detainees were kept in prison, and six of them were shot. Like Cánovas, Weyler was not too discriminating when it came to working-class radicals.

On June 7, 1896, after two years of relative calm, with Weyler packed off to Cuba, a French anarchist named Girault tossed a bomb into a religious procession as it wound its way down Cambios Nuevos Street in Barcelona. Six people died, and many more were wounded. The author of the crime fled to France and then to Argentina. But Cánovas did not allow the absence of the real criminal to stop him. He ordered the mass arrest of workers in Barcelona. The police threw dozens of workers into the dungeons of Montjuich, which again echoed with the cries of the tortured. People lucky enough to have attended the Olympic diving competition in 1992 enjoyed a spectacular view of Barcelona from the slopes of Montjuich, fitted out with pools and stadium seating, all surrounded by museums and parks. A hundred years earlier, however, the name Montjuich stood for barbarism, a place of pain and horror for the poor men and women unlucky enough to be sent there. The detainees charged with participating in the bombing at Cambios Nuevos were kept for days without food or water. Their jailers later fed them unprepared salt cod to make their thirst all the more unbearable. They stripped the detainees and forced them to remain awake, marching about their cells while holding their leg weights. Then after they collapsed into unconsciousness, they awoke them by burning their senseless bodies with hot irons. The torturers pulled out the workers' toenails, crushed their genitals and feet, used diabolic devices to compress their jaws and craniums, passed electricity through their bodies, and snuffed out cigars on their martyred flesh.[9]

By December they had their confessions. However, so many had proclaimed themselves the author of the bombing that the prosecutor initially had to ask for twenty-eight death sentences and fifty-nine life sentences. Even the military tribunal judging the case could not accept the absurdity of so many perpetrators. It handed down five sentences of death, which were carried out on May 4, 1897. Another twenty men received jail terms. The remaining sixty-three prisoners were absolved but deported nonetheless.[10]

The deportees were allowed to emigrate to France or other European countries, where they instigated a propaganda campaign against the Spanish regime. Articles appeared in the world press detailing the "crimes of Montjuich." Fernando Tarrida del Mármol, a Cuban-born anarchist and one of the victims of the Montjuich terror, wrote an influential book, Les inquisiteurs d'Espagne (Montjuich, Cuba, Philippines), which made a large audience familiar with the barbarism of the Spanish government. Already under pressure internationally for its treatment of Cuban civilians, Madrid lost whatever goodwill remained abroad. The martyrs of Montjuich appeared before packed meeting halls in Britain, the United States, and elsewhere to reveal their scars to sympathetic audiences. They were the living signs of Spanish barbarism. And they were celebrities. People witnessed with mute, appalled, horror the marks of torture. Then the silence gave way to cries for revenge.

Delegates of the Cuban revolution active in Europe sheltered the anarchist workers. Anarchism was almost as important in Cuba as it was in Spain. Cuban anarchists had not always gotten along with the separatists, but Martí's collaboration with the workers in Florida and the arrival of Weyler in Cuba had helped to change that. Anarchists the world over knew of Weyler's repression of the workers of Barcelona in 1894. To them, he was "the Butcher," and they hated him almost as much as they hated the man behind him, Cánovas, "the Monster." By 1896 the many serious differences that existed between Cuban bourgeois patriots and Cuban anarchists were subsumed in their common loathing of Weyler and Cánovas.[11]

In Paris, the Cuban Revolutionary Party (PRC) branch set up by the Puerto Rican patriot Dr. Ramón Betances took in Spanish anarchist exiles, but the French government, itself the object of anarchist violence, soon drove them out. Still, Betances helped to organize a public campaign in Paris against Spanish barbarism and backwardness, always favorite topics in France. The London Committee of the PRC, founded by Francisco J. Cisneros and José Zayas Usatorres in 1895, organized a mass meeting in Hyde Park. Following this, a group of British anarchists calling themselves "The Spanish Atrocities Committee" organized a giant meeting in Trafalgar Square on May 30, 1897. The purpose had become not only to condemn the tortures at Montjuich but to bring pressure to bear against the Spanish regime in Cuba. In this way, all around the world, a kind of "popular front" against Spain arose that brought together workers and middle-class sympathizers for the Cuban cause.[12]

The United States was not immune to this movement. People who had not seemed to care in the least when the U.S. government killed anarchists on trumped-up charges following the Haymarket Square incident in 1886 found themselves in a furious rage at the barbarism of the Spanish government in Barcelona. In Philadelphia, the noted American anarchist and feminist Voltairine de Cleyre issued a pamphlet titled *The Modern Inquisition in Spain*, which aimed, among other things, to convince the American public of the need to intervene against the Spanish regime in Cuba. She sold every copy printed. In New York, Emma Goldman and other American anarchists organized a demonstration in front of the Spanish embassy. Asked whether she thought someone should kill the Spanish diplomats in the embassy, she replied: "No, I don't believe that any Spanish diplomat in America is important enough to kill, but if I were in Spain now, I would kill Cánovas del Castillo."[13]

Michele Angiolillo was thinking the same thing. A handsome, intelligent, reserved young man of twenty-seven from southern Italy, Angiolillo had fled the country of his birth in 1896, pursued on a charge of writing subversive literature. From France, he went to Switzerland, where he again attracted the police. He then made his way to Barcelona, where he stayed with local anarchists, who gave him all the gory details of recent events at Montjuich. In 1897 Angiolillo went to London, where he worked in a printing establishment and resided in the home of a Spanish anarchist in exile, Jaime Vidal. Angiolillo formed part of the audience at Trafalgar Square when the martyrs of Montjuich paraded themselves before the sympathetic crowd. Later that night, at Vidal's place, two of the victims of Montjuich, Juan Bautista Ollé and Francisco Gana, showed their wounds again and spoke in intimate details of their ordeals. Angiolillo suddenly stood up, and without a word, he left the house. No one ever saw him alive again.

Angiolillo made his way to the Paris office of Ramón Betances, the leading figure of the PRC in Europe. They met twice to discuss a plan to assassinate Cánovas. According to an account by Betances, Angiolillo initially wanted to kill the child-king or the boy's mother, the queen regent, and it was Betances who convinced him to make Cánovas the target. Although there is no firm evidence for the frequently repeated story that has Betances supplying Angiolillo with 1,000 francs (an enormous sum for a one-way, third-class train ticket to Spain), the connection between the anarchist and the Puerto Rican patriot is firmly established. Angiolillo left Betances's office on July 30, 1897, and took a train to San Sebastián.[14]

Cánovas had just left that beautiful city on the Bay of Biscay after holding a conference with the queen regent. Cánovas took the mountain road inland to Mondragón, a little town in the Basque interior, home to the spa of Sánta Agueda, where thermal waters and fresh mountain air rejuvenated weary rich men and women up from Madrid's hot summer. Angiolillo followed him. He checked in as a guest of the spa on August 4 and attracted some attention as a foreigner with less than regal attire. Then everyone, including the security detail guarding Cánovas, made the mistake of forgetting about the shabby Italian stranger. On Sunday, August 8, 1897, as Cánovas sat down just after the noon hour to read the newspaper on a bench outside the spa's hotel, Angiolillo approached stealthily and fired a pistol at point-blank range into his right temple. The bullet passed through his brain and exited out his left temple. Angiolillo fired again into his victim's chest. Already dead, Cánovas fell forward. Angiolillo fired one more shot into the back of "the Monster" before police and Cánovas's wife arrived on the scene. Angiolillo surrendered his arm, saying: "I have done my duty and I am at peace. I have avenged my brothers of Montjuich."[15]

The death of Cánovas dramatically altered the political situation in Spain and Cuba. The Liberal Party under Praxedes Sagasta had been in opposition since the spring of 1895 and itched to return to power. Liberals and Conservatives had only minor differences between them in normal times. However, the Cuban war and the looming threat from the United States created an abnormal situation and exerted an interesting influence on Spain's evolving two-party system. The parties began to engage in a genuine foreign-policy debate, as if it might matter in coming elections. Indeed, the growth in Barcelona and other cities of a republican movement led by the popular demagogue Alejandro Lerroux, together with a press campaign by republicans, socialists, and others critical of the war effort, had begun to push the Liberal Party to the Left, at least in terms of its foreign policy, in 1896 and 1897. The Liberals never went so far as some radical critics of the government. For example, they never advocated unilateral withdrawal from Cuba and independence for the island, but they did borrow the language and tone of the populist critique as a way to distinguish themselves from the Conservatives. They demonized Weyler as a butcher who needed to be removed in the name of humanity, echoing and supporting the critique of Weyler emanating from Cuba and the United States.[16]

In the spring of 1897, the old man of the Liberal Party, Praxedes Sagasta, had finally taken off his gloves in the fight against Cánovas. Dropping his earlier tendency to outdo Cánovas's call to fight to the last peseta and the last drop of Spanish blood, he attacked the Conservative hawks in the Congress of Deputies. On May 19, 1897, Sagasta proposed an alternative course of action. "After having sent 200,000 men and having spilled so much blood, we are masters in Cuba only of the ground on which our soldiers stand." Perhaps, he suggested, it was time to use a carrot instead of a stick. Perhaps it was time to negotiate. On July 19, Segismundo Moret, a well-known economist, Liberal light, and inveterate enemy of Weyler and reconcentration, informed the Spanish Congress that if the Liberal Party were brought in to govern, it would move immediately to introduce a statute granting Cuba autonomy. With the death of Cánovas, everyone expected the Liberals to assume power and make good on these pledges. Thus, the stage had been set by Angiolillo for a unilateral Spanish peace initiative.[17]

The Cubans followed events in Spain closely. Moret's speech and the death of Cánovas generated renewed enthusiasm among the insurgents, who mounted an impressive offensive in August 1897.[18] Calixto García took 1,800 men and struck at the town of Las Tunas. The small Spanish garrison of seventy-nine men plus local Volunteers possessed a few antiquated field pieces that were ruined after fifty shots. García, in contrast, had new cannon and machine guns from the United States worked by American gunners. On August 30, overcome by superior firepower and weight of numbers, Las Tunas surrendered.[19] The loss of Las Tunas, a town of 4,000 inhabitants with no strategic importance, was not in itself a great material blow, but Weyler, in the waning days of his command, understood the moral implications. García had the pro-Spanish Volunteers at Las Tunas summarily executed, and support for the Spanish in the area, tenuous already, evaporated. The loss of Las Tunas erased whatever prestige Weyler still had.

Sagasta's Liberals formally assumed power on October 4, 1897, with Moret taking over the colonial ministry. The first thing the new government did was relieve Weyler, Moret announcing the news on October 9, 1897. Sagasta reversed everything Cánovas had done. A new slogan became attached to the Liberals, "not a man nor a peseta more," the reverse of the one Cánovas had adopted.[20] Cuban patriots had cause to rejoice. Weyler had almost destroyed the Cuban independence movement, along with a great part of the Cuban population. Weyler's replacement, Ramón Blanco, promised to take a gentler approach. He ended reconcentration almost immediately, though the suffering of the reconcentrados continued for months and even worsened for a while, as we have seen.

Blanco stopped sending columns out in search of the enemy and removed troops from forward positions in the hope of avoiding skirmishes that might impede peace negotiations with the Cubans.

Washington had done its part to ensure that the Liberals did not renege on their promises with regard to Cuba. The McKinley administration stepped up its pressure on the Spanish government in a way it had not done while Cánovas was in charge. McKinley, through U.S. ambassador Stewart L. Woodford, offered America's "good offices" to convince the Cubans to lay down their arms, if Spain would agree to a series of demands. If Spain ended reconcentration, pardoned the rebels, and conceded a significant degree of self-government to Cubans, then the situation might be resolved peacefully, and a Spanish-American war might be avoided. And so Spain did everything the Americans demanded. With Cánovas gone, it is what the Liberals wanted to try anyway.[21]

In November the Liberal government promulgated a new constitution granting autonomy to Cuba. A government took formal power in Cuba on January 1, 1898. Along with President José María Gálvez, there were secretaries of justice, treasury, education, public works, and agriculture and commerce. Spain still appointed the captain general, with control over military, naval, and foreign affairs, as well as veto power over the work of the Cuban government. Perhaps most significantly, final approval of the budget and taxes lay in the hands of the Spanish Congress. Autonomy had strict limits. Nevertheless, the new autonomy government represented a danger to the separatists. Elections scheduled for May 1898 promised to give Cuba's autonomous regime added legitimacy. What if the United States were satisfied with the outcome of the election? And what of the rest of the world? Would the insurgents find themselves redefined as terrorists and bandits fighting against a legitimately elected regime?

The Cuban separatists understood the danger, and they responded quickly to Spanish initiatives with their own reforms. The republic-in-arms drafted a new constitution eliminating Gómez's independent power and placing the conduct of the war firmly in the hands of civilians. They did this to convince critics that an independent Cuba would not slide into a military dictatorship under Gómez. Tomás Estrada Palma, the insurgents' delegate in the United States, lobbied vigorously to counter the public relations threat from autonomy. He knew that the American people and government must not be allowed to think that Cubans would accept half measures. That would constitute an emergency of the highest order, for the Cubans depended more than ever on the material and moral backing of the American public.[22] Estrada Palma, never so wary of America as Martí had been, professed to have "no fear" that McKinley would "back track" and support autonomy as a solution for Cuba. In Estrada Palma's view, McKinley was only pretending to go along with the Spanish Liberals to gain time. He wrote: "As for President McKinley, my confidential sources make me believe that he is not disposed to being duped by the shady politics of the Spanish government. For its part, the Congress will give its full support to the president or will force him" to go along, should his resolve fail.[23]

In fact, Estrada Palma's frenetic activity in the fall of 1897 against autonomy suggests that he had at least some concerns about the position the U.S. government might adopt. He got the Cubans in New York to march against autonomy. He encouraged Cuban émigrés to sign a petition pledging their "unconditional support of the Liberation Army to fight without truce until the work of redemption was crowned" with absolute victory. He called emergency meetings. On Monday, November 1, 1897, about 200 men met in the house of John Jacob Astor. There were speeches by Manuel Sanguily, Enrique José Varona, Dr. Diego Tamayo, and others. Estrada Palma assured everyone present that he would demonstrate to the American public that autonomy was a plot to keep Cuba in chains. The New York junta mass-produced a pamphlet to that effect, released it to the press, and sent it to every member of the U.S. Congress.[24]

While Estrada Palma had his hand on the pulse of American politics, Spain's ambassador to Washington, Enrique Dupuy de Lôme, clearly did not. American officials, such as Secretary of State William R. Day, continued to trick Dupuy into believing that McKinley was fully satisfied with autonomy. On December 17, 1897, Dupuy wrote to the Spanish minister of state that McKinley would not intervene, "leaving Spain to develop a policy that he approves and that merits his sympathy." Day had told him that "in view of the change of government [in Madrid], the policy of the Republican President had changed, and there was no longer any reason for intervention or mediation." In bold type, Dupuy added in his dispatch to Madrid: "The United States will not intervene in Cuban politics."[25]

There is some doubt about McKinley's position in late 1897 and early 1898. We do know that his administration never tried seriously to interdict the supplies of weapons reaching the Cuban Liberation Army, never mediated with the Cubans, and did nothing else to help bring an end to the war through negotiation. But does this mean that McKinley knew ahead of time that autonomy would fail? Was he pretending to support it as a way to gain time while he prepared the United States militarily and politically for war?[26] The likely truth about McKinley is that he had not yet made up his mind about Cuba. He knew that the rebels would not accept autonomy, but he was not so foolish as to confuse the insurgency with the entirety of the Cuban people, and he wanted to see how they responded. Dupuy may not have been aware of McKinley's doubts, but the

Cuban lobby in the United States clearly was, and the evidence of this is that they worked so hard to discredit autonomy with American officials and the public.[27]

In fact, autonomy was making inroads even among Cubans previously committed to the war. The number of Cuban deserters presenting themselves to Spanish officials grew at an alarming rate in early 1898. On January 17, 1898, Captain Nestor Alvarez convinced his whole squadron to surrender at Zarza. He planned to keep them together as a guerrilla force fighting in defense of the autonomous government, which he saw as legitimate. Ramón Solano, Alvarez's immediate superior, got wind of the treason and detained Alvarez and his co-conspirator, Sergeant Tomás Orellane. He had them both summarily shot. Solano reported the action to his superior, to warn him of "the extent of the treason" in the regiment, so that he could "take precautions as we all must in these days who have a command."[28]

Even some important officers, including Bartolomé Masó and Cayito Alvarez, had decided to go over to the Spanish.[29] One such officer was Colonel López Marín. Long frustrated with the racial politics of the insurgent forces and the behavior of Gómez, López Marín had become convinced that the war in western Cuba had been lost, and he thought that accepting the autonomous regime was "an honorable transaction." On January 28, 1898, he explained all this in a letter to a friend. He had hated Weyler, and this had kept him fighting for Cuba, despite the crimes of the "Cuban huns — the eastern invaders." Even the "infuriating racism" of the insurgency had not caused him to give up the fight. He wrote of the invasion of Pinar del Río, when "the brutal negro element" had gained the upper hand and the white population found itself "policed by blacks." This emerging "negro republic" did not even trust its own white officials, assigning black second officers to spy and report on their white superiors. Even this had not been enough to cause him to go over to the enemy, said López Marín. Now, however, with the West pacified and Weyler gone, what he saw in Cuba was a ruined country, where the vast majority of the population wanted peace but was forced by an "ignorant and inhumane" armed minority to remain at war against an autonomous regime that really was not that bad. This constituted a "horrible menace to the future of Cuba." Only autonomy could save the situation. Mayía Rodríguez thought López Marín must have suffered a "brain seizure." But the desertion of an important officer like López Marín reminds us of some important facts: race and racism continued to divide and weaken the insurgency, and military defeat in the West had, in fact, left much of Cuba pacified.[30]

With Weyler gone, with reconcentration ended, with the grant of autonomy, and now with the growing dissent in the ranks of the Liberation Army, the future of the Cuban republic-in-arms appeared uncertain. Given this situation, it is not surprising that McKinley hesitated.

Nevertheless, it must be stated clearly that, despite some desertions and divisions, most officials and soldiers in the Liberation Army remained faithful to the ideal of independence. Gómez, García, and other Cuban leaders were adamant about this. They refused to talk to the other side, unless the subject were the immediate surrender of Spanish forces. And their prospect for success was actually reasonably good. The passive attitude adopted by the Spanish in Cuba after Weyler's removal provided a breathing space in which the Liberation Army could rebuild. Although it never regained the strength it had enjoyed in its heyday during the winter of 1895–96, the Cuban army at least retained control over most of the East.[31] Indeed, by the spring of 1898, García and Gómez had approximately 4,000 men active in the East.[32]

The leaders of the Cuban revolution were committed to independence without negotiations, and much of the rank and file shared their resolve. A trooper named Orencio wrote to his sweetheart Carmela Viñagera in Matanzas: "I am doing relatively well. I am anxious to make an end (with independence, of course) to this interminable war. For, my friend, it is high time that this savage life, full of misery and unpleasantness, end." Nevertheless, he assured Señorita Viñagera, "we are ready to conquer or die trying. We laugh at all the undignified Spanish offers [of amnesty], and we have no doubt that we will obtain complete success soon."[33]

Most of the leaders of the Liberation Army and most of the soldiers stood as firm as Orencio, so the only practical effect of the autonomy regime's unilateral initiative to grant amnesty in exchange for peace was that it gave the insurgents a much-needed respite and alienated Spain's hard-line supporters. At that point, with Spanish forces withdrawn to defensive positions, the Cubans began to operate more freely: The failure of the Liberal Party's "carrot" became obvious to everyone. This, in turn, convinced McKinley that the war in Cuba would not end anytime soon. Knowing that the Cuban insurgent leaders would never accept autonomy, it became clear that only American intervention could break the stalemate.

This is how the Liberal program of autonomy and negotiation served as a halfway house toward Cuban independence. Because autonomy became possible only after Cánovas's death, scholars such as Donald Dyal conclude that the Spanish-American War would not have happened had Cánovas lived.[34] For this reason alone, one may say, with historian Frank Fernández, that Cuban independence in 1898 was in some measure the product of Angiolillo's three bullets.[35]

The same three bullets that killed Cánovas also brought the American battleship *Maine* to Havana on January 25, 1898. And the destruction of the *Maine* provided the immediate pretext for American intervention. This is how it happened.

When the Liberals in Spain removed Weyler, it alarmed Cuban supporters of Spanish rule. During the previous three years, these *integristas* had staked everything on a Spanish victory. They had fought for Spain, had even committed crimes in Spain's defense, and now they felt betrayed by the Mother Country. They viewed autonomy as a step toward full independence, and they anticipated nothing but rough treatment in an independent Cuba. Together with Spanish army officers, they did their best to undermine the Liberal program of reform and compromise.

Already in early October reports began to surface of an extensive organization of Civil Guards and other Weyler partisans preparing to organize a counter-demonstration upon the arrival of Ramón Blanco. U.S. consul Fitzhugh Lee became aware of planned protests against what the *integristas* viewed as Madrid's subservience to the United States.[1] The ugly mood in Havana spread to other western cities — Matanzas, Pinar del Río, Cárdenas, Cienfuegos. Ramón Blanco became alarmed. In a top secret memo to the civil governor of Matanzas on December 12, 1897, Blanco warned that *integristas* were planning attacks against property, citizens, and resident aliens in the town of Matanzas, and "even against the official residences of representatives of friendly nations, especially against the United States." These sorts of actions anywhere they might occur would be extremely dangerous because they might lead the United States to intervene immediately in defense of its citizens' lives and property.[2] On December 22, Fitzhugh Lee wrote to the U.S. State Department to request that one or two naval vessels be sent to Havana to protect Americans.[3]

The Weylerites hated the Liberal press even more than they hated the Cuban insurgents and the Americans. The Cuban press flourished under Blanco, because he lifted the censorship Weyler had imposed. In the winter of 1897–98, newspapers like *El Reconcentrado* and *La Discusión* ran articles vilifying Weyler and his supporters. One article in *El Reconcentrado*, under the headline "Fuga de Granujos," wished good riddance to Weyler's cronies and depicted their departure for Spain as the homeward flight of low-born, cowardly thieves and adventurers. This was too much for the hard-line integristas in Havana. Exasperated by the "criminal campaign" of the Liberal and autonomist press, approximately 100 Spanish officers and other Weylerites assaulted the office of El Reconcentrado on the morning of January 12, 1898, destroying the presses and files. Then they did the same thing to La Discusión. Blanco forced the crowd to disperse, but they soon reformed, shouting "Death to Autonomy," "Viva España," and "Viva Weyler." They marched next to the offices of the major daily, El Diario de la Marina, but it had already been sealed in anticipation of an attack and only suffered a few broken windows.

In this new environment, the United States decided to respond to Fitzhugh Lee's repeated requests that a warship be sent to Havana. And that is how the three bullets that took out Cánovas and Weyler produced a riot among dissatisfied hard-liners in Havana that brought the battleship Maine into the harbor of the Cuban capital. Madrid and Washington explained the arrival of the Maine as a symbol of renewed friendly relations between Spain and the United States. Some historians have repeated this official line as if it were true,[4] but members of the autonomy government, such as José Congosto, were not so naive. They knew that the presence of the Maine was part of a process of increasing tension between Spain and America. For example, when it sent the Maine to Havana, the United States also ordered its North Atlantic Squadron to the Gulf of Mexico for "battle exercises."[5] At the time, no one in Havana mistook these acts for friendly gestures.

Ramón Blanco tried to keep the visit of the Maine a secret until the last possible moment because he also knew it would be interpreted as a hostile act. Even members of the autonomy government only learned of the ship's scheduled stop on January 24. Blanco did not want the news to leak and give hard-liners time to organize an anti-American demonstration.[6] On January 25, the day the Maine docked, Lee wrote to Congosto urging him to provide additional security at the American consulate, in the vicinity of the public square, at the Hotel Inglaterra, and anywhere else Americans congregated, because his information also indicated that some sort of organized anti-American activity was in the works. He warned Congosto that "such a demonstration would bring matters to a head at once."[7] In fact, over the next two weeks, nothing untoward occurred in Havana, though the climate remained tense. The impressive sight of the Maine in the harbor even caused some enthusiasm among Habaneros. A steady stream of Cuban visitors toured it in late January and early February, and a few Spanish officers were invited aboard to view the ship under close escort. Members of the autonomy government made their own inspection on February 14.

The following evening, just before ten P.M. the *Maine* exploded, blowing debris and bodies high into the air and breaking windows in the city. The blast killed 266 Americans and injured many others, some severely. Most officers escaped serious injury. Some were ashore. Others, including Captain Charles Sigsbee, were in their cabins aft, far from the source of the explosion, and escaped injury.[8]

Experts now conclude that an accidental explosion aboard the *Maine* triggered by a coal fire probably caused the ship's destruction. Due to technical and design flaws, such fires broke out regularly aboard ships of the *Maine* class, especially in tropical waters, and above all when they were loaded, as the *Maine* was, with volatile bituminous coal. Inspectors had twice reprimanded Sigsbee for keeping a disorderly ship and violating ordnance protocols. These were serious infractions because the placement of the coal depot next to the ammunition magazine aboard ships like the *Maine* meant that the utmost caution had to be taken to monitor the coal for spontaneous combustion. A board commissioned in 1975 by Hyman Rickover, father of the nuclear navy, reopened the case and concluded that there was no evidence for an explosive device external to the hull. The problem had been internal and entirely avoidable with proper vigilance.[9]

In 1898 almost nobody in the United States saw the matter in this light. The idea of Spanish "perfidy" had become too fixed in people's minds for them to believe anything but evil of Spain. Not even a week previously, on February 9, Hearst's *Journal* had published a letter written by the Spanish ambassador, Enrique Dupuy de Lôme, that insulted President McKinley and the American people. Surely, a people capable of the wholesale slaughter of Cuban innocents would not balk at blowing up a battleship. It did not help that the only account of the disaster to reach the United States that night, aside from Sigsbee's anodyne official message about the loss of his ship, was the report of Sylvester Scovel. Scovel had made a career out of working closely with the Cuban insurgents to provide sensational reports of sinister Spanish doings, and his message of February 16 intimated that the explosion might have been caused by an external device. The headline in Pulitzer's *World* seemed noncommittal: "It Is Not Known Whether Explosion Occurred On or UNDER the *Maine*." But the capitalization of the word "under" gave readers a clue about what to think.[10]

Not to be outdone, the *Journal* ran banner headlines on the following day that read: "Destruction of the Warship Maine Was the Work of an Enemy" and "The Warship *Maine* Split in Two by an Enemy's Secret Infernal Machine." The enemy remained unnamed, but everyone knew that it meant Spain. The *Evening Journal* claimed to have information that the so-called infernal machine was not a mine, as the article in the Journal claimed, but a torpedo. The Journal insisted that it was a mine and purported to have information that the Spanish had planted it to explode at night in order to maximize casualties. What more proof was needed to prove the "brutal nature" of the Spanish? The World, less certain of the cause, asked in its banner headline, "Maine Explosion Caused by Bomb or Torpedo?" What had disappeared from view within the first two days following the disaster was the alternative explanation, the one that we now know to be most likely, that the explosion had been caused by an accidental coal fire, which set off an ammunition magazine. Instead, the debate focused on when the mine had been placed or whether it had in fact been a torpedo fired at the hull.[11]

Additional details added color to the story: the World claimed that Spanish officers responded to the tragedy by celebrating and boasting that they would do the same to any other American ship that visited Havana, an affront to the true response of Spanish officers and seamen who worked tirelessly to rescue survivors on the night of February 15. The line taken by the major dailies was too profitable to be changed, however. In the week following the disaster, Hearst increased the circulation of the Journal from 400,000 a day to 1 million. The destruction of the Maine had become a casus belli, and just as important, a cash cow more productive even than reconcentration had been. The problem now was to find some evidence of Spanish involvement.[12]

The U.S. Navy formed a court of enquiry to determine the cause of the blast. Scholars now agree that, through influence-peddling, the court issued a "managed verdict" blaming an external explosion. Secretary of the Navy John Long made certain to exclude proponents of the accident theory, which included the leading expert on the navy's own Bureau of Ordnance, and the court, presided by Admiral William T. Sampson, suppressed evidence that indicated an internal explosion. Captain Sigsbee, one of the main witnesses, had a personal motive to rule out an accidental cause, and although his testimony demonstrated an unfamiliarity with his ship and an utter negligence of its daily operations, the court agreed with him that none of the officers or men of the Maine bore any responsibility. Curiously, however, when Sampson became commander of the North Atlantic Squadron during the war with Spain, he assigned Sigsbee to command a converted commercial boat, the St. Paul. Another member of the court, French Ensor Chadwick, commander of the New York during the war, made certain to install extra bulkheads between the coal bunkers and the powder magazines in his ship. These details suggest that the court knew the real cause of the explosion: the negligence of Sigsbee and design flaws inherent to the Maine. What it announced to the world, though, was something quite different. The report that went to McKinley on March 25 and that McKinley announced to Congress on

March 28 confidently pronounced the destruction of the *Maine* to be the result of "the explosion of a submarine mine." [13]

There were a few dissenting voices. Of course, the Spanish argued that the explosion had been internal. More significantly, Captain Philip Alger, the leading American expert on explosives, also thought the explosion had probably resulted from a coal fire. The fact that he said so publicly, however, earned him no friends. Theodore Roosevelt, the assistant secretary of the navy, had already concluded that the tragedy had been "an act of dirty treachery" by the Spanish, and he accused Alger of taking the "Spanish side." The story of Spanish perfidy was too convenient for the powerful party of jingoes — Henry Cabot Lodge, Theodore Roosevelt, Alfred Thayer Mahan, Senator Redfield Proctor, and Admiral William T. Sampson — who had been pushing for war for years. They simply refused to listen to inconvenient facts. With William Randolph Hearst and millions of other Americans, their motto now was "Remember the *Maine* and to hell with Spain." [14]

Even with the findings of the naval court of enquiry in his hands, McKinley hesitated. He still hoped for a negotiated end to the Cuban war, and on March 29 he pressed the Spanish government to make a number of additional concessions and to declare a unilateral armistice, which, given the intransigence of Gómez and the Liberation Army, would have been tantamount to a Spanish surrender. Even so, the Sagasta government conceded every point and promised to pursue an armistice as well, merely asking for a delay of several weeks, due to internal political considerations: the first free elections in autonomous Cuba were scheduled for early May, and Sagasta wanted the Cuban regime to be involved in the peace process.

U.S. congressmen, however, would brook no more delays. They had reasons for wanting to move before the installation of the first Cuban government elected under the autonomy statute. Such a government would have had a strong claim to legitimacy and would have opposed American intervention. This would have removed some of the veneer of democratic liberation from the planned invasion, and complicated public relations. A revolt against McKinley's measured approach spilled over into a debate on the floor of Congress in early April. The Sagasta government realized it would have to suspend hostilities or face war with the United States. On April 9 the Spanish declared a unilateral cease-fire, but by then nothing would satisfy the U.S. Congress. The idea of a war had become massively popular in the United States, and senators and representatives knew that their reelection would depend on their having demonstrated a virile determination to punish the Spanish.

On April 13 the House of Representatives authorized McKinley to intervene in Cuba to establish a friendly government there. Three days later, the Senate also authorized intervention, but an amendment by Senator David Turpie asked that the current revolutionary republic be recognized as the legitimate government of the island. McKinley found this condition unacceptable. He did not consider the Cuban republic-in-arms a legitimate government, and he did not want to be hampered by having to operate with the Cubans' say-so. This has been taken by some to indicate that McKinley had nefarious designs on Cuba: that he wanted a free hand to operate without regard for Cuban wishes, because he had all along wanted to annex Cuba.[15]

In fact, however, McKinley's position was not that unreasonable. No commander in chief would have wanted to work through the revolutionary republic of Cuba in 1898, because it had so little power and no claim to represent the majority of Cubans. Even Máximo Gómez did not like to work with the government, and he concurred with McKinley that it was not legitimate. In a letter he wrote to Tomás Estrada Palma in June, Gómez laughed at "those people" in the Cuban government whose "big nightmare" was that McKinley was refusing to recognize them. He sympathized with McKinley because the Cuban governing authorities "do not in fact constitute more than a revolutionary government, not a government of the republic." He added that he had always considered it "an absurdity when [he] read Republic of Cuba" in official correspondence. The fact was that the Cuban insurgents had little enough control over their own forces, much less the ability to govern the island. Again, we can allow Gómez himself to speak to this issue. In a letter he wrote in May to the Cuban interim secretary of war, Gómez gave notice of the anarchy that reigned in the handful of towns that had fallen under the control of insurgent forces as the Spanish withdrew outlying garrisons to prepare for the American attack. "If you want to convince yourself of the truth of what I say, mount a horse and go to the cities abandoned by the enemy and now in our power and you will see that they are all centers of immorality." The crimes taking place in the republican zone against people and property were "natural results of the war," in which starving guerrilla soldiers sacked and looted towns that had long been protected by Spain and its Cuban allies. We "still do not have peace, and we do not have the Republic which will normalize everything." Until such a time, thought Gómez, the Americans were right to insist on working without regard to the Cuban government.[16]

The U.S. Congress reached a compromise. The Teller amendment gave McKinley a free hand to intervene and denied recognition to the insurgent government, but it also promised in the near future to return "the government and control of the island to its people." Based on this formula, on April 19, the Congress passed a joint resolution authorizing war, which McKinley signed on the following day. The U.S. Navy, already in place, began to blockade Cuban ports on

April 22. On April 25 the U.S. Congress formally declared war on Spain but dated the declaration retroactively to April 21 to legalize the blockade that was already in place.[17]

In supporting a war with Spain over Cuba, Americans had a variety of motives, power and profit not the least among them. American expansionists had eyed Cuba since before the United States existed. During the American War of Independence, despite the fact that Spain aided the thirteen colonies against Great Britain, American leaders talked about incorporating Spain's Florida and Louisiana territories. Florida at that time was a province of Cuba, governed from Havana, so why not take Florida and the much greater prize of Cuba itself? Jefferson, for one, wanted to do just that, fantasizing about "rounding out" the union by incorporating Cuba as a new state. In 1823 Secretary of State John Quincy Adams expressed similar ideas in a letter to the American ambassador in Madrid: "It is scarcely possible to resist the conviction that the annexation of Cuba to our federal republic will be indispensable to the continuance and integrity of the Union itself. . . . But there are laws of political as well as of physical gravitation; and if an apple severed by the tempest from its native tree cannot choose but fall to the ground, Cuba, forcibly disjoined from its own unnatural connection with Spain, and incapable of self support, can gravitate only towards the North American Union, which by the same law of nature cannot cast her off from its bosom."[18]

In 1825, now president, Adams offered to purchase Cuba. The Spanish responded indignantly. Adams and other American officials pretended not to understand the Spanish reaction. After all, Spain had parted a few years earlier with Florida without much fuss. They ought to have known, however, that Cuba was different. Columbus had landed there in 1492. For almost 400 years Havana had been one of the most important centers of Spanish culture in the New World. Spaniards may not have known the real Cuba, but the fantasy of a terrestrial paradise and fount of wealth in the Antilles had become a part of Spanish identity. Nobody in Spain ever considered seriously giving up the island for money or without a fight. Nor should this be surprising to us. No European power voluntarily surrendered colonies until after World War II. Even the fact that the Spanish court had discussed the subject had to be kept secret for fear of causing a riot.

In 1847 the Polk administration pledged $100 million for the island. This was no mean bid: Twenty years later the United States acquired Alaska from Russia for $7 million. Strapped for money as Spain was, the sale of Cuba must have been tempting. Yet no one considered it seriously. The place was emotionally valuable to Spaniards in ways not encompassed by John Quincy Adams's laws of political gravitation. Pierce's government made another offer in 1854, and

Buchanan tried to renew negotiations in 1858. In 1859 the U.S. Senate reported that "the ultimate acquisition of Cuba" had become a goal "in regard to which the popular voice has been expressed with a unanimity unsurpassed on any question of national policy which has hitherto engaged the public mind." The Civil War and westward expansion distracted the public mind for the next thirty years, but by 1890, the year in which the census declared the frontier officially closed, Americans had begun to cast about for new fields of conquest.[19]

In the meantime, the United States had pursued the economic colonization of Cuba without direct rule. The Sugar Act of 1871, for example, allowed sugar prices to be determined in the United States, placing Cuban producers in a neo-colonial situation in which they depended upon the goodwill of business interests in New York.[20] In 1881 the United States and Spain signed a treaty of reciprocity that opened up Cuba and Puerto Rico to American industrial exports. In exchange, the United States promised to buy goods, mainly agricultural products, from Spain and the Spanish Antilles. With this act, the United States bound Cuba and Puerto Rico tightly to its will. The State Department's main negotiator, John Foster, said as much when he reported on the treaty that "it will be annexing Cuba in the most desirable way."[21]

In the early 1890s, as the peculiar world "depression," characterized by too much innovation, overproduction, excess savings, and low prices, entered its third decade, the U.S. government faced pressure from every quarter to seek out new fields for trade and investment to relieve Americans of their extra products and cash. "Merchants now saw in the acquisition of colonies a partial solution of the disposal of surplus" goods and savings.[22] The need for colonies around the world became acute for this reason alone.

Benjamin Harrison's secretary of state, James G. Blaine, agitated constantly for expansion, advising his boss in 1891 simply to take Hawaii, Cuba, and Puerto Rico.[23] During the next few years the United States did just that. In 1893, during the second Cleveland administration, white planters and American troops deposed Queen Liliuokalani to prevent the adoption of a new democratic constitution that would have given power to the native Hawaiian majority. Washington was satisfied with the arrangement, but white elite rule proved fragile, and the United States annexed Hawaii directly in 1898. McKinley's seizure of Cuba and Puerto Rico can be seen as part of this process. In a Columbus Day speech in 1898 at the Trans-Mississippi Exposition in Omaha, McKinley said: "We have good money, we have ample revenues, we have unquestioned national credit, but we want new markets, and as trade follows the flag, it looks very much as if we were going to have new markets." There were a great many factors other than the need for markets that played into McKinley's decision to go to war over

Cuba, but he certainly was glad to take credit after the fact for opening up new markets by defeating the Spanish.[24]

It is also important to realize that the economic motives for the war with Spain went well beyond the attractions of Cuba itself. In the age of coal-fired steam power, countries sought possessions around the globe to establish coaling stations in order to preserve freedom of movement for commercial and naval vessels. The United States had obtained Midway and Alaska in 1867 and the rights to maintain a coaling station in Samoa in 1878. Washington sought through purchase to acquire territories in Haiti, the Dominican Republic, and other Caribbean and Pacific islands in the 1880s, but to no avail. Stations in Cuba and Puerto Rico seemed like perfect jumping-off points for all of Latin America. Then, too, there was the issue of the Philippines. Although the Spanish-American War was fought primarily over Cuba, American jingoes were eager to acquire markets and perhaps territorial concessions from Asia, and the acquisition of the Philippines seemed a great prize.

The Republican Party, in particular, had pledged itself to "the achievement of the manifest destiny of the republic in its broadest sense." For the Republican jingoes this meant territorial aggrandizement on a fantastic scale. Henry Cabot Lodge predicted that the United States would take over Canada, Cuba, and Hawaii and build a canal through Central America so that the country could compete for the "waste places of the earth," by which he seemed to have in mind Latin America and Asia. The Europeans and even the Japanese were winning the struggle for survival, and the United States had to make up ground. American supremacy was a given, a result of "natural selection," but the government must act. Through prompt action now, Lodge continued, "four-fifths of the human race will trace its pedigree to English forefathers" in the future, and that was as it should be: American imperialism would lead to the perfection of the human species. Josiah Strong, another jingo and social Darwinist, predicted that the Anglo-Saxons would take over all of Latin America and Africa. There would be great conflicts resulting from this empire building, but the outcome would be the "survival of the fittest," and Strong had no doubt that white Americans were the fittest humans. This struggle would be genocidal, but it was natural and unavoidable. There was "no human right to the status of barbarism." On the contrary, the right thing was for civilized peoples to overcome barbarians.[25]

Racist and economic motives for expansion were supplemented by domestic political motives. The United States faced difficult challenges in the 1890s. According to the popular thesis put forward by Frederick Jackson Turner, the presence of a frontier had kept America free and democratic. Its closing, therefore, posed a grave threat to democratic institutions. What America needed to preserve democracy was a new frontier. Through this line of reasoning it became possible for America to be both a firm supporter of popular government and an imperialist, a combination that had proved potent in ancient Athens, Rome, Revolutionary France, and Great Britain, before the United States took up the game.[26]

A different sort of threat to political stability came from the Populists, who were challenging the eastern establishment in the 1890s with a radical platform of more democracy. Western farmers, northern laborers, and many other working people suffered terrible privation in the 1890s. Neither the Democrats nor the Republicans could really give them what they wanted — higher farm prices and better wages and working conditions — without at the same time alienating interests in their own power bases. On the other hand, people could be given an empire. The use of foreign adventures to divert people from domestic issues was a hallowed tradition by 1898. House member Thomas M. Paschal of Texas expressed this use of "social imperialism" well in a letter to Secretary of State Richard Olney in 1895: "Why, Mr. Secretary," explained Paschal, "just think of how angry the anarchistic, socialistic, and populistic boil appears on our political surface. . . . One cannon shot . . . will knock more pus out of it than would suffice to inoculate and corrupt our people for the next two centuries." Washington used conflicts with Great Britain over Venezuela, for example, in order to derail the domestic agendas of political opponents, especially the Populists and free-silver Democrats. A war with Spain would do the trick even better. It would bind up the lingering wounds of the Civil War, joining North and South, East and West in a great national project. It would bring workers and farmers into league with industrialists and financiers. A good war could reforge the nation.[27] In short, the Republican administration, despite McKinley's native caution, together with the majority in Congress and many powerful interests in the United States, were in the mood for expansion in 1898, if not to solve immediate economic problems then to claim a "place in the sun" for the future and to address political problems at home.[28]

Reconcentration and the *Maine* disaster served the agenda of the jingoes well by making it possible to mobilize the American people for war. Even authoritarian regimes find it convenient to use propaganda to bring their subjects around to the idea of war. How much more necessary in a republic? Some scholars are skeptical about the role of reconcentration and the explosion of the *Maine*. The "real" cause of intervention, they say, was the need for markets and imperial grandeur, not the human rights campaign over reconcentration or outrage over the *Maine*. Some have even suggested that all the fuss over the destruction of the *Maine* just serves to distract us from looking at the deepest cause of intervention: the long-term interest of the U.S. government in expanding into Cuba. In fact, these sorts of controversies are the real distraction. What made 1898 most "splendid" from the point of view of the American jingoes who wanted a war for economic, political, and strategic reasons is that the twin tragedies of reconcentration and the *Maine* mobilized their countrymen. The jingoes could have their way under the guise of a humanitarian mission to save Cuba and avenge the *Maine*. The "mere events" of 1895–98 should not be written out of the history of American intervention in some puerile effort to find the "underlying" causes of the war with Spain. To do that is to miss the real texture of a great and tragic historical moment.

Following the *Maine* catastrophe, Spaniards girded themselves for yet another war. Life went on in Madrid. Richard Strauss performed as guest conductor of the symphony. The long drought affecting Castile served as a constant topic of conversation. But pervading all of this was a sense of patriotic exaltation. Bullfight fans in the Spanish capital organized one of the more comical expressions of popular patriotism and antipathy toward the United States. The aficionados arranged a fight between a bull, symbolizing Spain, and an elephant, understood to symbolize the United States. (Employing a pig in the role apparently struck everyone as not quite sporting.) It turned out to be a tedious match, however, with the bull "frankly cowardly, and the elephant, in truth, gentlemanly." There was no fight, and the crowd left in a black mood.[1]

The Madrid aficionados became even more despondent when their great idol, Frascuelo, passed away on March 8, 1898.[2] Lovers of the bullfight consider Frascuelo, whose true name was Salvador Sánchez, one of the greatest toreros of the nineteenth century. He was certainly the most popular. One biographer described him as Spain's "Messiah" and "Savior," inspiring frenzied devotions that eclipsed those offered to Jesus Christ.[3] In the ring, Frascuelo worked in an idiom that was muscular and dramatic, while rivals fought in the classical style, marked by control and technical prowess. Other bullfighters tried to exit fights as they entered them, with every hair in place and their suits-of-light unsoiled. Frascuelo habitually left the ring with his clothes torn and drenched in his own or in bulls' blood. He did not please traditionalists, but he thrilled the crowds. Frascuelo dared bulls to gore him, and they obliged twenty-four times during a twenty-four-year career that ended in 1890.

Frascuelo's sudden death from pneumonia, therefore, produced an astounding wave of grief. Spaniards, especially Madrileños, loved Frascuelo, because they saw reflected in him two cherished elements of Spanish national self-esteem in the modern era: laconic bravery in the face of danger and an emphasis on bravado rather than on technique. Like many bullfighters, Frascuelo came from a humble background, but that just intensified Spain's love affair with him, for he also represented the individual's ability to rise in society based on nothing but raw courage. So it was that thousands of people, from the most distinguished men and women of the royal court to peasants from nearby villages, turned out for the funeral in Madrid.[4]

In death as in life Frascuelo served as a national archetype. A man who had faced oblivion hundreds of times and who had survived terrible gorings succumbed finally to illness, just as Spanish soldiers like Eloy Gonzalo had fought heroically only to die of tropical diseases. The parallels with the Cuban situation were too obvious to go unnoticed. And so it was that Spaniards poured out their grief for Frascuelo in a cathartic lament for the failure in Cuba of martial virtue when faced with implacable microbes.

Yet Spaniards also celebrated Frascuelo and the national qualities of bravery and insouciance that he embodied. In March, Spaniards still had some hope that the old military virtues would provide redemption, that bravery and stoic heroism could overcome power, technology, and wealth. The Portuguese poet Abilio Manuel Guerra Junqueiro captured something of the way Spaniards perceived the approaching conflict when he characterized the war of 1898 as "the strange and extraordinary fight between Frascuelo and Edison." In such a contest, who knew what might happen?[5]

Spaniards had been expecting an American declaration of war for some time, and they accepted the event with a kind of relief. If we trust the memory of Manuel Corral, a soldier fighting in Santiago, the troops in Cuba received the news of war with the United States with "indescribable joy."[6] This may seem odd to us, at a distance of more than 100 years and knowing, as we do, that Spain was entering one of the most one-sided wars in history on the wrong side. But did Spanish political and military leaders realize this at the time? Scholars usually answer this question affirmatively: Spain's rulers knew that war with America was a forlorn hope, but they fought anyway, because they were convinced that to accept an American diktat without a fight would so dishonor the regime that it would result in the overthrow of the Bourbon monarchy by disgruntled patriots and army officers.[7]

Admiral Pascual Cervera's assessment of the military situation seems to support such an argument. Commander of the Spanish squadron sent to Cuba, Cervera had no illusions that he could defeat the American fleet or harry the eastern seaboard of the United States, as called for by the fanciful strategic plan of Segismundo Bermejo, Spain's minister of the navy. Likewise, he thought that Spanish land forces had already been defeated by the insurgents and were in no condition to fight the Americans. In short, he thought that war with the United States would "surely cause the total ruin of Spain."[8]

There is also some evidence in the diplomatic correspondence to suggest that Spain went to war for internal political reasons without any expectation of victory.

On February 26, American ambassador Stewart Woodford wrote to McKinley to report that Spanish officials felt that they could "not go further in open concessions to us without being overthrown." They especially feared the ultra-patriots in the army, who might form an alliance with the Carlists, supporters of a different, more absolutist, branch of the Bourbon family tree. "They want peace if they can keep peace and save the dynasty," but they "prefer the chances of war with the certain loss of Cuba to the overthrow of the dynasty." On March 9, Woodford wrote McKinley again to report a conversation he had at a formal dinner with an important Spanish businessman who was "talking for a purpose" and had informed him of two things. First, Spain had done all she could to appease the United States. And, second, Spain would never sell Cuba. According to his informant, the Spanish government knew they would be beaten but "would accept the issue of war without hesitation," in order to avoid the dishonor and potential revolutionary consequences of a unilateral withdrawal.[9]

There is a strange attraction to seeing Spain as a kind of Don Quixote sallying forth to do hopeless battle with the American giant. In fact, however, aside from the views of the pathologically pessimistic Cervera and a few others, most Spanish officials seemed to believe that victory was at least possible. So did the Spanish press. And so did a large part of the public. There were several reasons for confidence, some of them striking us today as ridiculous, others quite reasonable.

As we have seen, the Spanish military held an exceedingly high opinion of itself, of Spanish soldiers, and of Spain's "national character." This high self-regard had been communicated to them and by them to others through the press, literature, Sunday sermons celebrating anniversaries of historic victories, and other means. According to the national mythology, Spaniards possessed a bred-in-the-bones genius for war, especially for guerrilla warfare.

The belief in Spanish *guerrillerismo* goes back at least to the struggle against Napoleon, when guerrilla bands did indeed perform effectively against French regulars. Out of this experience evolved a tribal myth that held the Spanish people to be fiercely independent, capable of enduring great hardship, and recklessly generous with their own lives in defense of honor. The historian Francisco Rodríguez-Solis expressed this idea in an aphorism: "When the Spaniard is born, so is the guerrilla."[10] Felipe Navascués agreed that "our soldier has the reputation of being the best in the world."[11] According to Vicente Cortijo, all nations "envy our soldiers, and our officers are the most well schooled in Europe."[12] Another Spanish military writer, Florencio León Gutiérrez, grimly reassured his audience that the Spanish infantryman "fights tenaciously" and, if overwhelmed, knows how to die well, "with his strong hands gripping his weapon, with the courage of the race etched on his face and with the smile of a martyr on his lips." But Spain would not be defeated. "God, always great, always beautiful, and always Spanish will guard Spain and will not permit Right, Reason, and Justice to be mocked" by the Yankees.[13]

Racial and religious thinking combined in interesting ways in self-characterizations by Spanish military authorities. Carlos Gómez Palacios, for example, theorized that God had given each race its own peculiar "spiritual organization, formed to accomplish distinct ends" on earth. God had given the "Latin race" courage, honor, duty, strength, and dignity, "all that he denied to other races, especially the Saxons." These moral and physical qualities gave the Spanish their superiority on the battlefield. In the end, as light conquers darkness, Spain would overcome the barbaric North Americans, whose only god was money. All history of human spiritual progress was the history of the Latin race, God's chosen people. God would not abandon Spain now against the worshippers of Mammon.[14]

Meanwhile, according to the Spanish, the American people was a shapeless mass "formed by emigrants who, with a few honorable exceptions, were and remain the worst sort from each nation." The United States was a place "without traditions, without anything properly its own," a country "without science, art, or literature." The only thing Americans excelled at was commerce. They were "modern Carthaginians" attempting to take on something that was beyond them, the role of command. Everyone knew that "humanity is an exotic plant in the Yankee race," and "if they do not understand human sentiments, due to the moral defects of their constitution, they would never possess the sentiment of glory, which is the opposite of self-interest," which everyone knew was the only salient feature of the Anglo-Saxon mind and spirit. The Americans, "composed of the world's refuse," could not form a coherent and effective army. Indeed, one could not even "give the name of army to such an immense conglomeration of men who had no military discipline, no love of the military, nor any love or respect for those who command." Like their soldiers, American officers lacked any qualifications. They "understand business" better than war. People thus raised to value only profit and self-interest would never risk themselves in combat. "We have only to display our virtues" to "roll back and vanquish" such a foe.[15]

It was not only the military writers who predicted a Spanish victory. The Spanish press also rallied confidently behind the war effort and predicted victory. It could hardly have been otherwise. The American condemnation of Spanish barbarism in Cuba had injured Spanish pride, leading to popular demonstrations against the United States. This made it impossible for newspapers to adopt anything other than a shrill anti-American tone if they wished to stay profitable.[16] Even the liberal press found itself playing the game. Thus, on December 27, 1896, even as it condemned Weyler and the hard-line policy adopted toward Cubans, El Liberal delighted readers by recounting the fascinating story of the "Honeymoon of Mr. Big Pig." An American couple had come to Cádiz on honeymoon. The groom, Mr. Big Pig, cared only for money and wanted to return home immediately so he could get back to work. In the meantime, his young bride, who played tennis and was on her way to becoming as manly as other American women, began to experience a transformation in Cádiz. In the presence of the Spanish male, she became female. "Discarding her rough clothes and masculine hat, she started dressing in silk" and wearing flowers in her hair. She fell in love with Spain and, more to the point, with Spanish men, and she lost interest in the tedious and effeminate Mr. Big Pig.[17] Such depictions of American women as disconnected from their femininity are easy to find in the Spanish press in the 1890s. So, too, is the porcine imagery of American men. The first prize in the Madrid Carnival in 1898 went to someone costumed as a giant pig decked out in red, white, and blue.[18] How could one fear an unnatural country made up of masculine women and feminine and swinish men? How could one do anything but laugh?

After the American declaration of hostilities, even the radical press that had called for Cuban independence adopted a bellicose line. Blasco Ibáñez, the indefatigable republican opponent of the government, adopted the language of exalted nationalism, condemning the actions of the "arrogant Yankee" and defending his own "noble nation."[19] El Imparcial began to publish articles in praise of the Spanish army, previously its favorite target. The sacrifices in Cuba were now seen as exemplary of the "tenacity of a race that only counts victories when they are difficult."[20] The paper assured its readers that the approach of war was already dividing the United States along North-South lines. On April 19 the paper published a letter supposed to have been written by the widow of Jefferson Davis, complaining that "we, the inhabitants of the southern United States, have to suffer all the weight of the campaign. . . . Our cities and our coasts will be destroyed," while the North went untouched. Most southerners, she said, "abhor the idea of a war, which in the end will only favor those miserable Cuban mulattoes." The letter from Davis's widow expressed "most eloquently . . . the irritation that predominates in the southern states against the other states."[21]

This kind of wishful thinking went to extraordinary lengths. General Luis M. de Pando thought that something like 20,000 Cubans could be mobilized in Pinar del Río alone to repel an American invasion, if only Spain could provide them with arms and ammunition.[22] Cubans "preserve an affection for Spain . . . that can be fostered and increased" to produce Cuban regiments, now that the

United States had shown its true colors.[23] Other Latin Americans would also rally to a Spanish defense of the Americas against the Yankee menace.[24] Another author added that Europeans were also likely to weigh in to stop the North American colossus. Spain could then go on the offensive and reclaim Spanish territory in Florida with 100,000 men. The Americans would have their hands full with the insurrection of the Sioux and the 100,000 Mexicans said to be marshaling along the southern U.S. border.[25] Even the Spanish minister of war had his modest fantasies: In a letter to Blanco in June he wrote that he might be able to recruit 1,300 Mexicans to fight in Cuba.[26]

In fact, Spain had no allies in 1898, and it was in good part the fault of Cánovas, whose most famous pronouncement on foreign affairs had been that the "best foreign policy Spain can have is to have none."[27] As a result, Spain had little voice or standing in the international community, and no one offered the least aid in its war with the United States. Or almost no one. A Catholic Congress in 1896 offered the aid of Saint James, but as there were no sightings of the old "Moor killer" around Santiago or on any other Cuban battlefield, we can only assume that his holy assistance made no practical difference. Pope Leo XIII blessed Spanish armies, but this, too, seemed to have no effect against bullets or disease. Finally, the pope offered to provide arbitration with the United States in 1898, but this went nowhere, primarily because no one bothered to consult the Cubans.[28]

Far from offering any assistance, the European powers had lined up to take advantage of Spain's defeat. The British, for example, planned to seize the entire Bay of Algeciras, in effect extending its sovereignty over Gibraltar to adjacent areas, and to demand that Spanish artillery within striking distance of Gibraltar be dismantled. The British and the French expected a colonial redistribution to take place, and the Spanish belief that the two great powers would come to Spain's defense was sadly misplaced.[29] British plans called for the United States to occupy the Philippines, as well as Cuba, Puerto Rico, and the Canaries. In compensation, the French and Russians would partition the Balearic Islands while Britain took Spain's North African possessions and established an informal protectorate over the rest of Spain.[30]

When their isolation became apparent, Spaniards responded with a resounding: "no importa." Spaniards with their peculiar genius for guerrilla warfare became truly dangerous when fighting alone for their survival. Better to go it alone. The popular attitude, as Fernández-Rua summed it up, was, "So, the United States wants war? Well, it's about time. For a people who knew how to defeat the armies of Napoleon, McKinley will count for very little."[31] Spaniards came up with harebrained ideas for raising money to help the cause. The illusionist Doctor Fittini offered to take his popular show on the road and donate all proceeds to the army, a sign not only of patriotism but of the popular awareness of how badly the government needed funds to support the army in Cuba. Toreros and picadors in Madrid wanted to hold a special patriotic bullfight and donate the gate to the army. José Crespo planned to produce his own theatrical works and send the price of admission to the government. Others sent money to veterans and war widows. A letter of April 2, 1898, to the editor of El Imparcial from a reader in Granada enclosed five pesetas to aid the wounded. "There are many readers who hope that El Imparcial will request money for ships of war," the letter read, "because we do not trust others, least of all the politicians," to use public funds to purchase naval vessels.[32]

In the absence of funds, appeals to God might work. A woman calling herself "Crazy Mary" thought that divine intervention might be invoked to save Cuba. Writing to the Spanish king, she called upon him (though he was just a child) and other members of the Bourbon household to lead a holy crusade to redeem "the race of el Cid." If this course of action were followed, she suggested, surely it would bring divine favor and result in victory, just as it did in the chivalric romances she had read.[33] Others offered more practical "secret weapons." A letter written in June 1898 from a primary school teacher to the editor of El Imparcial contained a remarkable offer. The teacher had a colleague who was also an inventor and could offer two new devices to the Spanish navy, if only the government would listen to him. First, he had designed life jackets that were much better than anything the navy currently had. And, second, he had designed a small submarine that was so inexpensive that for the cost of a single surface ship the government could manufacture a whole squadron of submarines "sufficient to defeat the most powerful" enemy.[34] Doubtless, the Spanish navy could have used both devices, especially the first, but it was too late. On May 1 Admiral George Dewey had annihilated the Spanish Asiatic Squadron in Manila Bay, and by June two American squadrons in the Atlantic were hunting for the rest of the Spanish fleet.

Even after Dewey's victory in Manila, people attending mass in Madrid's cathedral listened attentively to a sermon praising Spanish resilience and fighting ability. The news of the naval defeat was everywhere, but it would not affect the resolve of Spain's forces on land, both in the Philippines and in Cuba. They would hold out and teach the Americans the meaning of hard fighting. The sermon compared 1898 to 1808, when Spaniards rose up against Napoleon in Madrid, Zaragoza, Gerona, Sevilla, and other cities. People commonly made this comparison. In July, upon hearing that the Americans had surrounded Santiago, Blanco remarked that "we are descended from the immortal defenders of Gerona and Zaragoza," presumably in the expectation that the people and soldiers of Santiago would fight house to house with knives against the U.S. troops. Santiago turned out to be no Zaragoza, and it was wishful thinking to believe it ever could be. But that is what Spaniards seemed to specialize in during the spring of 1898 — wishful thinking.[35]

Sometimes patriotism blended into veiled threats against a government that many judged to be too weak to stand up to American insults. Leopoldo Bararille Corral, a student in Ciudad Rodrigo, expressed these sentiments well in a poem, part lament, part boast, and part ambiguous threat: "Your glory ended on earth / 'Spain's End' will I place on a sign / If on the Yankee / You do not declare war. Because the lion is sleeping / And if he awakens . . . God help you."[36]

Some attempts have been made to demonstrate that Spaniards did not really support the war.[37] This argument has not been convincing, however. In fact, it is difficult to find signs of opposition to the war. Rather, the evidence suggests that the incidence of desertion and draft evasion was remarkably low and actually declined between 1895 and 1898.[38] Some scholars have argued that Spanish nationalism emerged only after 1898 and that popular support for the war was an invention of the monarchist press.[39] There is something to this argument. But we must be careful not to exaggerate. Because the government manipulated and suppressed popular opinion in Spain, it is difficult to provide any definitive answer about the popularity of the war. Yet, for all the worrying that monarchist politicians did in 1898, the insubordination and mutinies so common among the "patriotic" French and German troops who fought in World War I had no counterpart among the Spanish troops in Cuba. The domestic disturbances that did occur in 1898 were related to a terrible drought and high food prices. They were not antiwar protests.

Whatever the case is with regard to the popularity of the war with America, Spaniards had at least some reasons to be confident. The U.S. Army, with barely 25,000 men, lacked the requisite size to constitute a serious threat to the 150,000 Spaniards still in Cuba, or so people thought. Also, the Spanish possessed a better basic rifle than that used by the Americans. It is true that with the establishment of the Army Gun Factory and the growth of private manufacturers like Colts, the U.S. Army had begun in the 1890s to address the long-standing problem of inadequate arms production. The United States had also begun to manufacture a first-rate weapon: a version of the Swedish-designed Krag-Jorgensen rifle, which fired at a high velocity, used smokeless powder, and had a range only slightly inferior to the Spanish Mauser. However, the army had barely enough Krags for the 25,000 regulars, and even these lacked sufficient ammunition. Had the war gone on for a few months longer, the American army would have faced a serious shortfall of cartridges. Doubtless, American industry would have retooled quickly and made good on the shortfall, but initially, at least, the arsenal of the U.S. Army did not appear to be well stocked. As a result, almost all of the American volunteers had archaic Remingtons and Springfields that had to be fired at a closer range and used black powder, providing the enemy with nice clues about their targets even as they choked and blinded the riflemen who used them. These problems were not unknown to the Spanish. Indeed, even after the Spanish surrender, General Pando protested that the "military power of the United States was not, and still is not, sufficiently strong or established to impose conditions on Spain or on anyone else."[40]

On the other hand, the stark reality of America's potential power became obvious when Congress easily appropriated $50 million in March for the coming campaign. Driving home the point, McKinley's call for 125,000 volunteers produced over a million applicants. The army turned most of them away, of course, but overnight the United States had more than enough personnel to fight Spain. These were ominous signs. Still, problems remained that could give Spaniards some cause for optimism. For example, the United States did not have enough officers to drill its meager existing force, much less to organize and train a European-sized army on such short notice. Indeed, the U.S. Army had not drilled a brigade-sized force (4,000–6,000 men) in thirty years and had no operational provisions whatsoever for anything of divisional size (8,000–12,000 men). Put simply, the Spanish were not entirely delusional to think that in ground combat they might defeat the Americans.[41]

This is one reason that soldiers in Cuba treated the American declaration of war "with indescribable joy." They hated America for having covertly aided the insurgents for three years, and they believed that in a frontal war against U.S. troops they could finally display their real martial virtue.[42] The Spanish belief in their own superiority and in the weakness of Americans seems impossibly quaint today. In the battles outside Santiago, one Gatling gun counted for more than all of the Spanish bravery combined, and the Americans had several of the devastating new weapons against none for the Spanish.

Ironically, it was in naval combat, where the United States turned out to have an overwhelming superiority in firepower, that the Spanish had the greatest cause for confidence. Not only that, but the Americans had some doubts about their own naval superiority.

According to the standard interpretation of the Spanish-American War at sea, Spain, due to its underlying economic and cultural backwardness, had a navy that was hopelessly out of date, and everyone knew that the modern Americans with their new navy would be victorious. This assertion has been a comfort to people in several ways: It reinforces our faith in the modern gods, Technology and Progress;

it confirms the almost universal assumption that historical outcomes — by which we ultimately mean ourselves — are inevitable end products of some inexorable process called modernization; and it undergirds lingering and rarely spoken racist assumptions about the comparative cultural fitness of the Latin and Anglo peoples. The Spanish had fallen behind the times, because it was in their nature to do so. As Latins, they had a "medieval" mentality. And this incapacitated them in the struggle for survival among modern nations. The United States, in contrast, was the paragon of modernity and technological prowess. The American defeat of Spain was, therefore, a foregone conclusion, a confirmation of the correctness of the Promethean struggle of man, a necessary step on the path to us.

In fact, however, the fundamental imbalance between American and Spanish naval forces did not result from any cosmic and inexorable process. Instead, a series of political and technical decisions made in each country about ten years prior to the war created two very different navies. Moreover, the inequality of the two forces was not really that striking to contemporaries.

The United States in the 1870s had a third-rate navy. It probably could not have stood up even to Spain's, and the Spanish navy was itself in a state of decay.[43] Americans had always relied upon the idea of a "brown-water" navy, that is, small ships that would defend the coasts and river estuaries of the United States. Then, a series of new technologies — better coal-fired engines, steel hulls, and more accurate heavy artillery — produced a revolution in ship design. The age of steel warships had begun, with Great Britain leading the way. The United States soon followed the British lead. In 1883 the U.S. Congress authorized the construction of the country's first steel-hulled ships: three cruisers and a dispatch vessel, the so-called ABCDs, after their names — *Atlanta, Boston, Chicago,* and *Dolphin.* The following year, Commodore Stephen B. Luce founded the Naval War College to train a new generation of officers in the study of war at sea. The college's second president, Alfred Thayer Mahan, turned the institution into a national pulpit for a "blue water" navy of big battleships that he fervently believed America needed if it were to become a great power. Mahan's influence went a long way in Gilded Age America — Roosevelt, Lodge, and many others were Mahanites. In 1890 one of Mahan's admirers, Secretary of the Navy Benjamin F. Tracy, called for an ambitious program of naval building, and Congress responded by authorizing nine capital ships in the next few years.[44]

This thumbnail history is important because it highlights how very new the American fleet was in 1898. Many of the ships in the U.S. Navy had barely been tested. The officers and seamen were also inexperienced. Aside from Mahan and a handful of men who had promoted the new navy, nobody knew what to anticipate from it, not in America and not anywhere else in the world. The power of the U.S. Navy, which in hindsight was clearly awesome, was a great unknown to contemporaries, even experts in naval affairs. John D. Long, secretary of the navy during the Spanish-American War, recalled that before 1898, Spain's fleet "appeared formidable in comparison with our own. The battles of Manila and Santiago" were what opened everyone's eyes.[45]

Spain entered the 1880s with a navy almost as worthless as that of the United States.[46] A reform-minded Liberal cabinet proposed a long-term project for creating modern, private shipyards capable of creating the new generation of steel ships. The first, La Carraca, opened at the port of Cádiz working on government contracts. The Liberals wanted to provide a boost to the economy, create a skilled workforce of engineers and mechanics, and make Spain a naval power for the long haul. Navy minister Juan Bautista Antequera sent to the Spanish Congress a naval construction bill in 1885 that would have given La Carraca and other shipyards contracts to build twelve new battleships and a variety of other vessels in a program that would have spanned ten years and cost 231 million pesetas.

The plan went nowhere for several reasons. First, Spanish governments shuffled navy ministers as if it were a game, as indeed Restoration politics was, in some ways. Between 1876 and 1898 Spain had twenty-six navy ministers, many of them serving more than once. This wrecked any chance for continuity in the planning and execution of building programs, something that is fundamental when it comes to the construction of a navy. Predictably, Antequera fell from grace, and a new government scotched his plan.

Second, the government in Spain lacked funds. This problem afflicted Madrid throughout the nineteenth century, but it was especially pressing in the 1880s. In the midst of the long world depression, the Spanish government could not afford to be as ambitious as Antequera wanted. Moreover, the poverty of the Spanish government occurred just at the moment in history when ship design changed most rapidly. Battleships and carriers of Korean War vintage performed reasonably well in the first American war against Iraq, and the wooden ships of the eighteenth century fell victim to worms and rot long before they became obsolete. In contrast, the pace of technological change in ship design in the late nineteenth century was so rapid that a ship could go from first class to obsolete during the time it took to build it. In this context, governments naturally hesitated before investing in the new generation of big ships. Poorer countries like Spain gambled that it would be best to wait a few years until ship design — especially armor and weapons systems — stabilized. This was a gamble they lost, as we all know, but it was not the result of any peculiar Spanish irrationality or "medieval" mind-set. Third, and reinforcing the problem of resources, the army in Spain competed with the navy for available funds, and the army won, because it was vital to the maintenance of internal peace in Spain and so could reasonably argue that it deserved to be fully financed.

Fourth, Spain had committed itself to the *jeune école* theory of naval warfare associated with the work of Admiral Hyacinthe-Laurent-Théophile Aube in France. The jeune école scoffed at the ideas of Alfred Thayer Mahan and the blue-water school in Great Britain and the United States. Where Mahan predicted that naval contests of the future would be decided by big battleships blasting away at each other from great distances on the high seas, Admiral Aube's followers thought that the navies of the future would become smaller. Battleships would be dinosaurs harried by fast gunboats and destroyers that would sink them with torpedoes, a new and frightening weapon in the late nineteenth century that everyone tended to overvalue. The implication of Aube's theory was that poor countries like Spain should not try to mimic the British and American naval building programs. The new battleships were not only too costly, they were ill-conceived, because for the price of a single expensive battleship one could produce a squadron of small and lightly protected, but fast, gunboats armed with deadly torpedoes. The naval warfare of the future would be a "true guerrilla war at sea," as the Spanish commission charged with upgrading the navy insisted. The torpedo was an "armament that today creates a new equilibrium between the navies of the weakest nations and the battleship fleets [of the stronger]." [47]

In the late 1880s, at a time when France itself had already abandoned Aube's theory, Spanish naval experts were coming to believe fervently in it.[48] Articles on naval strategy in the quasi-official journal *La Correspondencia de España* began to laud the superiority of "subtle forces," that is, torpedo boats and light destroyers, against battleships.[49] Navy Minister Rafael Rodríguez Arias presented a project in 1887 that called for the construction of 120 torpedo boats, 10 small cruisers armed with torpedoes, and 11 larger cruisers that would be lightly armored and fast. There was not a single battleship in the plan. Thus, for a variety of reasons, none of them having to do with Spain's backward mentality and America's modern mind-set, Spain had a different sort of navy from that of the United States.

By 1898 the theory of the jeune école had been tested only once. In 1894 at the battle of Ya-lu, a fleet of Japanese battleships destroyed a Chinese fleet of cruisers and other small ships, blasting them out of the water from a distance before the Chinese could speed close enough to do the least bit of damage. Some observers realized the implications: Light cruisers, destroyers, and torpedo boats were useless against battleships. Only fully armored big ships could take and deliver the pounding of modern naval warfare. A few experts, among them the science editor of El Imparcial, understood the meaning of Ya-lu, but the government did not listen.[50]

Most naval experts chose not to generalize based on the battle of Ya-lu. For one thing, no one could be certain that Ya-lu would not prove to be an exceptional case. They reasoned, too, that the Chinese squadron was not up to the quality of Spain's, and Chinese sailors were not the equivalent of the Spanish. And, anyway, a combat among Asians halfway around the globe could not be taken as a serious challenge to the naval paradigm among white Europeans. Racism and cultural arrogance in this case served to blind the Spanish — and many others in Europe — to the obvious lesson of Ya-lu. In 1895 Felipe Navascués, the popular writer on military affairs, even knowing the details of Ya-lu, still thought that numerous and rapid cruisers were the best ships for fighting the "commercial war of the future" that he predicted. They would blockade enemy ports and destroy civilian shipping, thus crippling the economy of the foe and bringing the war to a conclusion. Battleships were too big and too few to carry out this task, and they would not be able to withstand the attack of small torpedo boats.[51]

The Spanish faith in their torpedo boats had its counterpart in an obsessive American fear of them. It was the one area of vulnerability in the U.S. Navy. Who knew if the jeune école might not prove correct after all? Henry Cabot Lodge complained bitterly in 1898 about the unpreparedness of the U.S. Navy in an address to the Senate and President McKinley: "Mr. President, if we had to-day, as we ought to have, twenty battle ships and a hundred torpedo boats, there never would have been a Cuban question; we should have been so ready and so strong that we could have laid our hands on the shoulder of Spain and said, 'You must stop;' and the contest would have been so hopeless that it never would have been entered upon. But, Mr. President, more conservative principles prevailed and we have not the large Navy we ought to have."[52] Considering Lodge's words carefully, one can conclude several things, among them that he did not consider Spain's position hopeless and that he valued the torpedo boat very highly.

Other American naval officers also had their worries about Spain's small boats. Captain French Ensor Chadwick thought the stealthy Spanish might use their torpedoes in a sneak attack to destroy America's great battleships, just as they had apparently sunk the Maine.[53] Richmond Pearson Hobson, one of America's leading experts on new naval technologies, issued a memorandum to Admiral William T. Sampson in May warning that the fleet was particularly vulnerable to torpedo attack.[54] Indeed, it was this fear that caused Hobson to make his famous attempt to block the mouth of Santiago harbor in June, an event we will touch upon later. Charles E. Clark, who captained the Oregon on its epic voyage from the West Coast around Cape Horn to the Caribbean, worried above all about an attack by the torpedo boat *Temerario*, known to be cruising off the coast of Chile or Argentina.[55] And when Spain sent six of its hybrid destroyer-torpedo boats to the Canaries in preparation for the outbreak of hostilities, American officials became obsessed with tracking and locating them.[56] Washington feared sending troop transports to Cuba until the whereabouts of the Spanish ships could be confirmed. This was only prudent, but it delayed the invasion of Cuba by several weeks.

Like their officers, American sailors had great confidence in the ability of their own battleships to defeat the Spanish big ships, but they feared the torpedo boats. Henry Williams was a young ensign aboard the *Massachusetts*, one of the best battleships in the American fleet. Along with the battleships *Texas* and *Iowa* and some smaller vessels, *Massachusetts* formed part of the so-called Flying Squadron, commanded by Commodore Winfield Scott Schley. Stationed at Hampton Roads, Virginia, the Flying Squadron steamed for Cuba in late April. In a voluminous correspondence with his father, Williams recorded every detail of life aboard ship, but his obsession was the fear everyone shared of the Spanish torpedoes. Having established a blockade of the port of Matanzas, on the night of May 21 the crew took "every possible precaution against torpedo attack [with] lookouts all over. All the guns are loaded, the crews by them, and hands by the searchlights. We stand our watches with a night glass in our hands all the time," so he felt confident they could detect the approach of a torpedo boat in time to avoid the worst. Still, the fear of torpedoes caused constant alarms and fatigued the sailors aboard every ship in the Flying Squadron.[57]

On May 29 Schley learned conclusively that the Spanish fleet had gone to Santiago, and he established a blockade of the city. "We have the Spanish fleet bottled in here," Williams wrote his father on May 30. He predicted its destruction,

> unless some of the torpedo boats sneak out and blow us up at night. Now we are busy looking for torpedo boats. We have the Marblehead and Vixen inshore of us scouting and looking out for torpedo boats, and we hope to have a lot more small fry to help in the scouting. It takes a great load off of us and is really the only safeguard against torpedo boats. Last night the Vixen fired the torpedo alarm (two red and one green rocket) and we promptly turned on our search lights and went to general quarters. I had just turned in, as I had the mid watch. We fired two shots just to let them know we were awake, and the other ships were banging away at a great rate at about 10:30.

The incident turned out to be no great thing. The men on the *Vixen* had seen the smoke and heard the racket of a steam engine being used near the beach, and having been instructed to be on high alert for the possibility of a Spanish torpedo attack, they made the assumption that the noise and smoke were caused by a torpedo boat.

This concern for torpedo attacks led to several nighttime incidents where small American vessels suffered damage by friendly fire. One tugboat hired by a New York newspaper approached a ship at night and barely escaped being blasted out of the water. The captain of the tug reported the incident, but far from eliciting sympathy, he became the brunt of seamen's jokes for having frightened everyone. "The tugs are in a bad way if they fool around at night," Williams wrote, when "they get fired on sure, because there are too many torpedo boats to stand on ceremony."

On June 8 Williams again wrote of his fear of the Spanish torpedo boats. The "small fry" he had alluded to earlier had by then set up a solid cordon between the big American ships and the mouth of Santiago harbor. Each speedy scout ship had small guns to repel torpedo boats, but Williams still thought that the battleships would suffer greatly if they were ever attacked under cover of darkness: "It's torpedo boats that worry us to death. We have nervous prostration every night watch on this account. It would be touch and go if one of them started at us." He reported that two torpedoes had been "picked up floating around. It is thought they were fired . . . during one of our numerous torpedo attacks. Anyhow, there they are, and we don't let floating objects lack for a fair share of attention." The Americans plucked these dangerous objects from the water. On June 15 Williams received orders to serve aboard one of the ships performing picket duty against the torpedo attacks. Now, for the first time, he learned that all of the alarm had been overblown, because the Spanish were not, in fact, attacking every night with torpedoes. "They have lots of torpedo boats," he commented, "and why they don't try to make a dash some night I don't understand."

In fact, the Spanish had only a few torpedo boats at Santiago, because so many of those in the Spanish fleet were under repair or had been unable to make the Atlantic crossing. Those that were available at Santiago did no good. On May 31 *Pluton* and *Furor*, which were fast destroyers armed with torpedoes, attempted to come out and attack Sampson's squadron, but against the intense American fire they did not get close enough to take a shot. On June 16 a Spanish boat exited the harbor long enough to fire a single torpedo at the scout ship *Porter*. But the torpedo traveled at such a slow pace that an ensign jumped into the sea, swam to the torpedo, disarmed it, and brought it aboard the ship. On June 22 *Terror* dashed out of San Juan, Puerto Rico, to attack *St. Paul*, but it was smashed to bits by the American ship's big guns before it could get into torpedo range.

In short, torpedoes proved to be less fearsome than anticipated. The same was true of the American torpedo boats. On May 11 *Winslow* bombarded Cárdenas, but a light cannonade from the shore batteries ravaged the torpedo boat, killing five sailors and wounding five more in the twenty-one-man crew, while *Winslow*'s own weapons did little damage. This kind of performance led the Boston *Herald* to observe that "not a single torpedo boat has inflicted five-cents worth of damage upon the Spanish." It is notable that, despite all the precautions Sampson took against the Spanish torpedo boats, he did not think enough of his own torpedo boats to make use of them in the blockade of Santiago.[58]

It was Spain's destiny to prove Mahan right and Aube wrong. Torpedo boats turned out to have no impact on the course of the naval battle at Santiago, as we shall soon see. But no one knew that until after the battle occurred. People everywhere felt uncertainty about how the contest would develop. As Spain's leading authority on naval history put it: "In 1898 the naval inferiority of Spain compared to the United States was obvious only to a few exceptionally well-informed observers."[59] In May and June 1898 reasonable Spaniards could at least hope for a chance to defeat the American fleet.

Spain had a problem maintaining and supplying the ships it did have. Most of the ships present in Cuba in 1898 had some sort of defect. Blanco complained in January that most of his vessels were in dry dock undergoing repairs. Some of Cervera's ships lacked part of their weapons systems or had suffered damage to their propulsion systems that made them lumbering hulks.[60] All of the Spanish crews were so short on artillery shells that they could not practice their gunnery, making the Spanish ships that much less battle worthy.[61]

These problems also resulted from choices made by political and military leaders, not by congenital defects of the Spanish personality. In the 1890s, ministries more concerned with quickly acquiring good ships than with the long-term development of a ship-building industry decided to purchase vessels abroad rather than give contracts to inefficient and inexperienced Spanish builders. That is why Spain lacked a modern shipyard in 1898.

The yard at La Carraca, in Cádiz, was Spain's newest and best, and it was a disaster. In a series of essays in October 1896, *El Liberal* documented the travails of La Carraca during the scheduled launch of the big cruiser *Princesa de Asturias*. Designed for a 2,000-ton ship, the dock slowly sank under the 7,000-ton weight of the *Princesa*. As a result, the grade for the launch became too shallow. Instead of rolling smoothly into the sea, *Princesa* got hung up when it was launched on October 8. The prow cleared the dock and was left suspended in midair over the water, much to the disappointment of the crowd that gathered for the exciting event. This perilous balancing act lasted over a week, by which time the unsupported section of the ship began to come apart at the seams from its own weight. Finally, an unusually high tide on October 18 resolved the crisis. The ship launched spontaneously in the middle of the night under the astonished gaze of a few workmen.

It is interesting to note how the editors of El Liberal explained the botched launching of the Princesa. It was, they wrote, emblematic of "our characteristic lack of foresight" as a people. Spain was afflicted, according to El Liberal, with a "terrible chronic illness" that destined the country for a "bad end." The specific failings of La Carraca became symbolic of national problems. Recalling satirist Mariano José de Larra's famous phrase, but with none of his irony, the newspaper explained to its readers that disastrous launchings, failed test runs, and slow production schedules in the naval yards were to be expected, that they were cosas de España, that is, Spanish peculiarities, as if the Spanish were naturally incapable of producing a modern ship.[62]

Why bother, then, to develop a native cadre of engineers and mechanics? Better to purchase ships abroad, where they could be produced more efficiently. Ironically, the finest ship purchased abroad, Reina Regente, of British manufacture, sank in rough seas in 1895. The best ship Spain had in 1898 was Cristóbal Colón. A new ship of Italian manufacture, Colón may have been the best armored cruiser in either navy. In 1898 the ship was being refitted and repaired, but the Spanish thought that the various works could be completed quickly, so that Colón would be in top form for any possible conflict with the United States. Technical problems with some of the firing systems caused the work to be delayed, however. In the end, the ship was whimsically reclassified as a battleship as if that might increase its value, and it went with Cervera, but it's heavy guns were not functioning.

On the American side, some of the battleships had faults of their own. In an age of rapidly changing ship design, new vessels required frequent spells in dry dock for repairs and refitting, and the U.S. Navy did not escape this technological imperative. Some of the American ships lacked sufficient armor on their prows and sterns, and they did not have adequate light artillery to ward off torpedo boats. The bigger guns fired very slowly — one shot every ten minutes on average — and they were not that accurate. They could not be fired in salvos like the later Dreadnoughts. In fact, the big guns were designed to deliver the coup de grâce at close range after the medium guns did the work of knocking out the enemy ships' mobility. American torpedo tubes had only one torpedo each, compared to the Spanish standard of three per tube. And Spanish cruisers had eight torpedo tubes, more than the typical American boat had. Indeed, a neutral assessment by British, French, and German experts predicted that the Spanish could defeat the Americans if the smaller Spanish ships struck at night and got in close to the American battleships.[63]

As always, Spanish military propaganda made too much of these sorts of neutral assessments and painted a rosy picture of the situation. An issue of Blanco y Negro in March 1898 compared the two navies and concluded that the U.S. Navy might be slightly superior but that this deficiency would be made good by Spanish sailors, who were "a hundred times better than [the Americans] are."[64]

This comforting fiction became harder to maintain after May 1. On that day, Admiral George Dewey, after a voyage from his station in Hong Kong, entered Manila Bay with six good ships, four of them steel cruisers with decks protected by armor plates. Admiral Patricio Montojo had seven ships in his squadron, but none was protected, and the largest, the Castilla had a wooden hull. Moreover, the American eight-inch guns could fire upon the Spanish from a safe range, because the Spanish had nothing equivalent. Indeed, many of the Spanish guns were old muzzle-loading cannon, useless in modern warfare at sea. The battle commenced at 5:40 A.M., with Dewey's famous instructions to the commander of his flagship, the Olympia: "You may fire when you are ready, Gridley." From a safe distance, the American ships pounded the Spanish squadron to bits. The Spanish did score a few hits when Dewey risked a closer pass to the wounded enemy vessels, but these were insignificant. No American sailor died. Nine were wounded. The Spanish lost every ship, 161 men killed, and 210 wounded. It was one of the most one-sided naval combats in history. But worse was to come.[65]

Talk in Spain now turned to the desperate idea of fighting a corso, that is, a kind of guerrilla war at sea against American shipping that would cripple the giant and force it to make peace.[66] Perhaps it was true that in an open contest between big ships, American technology would overwhelm Spanish courage, but a different kind of warfare might suit Spain better. Spain could attack American merchant vessels and sneak into eastern ports to wreak havoc. A corso like this would take advantage not only of the presumed innate guerrilla genius of the Spanish but of the kind of ships Spain had available. In the age of the battleship, and before the age of submarine warfare, a war of corsairs on the high seas proved to be a chimera. But it was not an absurd notion, merely an untested one. Every navy, even the British Royal Navy, had some officials who were slow to realize the new environment of war at sea in the age of steel. For example, it is a remarkable though little known fact that the British still equipped ships with grappling hooks as late as 1905 and trained seamen to board enemy vessels for hand-to-hand combat. Thus, the concept of a corso against the United States may have been a sign of desperation, but it was not a product of any peculiar backwardness in Spain.

So it was that before Manila and even after that debacle, a rational comparison of the naval forces of the United States and Spain would not have left

Spaniards thinking that they had no hope of victory. And where they were deficient, it was the result of rational, though incorrect, choices made by naval experts. After May 1, Spanish observers still persisted in thinking that "with our veteran and disciplined seamen, God will protect us and will send us days of peace and glory for our beloved Spain." [67] It was now that soldiers in Santiago were given "picture albums where a fantastic number of ships appeared," ships Spain lacked but that nonetheless "served to trick the fools." [68] On April 7 Minister of War Manuel Correa, perhaps understanding the futility of measuring Spain's navy against that of the United States, remarked: "I wish to God that we didn't have a single ship! That would satisfy me best. Then we could say to the United States from Cuba and from the Peninsula: Here we are! Come whenever you like! . . . Here we are, prepared not to lose even an atom of our territory." [69]

From the top to the bottom of society, the Spanish misconception of themselves and of their enemy could not have been more complete or more dangerous. As one Cuban author put it soon after the war's end, "Of a people that gives itself to such delusions one can say with confidence that it is capable of committing suicide . . . epically." [70] Spaniards went into a suicidal war of epic proportions, it is true, but they did not realize it at the time. They were deluded by their own myth of *guerrillerismo* and mistaken ideas about their enemy's softness of character, and by the false hope they placed in the theory that small, fast ships could overwhelm larger ones.

What of events in Cuba? On March 27, the day before McKinley made the naval court's findings on the *Maine* public, Ramón Blanco summarized the Cuban situation in a cable to Madrid. "Never has the war gone better than it is at these moments," he wrote. Máximo Gómez and the Cuban insurrectos "think only of hiding from our columns." He had sent five columns to Oriente, and they had "driven the enemy out of their positions in the Sierra Maestra and the Chaparra mountains, destroying their crops, their industries, and all of their resources. . . . Calixto García flees." [71] Similarly, Máximo Gómez and other leaders of the Cuban insurgency claimed that they had never been stronger than in the first few months of 1898. The Spanish were "packing their bags," and victory was around the corner. The truth about both armies is somewhat different.

The Spanish suffered terribly from disease and hunger, as they had throughout the war. Morale took a further hit when the Spanish mission was reduced to waiting and surviving, rather than engaging the enemy, after Weyler's dismissal. Nevertheless, until the American declaration of war in April 1898, the condition of the Spanish was far from desperate. General Antonio Pareja arrived in Guantánamo on December 27, 1897, and divided 550 men into three columns, which he used to destroy the houses and crops of the people living outside the zone of Spanish control. He also employed the men in building a new trocha to protect the zone of sugar mills and farms on the outskirts of the town. The soldiers had become day laborers, an abuse not unusual in the Spanish military, and, anyway, they had nothing else to do. Between January and April, Pareja encountered no resistance whatsoever from the insurgents, so there was no soldiering to be done.[72] Some of the Cubans began to entertain the thought of holding talks with the Spanish.

Around Holguín, in February 1898, Spanish forces cleared twelve villages or towns considered occupied by the enemy. They faced some sniper fire but no combat.[73] In March these troops, as well as the forces at Santiago and Manzanillo, made additional "conquests" against an insurgency that hardly fought back. According to the general in charge, "the insurrecto forces of the East had to abandon their principal centers and take refuge in Las Tunas, with only 1,200 men of the 5,000 they counted in November 1897."[74] In January 1898 the Máximo Gómez regiment included 116 armed and another 52 unarmed officers and troops, not even the equivalent of two companies. Only a few had died or been injured that month, because combat had become so rare. However, forty-two men had deserted to the enemy, taking their weapons in exchange for a pardon. The situation was worse in other regiments. Lieutenant Colonel Antonio Jiménez, head of the Honorato regiment of cavalry, had only eighty-four men under him, including sick, wounded, and unarmed individuals, too few to seek combat.[75] Everywhere one looked, the insurgents had melted away, as was the useful custom of the Liberation Army during periods of Spanish aggression. Of course, the insurgents had not finished with the Spanish. They merely waited for a better strategic situation.

The American declaration of war in April provided it. Indeed, the Spanish cease-fire on April 9 had already altered the situation for the insurgents dramatically. In March, according to an insurgent fighting in Matanzas, the Cubans were living in swamps and starving. Then with the proffered truce on April 9, they found over night that the Spanish were no longer to be seen. Suddenly they "could camp 500 meters from any city" without any danger that the Spanish would fire upon them.[76] Two weeks later, hearing that America had joined the fray, the insurgents in Puerto Príncipe came out of hiding, too, and began once again to "fire upon the forts of the trocha," which had not seen action in months. They "even attempted to assault it at various points, which obliged us to reinforce its defense and establish patrols," according to a Spanish officer. The Cubans "did not leave us alone day or night appearing continually where one least expected them." Most of the time the men along the trocha were employed in putting out fires in the cane fields. As usual, the Cubans did not inflict many losses, but they did occupy troops in onerous duties in an area where the deadly mosquito continued to do great damage. And they worked as best they could to prevent food from reaching the cities.[77]

Blanco, and Weyler before him, had all along expected an American intervention, or so they claimed later.[78] On April 17, anticipating the American declaration of war, Blanco reported that he had already ordered his forces in Oriente to reconcentrate, abandoning their forward positions in order to meet the approaching menace of an American landing. This also helped the insurgents regain their footing.[79] In the East, "where the insurgent bands had begun to fragment and scarcely opposed our columns" in March, they took the initiative again in April.[80]

The insurgents under Gómez in western Cuba, on the other hand, were beyond saving. When the government questioned Gómez's inaction during the Santiago campaign, he complained to Vice President Domingo Méndez Capote that he lacked officers, men, equipment, and food and that he could do nothing to aid García or the Americans in the East. Though annoyed, he had a "clear conscience" about his inaction and protested: "I will not give an explanation to the public, because it is not my fault that I can do nothing more. With an army that can't be mobilized and with Generals that can do nothing, one cannot go anywhere." He wanted the provisional government to come west to be near his headquarters, but he recognized that as far as getting across the trocha, "one could not even think of it, at least for now," because it was impassable. Ten days later, however, his isolation complete, Gómez ordered some of the eastern chiefs to cross the trocha anyway, "even though it be with their guts in their hands." He told them that he had asked the Americans to provide him with food, for that was what his starving men needed above all else before they could become an army again.[81] Gómez did eventually receive some relief from the United States, although the Americans had to abandon a plan to land a major shipment of supplies when they discovered that Gómez could not provide security for the operation.[82]

The fact of Cuban strength in Oriente and weakness in the West had profound consequences, for it helped to determine the site for the American invasion. As early as April 7 Spanish minister of war Manuel Correa cabled Blanco: "We know from source inside United States that various transports with troops are ready to leave Punta Gorda to disembark Santiago Cuba protected six cruisers Tortugas squadron. Insurgents will help disembarkation points near city."[83] The stage was set for a showdown in Santiago.

After lumbering across the Atlantic at eleven knots, Admiral Cervera eluded the American blockade of Cuba and put in at Santiago on May 19 with the best vessels in the Spanish fleet. Short on coal and pursued by two American squadrons, each superior to his own, Cervera had little choice but to do what he did.

Rumors of Cervera's presence at Santiago alarmed McKinley, because it posed a potential risk to the American plan to land an army in the area.[1] Commodore Schley steamed to Santiago, confirmed the Spanish presence there on May 29, and initiated a full-scale blockade of the port. Wanting to prevent Cervera's escape and safeguard against a sortie by torpedo boats, Admiral Sampson decided on June 3 to sink the collier *Merrimac* at a narrow spot in the channel entrance to the harbor. Fierce fire from Spanish shore batteries prevented Captain Hobson from scuttling his vessel in the appropriate place, but his bravery in the attempt made him a celebrity back home.[2]

Some Spanish and American authorities argue that Cervera made a mistake when he decided to put in at Santiago. His choice, they say, determined that the American invasion would take place in the East, a region the Spanish had never controlled, and where the Cubans under Calixto García could provide valuable assistance.[3] Indeed, the Spanish had fewer forces than usual in the region, because Blanco had just shifted troops from Santiago to cover the western ports of Cárdenas, Cienfuegos, Havana, and Matanzas.[4] In the East, Blanco had thirty-two battalions, in the West, seventy-eight, and these were fresher, better fed, and better equipped.[5] Scholars speculate that if Cervera had gone anywhere but Santiago, the ensuing campaign might have taken place in the West, with the advantage going to the Spanish. As it was, the U.S. Army faced only the starving shell of the garrison at Santiago, and Spanish defeat was ensured.

In fact, this argument makes no sense, because the Americans had decided to land at Santiago before they ever knew of the Spanish naval presence there. As we have seen, Blanco had received some indications in early April, before war with the United States had been declared, that the Americans were thinking of an invasion in the East. Major General Nelson Miles, who, with Secretary of War Russell Alger, ran the War Department, never liked the idea of a landing in the West. He knew that the U.S. Army was in no condition to measure itself against the veteran Spanish field armies stationed around Havana. That is why Miles favored an indirect approach. He proposed various schemes and, after some hesitation, selected Santiago as the best landing site. The Americans had good intelligence about the situation in eastern Cuba because García had sent several officers to Washington to help the Americans plan the invasion. In the West, the Americans would have been fighting in the midst of a countryside where the Spanish had many partisans and moved about freely. In the East, García and his 3,000 men could provide assistance and intelligence. Ultimately, this was the major factor that determined that Santiago would be the theater of American operations, not Cervera's decision to shelter in that port. In short, the decision to land at Santiago had been reached in April, and the plans were laid at least as early as May 28, one day before Schley confirmed Cervera's presence at Santiago. Army officers always like to blame the navy for everything, and vice versa. So Spanish military officials — and some scholars — blamed Cervera. The scapegoat admiral had many faults, but he was not responsible for drawing the Americans to Santiago.[6]

The real source of Spain's poor military performance against the Americans was the lack of strategic imagination displayed by her army officers. They remained locked in the paradigm of counterinsurgency warfare that had served them for the past three years. In their efforts to combat an elusive enemy that rarely gave battle, the Spanish had placed a majority of their troops in static positions, guarding cities, towns, and key roads and railroads. In April, when Spain attempted to forestall American intervention by declaring a unilateral cease-fire, this static mission became even more pronounced. The Spanish abandoned small garrisons and perfectly defensible positions to concentrate upon a handful of important cities in the hope that this would allow them to avoid the Cubans while they negotiated with the Americans. At Guantánamo, for example, a Spanish brigade of 7,086 officers and men under General Pareja relinquished its hold on outlying garrisons to regroup along a perimeter of fortifications around the city. They remained in this position from April to August, never attempting to take offensive action. Thus, 7,000 men became unavailable to face the American concentration of forces at Santiago, a short distance to the west.[7]

It is an exaggeration to say that Cuban forces had the Spanish "pinned down" at Guantánamo or anywhere else in Oriente, as some scholars claim.[8] The bulk of the Cuban forces in the East consisted of the 3,000 men under García's direct command at Santiago. García's correspondence indicated that at most there might have been another 1,000 men under arms in the rest of Oriente, but they did not present much of a challenge to the Spanish, "due to the utter exhaustion of the infantry and the great shortage of food for so many people."[9] There is no evidence in any accounts of the actions at Guantánamo of a sizable Cuban force operating in the vicinity, nor would the Cubans have been able to feed and arm a force capable of pinning down Pareja. And why would they bother? Pareja's orders to defend Guantánamo against a possible attack by the United States had him "pinned down" already. It took only a few guerrilla squadrons guarding the roads to prevent Pareja from communicating by courier with Santiago and other garrisons. That was the vital Cuban contribution to the isolation of Guantánamo and other Spanish garrisons in the East.

The campaign began on June 7, when the American cruisers *Marblehead* and *Yankee* entered Guantánamo Bay. The Spanish forts defending the mouth of the harbor did not serve to deter the landing in the slightest. Their ancient, muzzle-loading bronze and iron cannon included one artifact cast in 1668 that had a laughable range of 750 meters with the help of a stiff breeze.[10] The Spanish therefore had no way to respond to the shelling that quickly reduced their defenses to rubble. Ground combat began when a small force of American marines and sailors landed at Punta del Este and destroyed the cable station there. This completed Pareja's isolation. On June 10 the Americans landed in force — the first large-scale landing in Cuba. The First Marine Battalion, an elite force of 647 officers and men equipped with rapid-fire artillery, a Gatling gun, and modern Krags, occupied the hills east of the city. Joined by a few hundred insurgents, they pushed back a Spanish attack with the help of artillery fire from the *Marblehead* and the *Yankee*. Once the combined Cuban and American force secured this position, they began to probe Pareja's outer defenses, an extensive system of trenches and forts built to protect a zone of cultivation around Guantánamo.

Pareja considered it crucial to hold this perimeter because the crops planted inside it provided the Spanish with their only sustenance. Since the start of the American blockade on April 22, one German vessel had unloaded 1,700 sacks of rice at Santiago, allowing its garrison to survive, barely, on two cups of boiled rice a day for the next twelve weeks. But the men at Guantánamo did not have even this much to eat. When the blockade began, the food supply was day-to-day. Pay was nine or ten months behind, so soldiers could not afford to purchase anything on the black market either.[11] The garrison did not lose an inch of ground, but the defense of the cultivation zone absorbed all of Pareja's energies. Breaking out to do anything useful was the last thing on his mind.

Still there was not enough food to go around. On June 14 two Spanish deserters confessed to their American captors that they had not eaten in three days.[12] And it only got worse in July. Pareja later cabled Blanco a heart-breaking account of the ordeal his men had faced: "Resources gone, embargo on commerce. I used horses, mules, green corn to feed forces. Privations all around, especially outer trenches, mortality rising terrible rate. From May end July 756 dead rising this month 400 result work [and] poor diet. Nine emissaries sent Santiago giving account situation hanged [by the Cubans]. I knew nothing until July 25 when I received order from General Toral [in Santiago] to capitulate name of Government and Your Excellency. I obeyed lack of means subsistence." In combat, Pareja had lost 19 dead, 98 wounded, and 18 missing during all that time. But 1,156 men, 16 percent of his brigade, had perished from starvation and disease, not to mention the thousands laid low by sickness.[13]

Even then the insurgents and the American marines did not possess forces sufficient to stop Pareja from breaking out, if he had tried. But with no information reaching him from outside, he was not willing to take such a drastic step against previous explicit orders to stay put. Had he known about the American advance on Santiago during the last week of June, or had he possessed sufficient imagination and initiative, he might have attempted to march upon Santiago, catching the Americans between two fires. But that is not what happened. He followed orders and starved, helping to make the end in Cuba mercifully brief. Thus, the brigade at Guantánamo was hors de combat, not essentially because of anything the Cubans and Americans did, but because Pareja adhered to the poor strategy laid down by Blanco of protecting many points at once. As a result, the great blow that was about to fall on Santiago found the Spanish garrison there quite alone and unprepared.

On June 14, 819 officers and 16,058 American enlisted men departed Tampa Bay, arriving off of Santiago on June 20. The commander of the expedition, Major General William Shafter, together with Rear Admiral William Sampson, in charge of the Atlantic Squadron, went ashore with a small party about twenty miles west of Santiago. There they met with Calixto García to strategize about the landing. García recommended that the American troops land at Daiquirí beach, a few miles east of Santiago, and he promised to secure the area ahead of time to assist the invasion force. On June 22, 6,000 American troops rowed to shore. They advanced immediately to a place called Las Guásimas on the road to Santiago, allowing the remaining American forces to debark at Siboney, a point on the coast five miles closer to Santiago as the crow flies. Within four days the entire expeditionary force had been landed.

Observers found much to criticize in this exercise. The army lacked enough transports, so the landing took four days, a long period during which an enemy less passive than the Spanish could have launched a counterstrike. The Americans made poor use of their field artillery, though their Gatling guns proved a decisive advantage. In command of the field army, the old Confederate general Joseph Wheeler acted like a cowboy, exceeding his authority and endangering troops at Las Guásimas all in order to garner the glory of drawing first blood. And it was all unnecessary, because the Americans had good intelligence that the Spanish intended to evacuate Las Guásimas shortly. The Rough Riders, who had never fired their weapons in anger, committed a tactical blunder at the beginning of the encounter, placing themselves in a precarious position, so that they had to be rescued by the regulars of the Tenth Cavalry, the black troopers who would do so much of the hard fighting in America's imperial wars in Cuba and the Philippines.

The U.S. Army provisioned its men in scandalous fashion. The government allowed criminal speculators, a species characteristic of the freewheeling capitalism of Gilded Age America, to supply the rations, and they provided food unfit for swine.[14] One meat supplier even induced the government to accept what was essentially embalmed beef that made the men sick. A trooper named John Kendrick, who had worked as a meat packer, did not recall encountering this particular problem, but he remembered being forced to eat what he called "slunk," the tasteless, leathery, nutritionally useless tissues left after already unmarketable by-products had been rendered into beef tea.[15] All of these and other criticisms hit the mark perfectly. Had the Spanish army in Cuba not been a half-starved, sick, and dispirited remnant of the army of 1897, and had it put up a better fight at Santiago, then the various problems plaguing the U.S. Army might have had tragic consequences.

As it was, the Americans under Wheeler advanced quickly from Las Guásimas to the San Juan Hills during the last week of June, bringing up their entire force before the Spanish on July 1. General Arsenio Linares had been "absolutely incommunicado" with Guantánamo and other nearby forces since early June because the roads had been made impassable by the summer rains and because the Cubans patrolled the few routes that remained open.[16] The Spanish sent local inhabitants as couriers, but they never returned. Scouting parties could not be risked to gather intelligence. In effect, because of the weather, the Spanish strategy, and the vigilance of the Cubans, the Spanish operated under the fog of war even before the Americans landed, and this affected their ability to respond. Linares had 319 officers and 9,111 men at Santiago, a considerable force, on paper. It was an army of veterans who would not shrink under fire. On the other hand, many of them were starving and feverish wrecks by June 1898. Between fifteen and twenty men died each day in late June.[17] Conscripts who had naively viewed their posting to Cuba as a "pleasure trip" learned the meaning of misery, made so much worse because of the two-month blockade that preceded the

American assault. Veterans who had greeted the news of war with the United States with glee, hoping to see regular combat in place of the constant skirmishing and sniping of the Cubans, had a change of heart. Morale plummeted. Cut off from the world, on minimum rations of rice and water, and waiting for who knew what from the Americans, a spirit of defeatism infected the men.[18]

Incredibly, Linares did not place the healthy troops he did have in position to face the approaching Americans. Instead, he spread them out in a thin perimeter around the city, even though he knew the Americans were marching from Daiquirí. Perhaps Linares, accustomed by years of fighting an enemy that never attacked strongly defended trenches and towns, could not adjust to the idea of a regular war. Whatever the cause, Linares held the defensive line east of Santiago with a light force. He placed some 500 men at Kettle Hill and the San Juan Heights and an equal number at the height of El Caney, a few miles to the north. Against them, the Americans threw 8,000 troops.[19]

With these odds, defeat was certain when the Americans attacked on July 1. The Spanish, entrenched at El Caney and Kettle Hill, fought valiantly for a time. Their Mausers had a greater range than the American Krag-Jorgensens, and in the first minutes of battle the Spanish brought down hundreds of American troops. But the Americans had another decisive advantage beside numbers. Although they bungled the job of bringing up their artillery, they brought four Gatling guns. Once in place, these were so effective that the Spanish could not even raise their heads above their trenches to watch the charge of Teddy Roosevelt and the dismounted Rough Riders.[20] An assault on El Caney had similar results, with the Spanish falling back to the city of Santiago after one day of sharp battle. The Spanish lost 95 men killed, 376 men wounded, and 123 men captured in these encounters, a casualty rate of nearly 60 percent of the forces engaged.[21] They gave as good as they got, however, with the Americans suffering 441 casualties at El Caney and 1,385 in the storming of the San Juan Heights.[22]

Now completely surrounded, Spanish troops stood in trenches filled with water and shivered with hunger, cold, and fever as they awaited the end.[23] Unless the city received reinforcements and supplies or the Spanish fleet bottled up in the harbor achieved some prodigy to break the blockade by sea, the situation was hopeless. In fact, a Spanish relief column of nearly 3,500 men under Colonel Federico Escario had departed Manzanillo on June 22, but it took the column thirteen days to make the 200-mile trip. Escario's bedraggled troops arrived in Santiago on July 3, too late to make any difference and lacking the necessary supplies to provide any relief. Indeed, the additional mouths to feed added to the subsistence crisis. Had the column arrived before July 1, and had it been deployed at the San Juan Hills, it might have achieved something. But this, of course, is mere speculation.

The Cuban insurgents deserve part of the credit for Escario's slow march, for they harassed the Spanish the whole way, forcing them to halt and form up for defense on several occasions. Some historians make a great deal of this episode, even going so far as to claim that the insurgents stopped Escario from turning the tide of battle at Santiago. This is an untenable argument, however. The Cubans did not decimate the Spanish troops, as Cuban authorities claimed at the time and some historians still argue.[24] In fact, Escario lost twenty men killed and seventy wounded on the march. This was bad enough, and the wounded certainly slowed Escario's progress. However, the real cause for the delay was the parlous state of the roads between Manzanillo and Santiago. The rains had made them impassable, so much so that Escario decided to bypass them, attempting instead to hack his way through the jungle following river courses across very rugged terrain. This proved to be a terrible blunder, a shortcut that added days to the journey. Even so, it is hard to see how Escario's men could have tipped the balance in the battle for Santiago. When they arrived, they merely burdened the city's already stretched resources.[25]

The arrival of Escario, though it proved meaningless in the long run, contributed to a widening rift between the Americans and the Cubans. Shafter had learned of Escario's approach and gave Calixto García's 3,000 men the job of stopping him. When Escario brushed off García's forces and entered the city almost unmolested, it sent Shafter into a rage.[26] Having heard for years about epic battles won by the Cubans, Americans expressed astonishment when they saw that the insurgents did not fight well in a regular war of fixed positions. Experts at ambush and harassing actions, the Cubans had no experience with large-scale siege operations or battles. This is no slur against García's men, just a recognition of reality, but the Americans behaved as if the easy entry of Escario into Santiago were an indictment of Cuban honor and courage.

In his defense, García claimed, quite rightly, that the American plan worked out by General Shafter did not allow him the flexibility to go out to meet Escario, so that he could ambush the column in the mountains, as was his custom. This is a sensible explanation of the case. Shafter misunderstood and misused his Cuban allies, preventing them from functioning in the way they knew best: as guerrillas. But García also exaggerated his abilities to the Americans for political purposes, when he might simply have admitted his inability to stop a strong column such as that led by Escario. This was part of a pattern with García. For example, he later pretended that he had fought "always in the vanguard" at El Caney and the San Juan Hills, when in fact the Cubans hardly took part in these combats.[27]

This controversy over the role of the Cubans in the combats of 1898 may seem rather meaningless now, but it was a matter of grave concern at the time. The

Americans tried to take all of the credit for the liberation of Cuba as a way to help justify both their intervention and their continued occupation of Cuba after the Spanish defeat. The Cubans claimed sole credit for the victory for the opposite reason: they wanted to depict American intervention as an unnecessary meddling in Cuban affairs by an imperial power.

In fact, the Cuban and American men who fought all deserve credit for Cuba's liberation. There can be no question about the responsibility of the Cubans. We must not allow a focus on the Santiago campaign to mask their fundamental contribution to Spain's defeat. For over three years they had fought to gain control of the civilian population and its resources. They had exhausted the Spanish, harassing them and letting mosquitoes deal their dirty death. The Cubans had never fielded large armies capable of set battles, and they could not suddenly be expected to do so in 1898, particularly when they were half-starving and lacked clothing, shoes, and proper equipment. It should not offend Cuban honor to recognize the truth of this. On the contrary, it is a tribute to the men of the Liberation Army that, lacking resources, they had been able to continue the fight for so long, placing the Spanish in a position to be defeated by the rather small American expeditionary army.

American troops also liberated Cuba. Even after their partial recovery in April 1898, the Cuban insurgents could never have defeated large Spanish forces in places like Santiago. The Cuban attempt to claim credit for "pinning down" Spanish forces during the advance on Santiago is farcical. The insurgents participated in the fighting at Daiquirí, Guantánamo, Santiago, and elsewhere, but their role seems to have been insignificant.[28] Only the Americans could have destroyed the Spanish army at Santiago, and to claim otherwise is delusional.

Moreover, the revival of the Cuban insurgency in the spring of 1898 cannot be understood solely as a function of Cuban patriotism and sacrifice. The U.S. government and people, together with the antiwar movement in Spain itself, also deserve some of the credit. The Spanish Liberal government replaced Weyler with Blanco, ended reconcentration, granted Cuba autonomy, withdrew garrisons, and avoided offensive action during the winter campaign of 1897–98 in order to appease McKinley abroad and antiwar Liberals at home. When this was not enough to satisfy the Americans, the Liberal government tried a unilateral cease-fire on April 11. All of these actions taken together are what gave the Cuban Liberation Army a chance to regroup.

With the city of Santiago threatened by American troops, Ramón Blanco became increasingly impatient with Cervera's unwillingness to make a sortie from the harbor. Finally, he took direct command over the fleet and ordered it into combat. On July 3, at 9:35 A.M., the Spanish ships began to exit the harbor. The result is well-known. In 2½ hours of fighting along fifty miles of coastline west of Santiago, every ship in the Spanish squadron sank or ran aground. Only three of the seven American ships suffered any damage, and that very minor. One sailor died, and another was wounded.[29] In contrast, Cervera lost six ships and 323 men killed and 151 wounded out of the 2,227 men under his command.[30]

Despite the one-sided nature of the battle, the Americans actually missed with most of their shots (only 122 out of the 9,433 shells fired hit a target), but it was enough.[31] Five things produced the overwhelming American victory. First, Spanish gunnery was even worse than the American. Many of their guns did not function. Others lacked shells. And the crews had not been allowed to expend precious ammunition in gunnery practice, so it comes as little surprise that they were poor shots. Second, because the mouth of the harbor was so narrow, the Spanish ships had to exit one by one, allowing the Americans to concentrate on each ship in turn. Third, Cervera made his dash to the sea during broad daylight, although his best chance, according to the estimation of every naval authority then and since, would have been to make his escape at night. The explanation for this choice seems to be that Cervera, always a pessimist, decided to exit Santiago on a bright and sunny morning, because, certain of failure, he wanted his men to have the best possible chance to swim ashore and make their way back to Santiago. Fourth, the Spanish had used up their high-grade coal during the transatlantic journey to reach Cuba, leaving them no choice but to use the cheap stuff available in Santiago. This left their engines running below capacity and made it impossible for them to outrun or outmaneuver the Americans, an unlikely scenario in any case. And, finally, the Spanish ships had armored hulls, but their decks and superstructures were wooden. A few hits turned their topsides into infernos, causing panic among the crews, who were forced to fight fires rather than the enemy.[32] After running his flagship aground, Cervera fell captive, but the Americans allowed him to communicate the result of the battle to Madrid. "We have lost everything," he reported, adding later that the outcome was "an honorable disaster" and that "the country has been defended with honor and the satisfaction of having done our duty, leaving us with clear consciences."[33]

With the squadron a complete loss, and with Santiago starving and surrounded, the garrison's surrender became the only option. Linares had been gravely wounded in the battle for the San Juan Heights, and his replacement, General José Toral, held out for several days. He accepted a cease-fire to allow civilians inside Santiago to leave the city. Twenty-thousand starving wretches fled to the American lines, and then the siege was renewed. Now the big guns of the American ships joined the fire from artillery and Gatling guns that poured into the Spanish positions. The troops could scarcely raise their heads above their trenches to fire their own weapons. On July 13 Generals Shafter and Miles met with Toral to ask for his surrender. The Americans had begun to contract yellow fever and other diseases that would have laid the expeditionary army low in a few more weeks, but luckily for everyone concerned, the Spanish commander did not realize it. In any case, his own men were in even worse shape. On July 14 Toral surrendered the city.[34]

Crushing defeats on land and sea convinced the Spanish that continued war with the United States was futile. Though it took some time for Madrid formally to request peace negotiations, the Sagasta government had been working for weeks to prepare public opinion for a complete surrender. On July 26 the Spanish proposal reached Washington, followed by two weeks of negotiations that produced the Peace Protocol of August 12, 1898. The war was over. The formal treaty of peace came later, on December 10, 1898, following further negotiations held in Paris. Spain surrendered Cuba, Puerto Rico, the Philippines, and Guam and two weeks later sold several small islands in the Pacific to Germany. It was a dismal end to an empire that had once been the largest in the world. For the United States, which suddenly acquired its own far-flung empire, the Cuban conflict had been, in the words of John Hay, U.S. ambassador to Great Britain, "a splendid little war."

The period between the signing of the peace protocol on August 12 and the completion of the Treaty of Paris on December 10 casts an interesting light on the nature of the war and the peace that followed. After the capitulation of Santiago, Spanish forces elsewhere did not immediately surrender. Even General Pareja's brigade in nearby Guantánamo, which had been included by Toral in the capitulation, continued to fight. Indeed, the news from Santiago did not reach Pareja until July 25, but even then he at first refused to obey Toral and did not surrender until August 16. As he later explained to Blanco: "My brigade has not capitulated, it has not obeyed the surrendering Divisional General [Toral] but the government of his majesty and its General in Chief [Blanco]." Orders from Blanco and Madrid, not the loss of Santiago, made Pareja lay down his arms. It went the same elsewhere. Blanco worked to convince disgruntled officers and men who still wanted to fight the Americans to respect the peace protocol signed on August 12. Finally, he "found himself obliged to remove some officials" and to take strict measures against townspeople who still seemed intent on continuing the fight.[35]

None of this applied to the Cuban insurgents, however. As Blanco said, "they are not belligerents." He considered them bandits not included in the peace protocol. Indeed, "no pact with them could be reached." Blanco "reserved the right to operate against them," even after August 12.[36] For their part, the Cubans also

continued to attack Spanish positions in late August. As Blanco reported: "Insurgents continue hostilities, attacking towns, robbing and sacking."[37] On August 19 a Spanish foraging party repulsed an attack by Cuban insurgents near
Matanzas.[38] On September 10 Cuban guerrillas still prevented food from reaching the city of Puerto Príncipe, and Blanco was tempted, despite the delicacy of
the ongoing peace negotiations with the Americans, to mount a full-blown offensive against them, if nothing else to prevent the city from starving. As late as
October 1, the Cuban insurgents still kept livestock and produce out of Holguín,
and there were skirmishes around that city as well. The Americans did not have
enough men in Cuba to occupy the country, and they did not trust the Cubans to
do it. So an awkward situation arose in which the Spanish continued to govern
the cities with American consent and oversight, while the Cubans who had
fought so long for their freedom were left out in the cold. This situation was
bound to produce conflict.[39]

The Americans, it seemed, had experienced a change of heart about the insurgents. In part, it was simply a matter of the racism of white officers and soldiers reasserting itself. It must be remembered that the rank and file of the Liberation Army, especially in Oriente, were Afro-Cubans. Meanwhile, despite the
key role of black soldiers in the American expeditionary army at Santiago, American officers and most of the troops were white, and many came from the Jim
Crow South. They had little truck with the black Cuban insurgents. As one
American historian put it: "This was a white man's army, with no use for foreign
'niggers.'" Thus, General Samuel Young thought the insurgents were "degen-
erates, absolutely devoid of honor or gratitude. They are no more capable of self-
government than the savages of Africa." Grover Flint, who had been fighting
with Gómez for some time, thought that the Cuban "buffalo soldiers" fighting
in Oriente were comical, "continually grinning, and showing their ivory teeth
and white eyeballs." These were the men who had the audacity to claim the right
of victors and the right to self-government. The situation was explosive.[40]

Racism aside, the Americans also expressed genuine surprise at the destitu-
tion of the Cuban guerrilla forces. In a sense, the Cuban campaign of propaganda that had presented the rosiest picture to American audiences now came
back to hurt the Cubans. One soldier recalled thinking that the insurgents were
"the toughest crowd of people that I ever had the fortune to see. Most of them
didn't have clothes to cover their nakedness, and what they did have were
rags."[41] In American eyes, the Cubans were "a canaille, cowards, and bandits,
people more expert at highway robbery than at war." They were even known to
rob from the American troops, which is not surprising given their straightened
circumstances.[42]

McKinley had never considered it "wise or prudent" to recognize the Cuban wartime republic for fear that it would not be able to maintain the peace after hostilities ended. That fear now seemed well-founded to the Americans at Santiago. According to Shafter, the insurgents threatened not only the Spanish but also the Cuban people, many of whom had stayed in the cities and sided with the Spanish throughout the war. The leaders were "sore because they were not permitted to take part in the conference leading to the capitulation and because I will not permit them to go into the city armed." But Shafter feared that they would sack Santiago and murder the residents, especially the Spanish-born. These Spaniards were the judges, constables, clergymen, and other local government officials that the Americans needed to help them occupy the island. Shafter realized that after such a long civil war bad feelings were natural and justified, but he planned to take every precaution to keep the insurgents from creating a bloodbath in the cities.

The trouble, according to Shafter, was that "there was nothing for men to do in the country. It has absolutely returned to its wild state and has got to be settled and made anew. The attitude of the pronounced Cubans is hostile. They so far show no disposition to disband and go to work" in peacetime occupations. A war of pillage and ambush had become a habit with too many men. And when they could not immediately adjust to civilian life, the Americans dismissed them as inherently ungovernable.[43]

In anger at being prevented from immediately establishing Cuban rule at Santiago, García marched his men off for the interior, where his union with Gómez promised to create "complications of a grave character," according to Shafter. It might even become necessary, thought Shafter, to take military action against the Cubans. For their part, the Cubans, fearing that the United States would renege on its promises of April 1898 to allow Cubans to govern themselves, began to speak of the need to renew the war of liberation, this time against the United States. Fortunately, Gómez, whose influence and prestige remained for a while unchallenged, stood fast against this suicidal current of opinion. "I believe that thinking that the Americans intend to annex Cuba is an insult to the great nation freed by Washington," he intoned. And so a new conflict was avoided. Cuban nationalists would later take Gómez to task for acquiescing in the marginalization and ultimate demobilization of the Liberation Army at this critical juncture in Cuban history, but the truth was that he didn't have much of an army left to dismantle and few resources with which to feed and clothe the men he did have.[44]

Meanwhile, U.S. troops had a very different reaction to the erstwhile barbaric Spaniards. They were brave and honorable and had served as bulwarks of

QTY	ISBN	AUTHOR/TITLE	LIST$	DISC$	QTY	ISBN	AUTHOR/TITLE	LIST$	DISC$
____	-2673-1	Rable, FREDERICKSBURG! FREDERICKSBURG!	45.00	36.00					
____	-5662-2	Rankin, NC CONTINENTALS p *New in paperback!*	19.95	15.96					
____	-5461-1	Reardon, PICKETT'S CHARGE/HIST & MEMORY p	18.95	15.16					
____	-4938-3	Renda, TAKING HAITI p	19.95	15.96					
____	-2928-5	Rubin, SHATTERED NATION	34.95	27.96					
____	-2867-X	Schultz, WOMEN AT THE FRONT	34.95	27.96					
____	-2440-2	Simpson & Berlin, SHERMAN'S CIVIL WAR	55.00	44.00					
____	-5579-0	Smith, BLACK SOLDIERS IN BLUE p	19.95	15.96					
____	-5507-3	Stoler, ALLIES AND ADVERSARIES p	21.95	17.56					
____	-4914-6	Sweeney, SECRETS OF VICTORY p	18.95	15.16					
____	-3006-2	Tone, WAR & GENOCIDE IN CUBA *New!*	35.00	28.00					
____	-5607-X	Walker, PROMPT/UTTER DESTRUCTION/REV p	16.95	13.56					

Additional UNC Press titles may be ordered at the 20% convention discount:

_____

_____

_____

civilization against the insurgents. Above all, they turned out to be white. The Spanish, in turn, had a similar admiration for the Americans, once the fighting ended. Both sides fraternized "in a spirit of mutual admiration" and disregard for the Cubans.[45] Pedro López de Castillo, an infantrymen in the Santiago garrison, wrote an eloquent, open letter to the Americans on August 21, 1898, that read in part: "You fought us as men, face to face, and with great courage." This, said López, was "a quality which we had not met with during the three years we have carried on this war." López assured the Americans that Spaniards felt nothing but a "high sentiment of appreciation" for the American arrival. For now, the "white man's burden" would fall to the United States. He concluded by wishing the new occupiers "all happiness and health in this land" but warned that "the descendants of the Congo and of Guinea" would not be "able to exercise or enjoy their liberty, for they will find it a burden to comply with the laws which govern civilized communities."[46]

The stage was thus set for the United States to meddle in Cuban affairs during the first half of the twentieth century on the pretext that it was in the best interest of Cubans. America had come to Cuba with a "civilizing mission," one of the oldest and most useful imperial myths. In 1902 the United States evacuated the island, but not before securing a base at Guantánamo Bay as a reward for its sacrifices in the war, and inserting a clause in the Cuban Constitution that granted the United States the right to intervene in Cuban affairs to protect property and life if it were threatened by a new rebellion. In some ways, therefore, the Cubans were robbed of the redemption that Martí had supposed to be at the center of the island's great war of independence. This is just one way among many in which the splendid story of Cuban insurgency and independence has also to be read as a story of disaster for Cubans.[47]

The war had a dramatic impact on the United States as well. Indeed, in terms of its long-term effects, the Spanish-American War may have been as crucial to America as the World Wars of the twentieth century.[48] The war united the country as nothing ever had. The "blue and the gray" had fought together, overcoming the sectional differences that had torn the country apart only thirty-five years earlier. America acquired territory in the Caribbean that positioned it to play an imperial role in Latin America, and it acquired the Philippines and other territories in the Pacific that made the United States a counterweight and a threat to the rising power of Japan. All that power abroad helped to distract Americans from trouble at home, soothing the wounds of social and economic inequality in Gilded Age America with the salve of empire. In Cuba, American public health officials, led by William Gorgas, acted upon the theory of Cuban physician Carlos Finlay and put into place antimosquito measures that wiped out yellow fever, making an American occupation of the island infinitely less deadly. A few years later, Gorgas followed the same procedures in eradicating yellow fever from the Panama Canal zone, a key acquisition for the American empire.

And what of Spain? Among Hispanists, the current dogma is that the outcome of the war was not that bad for Spain. The economy recovered quickly after 1898. Intellectual life blossomed. The political system survived the shock. The greater disaster for Spain lay in the future, in the civil war of 1936–39 and its aftermath, when the country was torn apart and set back a generation. All of this is true. Nevertheless, Spaniards who lived through the Cuban war knew it as an unparalleled catastrophe, and we have tried not to ignore their voices. There is an authenticity to lived experience on which historians must insist if they wish to remain historians.[49]

Spain lost an army, a fleet, and an empire between 1895 and 1898. Even beyond this, however, the defeat in Cuba had long-term consequences of a psychological and institutional nature. Spaniards lost their bearing in the world. In the age of social Darwinism, it was considered natural and healthy that nations and races should struggle so that only the fittest would survive. Spaniards, who had spread their language, culture, and genetic material across half of the globe, had proved themselves unfit in Cuba, had shown that they were a "dying race," to use the phrase in vogue back then. The loss of prestige and confidence was felt mostly by elites, and this helped to produce elite institutions — crown, church, military — with a prickly and defensive sense of their mission to regenerate Spain. This reactionary culture lasted a long time. It helped to produce the civil war in 1936 and haunted the country until Franco's death in 1975. Even after that event, it continued to manifest the occasional phantom, as during the botched right-wing coup of 1981 against a democratic Spain then in its infancy.

The impact of the Cuban war on Spain's military institutions was especially dramatic. Cuba was Spain's Vietnam, with a difference: The Spanish army did not face the kind of widespread cultural rebellion against the war that challenged American military doctrine in Vietnam. True, a small number of Spaniards did voice their opposition, some heroically and eloquently out of genuine humanitarian concern, others from calculation: Being antiwar was almost the only thing that distinguished Liberals from Conservatives in 1897. This Liberal opposition to the war came to play a part in the unraveling of the Spanish regime in Cuba, as we have seen. In the aftermath of the crucial bullets fired by Angiolillo, the Liberals were ready to assume power from Cánovas's party. Yet the critics of the Cuban war were a vanguard without followers. There was no broad antiwar movement to challenge the military. Responsibility for the loss of Cuba was placed entirely with the Liberal administration, which had seen fit to recall

Weyler and give in to the Americans. This is true, as far as it goes, but the military failed as well. It failed, in the first place, to deal with the Cuban insurgents in a timely way, and, second, it failed to deal with the Americans. Unfortunately, being able to blame politicians for the defeat, the army remained unchastened by the experience, and career officers who had fought in the war returned to Spain with their swagger tragically intact.

Or almost intact. Their pride had been injured and required a salve. What they needed, and quickly, were new enemies they could defeat. These were found in the insurrectionary Spanish workers and Basque and Catalan separatists, who were routed with depressing frequency in the early twentieth century, all without the trouble of having to reform the woeful Spanish military. Against these "foes," and against Moroccan tribesmen, veterans of Cuba helped create an inhumane military culture in Spain, whose elite soldiers would come in later years to call themselves "The Bridegrooms of Death," and whose callous battle motto, intoned as they slaughtered striking Spanish workers, was the absurd "long live death." The experience of the Spanish military in Cuba shaped the thinking of the next generation of Spanish officers, including Francisco Franco, whose quasi-autobiographical film, La raza, began, significantly, in Cuba, with the death of the protagonist's father. This death required endless avenging, ensuring that the Cuban war bore its rotten fruit for decades to come in Spain.

Notes

ABBREVIATIONS USED IN THE NOTES

AGM	Archivo General Militar (Segovia)
AHN	Archivo Histórico Nacional (Madrid)
AMM	Archivo General Militar de Madrid (Madrid)
ANC	Archivo Nacional de Cuba (Havana)
BN	Biblioteca Nacional (Madrid)
car.	carpeta (folder)
CGC	Sección Capitanía General de Cuba
div.	división (division)
EP	Sección Expedientes Personales
exp.	expediente (document)
GR	Sección Gobierno de la Revolución
HL	Huntington Library (Pasadena)
LCMD	Library of Congress, Manuscripts Division (Washington, D.C.)
leg.	legajo (box or bundle)
secc.	sección (section)

PREFACE

1. For an example of the old interpretation in which the Cubans played little role in their own liberation see the classic work by Frank Freidel, *The Splendid Little War*. The "black legend" of Spanish decadence is a theme I discuss in a later chapter. For an essay on the theme see López Ibor, *El español y su complejo de inferioridad*.

2. For a critique of the American project of "constructing the Cuban absence" see the chapter by that title in Pérez, *War of 1898*. This "history with the Cubans left out" never went unchallenged in America. See, for example, Philip Foner, especially in his *Spanish-Cuban-American War*.

3. The myth of the Cuban "people-in-arms" was consubstantial with the war itself. Nevertheless, at least two Cuban combatants knew better and fought against the myth. General Piedra Martel found risible the view that Cuban national consciousness had anything to do with the genesis or success of the Cuban war effort: "The national spirit of independence was never well developed in Cuba. Not in 1868, and not in 1895 . . . despite the fact that some historians want to see in them an already well defined separatist tendency. A heroic minority sustained the war of 68 . . . and the same thing happened in the war of 95." See Manuel Piedra Martel, *Campañas de Maceo*, 9–10. General Miró dismissed as absurd the "grave error" current in 1895 that claimed armed insurgents were naturally superior fighters because they embodied the innate spirit of the people. See Miró, *Cuba*, 23. Unfortunately, the wisdom of Miró and Piedra Martel found no place in the historiography.

4. The classic account in this vein is the work by Emilio Roig de Leuchsenring, especially his *Cuba no debe*, where the title says it all. For more recent examples of this traditional nationalist interpretation of the war, see Amado Palenque, *La campaña de invasión*, 10, where

the Cuban victory over Spain is attributed to the development of Cuban nationalism. See also Ibarra, *Ideología mambisa*, 10, 21, 49; Botifoll, *Forjadores de la conciencia nacional cubana*, 5; Opatrn'y, *Antecedentes históricos*, 58, 237, 243; and Bosch, *De Cristóbal Colón a Fidel Castro*, 560.

5. Pérez, *War of 1898*, 88–89. Manuel Moreno Fraginals (*Cuba/España, España/Cuba*, 282) denied the importance of disease in destroying the Spanish army, a view that is entirely at odds with the evidence. The notion that the Cubans defeated the Spanish on their own is now accepted by some Spanish scholars, notably Elorza and Sandoica, in their popular history, *La Guerra de Cuba*.

CHAPTER ONE

1. Information on Gonzalo, unless otherwise noted, is from AMM, EP, microfilm nos. 25 and 26.

2. Ferrer, *Insurgent Cuba*, 100; Steele, *Cuban Sketches*, on rural conditions in the East. On banditry see Pérez, *Lords of the Mountain*; Schwartz, *Lawless Liberators*; and Paz Sánchez et al., *El bandolerismo en Cuba*.

3. Engineer's report: "Trocha de Júcaro. Observaciones oportunas respecto a su deficiencia, sobre todo si sobreviniera una guerra," June 10, 1893, AMM, CGC, microfilm no. 14; Díaz Benzo, *Pequeñeces*, 66.

4. Burguete y Lana, ¡*La guerra!* 57–58; see also *Album de la trocha*.

5. Pando Despierto, "La defensa de Cascorro," 8–16.

6. Weyler, *Mi mando*, 2:18–19.

7. Diego, *Weyler*, 204.

8. Pan-Montojo, *Más se perdió en Cuba*, 320, plate 6.

9. See, for example, Pérez Guzmán, *Herida profunda*.

10. For one such exception, see Offner, *Unwanted War*.

11. Estimates of Spanish losses in Cuba vary widely. The published figures in the *Diario Oficial del Ministerio de Guerra* showed 3,101 killed in combat, 41,288 from disease. According to a report given to the Spanish Congress in 1899, 53,541 men died during the war, but this included losses at sea and in the Philippines and Puerto Rico, so the numbers from this report would not be very different from those published in the *Diario* (AMM, CGC, legs. 4, 155). The most conservative figure for deaths from all causes produced soon after the war by the Instituto Geográfico y Catastral de España was 32,247 dead, but this didn't count Spaniards resident in Cuba who fought and died for the regime. Nor did it take into account losses at sea and Spaniards who died on the return voyage. Some scholars accept a very high figure of about 100,000 Spanish deaths, but there is no evidence for this claim. A careful recent estimate places Spanish losses in Cuba at about 45,000 men, a figure that has the virtue of being based on sound evidence and of falling within the parameters of official estimates at the time (Maluquer de Motes, *España en la crisis*, 41–43).

12. Bergad, *Cuban Rural Society*, 314, 318.

13. Cuban scholars generally insist that the Cuban Liberation Army was on the road to victory without American intervention. This assertion is based on an exaggerated view of the plight of the Spanish troops (bad as it was) and the suppression of evidence about the poor condition of the insurgents. Souza (*Máximo Gómez*, 212), for example, argued that "the abandonment of the Island by Spain was only a matter of a few more months" at the time of the American intervention. The historian who most categorically asserted

an immanent Cuban victory without U.S. help was Emilio Roig de Leuchsenring, whose many works include the obviously tendentious *Cuba no debe*. Prestigious Cubanists today accept Roig's line of reasoning. See Pérez, *War of 1898*, 10–11. Not surprisingly, almost all of the firsthand accounts by Cuban combatants predicted victory, especially after it had been achieved. But, as we shall see, unpublished diaries and correspondence express pessimism until the winter of 1897–98, when political events in Spain and pressure from the United States caused the Spanish army to stand down and, ultimately, declare a unilateral cease-fire. Among the most important works by Cuban combatants are those of Bernabé Boza, José Miró, and Máximo Gómez.

14. Espinosa y Ramos, *Al trote*, 279.

15. See, for example, Trask's *War with Spain in 1898*, the best military history of the Spanish-American War, where the Spanish-Cuban conflict is efficiently reduced to a short introductory chapter.

16. For example, Moreno Fraginals, *Cuba/España, España/Cuba*, where the war from 1895 to 1898 is treated at the end in just a few pages under the significant chapter heading "La Guerra Inevitable."

17. Thompson, *Making of the English Working Class*, 12.

CHAPTER TWO

1. Thomas, *Cuba*, 1–71.

2. Moreno Fraginals, *El ingenio*, 3:35–38. There are good articles on the subject in Naranjo et al., *La nación soñada*.

3. Scott, *Slave Emancipation*, 7; Eltis, *Economic Growth*, 249; Tomich, "World Slavery and Caribbean Capitalism"; Schmidt-Nowara, *Empire and Antislavery*, 4. For two classic accounts of slave society in Cuba see Klein, *Slavery in the Americas*, and Knight, *Slave Society in Cuba*.

4. For a survey of this period see the first seven chapters of Pérez, *Cuba*. On railroads see Zanetti and García, *Sugar and Railroads*.

5. Durnerin, *Maura et Cuba*; Cayuela Fernández, *Bahía de Ultramar*.

6. Urquía y Redecilla, *Historia negra*, xiv, 3.

7. Fabié, *Mi gestión*, 27.

8. Tortella, *El desarrollo de la España contemporánea*, 155; Roldán de Montaud, "La hacienda cubana"; Maluquer de Motes, "El mercado colonial"; Giberga y Gali, *Apuntes sobre la cuestión*, 196.

9. See, for example, Ringrose, *Madrid and the Spanish Economy*, and Cruz, *Gentlemen Bourgeois and Revolutionaries*.

10. On the Spanish economy see Prados de la Escosura, *De imperio a nación*; Sánchez-Albornoz, ed., *Economic Modernization of Spain*. For an older, more pessimistic view see Nadal, *El fracaso de la revolución industrial en España*.

11. Classic political histories of Spain are Artola, *Los orígenes de la España contemporánea*, and Carr, *Spain*.

12. Serrano, *Final del imperio*, 4–5; López Segrera, "Cuba," 77–93.

13. Zanetti, "Las relaciones comerciales hispano-cubanas," 95–117, Table 1.

14. Durnerin, *Maura et Cuba*, 32–33.

15. Fabié, *Mi gestión*, 20.

16. Serrano, *Final del imperio*, 6; Pérez, *Cuba and the United States*, 2–12.

17. Pérez, *On Becoming Cuban*, ch. 1.

18. Le Riverend, *Historia económica*, 136. Roderick Aya (*Missed Revolution*, ix–x) got it right when, in his study of rural revolution in Sicily and Andalucía, he wrote: "What is striking is the moderation and weakness of proletarian-based agrarian movements by comparison with the defensive mobilization of peasants still possessed of self-owned productive means and close-knit community organization."

19. Cayuela Fernández, *Bahía de Ultramar*, 4–6.

20. Muñiz de Quevedo, *Ajiaco*, 32–40; Montesinos y Salas, *Los yankees en Manzanillo*, 11–12.

21. AHN, Sección Ultramar, leg. 4483.

22. See Barnet, *Biografía de un cimarrón*.

23. Gómez, *La insurrección por dentro*, 19.

24. "Cuestiones cubanas," BN ms. 20064/10; Ablanedo, *La cuestión de Cuba*, 17–20; Montesinos y Salas, *Los yankees*, 10–11.

25. Schwartz, *Lawless Liberators*, 40.

26. Armiñan, *Weyler*, 62–64.

27. Ferrer, "Rethinking Race and Nation in Cuba," 60–76.

28. Scott, *Slave Emancipation*, 27–46.

29. For an analysis of the economic impact of emancipation in Matanzas see Bergad, *Cuban Rural Society*, 188–89, 263–79.

30. Roldán de Montaud, "La hacienda cubana," 137; Mariano, *Cuestiones hispano-norte-americanas*, 9. According to one contemporary Cuban, the colonial government spent almost $11 million a year before the war servicing the debt, another $13 million on military and administrative expenses, and only $771,000 on everything else, leaving almost nothing for things like primary education (Izaguirre, *Asuntos cubanos*).

31. Estévez Romero, *Desde el Zanjón*, 24, 595.

32. See Ablanedo, *La cuestión de Cuba*. For other contemporary critiques of Spanish corruption see Blasco Ibáñez, *Artículos*; Moreno, *El país del chocolate*; and Merchan, *Cuba*.

33. Garralda Arizcún, "La guerra hispanocubana," 1221.

34. See Moreno Fraginals et al., eds., *Between Slavery and Free Labor*, especially the essays by Moreno Fraginals and Iglesias.

35. Pérez, *Cuba and the United States*, 74; LaFeber, *New Empire*, 286.

36. Menéndez Caravía, *La Guerra en Cuba*, 13.

37. Trask, *War with Spain*, 4.

38. Pardo González, *La brigada*, 13.

39. Peralta's correspondence in Garralda Arizcún, "La guerra hispanocubana," 1230–37.

40. Fabié, *Mi gestión*, 23.

41. *El Imparcial*, October 1, 3, 6, 8, 1894.

42. For some of these details, see AMM, CGC, microfilm no. 14.

CHAPTER THREE

1. Mañach, *Martí*.

2. Dirección política de las FAR, *Historia de Cuba*, 220–21.

3. Maceo to Juan Arnao, June 14, 1885, and Gómez to Arnao, January 20, 1885, Papers of Juan and Nicolás Arnao, LCMD. The text of Gómez's letter is interesting enough to quote at length:

> Dear friend: your letter of the 15th reaches me today, and I am informed of that which I already suspected: New York weak as always. . . . Marty [sic] from the first day he met me in New York, wanted to break with me . . . because he is not a man who can enter any sphere without trying to dominate it. . . . He said inside "with this old soldier I cannot dominate, and what is worse I may see myself in the end committed to follow him to the battlefields of Cuba. . . . This man cares little for orators and poets and asks for gunpowder, bullets, and men to go with him to the fields of my country to kill tyrants." This, my friend, is, neither more nor less, the thinking of that young man, whom we ought to leave in peace, while we go to fight to create a country for his children. Let's not worry any further about these small matters. They are atoms that have no influence in the destinies of peoples.

4. Martí, En los Estados Unidos, 10.
5. Mañach, Martí, 230.
6. Toledo Sande, Cesto de llamas, 189, 259–60.
7. Fernández, Cuban Anarchism, 24–35.
8. Pérez, ed., José Martí in the United States.
9. Poyo, "With All and for the Good of All."
10. Guerra y Sánchez et al., Historia de la Nación Cubana, 7:121.
11. Mañach, Martí, 325–28.
12. Guerra y Sánchez et al., Historia de la Nación Cubana, 7:119–22.
13. See Anderson, Imagined Communities; Hobsbawm, Nations and Nationalism since 1780; Hobsbawm and Ranger et al., Invention of Tradition; Anthony Smith, Theories of Nationalism; and Woolf et al., Nationalism in Europe.
14. Estrade, "José Martí," 17–88; Elorza, "El Sueño de Cuba en José Martí," 65–78.
15. Liss, Roots of Revolution, 49.
16. Sepúlveda Muñoz, "¡Viva Cuba Libre!" 263–77.
17. Tortella, El desarrollo, 34.
18. The best example of this sort of literature in English, though it dates from the early twentieth century, is Brenan, South from Granada.
19. Barón Fernández, La guerra hispano-americana, 23–24.
20. Juan Gualberto Gómez, Por Cuba Libre, 12–15. For another example see Manuel de la Cruz, Episodios de la revolución cubana, 1–2.
21. Izaguirre, Asuntos cubanos, 174–81.

CHAPTER FOUR
1. Consular reports in AMM, CGC, legs. 140, 141.
2. Heredia y Mota, Crónicas, 1:8–14.
3. Mariano y Vivo, Apuntes en defensa, 23.
4. Monfort y Prats, Historia de la Guerra, 33–46; Juan Gualberto Gómez, Por Cuba Libre, 45–48.
5. Cortijo, Apuntes para la historia, 19; Mariano y Vivo, Apuntes en defensa, 26.

6. Maura, *Proyecto de Ley*.

7. Diego, "Las reformas de Maura."

8. Tussell, *Antonio Maura*, 29. Tussell cites a letter from General Luque, who witnessed the demonstrations in support of Maura and Calleja, that reads in part: "I . . . know very well how to distinguish fabricated enthusiasm from the genuine article, and the enthusiasm, from Santiago to Havana, for the reforms [proposed by Maura] is truly impressive in its spontaneity."

9. Mañach, *Martí*, 317.

10. Durnerin, *Maura et Cuba*, 191; Souza, *Máximo Gómez*, 129.

11. Núñez Florencio, *El Ejército español*, 36–37.

12. Elorza and Hernández Sandoica, *La Guerra de Cuba*, 186.

13. Cuban accounts of the war sometimes treat Cuba as a "nation-in-arms" in 1895. See, for example, Palenque, *La campaña de invasión*; Ibarra, *Ideología mambisa*; or almost anything by Roig de Leuchsenring, for example, his description of the "war of the majority" against Spain in his introduction to Juan Gualberto Gómez, *Por Cuba Libre*, 68. This view originated with some of the combatants; for example, see Valdés-Domínguez, *Diario*, 3:84, where he suggests that the loss of all the revolution's leaders would not matter because the insurrection was the unstoppable emanation of the Cuban nation. Americans also exaggerated the "unanimity" of the Cuban people. Henry Proctor visited Cuba and reported on "the spectacle of a million and a half people, the entire native population of Cuba, struggling for freedom and deliverance" from Spain (Millis, *Martial Spirit*, 124). For a recent consideration of the power of the myth of the "people-in-arms" see Moran and Waldron, eds., *People in Arms*.

14. Helg, *Our Rightful Share*; Ferrer, *Insurgent Cuba*.

15. Miranda, *Antorchas de la Libertad*, 30.

16. Piedra Martel, *Campañas de Maceo*, 10, 13.

17. Giberga y Gali, *Apuntes sobre la cuestión*, 155.

18. Heredia y Mota, *Crónicas*, 1:10–37.

19. Maluquer de Motes, *España en la crisis*, 33.

20. Military assaults on periodicals became so frequent after 1895 that one historian characterized them as "the sport of the era." Eventually, the legal battles between civilians and officials over these assaults led to the creation of broad autonomy for military courts and the exemption of officers from the rule of law, with terrible consequences for the future of the country (Núñez Florencio, "Las raíces de la Ley de Jurisdicciones").

21. Núñez Florencio, *Militarismo y antimilitarismo*, 150–57.

22. Maceo, *Ideología política*, 1:346–47.

23. Souza, *Máximo Gómez*, 150–53.

24. AMM, CGC, microfilm no. 28.

25. One veteran thought Maceo had ordered Key's death, but then he suggested in a footnote that it was an accident. See Rosell y Malpica, *Diario*, 1:37.

26. Piedra Martel, *Campañas de Maceo*, 5–39; Foner, *Antonio Maceo*, 166–67; Monfort y Prats, *Historia de la Guerra*, 78.

27. Roig, *La guerra de Martí*, 29.

28. Curnow, *Manana*, 172.

29. Llorens y Maceo, *Con Maceo*, 20.

30. *Boletín oficial*, May 10, 1895.

31. Curnow, *Manana*, 178–79.

32. Bartolomé Masó was vice president, and Severo Pina, Santiago García Cañizares, Carlos Roloff, and Rafael Portuondo became the secretaries of finance, interior, war, and foreign affairs, respectively.

33. Ramiro Cabrera, *¡A Sitio Herrera!* 157–58.

34. "I want to leave the world/by the natural door:/When I die they should carry me/in a coach of green leaves/Don't put me in the dark/to die like a traitor/I am good, and as a good man/I will die facing the sun." [Author's translation]

35. Salas, *La Guerra de Cuba*, 11; Calleja Leal, "La muerte de José Martí"; Baquero, "Versiones y precisiones."

36. Curnow, *Manana*, 175–77.

37. Heredia y Mota, *Crónicas*, 1:39.

38. *Boletín oficial*, May 20, 1895; Monfort y Prats, *Historia de la Guerra*, 92–95.

CHAPTER FIVE

1. AMM, CGC, leg. 138; Miró, *Cuba*, 64.

2. Souza, *Máximo Gómez*, 3. Gómez's diary entry of August 25, 1877, stated: "Disorder continues and discipline is now lost." Later, the military leaders of the Cuban republic-in-arms forgot the ruinous state of the insurgency, allowing them to pin defeat on civilian politicians — a Cuban "stab in the back" equivalent to Ludendorff's myth of the socialists' "betrayal" of the German army. See Pérez Guzmán and Serrano, *Máximo Gómez*, 33–35.

3. Souza, *Ensayo histórico*, 72–73.

4. Foner, *Antonio Maceo*, 175. On Cuba and the Spanish economy see Cayuela Fernández, *Bahía de Ultramar*, and Maluquer de Motes, "El mercado colonial."

5. Pérez, *Cuba*, 163–64.

6. García-Cisneros, *Máximo Gómez*, 11.

7. José Gómez to Santiago García Cañizares, February 12, 1897, ANC, GR, leg. 16, exp. 2254.

8. García-Cisneros, *Máximo Gómez*, 11, 18; Souza, *Máximo Gómez*, 60–64; Griñan Peralta, "El carácter de Máximo Gómez."

9. Giberga y Gali, *Apuntes sobre la cuestión*, 153.

10. Weyler, *Mi mando*, 1:70–79; Giberga y Gali, *Apuntes sobre la cuestión*, 153; Palenque, *La campaña de invasión*, 3.

11. Foner, *Antonio Maceo*, 175.

12. Miró, *Cuba*, 175.

13. Heredia y Mota, *Crónicas*, 1:24.

14. Rodríguez Demorizi, *Papeles dominicanos*, 41–42, 48.

15. Foner, *Antonio Maceo*, 175.

16. García-Cisneros, *Máximo Gómez*, 15–16.

17. Pérez, *Cuba*, 124.

18. Buznego, *Mayor General Máximo Gómez*, 1:10.

19. Souza, *Máximo Gómez*, 169–72, 188.

20. José Maceo's log for June 1895 in ANC, GR, leg. 14, exp. 1892, makes apparent how important his role was in establishing the insurgency's authority in the East. See also his correspondence in ANC, GR, leg. 14, exp. 1863.

21. José Maceo to Severo Pina, October 10, 1895, ANC, GR, leg. 14, exp. 1893.

22. Emilio Latanlade, for example, had by himself collected $44,000 (Latanlade to José Maceo, February 16, 1896, ANC, GR, leg. 14, exp. 1924).

23. Records of some of these weapons purchases are in AMM, CGC, leg. 104.

24. Fernando Gómez, La insurrección por dentro, 15–17.

25. Circular of March 20, 1896, reproduced in Fernando Gómez, La insurrección por dentro, 21–23; Flint, Marching with Gómez, 25.

26. Roloff's order in AMM, CGC, microfilm no. 28.

27. Valdés-Domínguez, Diario, 3:85.

28. Boza, Mi diario, 52; Fernando Gómez, La insurrección por dentro, 15–17.

29. Boza, Mi diario, 30–31, 46–47.

30. Ibid., 169.

CHAPTER SIX

1. Izaguirre, Asuntos cubanos, 9–10. For a paranoid but interesting account of the role of Masonry in the overthrow of the Spanish colony in Cuba, see Villalba Muñoz, La gran traición.

2. Pando, Cuba's Freedom Fighter, 4.

3. Foner, Antonio Maceo, 2, 7–8, 20; Piedra Martel, Campañas de Maceo, 20–21.

4. Piedra Martel, Campañas de Maceo, 86.

5. Circular of Weyler in Boletín oficial, June 10, 1897.

6. Pando, Cuba's Freedom Fighter, 13. Martínez Campos's gloomy report has been cited, as it is in Pando's book, as an assessment of the situation in Cuba as a whole. He meant it to apply only to the East, as is clear from the context of the report.

7. Maza Miguel, "Between Ideology and Compassion"; Pardo González, La brigada; Vehráhz, Los Estados Unidos vencidos, 11. On African influences on religion in Cuba see Barnet, Afro-Cuban Religions.

8. Burguete y Lana, ¡La guerra! 74–76.

9. Pardo González, La brigada, 15.

10. Armiñan, Weyler, 113.

11. Saíz Cidoncha, Guerrillas en Cuba, 12.

12. Souza, Ensayo histórico, 109–10.

13. Corral, El desastre, 149.

14. Reparaz, La guerra de Cuba, 43.

15. Cortijo, Apuntes para la historia, 22; Mariano y Vivo, Apuntes en defensa, 10.

16. Amante de la nación, Estudio de la Guerra, 8.

17. Souza, Ensayo histórico, 65.

18. Gómez Núñez, La acción de Peralejo, 8.

19. Souza, Ensayo histórico, 54–55.

20. Cardona, Historia del Ejército, 116–17; Izaguirre, Asuntos cubanos, 15.

21. Piedra Martel, Campañas de Maceo, 26–35.

22. Gómez Núñez, *La acción de Peralejo*, 16. Miró gave a completely different version of this part of the battle, claiming that it was the Cubans who picked up ammunition from the dead Spanish soldiers. See Miró, *Cuba*, 74–81. There are two reasons to doubt Miró. First, although he pretended to have been present at the battle, we know that he was not. Second, Miró copied words and whole phrases from the 1895 account by the Spaniard Gómez Núñez, merely substituting "Cuban" for "Spaniard" at the necessary point in his 1909 narrative.

23. Souza, *Ensayo histórico*, 55.

24. Weyler, *Mi mando*, 1:24.

CHAPTER SEVEN

1. Souza, *Ensayo histórico*, 32; Souza, *Máximo Gómez*, 180–84.

2. Máximo Gómez to Rafael Portuondo, ANC, GR, leg. 11, exp. 1458.

3. Llorens y Maceo, *Con Maceo*, 28–30.

4. Fité, *Las desdichas de la patria*, 45.

5. Rodríguez Mendoza, *En la manigua*, 19.

6. Consular reports in AMM, CGC, leg. 159.

7. Adán, *El lobbyismo*, 5.

8. Juan Gualberto Gómez, *Por Cuba Libre*, 68.

9. Adán, *El lobbyismo*, 6–7.

10. Dupuy to minister of state, AMM, CGC, leg. 159.

11. AMM, CGC, microfilm no. 28.

12. Foner, *Antonio Maceo*, 173.

13. See Heredia y Mota, *Crónicas*, for revealing photos of Spanish vessels.

14. Rodríguez Mendoza, *En la manigua*, 28–70.

15. The story that follows is based on Rutea's captured diary in AMM, CGC, leg. 134, and on the published memoirs of fellow expeditionaries in Rodríguez Mendoza, *En la manigua*, and Ramiro Cabrera, *¡A Sitio Herrera!*

16. Order by Máximo Gómez in AMM, CGC, leg. 159.

17. Lubián, *Episodios de las guerras*, 53. See also Carrillo Morales, *Expediciones cubanas*.

18. Souza, *Máximo Gómez*, 187.

19. Crouch, *Yankee Guerrillero*, 23, 37, 110.

20. Numerous examples of Cuban officers' complaints about their men dispersing between engagements can be found in AMM, CGC, legs. 134–38.

21. Boza, *Mi diario*, 28.

22. Maceo's correspondence complaining of Masó's orders in AMM, CGC, leg. 135.

23. "Diario de las operaciones," Regimiento Infantería de la Habana no. 66, AMM, CGC, leg. 290.

24. Souza, *Ensayo histórico*, 108–9.

25. Saíz Cidoncha, *Guerrillas en Cuba*, 69.

26. Miró, *Cuba*, 95–99.

27. Rodríguez Demorizi, *Papeles dominicanos*, 47.

28. Piedra Martel, *Campañas de Maceo*, 47–48.

29. Weyler, *Mi mando*, 1:294.

30. Pérez, *Cuba*, 146.

31. Espinosa y Ramos, *Al trote*, 36–38.

32. Juan Gualberto Gómez, *Por Cuba Libre*, 224.

33. Maceo to Dimas Zamora, AMM, CGC, leg. 135.

34. Miró, *Cuba*, 28.

35. *Cuadros de la guerra*, 19. For similar characterizations see Francisco Cabrera, *Episodios de la Guardia*, 118, and Amante de la nación, *Estudio de la Guerra*, 1–2.

36. Piedra Martel, *Campañas de Maceo*, 48–53.

37. Souza, *Ensayo histórico*, 116.

38. Piedra Martel, *Campañas de Maceo*, 53–59; Miró, *Cuba*, 147–49; Weyler, *Mi mando*, 1:39–40.

39. Piedra Martel, *Campañas de Maceo*, 61–68.

40. Boza, *Mi diario*, 74.

41. Moreno Fraginals, *Cuba/España, España/Cuba*, 266.

42. Miró, *Cuba*, 200–201.

43. Foner, *Antonio Maceo*, 172.

44. Boza, *Mi diario*, 196–97.

45. Menéndez Caravía, *La Guerra en Cuba*, 5–11.

46. Piedra Martel, *Campañas de Maceo*, 10–13.

47. Weyler, *Mi mando*, 1:14.

48. Philip Foner insisted that "the Cuban Liberation Army was completely integrated," but it is hard to find any evidence for this claim. Indeed, as the war dragged on, whites and westerners replaced blacks and Orientales in positions of leadership in the army, a sign that racial and regional hierarchy had reasserted itself within the revolution.

49. It has been estimated that Afro-Cubans made up as much as 80 percent of the Liberation Army (Thomas, *Cuba*, 323). This percentage is probably too high. The figure of 60 percent may be closer to the truth. See Ferrer, *Insurgent Cuba*, 3.

50. Ferrer, *Insurgent Cuba*, 96–97.

51. Muñiz de Quevedo, *Ajiaco*, 42–43.

52. Captured regimental lists in AMM, CGC, leg. 136.

53. Bandera had a reputation for cruelty and immorality that finally ended his military career. Reports of his crimes reached Gómez, who dismissed him and refused to entertain any thought of reinstating him, citing his "recurrent immoral conduct" and "insubordination" (ANC, GR, leg. 11, exp. 1516). Ferrer, however, implies that the dismissal of Bandera was primarily racial in motivation. See Ferrer, "Rustic Men, Civilized Nation." See also Ferrer, *Insurgent Cuba*, 173–83.

54. Heredia y Mota, *Crónicas*, 2:50.

55. Saíz Cidoncha, *Guerrillas en Cuba*, 69.

56. Miró, *Cuba*, 122.

57. Miranda, *Antorchas de la Libertad*, 100, 243.

CHAPTER EIGHT

1. Some place the number of Spanish dead from illness at close to 50,000. See Rodríguez González, *Operaciones*, 22; Alonso Baquer, "El ejército español," 306; Feijóo Gómez, *Quintas*, 310–11; and "Casualties," 106–8. For published data on the health of the Spanish army, see Brunner, "Morbidity and Mortality," 409–12; España, Ministerio

de la Guerra, *Estados de las fuerzas*; Larra y Cerezo, *Datos para la historia*; and Larra y Cerezo, *Les hôpitaux militaires*. For the list of dead on the Cuban side, see Roloff, *Indice alfabético*.

2. Corral, *El desastre*, 73, 124.

3. Pando, *Documento*, 7.

4. Ramón y Cajal, *Recuerdos de mi vida*, 1:331–50.

5. Tone, "How the Mosquito (Man) Liberated Cuba," 277–308.

6. Montaldo y Peró, *Guía práctica*, 82.

7. Harrison, *Mosquitoes, Malaria, and Man*.

8. Correspondence of Martínez Campos and Ministry of War, November 15 and December 7, 1895, AMM, CGC, leg. 114.

9. Minister of war to Martínez Campos, AMM, CGC, microfilm no. 30.

10. Hernández Sandoica, "Polémica arancelaria," 279–319.

11. There is a correspondence between Martínez Campos and various Spanish cabinet members on this subject in AMM, CGC, leg. 114.

12. Frieyro de Lara, "La situación del soldado," 161–71.

13. Corral, *El desastre*, 18–24, 56–58.

14. Carrasco y Sandía, *Pequeñeces*, chs. 1–2.

15. Alonso Baquer, *El ejército*, 167–69.

16. Varela Ortega, *Los amigos políticos*.

17. The best work on the Spanish standard of living is Martínez Carrión, ed., *El nivel de vida*. The authors in this collection agree that the early stages of agrarian capitalism generated a sharp crisis, followed by slow recovery in the late nineteenth century and rapid progress after 1900.

18. See, for example, Núñez Florencio, "Las raíces de la Ley de Jurisdicciones," 185–98.

19. Ballbé, *Orden público*, 227–34.

20. Feijóo Gómez, *Quintas*, 116–24.

21. Núñez Florencio, *Militarismo*, 24.

22. Ballbé, *Orden público*, 248–52.

23. Díaz Benzo, *Pequeñeces*, 12–13.

24. Headrick, *Ejército y política*, 74–75. On the military see also Christiansen, *Origins of Military Power in Spain*.

25. Barado, *Nuestros soldados*, 43–47.

26. Feijóo Gómez, *Quintas*, 310–11; Ovilo y Canales, *La decadencia*, 13.

27. Serrano, "Prófugos y desertores." Serrano wants to show that Spaniards resisted the draft as part of a general opposition to the war, but his own statistics bring this assertion into question. See also the evidence presented by Feijóo Gómez, *Quintas*, 51, showing a decline in desertion and draft resistance during the war.

28. Ovilo y Canales, *La decadencia*, 9.

29. Jensen, "Moral Strength"; Jensen, "Military Nationalism."

30. Feijóo Gómez, *Quintas*, 287–89, 301–3, 313–14.

31. Letter to Weyler in AHN, Sección Diversos, Títulos-Familias, leg. 3177, no. 5.

32. Corral, *El desastre*, 34.

33. *El Imparcial*, December 31, 1896.

34. Cable to Weyler, AMM, CGC, leg. 159.

35. Larrea, El desastre, 163–69, 184.

36. Blasco Ibáñez, Artículos, 11.

37. Avelino Delgado, "Spanish Army in Cuba," 1:105. The quote is from Alonso Baquer, El ejército, 199–205.

38. Muñiz de Quevedo, Ajiaco, 171.

39. Rodríguez Mendoza, En la manigua, 91–92.

40. Vehráhz, Los Estados Unidos vencidos, 12.

41. Weyler, Mi mando, 1:43.

42. Album de la trocha, 11.

CHAPTER NINE

1. The Spanish campaign logs in AMM, CGC, 288–384, are poignant reading on this matter.

2. Letter of Bernardo Carvajal, September 21, 1895, AGM, secc. 6, div. 3, leg. K-4.

3. Flint, Marching with Gómez, 45; Corral, El desastre, 68–73.

4. Yriondo to Coronel Aldave, AGM, secc. 6, div. 3, leg. K-4.

5. Muñiz de Quevedo, Ajiaco, 28.

6. Corral, El desastre, 16–17.

7. Burguete y Lana, ¡La guerra! 57–58.

8. Letters of November 24, 1895; February 29, May 9, May 26, October 21, 1896, AGM, secc. 6, div. 3, leg. K-4.

9. Letter of Marcelino Soler, August 21, 1896, AGM, secc. 6, div. 3, leg. K-4.

10. José Aldave, orders of November 7, 12, 1895, AGM, secc. 6, div. 3, leg. K-4.

11. Weyler, Mi mando, 1:26–28.

12. Mariano y Vivo, Apuntes en defensa, 37.

13. An example of this approach is Pardo González, La brigada.

14. Estévez Romero, Desde el Zanjón, 4–6.

15. Forcadell Alvarez, "El lúcido pesimismo," 31–57.

16. Martínez Campos's letter is reproduced in Weyler, Mi mando, 1:28–32.

CHAPTER TEN

1. Boza, Mi diario, 74.

2. Miró, Cuba, 169–72. Piedra Martel commented on the deportment of the Spanish troops: "I must say, in defense of the Spanish army, that, neither before nor after, in the whole course of the campaign, did I see soldiers lose their morale and organization like those at Mal Tiempo" (Campañas de Maceo, 68–72); see also Piedra Martel, Memorias de un mambí, 76; and Souza, Ensayo histórico, 144–51.

3. Barnet, Biografía de un cimarrón, 154.

4. On Spanish losses see reports of operations, October to December 1895, AMM, CGC, leg. 290, and the discussion in Miró, Cuba, 144–45. Cuban losses were given by General Serafín Sánchez, cited in Dirección política de las FAR, Historia de Cuba, 397. Bernabé Boza reported slightly different numbers, four dead and forty-two wounded in Mi diario, 60.

5. Elorza and Hernández Sandoica, La guerra de Cuba, 227.

6. Boza, Mi diario, 41, 91.

7. Dumpierre, introduction to Gómez, Diario de campaña, 10–13. See also Roig, La guerra de Martí, 63.

8. Barquín, Las luchas guerrilleras, 10–11.

9. Clark, Cuba and the Fight for Freedom, 418–22.

10. Foner, Antonio Maceo, 20, 37, 174; Foner, Spanish-Cuban-American War, 1:19–26.

11. Joseph Smith, Spanish-American War, 12–13.

12. Carrasco y Sandía, Pequeñeces, ch. 13.

13. Jiménez Castellanos, Sistema, 30.

14. Barrios quoted in Souza, Máximo Gómez, 74–75.

15. Saíz Cidoncha, Guerrillas en Cuba, 48–49.

16. For a good contemporary discussion of the Spanish tendency to report inflated enemy casualties, see Larrea, El desastre, 193–207.

17. Souza, Ensayo histórico, 151.

18. Burguete y Lana, ¡La guerra! 95, 105, 137; Morote, En la manigua, 13–14.

19. Espinosa y Ramos, Al trote, 60, 78–79.

20. Gómez, Diario, 394.

21. Fuente y Hernández, El fusil mauser español.

22. Crouch, Yankee Guerrillero, 107; Flint, Marching with Gómez, 240.

23. Boza, Mi diario, 27.

24. Francisco Argilagos made this point well in Prédicas insurrectas, 32–48. The use of explosive bullets shows up in the records of military hospitals beginning in 1896. See, for example, AMM, CGC, legs. 172, 173, 174, 175.

25. "Reglamenta susinta," AMM, CGC, leg. 138.

26. Boza, Mi diario, 27.

27. Bellesiles, Arming America. Despite the campaign to discredit Bellesiles and his use of probate records, the thesis of Arming America — that the American love affair with guns was a purposeful social construction of the nineteenth century rather than an organic legacy of the colonial era — remains unassailed.

28. Feijóo Gómez, Quintas, 307–8; Corral, El desastre, 35–36; Cassola, Establecimiento de colonias, xi.

29. Jiménez Castellanos, Sistema, 96, 114–15.

30. Boza, Mi diario, 84.

31. Battle recounted in the letter of General Luque on display at the Army Museum in Madrid.

32. Guerra y Sánchez et al., Historia de la Nación Cubana, 6:230.

33. Crouch, Yankee Guerrillero, 68.

34. Cuadros de la guerra, 24, 31.

35. Battle reports, AMM, CGC, legs. 171, 172, 175.

36. See Larra y Cerezo, Datos para la historia.

37. Hospital reports, AMM, CGC, legs. 171, 180, and AGM, secc. 2a, div. 4a, leg. K1.

38. Battle reports, AMM, CGC, legs. 171–80.

39. Hospital reports, AGM, secc. 2a, div. 4a, leg. K1; AMM, CGC, leg. 173.

40. Muñiz de Quevedo, Ajiaco, 65.

41. Pardo González, La brigada, 24.

42. Souza, Ensayo histórico, 144.

43. Ibid., 149–50.

44. Martínez Campos to Sabas Marín, December 20, 1895, AMM, CGC, leg. 440.

45. Piedra Martel, *Campañas de Maceo*, 79–85.

46. Souza, *Máximo Gómez*, 202–4.

CHAPTER ELEVEN

1. Letter from Luisa to her mother, AMM, CGC, leg. 136.

2. "Diary of Fourth Corps, Second Div., Third Squad," AMM, CGC, leg. 140.

3. Miró, *Cuba*, 100–101.

4. Giberga y Gali, *Apuntes sobre la cuestión*, 147.

5. *New York Times*, June 6, 1896.

6. For a *longue durée* interpretation of Cuban nationalism and why national identity was more advanced than in Puerto Rico, see Ibarra, "Cultura é identidad nacional."

7. Diary of José Hernández, AMM, CGC, leg. 139; Arbelo, *Recuerdo*, 57.

8. Souza, *Ensayo histórico*, 32.

9. Flint, *Marching with Gómez*, 85–88.

10. Núñez Jiménez, "Los primeros en llamarse cubanos," quoted in Serrano, *Final del imperio*, 6.

11. On the subject of Cuba's problematic national identity see Fernández and Cámara Betancourt, eds., *Cuba, the Elusive Nation*.

12. Piedra Martel, *Campañas de Maceo*, 9–10.

13. Miró, *Cuba*, 23.

14. Giberga y Gali, *Apuntes sobre la cuestión*, 155.

15. *Daily Inter Ocean*, January 20, 1896.

16. Pérez Guzmán, *Herida profunda*, 33–34.

17. Correspondence of Lacret, AMM, CGC, leg. 140.

18. Fernando Gómez, *La insurrección por dentro*, 17–18.

19. Barnet, *Biografía de un cimarrón*, 163–65.

20. Rodríguez Mendoza, *En la manigua*, 75.

21. Weyler, *Mi mando*, 1:30.

22. Barnet, *Biografía de un cimarrón*, 158.

23. Rodríguez Mendoza, *En la manigua*, 148–49.

24. Souza, *Máximo Gómez*, 154–57.

25. Battle diary of Acosta, AMM, CGC, leg. 139.

26. "Documentos incautados del enemigo," AMM, CGC, legs. 138–40.

27. Monfort y Prats, *Historia de la Guerra*, 269.

28. Flint, *Marching with Gómez*, 80.

29. Arbelo, *Recuerdo*, 12–17, 43–44.

30. Crouch, *Yankee Guerrillero*, 118, 80–83.

31. See Roig de Leuchsenring's *Cuba no debe*, 23.

32. Barnet, *Biografía de un cimarrón*, 182–83.

33. Telegram from Manuel Rodríguez San Pedro, provincial governor of Pinar del Río, to Martínez Campos, AMM, CGC, microfilm no. 28, leg. 101.

34. Piedra Martel, *Campañas de Maceo*, 85–120.

35. Weyler, *Mi mando*, 1:65.

36. Amante de la nación, *Estudio de la Guerra*, 4–5.

37. "Extract from a Letter," Phillips Papers, LCMD.

38. Weyler, *Mi mando*, 1:28–31.

CHAPTER TWELVE

1. Diego, *Weyler*, 35–39.

2. Martínez Carrión et al., "Creciendo con desigualdad," 405–60.

3. Armiñán, *Weyler*, 137.

4. Cardona and Losada, *Weyler*, 20–23.

5. There appears to be no evidence to support the legend that places Weyler in these years in Washington, D.C., where he supposedly consulted with Sherman, among other veterans of the U.S. Civil War, on the subject of counterinsurgency. See Diego, *Weyler*, 59–61.

6. Diego, *Weyler*, 68–88.

7. Armiñán, *Weyler*, 145–46.

8. See Weyler's correspondence with Gago (especially no. 107), AHN, Sección Diversos, Títulos-Familias, leg. 3175.

9. Diego, *Weyler*, 178–79.

10. See Weyler's introduction to Fernando Gómez, *La insurrección por dentro*, viii.

11. Cardona and Losada, *Weyler*, 176.

12. Weyler, *Mi mando*, 1:116.

13. Cardona and Losada, *Weyler*, 177.

14. Weyler, *Mi mando*, 1:178.

15. Ibid., 130–31; Mariano y Vivo, *Apuntes en defensa*, 42–82.

16. Díaz Benzo, *Pequeñeces*, 25, 59–60.

17. Letters from local officials to Weyler, AGM, secc. 6, div. 3, leg. K-4; Corral, *El desastre*, 60.

18. Battle report, AMM, CGC, leg. 159.

19. Fernández, *Cuban Anarchism*, 17–18.

20. See Poyo, *"With All and for the Good of All."*

21. Boza, *Mi diario*, 171–72.

22. Ibid., 220.

23. Máximo Gómez to Carlos Roloff, April 13, 1896, ANC, GR, leg. 11, exp. 1444.

24. Ibid., April 28, 1896.

25. Hernández, ed., *Apuntes biográficos*, 137.

26. Weyler, *Mi mando*, 2:7–8.

27. Boza, *Mi diario*, 210–21.

28. Phillips Papers, LCMD.

29. Acosta Quintana, *Planos de comunicaciones*.

30. Weyler's dispositions regarding train travel in AMM, CGC, leg. 441.

31. Weyler to Suárez Inclán, AMM, CGC, leg. 441.

32. Captured correspondence of Maceo, AMM, CGC, leg. 136; diary of Baldomero Acosta, AMM, CGC, leg. 139.

33. Many of the details of this battle are drawn from *Cuadros de la guerra*, 15–35.

34. AMM, CGC, leg. 134.

35. In a cable to General Bernal, AMM, CGC, leg. 482, Weyler reported only sixty Spanish casualties. Hospital records show that forty-nine survivors required hospitalization, all of them from bullet wounds.

36. *Times* of London, June 3, 1896.

37. Weyler, *Mi mando*, 2:61.

38. Ibid., 1:341–42.

39. Rosell y Malpica, *Diario*, 1:33–37, 73–79.

40. Valdés-Domínguez, *Diario*, 2:5.

41. Calixto García to Máximo Gómez, December 19, 1896, ANC, GR, leg. 11, exp. 1402.

42. Flint, *Marching with Gómez*, 80.

43. Pando's report of Segura's activities, AMM, CGC, leg. 440.

44. Diary by unknown Cuban officer, AMM, CGC, leg. 134.

45. Aguirre's correspondence, AMM, CGC, leg. 136.

46. Martí's diary, AMM, CGC, leg. 136.

47. Fernando Gómez, *La insurrección por dentro*, 50.

48. Correspondence of Lacret, AMM, CGC, legs. 138, 140.

49. Weyler, *Mi mando*, 2:406.

50. Correspondence of Lacret, AMM, CGC, leg. 140.

51. A recent book highlights the role of the provisional government and its delegate in New York, Tomás Estrada Palma, in encouraging American intervention, but it should be added that many Cuban military officials, including even Maceo, as we shall see, thought at one time or another that American intervention would prove the likeliest path to success. See Hidalgo de Paz, *Cuba*.

CHAPTER THIRTEEN

1. José Maceo to minister of war, ANC, GR, leg. 14, exp. 1941.

2. Gómez to Maceo, ANC, GR, leg. 14, exp. 1946.

3. Foner, *Antonio Maceo*, 96–103.

4. Souza, *Máximo Gómez*, 237.

5. Weyler, *Mi mando*, 2:386–93.

6. Crouch, *Yankee Guerrillero*, 37.

7. Cuban estimates of Spanish losses are no more reliable than Spanish estimates of Cuban losses, but some scholars do not seem to realize this. See Elorza and Hernández Sandoica, *La guerra de Cuba*, 253.

8. Compare Bernal's estimate in Weyler, *Mi mando*, 2:304, to the medical report in AMM, CGC, leg. 175.

9. Rioja, *En la manigua*, 30.

10. Circular issued by Maceo, AMM, CGC, leg. 136.

11. For examples of Maceo's earlier attitude toward American intervention, see Griñan Peralta, *Maceo*, 193–95.

12. Loinaz del Castillo to Máximo Gómez, November 19, 1896, ANC, GR, leg. 11, exp. 1401.

13. Weyler, *Mi mando*, 3:22–30.

14. Fernando Gómez, *La insurrección por dentro*, includes accounts of Maceo's death by Miró, Nodarse, and Cosme de la Torriente. These sections of Gómez's work are also reprinted in Weyler, *Mi mando*, 3:256–85.

15. Alvarez Angulo, *Memorias*, 169–70.

16. José Maceo to Antonio Maceo, June 22, 1895, ANC, GR, leg. 14, exp. 1892.

17. Captured correspondence in AMM, CGC, leg. 136.

18. Valdés-Domínguez, *Diario*, 3:49.

19. Betancourt to Mayía Rodríguez, September 17, 1897, AMM, CGC, leg. 159.

20. Rodríguez Mendoza, *En la manigua*, 49–50, 64–75, 170, 184, 202.

21. Socorro to Mayía Rodríguez, August 16, 1897, AMM, CGC, leg. 159.

22. Fernando Gómez, *La insurrección por dentro*, 11.

23. Corral, *El desastre*, 91, 134. Similar descriptions of conditions are in Flint, *Marching with Gómez*, 21.

24. Barnet, *Biografía de un cimarrón*, 169.

25. Pérez to Carrillo, AMM, CGC, leg. 137.

26. Valdés-Domínguez, *Diario*, 3:63, 85, 161, 183–84.

27. Crouch, *Yankee Guerrillero*, 68, 85–87, 92, 100.

28. Mariano y Vivo, *Apuntes en defensa*, 95.

29. Barnet, *Biografía de un cimarrón*, 169.

30. Letter signed by Major General Francisco Carrillo, Colonel Rosendo García, and Lieutenant Colonel José Acosta, January 19, 1897, AMM, CGC, leg. 138.

31. Rodríguez Mendoza, *En la manigua*, 15.

32. García Cisneros, *Máximo Gómez*, 71.

33. Gómez to Cleveland, February 9, 1897, and to McKinley, March 1, 1897, AMM, CGC, leg. 136.

34. Elorza and Hernández Sandoica, *La guerra de Cuba*, 206.

35. Buznego, *Mayor General Máximo Gómez*, 2:8.

36. Souza, *Máximo Gómez*, 91.

37. Boza, *Mi diario*, 331–32.

38. Martí's correspondence, AMM, CGC, leg. 138.

39. Giberga y Gali, *Apuntes sobre la cuestión*, 180.

40. Diario of Comandante José Plasencia, AMM, CGC, leg. 138.

41. Mora to Gasset, September 4, 1897, BN, Ms. 21381/61.

42. Mayía Rodríguez to Gómez, October 6, 1897, AMM, CGC, leg. 159.

43. Fernando Gómez, *La insurrección por dentro*, 134–40. Gómez apparently took these numbers from the diary of Quintín Bandera.

44. Valdés-Domínguez, *Diario*, 4:45.

45. Correspondence from the Third Corps to government officials, ANC, GR, leg. 16, exps. 2270, 2273, 2285.

46. Roloff, *Indice alfabético*. The mortality figures are total deaths, 4,848; from sickness, 1,321; percent of deaths from sickness, 27 percent. These were revised and raised somewhat by later scholars to 8,617, 3,437, and 40 percent, respectively. See Foner, *Antonio Maceo*, 174.

47. Gómez to Portuondo, October 10, 1897, ANC, GR, legs. 11, 462.

48. Gómez to Mandulay, June 27, 1896, ANC, GR, legs. 11, 1147.

49. Mayía Rodríguez to Alejandro Rodríguez, October 20, 21, 1897, and January 9, 1898, ANC, GR, legs. 14, 1859.

CHAPTER FOURTEEN

1. Weyler's orders in AMM, CGC, leg. 114.

2. Pérez Guzmán, *Herida profunda*, 46–47.

3. Ibid., 17.

4. Morote, *En la manigua*, 4.

5. Chadwick, *Relations*, 2:493–94.

6. Pérez Guzmán, *Herida profunda*, 256.

7. AHN, Sección Diversos, Títulos-Familias, leg. 3176, no. 107; Fernando Gómez, *La insurrección por dentro*, 19.

8. Gutiérrez de la Concha, *Memoria sobre la guerra*, 89.

9. Circulars dated April 6, 8, and 26, 1870, AMM, CGC, leg. 61.

10. Weyler, *Mi mando*, 1:9.

11. Cardona and Losada, *Weyler*, 12.

12. Correspondence between Martínez Campos and the minister of war and the colonial minister, AMM, CGC, leg. 101.

13. The Cuban "deconcentration" orders may be found in AMM, CGC, leg. 138.

14. Espinosa y Ramos, *Al trote*, 69, 253.

15. Machado's correspondence, AMM, CGC, leg. 136.

16. Barnet, *Biografía de un cimarrón*, 162.

17. Weyler, *Mi mando*, 1:56.

18. Máximo Gómez to Rafael Portuondo, September 8, 1896, ANC, GR, leg. 11, exp. 1451.

19. General José M. Capote to Brigadier Cornleo Rojas, n.d., ANC, GR, leg. 16, exp. 2207.

20. Máximo Gómez to Rafael Portuondo, September 8, 1896, ANC, GR, leg. 11, exp. 1451.

21. Brigadier Javier Vega to Secretary of War Rafael Manduley, July 18, 1896, ANC, GR, leg. 16, exp. 2219.

22. Letter of April 3, 1896, Phillips Papers, LCMD.

23. Reports from Cuban commanders, AMM, CGC, leg. 140.

24. Maceo's orders, AMM, CGC, leg. 138.

25. *Times* of London, July 17, 1896.

26. AMM, CGC, microfilm no. 33.

27. Pardo González, *La brigada*, 36–37.

28. Trial records, AMM, CGC, leg. 136.

29. El Gobierno Civil del Estado de Oriente listed hundreds of names of prefects, subprefects, and other civil officials in 1897, in ANC, GR, leg. 14, exp. 1648.

30. Brigadier José Gómez to Santiago García Cañizares, February 14 and March 5, 1897, ANC, GR, leg. 16, exp. 2255 and 2262; Brigadier H. Espinosa to Cañizares, April 17, 1897, ANC, GR, leg. 16, exp. 2269.

31. AMM, CGC, leg. 138.

32. José María Rodríguez to General Miles, August 17, 1898, and Rodríguez to Bartolomé Masó, n.d., ANC, GR, leg. 11, exps. 1851, 1852.

33. Jesús Rabí to García Cañizares, September 19, 1898, ANC, GR, leg. 16, exp. 2197.

34. Castro's correspondence, AGM, secc. 6A, div. 3a, leg. K3.

35. Gómez to Portuondo, November 21, December 8, 1896, and Portuondo to Consejo de Gobierno, December 10, 1896, ANC, GR, leg. 11, exps. 1468, 1469.

36. Weyler's personnel file, AMM, EP, microfilm no. 53.

37. Various telegrams from the field, AMM, CGC, leg. 482.

38. AMM, CGC, leg. 440.

39. Corral, El desastre, 43–44, 81–85, 97.

40. Weyler's instructions in AMM, CGC, leg. 114.

41. Millis, Martial Spirit, 75–77.

42. See, for example, Espinosa y Ramos, Al trote, 156–57.

43. Romanones, Sagasta, 192; Francos Rodríguez, La vida de Canalejas, 156–58; Pérez Guzmán, Herida profunda, 10.

44. Offner, Unwanted War, 92–93. Lee later revised this estimate downward to 200,000.

45. Morgan, America's Road, 25.

46. Offner, Unwanted War, 42–48.

47. Russell et al., Illustrated History.

48. For examples, see Golay, Spanish-American War, 5; Pérez Guzmán, Herida profunda, 10; Romanones, Sagasta, 192–95; and Roig de Leuchsenring, Cuba no debe, 18–21, and La guerra libertadora, 145. Roig viewed reconcentration as "the extermination of the civilian peasant population by the barbaric Weyler and his hordes of assassins," and when it came to counting the victims of reconcentration, he chose the highest possible figures given by Blanco and Canalejas. The quotation is from Roig's introduction to Juan Gualberto Gómez, Por Cuba Libre, 45.

49. Pérez de la Riva and Blanca Morejón, "La población de Cuba"; Le Riverend, Historia Económica, 491, 563. Philip Foner also liked the figure of 200,000. See Foner, Spanish-Cuban-American War, 1:115. The number of dead could be increased further by rounding the population of 1895 up to 1,800,000 and that of 1898 down to 1,500,000, as Hugh Thomas seems to have done (Cuba, 423). Even this was not enough for Fernando Portuondo del Prado and Oscar Pino-Santos, who, using this same census data, insisted nonetheless that 400,000 reconcentrados died, a figure that far exceeds their own already generously rounded data. See Portuondo del Prado, Historia de Cuba, 578, and Pino-Santos, Cuba, 231.

50. Maluquer de Motes, España en la crisis, 39. Maluquer's discussion of the census data is the most skillful that I have seen.

51. Trask, War with Spain, 9; Joseph Smith, Spanish-American War, 19; Musicant, Empire by Default, 70; Pérez Castañeda, La explosión; Mesa-Lago, "El trabajo en Cuba," 36–77.

52. The data and the discussion that follows (unless otherwise indicated) come from reports on reconcentration in AMM, GCG, especially leg. 167, and AMM, Fondo Documentación sobre Cuba, leg. 61.

53. AMM, CGC, microfilm no. 45.

54. AMM, CGC, leg. 159.

55. Circular to prefects November 1897, AMM, CGC, leg. 136.

56. *New York World*, May 17, 1896. See also Wilkerson, *Public Opinion*, 29–40. Americans connected Weyler's behavior in Cuba with the murderous occupation of the Low Countries by the Duke of Alva in the late sixteenth century. It was then, according to Henry Cabot Lodge, that the English and the Dutch, representatives of civilization, had begun the work of dismantling the decadent Catholic empire of the Spanish Hapsburgs, and it would fall to the Americans to complete the job. "We represent the spirit of liberty," wrote Lodge, "and the spirit of the new time, and Spain is over against us because she is medieval, cruel, dying" (Lodge, *Intervention in Cuba*, 8–9).

57. Julian Juderías first used the term "black legend" for the title of his 1914 book, *La leyenda negra*. The timing of the work is interesting. Juderías had lived through the most intense period of "Spain bashing" the world had seen since the Thirty Years' War. An interesting essay on the image of Spain in America is Kagan, "Prescott's Paradigm."

58. Robert Cecil, Marquess of Salisbury, pronounced his "dying nations" speech in Royal Albert Hall three days after George Dewey destroyed Spain's Asian Fleet in Manila Bay on May 1, 1898. Later, in a fit of diplomatic sensitivity, he denied that Spain had been the subject of his discourse, but no one believed his retraction. The language of "living" and "dying" nations had already become familiar in the age of social Darwinism. And in the United States no one doubted which nation was living (the United States) and which dying (Spain). There is a nice analysis of the impact of this speech in Spain in Ballbé, *Orden público*, 175–79.

59. Thomas, *Cuba*, 336; Wilkerson, *Public Opinion*, 7–8, 29–32, 42. On this subject see also Wisan, *Cuban Crisis*. On the subject of bullfighting, Mary F. Lowell of the Temperance League argued in public forums that Spanish cruelty arose from the national festival, which produced monsters like Weyler who were inured to the most extreme violence and who were therefore more likely to employ it themselves in a routine way. Lowell's amateurish sociology received an interesting retort by the eminent Spanish writer Emilia Pardo Bazán, in *La vida*, 31–37.

60. Millis, *Martial Spirit*, 40–43.

61. *Daily Inter-Ocean*, February 10, 1896.

62. *New York World*, May 26, 1896.

63. Brown, *Correspondents' War*, 49.

64. Rea, *Facts and Fakes*.

65. *Times of London*, May 21, 1896.

66. Moret to Blanco, AMM, CGC, leg. 114.

67. Armiñan, *Weyler*, 15.

68. *New York World*, August 23, 1896.

69. LaFeber, *New Empire*, 287–88.

70. AMM, CGC, leg. 145.

71. Morgan, *America's Road*, 23.

72. Lee, "Cuba under Spanish Rule."

73. Pardo González, *La brigada*, 14.

CHAPTER FIFTEEN

1. For recent reassessments of Cánovas, covering every aspect of his life and times, see Bullón de Mendoza and Togores, eds., *Cánovas y su época*.

2. Conde Fernández-Oliva, "Sobre el pensamiento," 143–44.

3. Comellas, *Cánovas*, 95, 153, 330–34. On his view of monarchy, see also Raga Gil, "Cánovas ante la Gloriosa," 33–46.

4. Comellas, *Cánovas*, 130–31, 227; Raga Gíl, "Cánovas ante la Gloriosa," 44–45.

5. The following discussion rests on two excellent accounts of the political crisis of the early 1890s in Spain: Serrano, *Le tour du peuple*, and Alvarez Junco, *El emperador*.

6. Serrano Sanz, *El viraje*.

7. Anarchism was more complex than can be described here. See Alvarez Junco, *La ideología política del anarquismo*; Esenwein, *Anarchist Ideology*; and Kaplan, *Anarchists of Andalucía*.

8. Alvarez Junco, *El emperador*, 148.

9. Argilagos, *Prédicas insurrectas*, 32–48.

10. Alvarez Junco, *El emperador*, 154.

11. Fernández, *Cuban Anarchism*, 31–35.

12. Fernández, *La sangre*, 23–29.

13. Ibid., 30.

14. Ibid., 80–94.

15. Ibid., 34.

16. Mariano y Vivo, *Apuntes en defensa*, 93–95.

17. Sagasta's quote reproduced in Roig de Leuchsenring, *Cuba no debe*, 30.

18. Armiñan, *Weyler*, 165.

19. García Acuña, *Impresiones y antecedentes*, 6.

20. Pando, *Documento*, 6.

21. Offner, *Unwanted War*, 57.

22. Adán, *El Lobbyismo*, 11.

23. Estrada Palma to García Cañizares, AMM, CGC, leg. 155.

24. Estrada Palma's correspondence in AMM, CGC, leg. 155.

25. Dupuy correspondence in AMM, CGC, leg. 155.

26. This is the position of Robles Muñoz, 1898, 104–7.

27. See Offner, *Unwanted War*, for a detailed examination of diplomacy in this period.

28. Letter from Ramón Solano of January 22, 1898, AMM, CGC, leg. 138.

29. In Jiguaní, eleven insurgents turned themselves in during early February. In March Cayito Alvarez and other Cuban officers attempted to surrender but were intercepted and executed by another band of Cubans. In Sancti Spíritus in early April 1898, Colonel Rosendo García surrendered with three officers and twenty-two men, all armed and mounted. These are just a few examples of what was going on. As General Pando wrote to Blanco from Manzanillo on March 13, 1898: "Desertion continues and marked enemy demoralization in this jurisdiction" (AMM, CGC, legs. 155, 159).

30. López Marín to Gustavo, Guanajay, January 28, 1898, AMM, CGC, leg. 155.

31. Corral, *El desastre*, 136–38.

32. A detailed Spanish assessment of Cuban forces in AMM, CGC, leg. 159.

33. Orencio to Viñagera, AMM, CGC, leg. 155.

34. Dyal, *Historical Dictionary*, 10.

35. Fernández, *La sangre*.

CHAPTER SIXTEEN

1. Fitzhugh Lee to Blanco, AMM, CGC, leg. 155.
2. Blanco to the civil governor of Matanzas, December 6, 1897, AMM, CGC, leg. 155.
3. Rickover, Battleship, 27.
4. See, for example, Robles Muñoz, 1898, 7–8.
5. Díaz Plaja, 1898, 30; Offner, Unwanted War, 96.
6. Congosto to Moret, AMM, CGC, leg. 155.
7. Lee to Congosto, January 25, 1898, AMM, CGC, leg. 155.
8. Blanco's report, AMM, CGC, leg. 155; Dyal, Historical Dictionary, 200–202.
9. The best study of the Maine incident is Rickover, Battleship.
10. Milton, Yellow Kids, 220.
11. Ibid., 222–36; Brown, Correspondents' War, 114–28.
12. Feuer, War at Sea, 6, 8–10.
13. Rickover, Battleship, 43–74.
14. Golay, Spanish-American War, 12; Rodríguez González, Operaciones, 26–29.
15. See, for example, Foner, Spanish-Cuban-American War, 1:xi, 208–9, 217, 260.
16. Rodríguez Rodríguez, Algunos documentos, 32 n. 2, 35.
17. Offner, Unwanted War, 159–93.
18. Adams to Hugh Nelson, April 28, 1823, in Adams, Writings, 7:372–73.
19. Thomas, Cuba, 229. See also ibid., chaps. 17 and 18 on Americans' designs on Cuba in the early nineteenth century.
20. Moreno Fraginals et al., eds., Between Slavery and Free Labor, 19.
21. LaFeber, New Empire, 49.
22. Pratt, Expansionists, 276. Pratt emphasized the pressure to acquire markets after 1898, but it is clear that at least some American business leaders and politicians, responding to depressed demand at home for American products, were thinking about securing foreign markets earlier than 1898.
23. LaFeber, New Empire, 105–20.
24. Morgan, America's Road, 92.
25. Pratt, Expansionists, 2–9.
26. Williams, "Frontier Thesis," 379–95.
27. LaFeber, New Empire, 173–76, 264–81; Millis, Martial Spirit, 44; Golay, Spanish-American War, 33.
28. Damiani, Foreign Economic Policy. Damiani concluded that economic, racial, and political motives for empire were not very important and that reconcentration and the destruction of the Maine brought America and Spain to war.

CHAPTER SEVENTEEN

1. Francos Rodríguez, El año, 69.
2. Frascuelo's career, death, and funeral were the subject of every major Spanish periodical in the spring of 1898 until war with the United States pushed the torero's death into the background. A particularly good account appeared in El Liberal on March 9, 1898.
3. Ontañon, Frascuelo, 30.
4. Francos Rodríguez, El año, 79–96. See also Fernández-Rua, España.

5. "Otro Salvador, otro Mesías se presentaba al mundo." The quote from Guerra Junqueiro ("la pelea singular, extraña, entre Frascuelo y Edisson.") is used by Ontañon, *Frascuelo*, 105.

6. Corral, *El desastre*, 176. See also Urquía y Redecilla, *Historia negra*, viii–ix.

7. A few examples: Varela Ortega, "Aftermath of Splendid Disaster," 317–44; Torre, "El noventa y ocho español," 79–90; Feuer, *War at Sea*, 18; and Balfour, *End of the Spanish Empire*, 26.

8. Cervera to Victor Concas, February 26, 1898, in Concas y Palau, *Squadron*, 74–76. Cervera published his correspondence in *Guerra hispano-americana*. It was translated as U.S. Navy Department, *Spanish American War*. The opinions of Cervera have been cited in translation in many places, among them Joseph Smith, *Spanish-American War*, 65–69, and Trask, *War with Spain*, 60–71. The most pessimistic Spanish view of the matter was probably that published by the military writer Mariano y Vivo, who wrote a letter to the *Diario de Tarragona* on April 10, 1898, predicting that the United States would wipe out Spain and take Puerto Rico, Cuba, the Philippines, and the Canary Islands. A "war with the United States," he wrote, was a guarantee of "the absolute annihilation of our colonial power" (Mariano y Vivo, *Apuntes en defensa*, 5–6).

9. U.S. Department of State, handwritten notes, HL, Ms.

10. Rodríguez-Solis, *Los guerrilleros de 1808*, 2:27.

11. Navascués, *¡¡La próxima guerra!!* 4.

12. Cortijo, *Apuntes para la historia*, 32.

13. León Gutiérrez, *España y los Estados Unidos*, 6, 18.

14. Gómez Palacios, *La raza latina*, 5–6.

15. Ablanedo, *La cuestión de Cuba*, 51; Cortijo, *Apuntes para la historia*, 4; León Gutiérrez, *España y los Estados Unidos*, 7–8, 15–17, 24; Gómez Palacios, *La raza latina*, 13, 45.

16. Blasco Ibáñez, *Artículos*, 10.

17. *El Liberal*, December 27, 1896.

18. Tuñón de Lara et al., eds., *El desastre del 98*, 7.

19. Blasco Ibáñez, *Artículos*, 304–5.

20. *El Imparcial*, April 22, 1898.

21. Ibid., April 19, 1898.

22. Pando, *Documento*, 16.

23. Díaz Benzo, *Pequeñeces*, 110.

24. León Gutiérrez, *España y los Estados Unidos*, 17.

25. Lluhi y Taulina, *El conflicto de España*.

26. Minister of war to Blanco, June (n.d.) 1898, AMM, CGC, leg. 159.

27. Fernández-Rua, *España*, 7.

28. Roig de Leuchsenring, *La guerra libertadora*, 161.

29. Jover Zamora, *1898*.

30. Ballbé, *Orden público*, 389–457. See also Torre del Río, "La neutralidad británica."

31. Fernández-Rua, *España*, 4–5.

32. This correspondence in BN, ms. 21363/4.

33. BN, ms. 21356/3. Crazy Mary's letter to Carlos, in verse, was exceedingly long, and it included a note that read in part: "I am a prisoner in my own home for the past five days, under guard, all because I am crazy! They are doing terrible things to me at the

instigation of Father Canaya. I beg you to come [illeg.] to my rooms, Princesa street 47. The door is open, and although I am crazy, I do not bite."

34. Letter to *Imparcial* in BN, ms. 21363/4.

35. Francos Rodríguez, *El año*, 143, 231–32.

36. This letter is in BN, ms. 21356/3.

37. Serrano, *Le tour du peuple*, 39.

38. Serrano, "Prófugos y desertores."

39. Alvarez Junco, *El emperador*, 222.

40. Pando, *Documento*, 19.

41. Golay, *Spanish-American War*, 41.

42. Corral, *El desastre*, 176.

43. Long, *New American Navy*, 1:7.

44. Hobson, *Sinking of the Merrimac*, x–xi.

45. Long, *New American Navy*, 1:1–2.

46. The best works on this subject are Rodríguez González, *Política naval*, 61–65, and Gárate Córdoba and Manera Regueyra, *La armada*, 118–20. On the American blue water navy see Hagan, *People's Navy*.

47. Rodríguez González, *Política naval*, 175.

48. See Rapallo, *Ensayo de estrategía naval*, for a contemporary Spanish version of the jeune école theory.

49. Armiñan, *Weyler*, 162.

50. *El Imparcial*, October 19, 1894.

51. Navascués, *La próxima guerra*. Almost everything Navascués predicted about the "next war" failed to come true. In fairness to the author, he completed the manuscript of his book in 1892, before Ya-lu.

52. Lodge, *Intervention in Cuba*, 7–8.

53. Chadwick, *Relations*, 1:178.

54. Hobson, *Sinking of the Merrimac*, 3.

55. Feuer, *War at Sea*, 37–45.

56. Ibid., 17.

57. This and other quotations from Williams's correspondence comes from Henry Williams Papers, LCMD.

58. Feuer, *War at Sea*, 73, 96–99, 107, 150–56.

59. Rodríguez González, *Política naval*, 485.

60. Chadwick, *Relations*, 1:213.

61. Blanco to Moret, January 7, 1898, AMM, CGC, leg. 114; Feuer, *War at Sea*, 21.

62. *El Liberal*, October 9–18, 1896.

63. Rodríguez González, *Política naval*, 33–38.

64. Fernández-Rua, *España*, 12.

65. Trask, *War with Spain*, 101–5.

66. Francos-Rodríguez, *El año*, 125–28.

67. Ollero, *Teatro de guerra*, 28.

68. Pardo González, *La brigada*, 18.

69. Rodríguez Puértolas, ed., *El desastre en sus textos*, 21.

70. Miró, *Cuba*, 265–66.

71. Blanco to minister of war, AMM, CGC, leg. 155.

72. Pardo Gonzalez, La brigada, 44–47.

73. Battle reports, AMM, CGC, leg. 159.

74. Pando, Documento, 10–11.

75. Jiménez's correspondence in AMM, CGC, leg. 138.

76. Rodríguez Mendoza, En la manigua, 203, 207.

77. Pardo Gonzalez, La brigada, 56.

78. Blanco's correspondence to this effect in AMM, CGC, leg. 159; see also Weyler, Mi mando, 5:546–48.

79. Blanco's orders, AMM, CGC, leg. 159, car. 12.

80. Blanco to colonial minister, April (n.d.) 1898, AMM, CGC, leg. 159.

81. Rodríguez Rodríguez, Algunos documentos, 26–34.

82. Feuer, War at Sea, 138.

83. Correa to Blanco, April 7, 1898, AMM, CGC, leg. 156.

CHAPTER EIGHTEEN

1. Trask, War with Spain, 126.

2. Hobson, Sinking of the Merrimac.

3. Pando, Documento, 15; Trask, War with Spain, 335; Chadwick, Relations, 1:62.

4. Blanco's orders in AMM, CGC, leg. 159.

5. Blanco to Correa, May 6, 1898, AMM, CGC, leg. 159; Pando, Documento, 11–15.

6. Trask, War with Spain, 126–27.

7. Pardo González, La brigada, 57, 62.

8. Chadwick, Relations, 1:376–77; Balfour, End of the Spanish Empire, 40. One Cuban author in a flight of fancy wrote that García had 20,000 men under arms pinning down the Spanish in their garrisons (Torriente, Fin de la dominación, 19).

9. Academia de la Historia de Cuba, Parte oficial.

10. Pardo González, La brigada, 21.

11. Ibid., 36–37.

12. Feuer, War at Sea, 120–36.

13. Pareja's cable, AMM, CGC, leg. 67, car. 18.

14. Cosmas, Army for Empire, 5–11.

15. George Kendrick, "The Midsummer Picnic of 1898," HL, ms., 109–10.

16. Linares to Blanco, June 15, 1898, AMM, CGC, leg. 158; Pardo González, La brigada, 20.

17. Chadwick, Relations, 1:376–77.

18. Alvarez Angulo, Memorias, 178–201.

19. The disposition of Spanish forces is detailed in a document in AMM, CGC, 158. See also Chadwick, Relations, 2:72–73.

20. Pardo González, La brigada, 118; Golay, Spanish-American War, 59–63.

21. These are the official reported figures in AMM, CGC, leg. 155.

22. Trask, War with Spain, 237, 245.

23. Alvarez Angulo, Memorias, 225–28.

24. Balfour, End of the Spanish Empire.

25. Blanco to minister of war, July 3, 1898, AMM, CGC, leg. 159.

26. Golay, *Spanish-American War*, 74.

27. Academia de la Historia de Cuba, *Parte oficial*; Chadwick, *Relations*, 2:77, 85, 194.

28. Alvarez Angulo, *Memorias*, 221–25.

29. Trask, *War with Spain*, 265.

30. Concas y Palau, *Squadron*, 83.

31. Golay, *Spanish-American War*, 99.

32. See Rodríguez González, *Operaciones*.

33. Cervera to minister of war, July 4, 9, 1898, AMM, CGC, leg. 155.

34. Golay, *Spanish-American War*, 74–82.

35. Blanco to foreign minister, August 14, 1898, AMM, CGC, leg. 155.

36. Ibid., August 14, 1898.

37. Ibid., August 17, 1898.

38. Blanco to minister of war, August 19, 1898, AMM, CGC, leg. 159.

39. Blanco to March, September 10, 1898, and Blanco to Evacuation Committee, October 1, 1898, AMM, CGC, leg. 155.

40. Flint, *Marching with Gómez*, 20–21.

41. Diary entry of June 26, 1898, Henry Williams Papers, LCMD.

42. Corral, *El desastre*, 232–33.

43. Shafter to Adjutant General Corbin, July 18, 23, August 4, 17, 1898, *Correspondence*, 158, 175, 203, 231–32.

44. Rodríguez Demorizi, *Papeles dominicanos*, 73.

45. Millis, *Martial Spirit*, 362–63.

46. *Correspondence*, 249–50.

47. Espinosa y Ramos, *Al trote*, 279.

48. As argued by Donald Dyal in *Historical Dictionary*, viii–ix.

49. In 1998, scholarly articles and books raced to Spanish presses to take advantage of the centennial "celebration" of the Cuban disaster. Their quality varied greatly, but they all emphasized one point: Spain shrugged off the defeat rather easily so that 1898 was not so disastrous, after all. This new view quickly became so commonplace that a leading Spanish scholar, José María Jover, had to remind himself and his colleagues that "[w]e cannot and must not forget that [1898] was a catastrophe" (quoted in Núñez Florencio, "Menos se perdió," 11–13).

Bibliography

Archives and Manuscript Collections

CUBA
　Archivo Nacional de Cuba, Havana
　Museo Finlay, Havana
　Biblioteca Nacional José Martí, Havana

SPAIN
　Archivo General Militar, Segovia
　Archivo General Militar de Madrid, Madrid
　Archivo Histórico Nacional, Madrid
　Biblioteca Nacional, Madrid

UNITED STATES
　History of Medicine Archives, Bethesda, Md.
　Huntington Library, Pasadena, Calif.
　Library of Congress, Manuscripts Division, Washington, D.C.
　National Archives, Washington, D.C.

Books and Articles

Abellán, José Luís. *Sociología del 98*. Barcelona, 1973.

Ablanedo, Juan Bautista. *La cuestión de Cuba*. Sevilla, 1897.

Academia de la Historia de Cuba. *Papeles de Maceo*. 2 vols. Havana, 1948.

———. *Parte Oficial del Lugarteniente General Calixto García al General en Jefe Máximo Gómez el 15 de Julio de 1898 sobre la campaña de Santiago de Cuba*. Havana, 1953.

Acosta Quintana, Sebastian. *Planos de comunicaciones de las provincias de la Isla de Cuba*. Havana, 1884.

Adams, John Quincy. *Writings of John Quincy Adams*. 7 vols. Edited by W. C. Ford. New York, 1913–17.

Adán, José A. *El lobbyismo en la independencia de Cuba*. Miami, 1979.

Agramonte, Aristides. *The Inside History of a Great Medical Discovery*. Havana, 1930.

Album de la trocha: Breve reseña de una excursión feliz desde Cienfuegos a San Fernando recorriendo la linea militar, por cuatro periodistas, Junio 1897. Havana, 1897.

Alcalá, José. *La Artillería española en Santiago de Cuba*. Madrid, 1899.

Alcázar, José. *Historia de España en América*. Madrid, 1898.

Alger, Russel A. *The Spanish-American War*. Freeport, N.Y., 1971.

Allahar, Anton L. *Class, Politics, and Sugar in Colonial Cuba*. Lewiston, N.Y., 1990.

Allendesalazar, José Manuel. *El 98 de los americanos*. Madrid, 1974.

Almeida Bosque, Juan. *El general en jefe Máximo Gómez*. Havana, 2000.

Alonso, José Ramón. *Historia política del ejército español*. Madrid, 1974.

Alonso Baquer, Miguel. *El ejército en la sociedad española*. Madrid, 1971.

———. "El ejército español y las operaciones militares en Cuba (1895: La campaña de Martínez Campos)." In *1895: La guerra en Cuba y la España de la Restauración*, edited by Emilio de Diego, 297–318. Madrid, 1996.

————. "La guerra hispano-americana de 1898 y sus efectos sobre las instituciones militares españoles." *Revista de Historia Militar* 27, no. 54 (1983): 127–51.

Alvarez Angulo, Tomás. *Memorias de un hombre sin importancia.* Madrid, 1962.

Alvarez Junco, José. *El emperador del paralelo: Lerroux y la demagogia populista.* Madrid, 1990.

————. *La ideología política del anarquismo español (1868–1910).* Madrid, 1976.

Alvira, Francisco, et al. *La enseñanza militar en España, un análisis sociológico.* Madrid, 1986.

Alzola y Minondo, Pablo. *Relaciones comerciales entre la Península y las Antillas.* Madrid, 1895.

Amante de la nación. *Estudio de la Guerra de Cuba: sus errores y medios de hacer de vencer de acuerdo con las últimas disposiciones.* Madrid, 1896.

Amer, Carlos. *Cuba y la opinión pública.* Madrid, 1897.

American-Spanish War: A History by the War Leaders. Norwich, Conn., 1899.

Amster, Lewis J. "Carlos J. Finlay: The Mosquito Man." *Hospital Practice* 22 (May 15, 1987): 223–46.

Anderson, Benedict. *Imagined Communities.* London, 1983.

Andrés-Gallego, José, et al. *Historia General de España y América.* Vol. 16-2. Madrid, 1981.

————. *Un 98 distinto (Restauración, Desastre, Regeneración).* Madrid, 1998.

Aparicio, Raul. *Hombradía de Antonio Maceo.* Havana, 2001.

Arbelo, Manuel. *Recuerdo de la guerra de independencia.* Havana, 1918.

Arderíus, Francisco. *De mis recuerdos.* Madrid, 1914.

Argilagos, Francisco R. *Prédicas insurrectas.* Havana, 1916.

Armiñan, Luis. *Weyler.* Madrid, 1946.

Arnold, David, ed. *Warm Climates and Western Medicine: The Emergence of Tropical Medicine, 1500–1900.* Amsterdam, 1996.

Artola, Miguel. *Los orígenes de la España contemporánea.* Madrid, 1959.

Atkins, Edwin F. *Sixty Years in Cuba.* Cambridge, Mass., 1926.

Augustine, George. *History of Yellow Fever.* New Orleans, 1909.

Avelino Delgado, Octavio. "The Spanish Army in Cuba, 1868–1898: An Institutional Study." 2 vols. Ph.D. dissertation, Columbia University, 1980.

Aya, Roderick. *The Missed Revolution: The Fate of Rural Rebels in Sicily and Southern Spain, 1840–1950.* Amsterdam, 1973.

Azaña, Manuel. *¡Todavía el 98! El Idearium de Ganivet, Tres generaciones del Ateneo.* Introducción por Santos Juliá. Madrid, 1997.

Azcarate, Pablo. *La guerra del 98.* Madrid, 1968.

Bahamonde Magro, Angel, and José G. Cayuela Fernández. *Hacer las Americas: Las elites coloniales españolas en el siglo XIX.* Madrid, 1992.

————. "Trasvase de capitales antillanos y estrategias inversoras. La fortuna del marqués de Manzanedo (1823–1882)." *Revista Internacional de Sociología* 45 (1987): 125–47.

Balfour, Sebastian. *The End of the Spanish Empire, 1898–1923.* Oxford, 1997.

Ballbé, Manuel. *Orden público y militarismo en la España constitucional (1812–1933).* Madrid, 1985.

Bañon Martínez, Rafael, and Thomas M. Barker, eds. *Armed Forces and Society in Spain Past and Present.* New York, 1988.

Baquero, Gastón. "Versiones y precisiones en la muerte de Martí." In Baquero et al., *Indios, blancos y negros en el caldero de América*. Madrid, 1991.

Barado y Font, Francisco. *Nuestros soldados: Narraciones y episodios de la vida militar en España*. Barcelona, 1889.

Barnes, James. "Songs of the Ships of Steel." *McClure's Magazine* 11 (June 1898): 115–19.

Barnet, Miguel. *Afro-Cuban Religions*. Princeton, N.J., 2001.

———. *Biografía de un cimarrón*. Barcelona, 1968.

Barón Fernández, José. *La guerra hispano-americana de 1898*. La Coruña, 1993.

Barquín López, Ramón M. *Las luchas guerrilleras en Cuba: de la colonia a la Sierra Maestra*. Madrid, 1975.

Barrios Carrión, Leopoldo. *Apuntamientos de un curso de arte de guerra*. Toledo, 1892.

———. *Bosquejo geográfico militar de la provincia de Puerto Príncipe*. Barcelona, 1881.

Beals, Carleton. *The Crime of Cuba*. Philadelphia, 1933.

Beisner, Robert L. *Twelve against Empire: The Anti-Imperialists, 1898–1900*. Chicago, 1992.

Bellesiles, Michael. *Arming America: Gun Ownership in the United States*. New York, 2000.

Bergad, Laird W. *Cuban Rural Society in the Nineteenth Century: The Social and Economic History of Monoculture in Matanzas*. Princeton, N.J., 1990.

Blasco Ibáñez, Vicente. *Artículos contra la guerra de Cuba*. Edited by J. L. León Roca. Valencia, 1978.

Blinkhorn, Martin. "Spain: The 'Spanish Problem' and the Imperial Myth." *Journal of Contemporary History* 15 (1980): 5–25.

Bolado Argüello, Nieves. *La independencia de Cuba y la Prensa: apuntes para la historia*. Torrelavega, Cantabria, 1991.

Boletín oficial de la Capitanía General de Cuba. Havana, 1895–98.

Bonsal, Stephen. *The Fight for Santiago: The Story of the Soldier in the Cuban Campaign from Tampa to the Surrender*. New York, 1899.

Bosch, Juan. *De Cristóbal Colón a Fidel Castro: El Caribe, frontera imperial*. Santo Domingo, 1993.

Botifoll, Luis J. *Forjadores de la conciencia nacional cubana*. Miami, 1984.

Boyd, Carolyn P. *Praetorian Politics in Liberal Spain*. Chapel Hill, 1979.

Boza, Bernabé. *Mi diario de la guerra desde Baire hasta la intervención americana*. Havana, 1924.

Bradford, James C., ed. *Crucible of Empire: The Spanish-American War and Its Aftermath*. Annapolis, 1993.

Brands, H. W. *The Reckless Decade: America in the 1890s*. New York, 1995.

Brenan, Gerald. *South from Granada*. Cambridge, 1957.

Brès, P. L. J. "A Century of Progress in Combating Yellow Fever." *Bulletin of the World Health Organization* 64 (1986): 775–86.

Brown, Charles H. *The Correspondents' War: Journalists in the Spanish-American War*. New York, 1967.

Brunner, W. F. "Morbidity and Mortality in the Spanish Army in Cuba during the Calendar Year 1897." *Public Health Reports* 13 (April 29, 1898): 409–12.

Bullón de Mendoza, Alfonso, and Luis E. Togores, eds., *Cánovas y su época*. 2 vols. Madrid, 1999.

Burguete y Lana, Ricardo. *¡La guerra! Cuba: Diario de un testigo*. Barcelona, 1902.

Buznego, Enrique. *Mayor General Máximo Gómez: Sus campañas militares*. 2 vols. Havana, 1986.

Bynum, W. F. *Science and the Practice of Medicine in the Nineteenth Century*. Cambridge, Mass., 1994.

Cabot Lodge, Henry. *Intervention in Cuba. Speech of Hon. Henry Cabot Lodge of Massachusetts in the Senate of the United States, April 13, 1898*. Washington, D.C., 1898.

Cabrera, Francisco. *Episodios de la Guardia Civil de Cuba*. Valencia, 1897.

Cabrera, Ramiro. *¡A Sitio Herrera!* Havana, 1922.

Cacho Viu, Vicente. *Repasar el noventa y ocho*. Madrid, 1997.

Calleja Leal, Guillermo. "La muerte de José Martí en el combate de Dos Ríos." In Calleja Leal et al., *La presencia española en Cuba (1868–1895)*. Madrid, 1995.

Carbonell y Martí, J. *Estudio sobre las causas de la fiebre amarilla*. Havana, 1879. Ms. in History of Medicine Archives, Bethesda, Md.

Cardona, Gabriel. *Historia del Ejército: El peso de un grupo social diferente*. Barcelona, 1983.

———. *El problema militar en España*. Madrid, 1990.

Cardona, Gabriel, and Juan Carlos Losada. *Weyler, nuestro hombre en la Habana*. Barcelona, 1997.

Carr, Raymond. *Spain, 1808–1975*. Oxford, 1975.

Carrasco y Sandía, Felipe. *Pequeñeces de la Guerra de Cuba, por un español*. Madrid, 1897.

Carrillo Morales, Justo. *Expediciones cubanas*. Havana, 1936.

"Carta de Arturo Mora a Rafael Gasset." Ms. 21381/61, Biblioteca Nacional, Madrid.

"Cartas con motivo a la suscripción abierta por el periódico El Imparcial." Ms. 21363/4, Biblioteca Nacional, Madrid.

Carter, Henry Rose. *Yellow Fever: An Epidemiological and Historical Study of Its Place of Origin*. Edited by Laura A. Carter and Wade H. Frost. Baltimore, 1931.

Casas, Juan Bautista. *La guerra separatista en Cuba, sus causas, medios de terminarla y evitar otras*. Madrid, 1896.

Cassola, Manuel. *Establecimiento de colonias militares en Ultramar*. Madrid, 1883.

"Casualties." In *The Oxford Companion to American Military History*. Oxford, 1999.

Cayuela Fernández, José G. *Bahía de Ultramar: España y Cuba en el siglo XIX. El control de las relaciones coloniales*. Madrid, 1993.

———, ed. *España en Cuba: final del siglo*. Zaragoza, 2000.

Cervera y Topete, Pascual. *Guerra hispano-americana. Colección oficial referente á las operaciones navales durante la guerra con los Estados Unidos en 1898*. El Ferrol, 1899.

Chadwick, French Ensor. *The Relations of the United States and Spain: The Spanish American War*. 2 vols. New York, 1968.

Christiansen, Eric. *The Origins of Military Power in Spain, 1800–1854*. Oxford, 1967.

Churchill, Winston S. *My Early Life: A Roving Commission*. London, 1944.

Clark, James Hyde. *Cuba and the Fight for Freedom*. Philadelphia, 1896.

Cohen, Stan. *Images of the Spanish-American War, April–August 1898*. Missoula, 1997.

Comellas, José Luis. *Cánovas*. Madrid, 1965.

Companys Monclús, Julián. "La Carta de Dupuy de Lôme." *Boletín de la Real Academia de la Historia* 84 (September–December 1987): 465–81.

———. *España en 1898: Entre la diplomacia y la guerra*. Madrid, 1991.

Concas y Palau, Víctor M. *The Squadron of Admiral Cervera*. Washington, D.C., 1900.

Concha, Manuel. *Observaciones sobre táctica de guerrillas.* Madrid, 1874.

Conde Fernández-Oliva, Emilio C. "Sobre el pensamiento en relación a las fuerzas armadas de Cánovas del Castillo." In Bullón de Mendoza and Togores, eds., *Cánovas y su época,* 1:135–51.

Corral, Manuel. *El desastre: memorias de un voluntario en la campaña de Cuba.* Barcelona, 1899.

Correspondence Relating to the War with Spain. 2 vols. Washington, D.C., 1993.

Cortijo, Vicente. *Apuntes para la historia de la pérdida de nuestras colonias por un testigo presencial.* Madrid, 1899.

Cosmas, Graham A. *An Army for Empire: The United States Army in the Spanish-American War.* Columbia, Mo., 1971.

Costa, Joaquin. *Oligarquía y caciquismo, Colectivismo agrario, y otros escritos.* 2nd ed. Madrid, 1969.

Crespo, Pedro Z. *La administración de una colonia.* Philadelphia, 1886.

Crouch, Thomas, W. *A Yankee Guerrillero: Frederick Funston and the Cuban Insurrection, 1896–1897.* Memphis, 1975.

Cruz, Jesús. *Gentlemen Bourgeois and Revolutionaries: Political Change and Cultural Persistence among the Spanish Dominant Groups, 1750–1850.* New York, 1996.

Cruz, Manuel de la. *Episodios de la revolución cubana.* Havana, 2001.

Cuadros de la guerra: Acción de Cacarajícara por un testigo. Havana, 1896.

Curnow, Ena. *Manana: Detrás del Generalísimo.* Miami, 1995.

Curtin, P. D. *Death by Migration: Europe's Encounter with the Tropical World in the Nineteenth Century,* Cambridge, 1989.

Damiani, Brian P. *Foreign Economic Policy of the United States.* New York, 1987.

Davis, Richard Harding. *Cuba in War Time.* New York, 1897.

———. *The Notes of a War Correspondent.* New York, 1911.

Delaporte, François. *The History of Yellow Fever: An Essay on the Birth of Tropical Medicine.* New York, 1991.

Díaz Benzo, Antonio. *Pequeñeces de la Guerra de Cuba, por un español.* Madrid, 1897.

Díaz Plaja, Fernando. *1898.* Madrid, 1976.

———. *La historia de España en sus documentos. El siglo XIX.* Madrid, 1954.

Diego, Emilio. "Las reformas de Maura, la última oportunidad política en las Antillas?" In *1895: La guerra en cuba y la España de la Restauración,* edited by Emilio Diego, 99–117. Madrid, 1996.

———. *Weyler, de la leyenda a la historia.* Madrid, 1998.

———, ed. *1895: La guerra en Cuba y la España de la Restauración.* Madrid, 1996.

Dirección política de las FAR. *Historia de Cuba.* Havana, 1985.

Documentos presentados a las Cortes en la legislatura de 1898 por el Ministro de Estado. Madrid, 1898.

Documents de Cuba. Barcelona, 1968.

Domínguez, Francisco. *Carlos J. Finlay, Son Centenaire (1933), Sa Découverte (1881).* Paris, 1935.

Duran, Aleida. "Carlos J. Finlay Salvó Millones de Vidas." <<http://www.contactomagazine.com/finlay.html>>.

Durnerin, James. *Maura et Cuba: Politique Coloniale d'un Ministre Liberal.* Paris, 1978.

Dyal, Donald H. *Historical Dictionary of the Spanish-American War.* Westport, Conn., 1996.

Elorza, Antonio. "El Sueño de Cuba en José Martí." In *La nación soñada: Cuba, Puerto Rico y Filipinas ante el 98,* edited by Consuelo Naranjo Orovio et al., 65–78. Madrid, 1996.

Elorza, Antonio, and Elena Hernández Sandoica. *La Guerra de Cuba (1895–1898): Historia política de una derrota colonial.* Madrid, 1998.

Eltis, David. *Economic Growth and the Ending of the Transatlantic Slave Trade.* New York, 1987.

Escribano Iñigo, Bienvenido. *Exposición que dirigen al excelentísimo señor presidente del Consejo de Ministros D. Antonio Cánovas del Castillo los habitantes de los pueblos de Aldeatejada, Arapiles, Miranda de Azán, Las Torres, y Carbajosa de la Sagrada.* Salamanca, 1897.

Esenwein, George Richard. *Anarchist Ideology and the Working-Class Movement in Spain, 1868–1898.* Berkeley, 1989.

Eslava Galán, Juan, and Diego Rojano Ortega. *La España del 98: El fin de una era.* Madrid, 1997.

Espadas Burgos, Manuel. "El factor ultramarino en la formación de la mentalidad militar española." *Estudios de Historia Social* 47 (1988): 311–25.

España. Ministerio de la Guerra. *Estados de las fuerzas y material sucesivamente enviados con motivo de las actuales campañas a los distritos de ultramar.* Madrid, 1897.

Espinosa y Ramos, Serafín. *Al trote y sin estribos (recuerdos de la Guerra de Independencia).* Havana, 1946.

Estévez Romero, Luis. *Desde el Zanjón hasta Baire: Datos para la historia de Cuba.* Havana, 1899.

Estrade, Paul. "José Martí: Las ideas y la acción." *Estudios de Historia Social* 44 (1988): 17–88.

Fabié, Antonio María. *Mi gestión ministerial en la Isla de Cuba.* Madrid, 1898.

Faget, Charles. *Fievre jaune.* Paris, 1875.

Farhang, Mansour. *U.S. Imperialism: The Spanish-American War to the Iranian Revolution.* Boston, 1981.

Farrell, Jeanette. *Invisible Enemies: Stories of Infectious Disease.* New York, 1998.

Feijóo Gómez, Albino, *Quintas y protesta social en el siglo XIX.* Madrid, 1996.

Fernández, Damián J., and Madeline Cámara Betancourt, eds. *Cuba, the Elusive Nation: Interpretations of National Identity.* Gainesville, Fla., 2000.

Fernández, Frank. *Cuban Anarchism: The History of a Movement.* Translated by Charles Bufe. Tucson, Ariz., 2001.

———. *La sangre de Santa Agueda: Angiolillo, Betances, y Cánova. Análisis de un magnicidio y sus consecuencias históricas.* Miami, 1994.

Fernández Almagro, Melchor. *Política naval de la España moderna y contemporánea.* Madrid, 1946.

Fernández Bastarreche, Fernando. *El ejército español en el siglo XIX.* Madrid, 1978.

Fernández-Rua, José Luis. *España, 1898.* Madrid, 1954.

Ferrer, Ada. *Insurgent Cuba: Race, Nation, and Revolution, 1868–1898.* Chapel Hill, 1999.

———. "Rethinking Race and Nation in Cuba." In *Cuba, The Elusive Nation: Interpretations of National Identity,* edited by Damián J. Fernández and Madeline Cáamara Betancourt, 60–76. Gainesville, Fla., 2000.

———. "Rustic Men, Civilized Nation: Race, Culture, and Contention on the Eve of Cuban Independence." *Hispanic American Historical Review* 78 (1998): 663–86.

Feuer, A. B. *The Spanish-American War at Sea: Naval Action in the Atlantic.* Westport, Conn., 1995.

Field, James A., Jr. "American Imperialism: The Worst Chapter in Almost Any Book." *American Historical Review* 83 (June 1978): 644–83.

Figuero, Javier, and Carlos G. Santa Cecilia. *La España del desastre.* Barcelona, 1997.

Finlay, Carlos E. *Carlos Finlay and Yellow Fever.* New York, 1940.

Finlay, Carlos J. *Obras completas.* 6 vols. Havana, 1965–81.

———. *Trabajos selectos.* Havana, 1912.

Fité, Vital. *Las desdichas de la patria.* Madrid, 1899.

Flint, Grover. *Marching with Gómez.* Boston, 1898.

Foner, Philip. *Antonio Maceo: The "Bronze Titan" of Cuba's Struggle for Independence.* New York, 1977.

———. *The Spanish-Cuban-American War and the Birth of American Imperialism.* 2 vols. New York, 1972.

Forcadell Alvarez, Carlos. "El lúcido pesimismo del gobernador general de la isla de Cuba: La correspondencia de Martínez Campois con el Ministerio de Ultramar." In *España en Cuba: Final de siglo,* edited by José Cayuela Fernández, 31–57. Zaragoza, 2000.

Fradera, Josep M. *Gobernar colonias.* Barcelona, 1999.

Francos Rodríguez, José. *El año de la derrota, 1898, de las memorias de un gacetillero.* Madrid, 1930.

———. *La vida de Canalejas.* Madrid, 1918.

Freidel, Frank. *The Splendid Little War.* Boston, 1958.

Frieyro de Lara, Beatriz. "La situación del soldado en Cuba vista desde el parlamento." In *Antes del "desastre": orígenes y antecedentes de la crisis del 98,* edited by Juan Pablo Fusi and Antonio Niño, 161–71. Madrid, 1996.

Fuente y Hernández, José. *El fusil mauser español.* Madrid, 1894.

Fusi, Juan Pablo, and Antonio Niño, eds. *Antes del "desastre": Orígenes y antecedentes de la crisis del 98.* Madrid, 1996.

———. *Vísperas del 98: Orígenes y antecedentes de la crisis del 98.* Madrid, 1997.

Gago y Palomo, José. *El ejército nacional.* Granada, 1895.

Gallego García, Tesifonte. *La insurrección cubana, crónicas de la campaña.* Madrid, 1897.

Gárate Córdoba, José María, and Enrique Manera Regueyra, *La armada y la cultura militar en el siglo XIX.* Vol. 4 of *Las fuerzas armadas españolas,* edited by Miguel Alonso Baquer and Mario Hernández Sánchez-Barba. Madrid, 1987.

García Acuña, José. *Impresiones y antecedentes de la guerra hispano-yanqui.* Madrid, 1911.

García Barron, Carlos. *Cancionero del 98.* Madrid, 1974.

García Cisneros, Florencio. *Máximo Gómez: caudillo o dictador?* Miami, 1986.

Garralda Arizcún, José Fermín. "La guerra hispanocubana narrada por un español en la gran antilla." In *Cánovas y su época.* Vol. 2, edited by Alfonso Bullón de Mendoza and Luis E. Togores, 1215–53. Madrid, 1999.

Giberga y Gali, Eliseo. *Apuntes sobre la cuestión de Cuba por un autonomista.* Madrid, 1897.

Gibson, William M. *Theodore Roosevelt among the Humorists.* Knoxville, 1980.

Gil Alvaro de Trasmiera, Antonio. *Glorias del ejército español: Historia del regimiento inmemorial del Rey.* Madrid, 1911.

Golay, Michael. *The Spanish-American War*. New York, 1995.

Gómez, Fernando. *La insurrección por dentro. Apuntes para la historia*. Havana, 1897.

Gómez, Juan Gualberto. *Por Cuba Libre*. Havana, 1974.

Gómez, Máximo. *Diario de campaña*, Havana, 1969.

———. *Obras escogidas*. Havana, 1979.

Gómez Núñez, Severo. *La acción de Peralejo*. Havana, 1897.

———. *La guerra hispano-americano*. 4 vols. Madrid, 1899–1902.

Gómez Palacios, Carlos. *La raza latina*. Buenos Aires, 1898.

González Alcorta, Leandro. *Que pasa en Cuba?* León, 1896.

González Iglesias, Manuel. *Los novios de la muerte*. Madrid, 1968.

Goode, W. A. M. *With Sampson through the War*. New York, 1899.

Greenfield, Sumner M. *La generación de 1898 ante España: Antología de literaturea de temas nacionales y universales*. Lincoln, Neb., 1981.

Griñan Peralta, Leonardo. "El carácter de Máximo Gómez." In *Biblioteca de la Historia, Filosofía y Sociología*. Vol. 24. Havana, 1946.

———. *Maceo: análisis caracterológico*. Havana, 1935.

Guerra y Sánchez, Ramiro, José M. Pérez Cabrera, Juan J. Ramos, and Emeterio S. Santovenia, eds. *Historia de la nación cubana*. 10 vols. Havana, 1952.

Guiteras, Juan. *Sanidad y beneficiencia*. Santiago, 1909–10.

Gutiérrez de la Concha, Manuel (Marqués de la Habana). *Memoria sobre la guerra de la isla de Cuba*. Madrid, 1875.

Hagan, Kenneth J. *The People's Navy: The Making of American Sea Power*. New York, 1991.

Harrison, Gordon A. *Mosquitoes, Malaria, and Man: A History of the Hostilities since 1880*. New York, 1978.

Headrick, Daniel R. *Ejército y política en España, 1866–1898*. Madrid, 1981.

Healy, David. *The United States in Cuba, 1898–1902*. Madison, 1963.

Helg, Aline. *Our Rightful Share: The Afro-Cuban Struggle for Equality, 1886–1912*. Chapel Hill, 1995.

Heredia y Mota, Nicolás. *Crónicas de la Guerra de Cuba*. 2 vols. Havana, 1957.

Hernández, Berta, ed. *Apuntes biográficos del Mayor General Serafín Sánchez*. Havana, 1986.

Hernández, Eusebio. *Maceo: Dos conferencias históricas*. Havana, 1968.

Hernández Poggio, Ramón. *Aclimatación é higiene de los Europeos en Cuba*. Madrid, 1874.

Hernández Sandoica, Elena. *El colonialismo (1815–1873): Estructuras y cambios en los imperios coloniales*. Madrid, 1994.

———. "La navegación a ultramar y la acción del Estado: España, siglo XIX." *Estudios de Historia Social* 44 (1988): 105–13.

———. "Pensamiento burgués y problemas coloniales en la España de la Restauración, 1875–1887." 2 vols. Doctoral thesis, Universidad Complutense, Madrid, 1982.

———. "Polémica arancelaria y cuestión colonial en la crisis de crecimiento del capital nacional: España, 1868–1900." *Estudios de Historia Social* 22–23 (July–December 1982): 279–319.

Herr, Richard. *An Historical Essay on Modern Spain*. New York, 1971.

Hidalgo de Paz, Ibrahim. *Cuba, 1895–1898: Contradicciones y disoluciones*. Havana, 1999.

Hobsbawm, Eric J. *Nations and Nationalism since 1780*. Cambridge, 1990.

Hobsbawm, Eric J., and Terence Ranger, eds. *The Invention of Tradition*. Cambridge, 1983.

Hobson, Richmond Pearson. *The Sinking of the Merrimac.* Annapolis, Md., 1987.

Hofstadter, Richard. "Cuba, the Philippines, and Manifest Destiny." In *The National Temper: Readings in American Culture and Society*, edited by Lawrence W. Levine and Robert Middlekauff, 242–65. New York, 1972.

Ibarra, Jorge. "Cultura é identidad nacional en el Caribe hispánico: El caso puertorriqueño y el cubano." In *La nación soñada: Cuba, Puerto Rico y Filipinas ante el 98*, edited by Consuelo Naranjo, Miguel A. Puig-Samper, and Luis Miguel García Mora, 86–95. Madrid, 1996.

———. *Ideología mambisa.* Havana, 1972.

Ingalls, John J. *America's War for Humanity.* Portland, Ore., 1898.

Izaguirre, José María. *Asuntos cubanos, colección de artículos y poesías.* New York, 1896.

Jeffers, H. Paul. *Colonel Roosevelt: Theodore Roosevelt Goes to War, 1897–1898.* New York, 1996.

Jensen, Geoffrey. "Military Nationalism and the State: The Case of Fin-de-siècle Spain." *Nations and Nationalism* 6 (2000): 257–74.

———. "Moral Strength Through Material Defeat: The Consequences of 1898 for Spanish Military Culture." *War and Society* 17 (October 1999): 25–39.

Jiménez Castellanos, Adolfo. *Sistema para combatir las insurrecciones en Cuba, según lo que aconseja la experiencia.* Madrid, 1883.

Jover Zamora, José María. *1898: Teoría y práctica de la redistribución colonial.* Madrid, 1979.

Juderías, Julian. *La leyenda negra: Estudios acerca del concepto de España en el extranjero.* Madrid, 1914.

Jutglar, Antoní. *Ideologías é intereses en la España contemporánea.* 2 vols. Madrid, 1968.

Kagan, Richard L. "Prescott's Paradigm: American Historical Scholarship and the Decline of Spain." *American Historical Review* 101 (April 1996): 423–46.

Kaplan, Temma. *Anarchists of Andalucía: 1868–1903.* Princeton, N.J., 1977.

Kennan, George. *Campaigning in Cuba.* New York, 1899.

Klein, Herbert S. *Slavery in the Americas: A Comparative Study of Virginia and Cuba.* Chicago, 1967.

Knight, Franklin W. *Slave Society in Cuba during the Nineteenth Century.* Madison, Wisc., 1970.

LaFeber, Walter. *Inevitable Revolutions: The United States in Central America.* New York, 1983.

———. *The New Empire: An Interpretation of American Expansion, 1860–1898.* New York, 1963.

Laín Entralgo, Pedro. *El problema de España en el siglo XIX.* Madrid, 1957.

Laín Entralgo, Pedro, and Carlos Seco Serrano, eds. *España en 1898: Las claves del desastre.* Barcelona, 1998.

Lane, Jack C. *Armed Progressive: General Leonard Wood.* San Rafael, Calif., 1978.

Larra y Cerezo, Angel. *Datos para la historia de la campaña sanitaria en la guerra de Cuba (apuntes estadísticos relativos al año 1896).* Madrid, 1901.

———. *Les hôpitaux militaires de l'île de Cuba et notamment l'hôpital d'Alphonse XIII de la Havane pendant la guerre actúelle.* Madrid, 1898.

Larrea, Francisco [Efeele, pseud.]. *El desastre nacional y los vicios de nuestras instituciones militares.* Madrid, 1901.

Lebergott, Stanley. "The Returns to U.S. Imperialism, 1890–1929." *Journal of Economic History* 40 (June 1980): 229–49.

Lee, Fitzhugh. "Cuba under Spanish Rule." *McClure's Magazine* 11 (June 1898): 99–114.

León Gutiérrez, Florencio. *España y los Estados Unidos.* Sevilla, 1898.

———. *España sin sus colonias.* Edited by Fernando Tomás Pérez González. Cáceres, 1999.

Le Riverend, Julio. *Historia económica de Cuba.* Havana, 1967.

Lewis, Henry Harrison. "General Wood at Santiago. Americanizing a Cuban City." *McClure's Magazine* 12 (March 1899): 460–69.

Liss, Sheldon B. *Roots of Revolution: Radical Thought in Cuba.* Lincoln, Neb., 1987.

Llorens y Maceo, José S. *Con Maceo en la invasión.* Havana, 1928.

Lluhi y Taulina, Jaime. *El conflicto de España con los Estados Unidos y única solución digna para España.* Madrid, 1896.

Lodge, Henry Cabot. *Intervention in Cuba. Speech of Hon. Henry Cabot Lodge of Massachusetts in the Senate of the United States. April 13, 1898.* Washington, D.C., 1898.

———. *The War with Spain.* New York, 1899.

Long, John D. *The New American Navy.* 2 vols. New York, 1903.

López Ibor, Juan José. *El español y su complejo de inferioridad.* Madrid, 1960.

López Segrera, Francisco. "Cuba: Dependence, Plantation Economy, and Social Classes, 1762–1902." In *Between Slavery and Free Labor: The Spanish-Speaking Caribbean in the Nineteenth Century,* edited by Manuel Moreno Fraginals, Frank Moya Pons, and Stanley L. Engerman, 77–93. Baltimore, 1985.

Lubián y Arias, Rafael. *Episodios de las guerras por la independencia de Cuba.* Miami, 1984.

Maceo, Antonio. *Ideología política: Cartas y otros documentos.* 2 vols. Havana, 1998.

Macías Picavea, Ricardo. *El problema nacional, hechos, causas, remedios.* Madrid, 1899.

Madariaga, Salvador. *The Genius of Spain.* Oxford, 1923.

Mahan, Alfred Thayer. *Lessons of the War with Spain and Other Articles.* Boston, 1899.

Maluquer de Motes, Jordi. "El mercado colonial antillano en el siglo XIX." In *Agricultura, comercio colonial y crecimiento económico en la España contemporánea,* edited by Jordi Nadal and Gabriel Tortella, 322–57. Barcelona, 1974.

———. *España en la crisis de 1898: De la Gran Depresión a la modernización económica del siglo XX.* Barcelona, 1999.

———. "La formación del mercado interior en condiciones coloniales: la inmigración y el comercio catalán en las Antillas españolas durante el siglo XIX." *Estudios de Historia Social* 44 (1988): 89–103.

Mañach, Jorge. *Martí: Apostle of Freedom.* Translated by Coley Taylor. New York, 1950.

Mariano, Marqués de. *Cuestiones hispano-norte-americanas.* Barcelona, 1898.

Mariano y Vivo, Manuel [A + B, pseud.]. *Apuntes en defensa del honor del ejército.* Madrid, 1898.

Marimon Riutort, Antoni. *El general Weyler, governador de l'illa de Cuba.* Palma, Mallorca, 1992.

Marinas Otero, Luis. *La herencia del 98.* Madrid, 1957.

Martí, José. *En los Estados Unidos.* Madrid, 1968.

Martín Jiménez, Hilario. *Valeriano Weyler (1838–1930): De su vida y personalidad.* Santa Cruz de Tenerife, 1998.

Martínez Campos y Serrano, Carlos (Duque de la Torre). *España bélica: El siglo XIX.* Madrid, 1961.

Martínez Carrión, José Miguel, ed. *El nivel de vida en la España rural, siglos XVII–XX.* Alicante, 2002.

Massons, Josep María. *Historia de la sanidad militar española.* 4 vols. Barcelona, 1994.

Matthews, Franklin. "Under Water in the Holland. A Voyage in the Diving Torpedo Boat." *McClure's Magazine* 12 (February 1899): 291–98.

Maura, Antonio. *Proyecto de Ley Reformando el Gobierno y Administración de las islas de Cuba y Puerto Rico.* Madrid, 1893.

May, Ernest R. *American Imperialism: A Speculative Essay.* New York, 1968.

———. *Imperial Democracy: The Emergence of America as a Great Power.* New York, 1961.

Maza Miguel, Manuel Pablo. "Between Ideology and Compassion: The Cuban Insurrection of 1895–98, through the Private Correspondence of Cuba's Two Prelates with the Holy See." Ph.D. dissertation, Georgetown University, 1987.

McIntosh, Burr W. *The Little I Saw of Cuba.* New York, 1899.

Méndez Capote, Renée. *Relatos heróicos.* Havana, 1975.

Mendoza y Vizcaíno, Enrique. *Historia de la guerra hispano-americana.* Mexico City, 1902.

Menéndez Caravía, José. *La Guerra en Cuba. Su origen y desarrollo, reformas necesarias para terminarla é impedir la propaganda filibustera.* Madrid, 1896.

Merchan, Rafael M. *Cuba: Justificación de su Guerra de Independencia.* Bogotá, 1896.

Merk, Frederick. *Manifest Destiny and Mission in American History: A Reinterpretation.* New York, 1963.

Mesa-Lago, Carmelo. "El trabajo en Cuba en el período pre-revolucionario." *Moneda y Crédito* 136 (1976): 36–77.

Millis, Walter. *The Martial Spirit.* New York, 1931.

Milton, Joyce. *The Yellow Kids: Foreign Correspondents in the Heyday of Yellow Journalism.* New York, 1989.

Miranda, Luis Rodolfo. *Antorchas de la Libertad.* Havana, 1945.

Miró Argenter, José. *Cuba: Crónicas de la guerra, las campañas de invasión y de occidente, 1895–1896.* Havana, 1945.

Monfort y Prats, Manuel. *Historia de la Guerra de Cuba.* San Juan, P.R., 1896.

Montaldo y Peró, Federico. *Guía práctica, higiénica, y médica del Europeo en los paises tórridos (Filipinas, Cuba, Puerto Rico, Fernando Póo, etc.).* Madrid, 1898.

Montero y Rapallo, Manuel. *Ensayo de estrategía naval.* Madrid, 1892.

Montesinos y Salas, Enrique. *Los yankees en Manzanillo.* Manzanillo, 1898.

Morales, Salvador. "Los trabajadores y la liberación nacional en Cuba." *Estudios de Historia Social* 45 (1988): 149–59.

Morales Lezcano, Victor. *Africanismo y orientalismo español en el siglo XIX.* Madrid, 1989.

Moran, Daniel, and Arthur Waldron, eds. *The People in Arms: Military Myth and National Mobilization since the French Revolution.* Cambridge, 2003.

Moreno, Francisco. *El país del chocolate (la inmoralidad en Cuba).* Madrid, 1887.

Moreno Fraginals, Manuel. *Cuba/España, España/Cuba: Historia común.* Barcelona, 1995.

———. *El ingenio.* 3 vols. Havana, 1978.

Moreno Fraginals, Manuel, and José Moreno Masó. *Guerra, migración y muerte (El ejército español en Cuba como vía migratoria).* Gijón, 1993.

Moreno Fraginals, Frank Moya Pons, and Stanley L. Engerman, eds. *Between Slavery and Free Labor: The Spanish-Speaking Caribbean in the Nineteenth Century.* Baltimore, 1985.

Morgan, H. Wayne. *America's Road to Empire: The War with Spain and Overseas Expansion.* New York, 1965.

Morote, Luis. *En la manigua.* Madrid, 1912.

———. *La moral de la derrota.* Madrid, 1997.

———. *La problemática de un republicano (1862–1923).* Madrid, 1976.

Müller y Tejeiro, José. *Combates y capitulación de Santiago de Cuba.* Madrid, 1898.

Muñiz de Quevedo, José. *Ajiaco: Apuntes de un soldado.* Madrid, 1898.

Musicant, Ivan. *Empire by Default: The Spanish-American War and the Dawn of the American Century.* New York, 1998.

Nadal, Jord. *El fracaso de la revolución industrial en España, 1814–1913.* Barcelona, 1975.

Nadal, Jord, and Gabriel Tortella, eds. *Agricultura, comercio colonial y crecimiento económico en la España contemporánea.* Barcelona, 1974.

Naranjo Orovio, Consuelo, and Tomás Mallo Gutiérrez, eds. *Cuba la perla de las Antillas: Actas de las I Jornadas sobre "Cuba y su Historia".* Madrid, 1994.

Naranjo Orovio, Consuelo, Miguel A. Puig-Samper, and Luis Miguel García Mora, eds. *La nación soñada: Cuba, Puerto Rico y Filipinas ante el 98.* Madrid, 1996.

Navascués, Felipe de. *¡¡La próxima guerra!!* Madrid, 1895.

Nelan, Charles. *Cartoons of Our War with Spain.* New York, 1898.

Núñez, Clara Eugenia. *La fuente de la riqueza: Educación y desarrollo económico en la España contemporánea.* Madrid, 1992.

Núñez Florencio, Rafael. "Ejército y política bajo la Restauración." *Bulletin d'Histoire Contemporaine de l'Espagne* 16 (December 1992): 29–73.

———. *El Ejército español en el Desastre de 1898.* Madrid, 1997.

———. "Menos se perdió en Cuba." *Revista de libros* 21 (September 1998): 11–13.

———. *Militarismo y antimilitarismo en España (1888–1906).* Madrid, 1990.

———. "El presupuesto de la paz: Una polémica entre civiles y militares en la España finisecular." *Hispania* 49 (January–April 1989): 197–234.

———. "Las raíces de la Ley de Jurisdicciones: Los conflictos de competencia entre los tribunales civiles y militares en los años 90." In *Antes del "desastre": Orígenes y antecedentes de la crisis del 98,* edited by Juan Pablo Fusi and Juan Antonio Niño, 185–98. Madrid, 1996.

———. *Tal como éramos: España hace un siglo.* Madrid, 1998.

Offner, John L. *An Unwanted War.* Chapel Hill, 1992.

Ollero, F. *Teatro de guerra.* Madrid, 1898.

Ontañon, Eduardo. *Frascuelo ó el toreador.* Madrid, 1937.

Opatrn'y, Josef. *Antecedentes históricos de la formación de la nación cubana.* Prague, 1896.

Ortega y Gasset, José. *Textos sobre el 98: Escritos políticos (1908–1914).* Selección de Andrés de Blas. Introducción de Vicente Cacho Viu. Madrid, 1998.

Ortiz, Fernando. *Cuban Counterpoint: Tobacco and Sugar.* Durham, N.C., 1995.

Ovilo y Canales, Felipe. *La decadencia del ejército: Estudio de higiene militar.* Madrid, 1899.

Palazón Ferrando, Salvador, and Candelaria Saiz Pastor, eds., *La ilusión de un imperio: las relaciones económicas hispano-cubanas en el siglo XIX.* Alicante, 1998.

Palenque, Amado. *La campaña de invasión, 1895–1896.* Havana, 1988.

Pan-Montojo, Juan, ed. *Más se perdió en Cuba: España, 1898 y la crisis de fin de siglo.* Madrid, 1998.

Pando, Magdalen M. *Cuba's Freedom Fighter, Antonio Maceo, 1845–1896*. 1980. <<http://198.62.75.1/www2/fcf/antonio.maceo.ff.html>>. September 13, 2002.

Pando Despierto, Juan. "La defensa de Cascorro." *Historia 16* 254 (1997): 8–16.

———. *El mundo militar a través de la fotografía*. 3 vols. Madrid, 1994.

Pando y Sánchez, Luis Manuel. *Documento presentado al senado*. Madrid, 1899.

Pardo Bazán, Emilia. "Los Toros." In *La vida contemporánea (1896–1915)*, edited by Carmen Bravo-Vilasante, 31–37. Madrid, 1972.

Pardo González, Cándido. *La brigada de Guantánamo en la Guerra Hispano-Americana: Notas de mis cartera de camapaña*. 1930. Archivo General Militar de Madrid, Microfilm, roll 60.

Patterson, Thomas G. "United States Intervention in Cuba, 1898: Interpretations of the Spanish-American-Cuban-Filipino War." *The History Teacher* 29 (May 1996): 341–61.

Payne, Stanley G. *Politics and the Military in Modern Spain*. Stanford, 1967.

Paz Sánchez, Manuel, José Fernández Fernández, and Nelson López Novegil. *El bandolerismo en Cuba*. Santa Cruz de Tenerife, 1993.

Pérez, Louis A., Jr. *Cuba and the United States: Ties of Singular Intimacy*. Athens, Ga., 1990.

———. *Cuba between Empires, 1878–1902*. Pittsburgh, 1989.

———. *Cuba: Between Reform and Revolution*. New York, 1995.

———. *Lords of the Mountain: Social Banditry and Peasant Protest in Cuba, 1878–1918*. Pittsburgh, 1989.

———. *On Becoming Cuban: Identity, Nationality, and Culture*. Chapel Hill, 1999.

———. *The War of 1898: The United States and Cuba in History and Historiography*. Chapel Hill, 1998.

———, ed. *José Martí in the United States: The Florida Experience*. Tempe, Arizona, 1995.

———. *Slaves, Sugar, and Colonial Society: Travel Accounts of Cuba, 1801–1899*. Wilmington, Del., 1992.

Pérez Castañeda, Tiburcio. *La explosión del Maine y la guerra de los Estados Unidos con España*. Havana, 1925.

Pérez Delgado, Rafael. *1898, el año del desastre*. Madrid, 1976.

Pérez Garzón, Juan Sisinio. *Luis Morote: La problemática de un republicano (1862–1923)*. Madrid, 1976.

Pérez Guzmán, Francisco. *Herida profunda*. Havana, 1998.

Pérez Guzmán, Francisco, and Violeta Serrano Rubio. *Máximo Gómez: Aproximación a su cronología, 1836–1905*. Havana, 1986.

Pérez Rioja, Antonio. *Liquidaciones coloniales. La tragedia de América. Cómo empieza y cómo acaba*. Madrid, 1899.

Pérez de la Riva, Juan. *La Isla de Cuba en el Siglo XIX vista por los extranjeros*. Havana, 1981.

Pérez de la Riva, Juan, and Blanca Morejón. "La población de Cuba, la Guerra de Independencia, y la inmigración del siglo XX." *Revista de la Biblioteca Nacional José Martí*, May–August, 1971, 17–27.

Pertierra Serra, Enrique. *Italianos por la libertad de Cuba*. Havana, 2000.

Photographic History of the Spanish-American War. New York, 1898.

Piedra Martel, Manuel. *Campañas de Maceo en la última Guerra de Independencia*. Havana, 1946.

———. *Memorias de un mambí*. Havana, 1966.

Pino-Santos, Oscar. *Cuba: Historia y Economía*. Havana, 1983.

"Poesías patrióticas." Ms. 21356/3, Biblioteca Nacional, Madrid.

Polavieja, Camilo G. *Relación documentada de mi política en Cuba, lo que ví, lo que hice, lo que anuncié*. Madrid, 1898.

Portuondo del Prado, Fernando. *Historia de Cuba*. Havana, 1965.

Post, Charles Johnson. *The Little War of Private Post*. Boston, 1960.

Poyo, Gerald E. *"With All and for the Good of All": The Emergence of Popular Nationalism in the Cuban Communities of the United States, 1848–1898*. Durham, N.C., 1989.

Prados de la Escosura, Leandro. *De imperio a nación: Crecimiento y atraso económico en España (1780–1930)*. Madrid, 1988.

Pratt, Julius. "American Business and the Spanish American War." *Hispanic American Historical Review* 14 (May 1934): 163–201.

———. *Expansionists of 1898: The Acquisition of Hawaii and the Spanish Islands*. Gloucester, Mass., 1959.

Raga Gil, José Tomás. "Cánovas ante la Gloriosa." In *Cánovas y su época*. Vol. 1, edited by Alfonso Bullón de Mendoza and Luis E. Togores, 33–46. Madrid, 1999.

Ramon y Cajal, Santiago. *Recuerdos de mi vida*. 2 vols. Madrid, 1901.

Rea, George Bronson. *Facts and Fakes about Cuba*. New York, 1897.

Reparaz, Gonzalo. *La guerra de Cuba*. Madrid, 1896.

Reverter Delmas, Emilio. *Cuba española. Reseña histórica de la insurrección cubana en 1895*. 6 vols. Barcelona, 1897–99.

———. *La guerra de Cuba*. Barcelona, 1899.

Rickover, Hyman G. *How the Battleship "Maine" Was Destroyed*. Washington, D.C., 1976.

Ringrose, David. *Madrid and the Spanish Economy (1560–1850)*. Berkeley, 1983.

Rioja, A. *En la manigua: El Guao, Ceja del Negro y Guayabito*. Havana, 1896.

Robles Muñoz, Cristóbal. *1898: Diplomacia y Opinión*. Madrid, 1991.

———. "La lucha de los independentistas cubanos y las relaciones de España con Estados Unidos." *Hispania* 50 (January–April 1990): 159–202.

———. "La oposición al activismo independentista cubano." *Hispania* 48 (January–April 1988): 227–88.

Rodríguez Demorizi, Emilio. *Papeles dominicanos de Máximo Gómez*. Ciudad Trujillo, 1954.

Rodríguez González, Agustín Ramón. "De la utopia al desastre. Un análisis de la política naval de la Restauración." *Bulletin d'Histoire Contemporaine de l'Espagne* 16 (December 1992): 74–99.

———. *Isaac Peral: Historia de una frustración*. Cartagena, 1993.

———. *Operaciones de la guerra de 1898, un revisión crítica*. Madrid, 1998.

———. *Política naval de la Restauración (1875–1898)*. Madrid, 1988.

Rodríguez Mendoza, Emilio. *En la manigua*. Valparaiso, 1900.

Rodríguez Puértolas, Julio, ed. *El desastre en sus textos: La crisis del 98 vista por los escritores coetáneos*. Madrid, 1999.

Rodríguez Rodríguez, Amalia. *Algunos documentos políticos de Máximo Gómez*. Havana, 1962.

Rodríguez-Solis, Francisco. *Los guerrilleros de 1808*. 2 vols. Madrid, 1887.

Roig, Pedro. *La guerra de Martí*. Miami, 1984.

Roig de Leuchsenring, Emilio. *Análisis y consecuencias de la Intervención norteamericana en los asuntos interiores de Cuba*. Havana, 1923.

———. *Cuba no debe su independencia a los Estados Unidos*. Havana, 1950.

———. *La guerra libertadora cubana de los treinta años, 1868–1898*. Havana, 1952.

———. *Weyler in Cuba*. Havana, 1947.

Roldán de Montaud, Inés. "La hacienda cubana en el período de entreguerras (1878–1895)." In *Economía y Colonias en la España del 98*, edited by Pedro Tedde, 123–59. Madrid, 1999.

Roloff y Mialofsky, Carlos. *Indice alfabético y defunciones del Ejército Libertador de Cuba*. Havana, 1901.

Romanones, Alvaro Figueroa y Torres Conde de. *Sagasta; O, El político*. Madrid, 1930.

Rosell y Malpica, Eduardo. *Diario del Teniente Colonel Eduardo Rosell y Malpica (1895–1897)*. 2 vols. Havana, 1949.

Ruíz-Manjón, Octavio, and Alicia Langa, eds. *Los significados del 98: La sociedad española en la génesis del siglo XX*. Madrid, 1999.

Russell, Henry B., Redfield Proctor, and John M. Thurston. *An Illustrated History of Our War with Spain*. Hartford, 1898.

Saíz Cidoncha, Carlos. *Guerrillas en Cuba y otros paises de ibero-américa*. Madrid, 1974.

Saladariagas y Zayas, Enrique. *A Tribute to Finlay*. Havana, 1952.

Salas, Delfín. *La Guerra de Cuba, 1898*. Madrid, 1989.

Sánchez-Albornoz, Nicolás, ed., *The Economic Modernization of Spain, 1830–1930*. New York, 1987.

Santaner Mari, Joan. *General Weyler*. Palma de Mallorca, 1985.

Sanz, L. "Cuadro en el que se manifiesta los Hospitales por Departamentos." Havana, 1879. Ms. in History of Medicine Archives, Bethesda, Md.

Schmidt-Nowara, Christopher. *Empire and Antislavery: Spain, Cuba, and Puerto Rico, 1833–1874*. Pittsburgh, 1999.

Schwartz, Rosalie. *Lawless Liberators: Political Banditry and Cuban Independence*. Durham, N.C., 1989.

Scott, Rebecca. "Defining the Boundaries of Freedom in the World of Cane: Cuba, Brazil, and Louisiana after Emancipation." *American Historical Review* 99 (February 1994): 70–102.

———. *Slave Emancipation in Cuba: The Transition to Free Labor, 1860–1899*. Princeton, N.J., 1985.

Sepúlveda Muñoz, Isidro. "¡Viva Cuba Libre!: Análisis crítico del nacionalismo martiano." In *Antes del "desastre": Orígenes y antecedentes de la crisis del 98*, edited by Juan Pablo Fusi and Antonio Niño, 263–77. Madrid, 1996.

Serrano, Carlos. "1898, España en cuestión." *Estudios de Historia Social* 47 (1988): 387–93.

———. *Final del imperio: España, 1895–1898*. Madrid, 1984.

———. *Militarismo y civilismo en la España contemporánea*. Madrid, 1984.

———. *1900 en España*. Madrid, 1991.

———. "Prófugos y desertores en la guerra de Cuba." *Estudios de Historia Social* 22–23 (July–December 1982): 253–78.

———. *Le tour du peuple: Crise nationale, mouvements populaires et populisme en Espagne (1890–1910)*. Madrid, 1987.

Serrano Sanz, José María. *El viraje proteccionista en la Restauración. La política comercial española, 1875–1895*. Madrid, 1987.

Siles, José. *Memorias de un patriota: Relatos de guerra*. Madrid, 1905.

Smith, Anthony. *Theories of Nationalism*. Oxford, 1983.

Smith, Joseph. *The Spanish-American War: Conflict in the Caribbean and the Pacific, 1895–1902*. New York, 1994.

Soldevilla, Francisco. *Historia de España*. 10 vols. Barcelona, 1954.

Souza y Rodríguez, Benigno. *Ensayo histórico sobre la invasión*. Havana, 1948.

———. *Máximo Gómez, el generalísimo*. Havana, 1936.

Steele, James Williams. *Cuban Sketches*. New York, 1881.

Sternberg, George Miller. *Sanitary Lessons of the War and Other Papers*. New York, 1977.

Strode, George K., ed. *Yellow Fever*. New York, 1951.

Tedde, Pedro, ed. *Economía y colonias en la España del 98*. Madrid, 1999.

Thomas, Hugh. *Cuba; or, The Pursuit of Freedom*. New York, 1998.

Thompson, Edward P. *The Making of the English Working Class*. New York, 1966.

Toledo Sande, Luis. *Cesto de llamas: Biografía de José Martí*. Havana, 1996.

Tomich, Dale. "World Slavery and Caribbean Capitalism: The Cuban Sugar Industry, 1760–1868." *Theory and Society* 20 (June 1991): 297–319.

Tone, John Lawrence. *The Fatal Knot: The Guerrilla War in Navarre and the Defeat of Napoleon in Spain*. Chapel Hill, 1994.

———. *La guerrilla española y la derrota de Napoleón*. Madrid, 1999.

———. "How the Mosquito (Man) Liberated Cuba." *History and Technology* 18 (2002): 277–308.

———. "The Machete and the Liberation of Cuba." *Journal of Military History* 62 (January 1998): 7–28.

Torre del Río, Rosario de la. "La neutralidad británica en la guerra hispano-norteamericana de 1898." Ph.D. dissertation, Universidad Complutense, Madrid, 1985.

———. "El noventa y ocho español." In *Siglo XX, Historia universal. Las vísperas de nuestro siglo: Sociedad, política y cultura en el 98*. Madrid, 1983.

———. *Inglaterra y España en 1898*. Madrid, 1988.

Torriente, Cosme de la. *Fin de la dominación de España en Cuba (12 de Agosto de 1898)*. Havana, 1948.

Tortella, Gabriel. *El desarrollo de la España contemporánea: Historia económica de los siglos XIX y XX*. Madrid, 1994.

Touatre, Just. *Yellow Fever. Clinical Notes*. New Orleans, 1898.

Trask, David F. *The War with Spain in 1898*. New York, 1981.

Tuñón de Larra, Manuel, José Andrés Gallego, and José Luís Abellán, eds. *El desastre del 98*. Madrid, 1985.

Tussell, Javier. *Antonio Maura: Una biografía política*. Madrid, 1994.

Uría González, Jorge, et al. *Asturias y Cuba en torno al 98: Sociedad, economía, política y cultura en la crisis de entresiglos*. Barcelona, 1994.

Urquía y Redecilla, Juan [Capitán Verdades, pseud.]. *La guerra hispano-americana*. Barcelona, 1899.

———. *Historia negra: Relato de los escándalos ocurridos en nuestras ex-colonias durante las últimas guerras*. Barcelona, 1899.

U.S. Adjutant-General's Office. *Notes and Tables on Organization and Establishment of the Spanish Army in the Peninsula and Colonies*. Washington, 1898.

U.S. Havana Yellow Fever Commission, "Official Reports to the Commission, 1879." Ms. in History of Medicine Archives, Bethesda, Md.

U.S. Naval Institute. *Log of the Gloucester.* Annapolis, 1899.

U.S. Navy Department. *The Spanish American War: A Collection of Documents Relative to the Squadron Operations in the West Indies. Arranged by Rear Admiral Pascual Cervera y Topete.* Washington, D.C., 1899.

Valdés Domínguez, Fermín. *Diario de soldado.* 4 vols. Havana, 1972–74.

Varela Ortega, José. "Aftermath of Splendid Disaster: Spanish Politics before and after the Spanish American War of 1898." *Journal of Contemporary History* 15 (1980): 317–44.

———. *Los amigos políticos. Partidos, elecciones y caciquismo en la Restauración.* Madrid, 1977.

Vehráhz, Mister. *Los Estados Unidos vencidos por España.* Toledo, 1899.

Villalba Muñoz, Luis. *La gran traición.* Barcelona, 1899.

Warner, Margaret. "Hunting the Yellow Fever Germ: The Principle and Practice of Etiological Proof in Late Nineteenth-Century America." *Bulletin of the History of Medicine* 59 (1985): 361–82.

Watts, Sheldon. *Epidemics and History: Disease, Power, and Imperialism.* New Haven, 1997.

Weyler y López de Puga, Valeriano. *En el archivo de mi abuelo: biografía del capitán general Weyler.* Madrid, 1946.

Weyler y Nicolau, Valeriano. *Mi mando en Cuba.* 5 vols. Madrid, 1910–11.

Wheeler, Joseph. *The Santiago Campaign 1898.* New York, 1898.

Wilkerson, Marcus M. *Public Opinion and the Spanish-American War: A Study in War Propaganda.* New York, 1932.

Williams, William A. "The Frontier Thesis and American Foreign Policy." *Pacific Historical Review* 24 (November 1955): 379–95.

Wilson, H. W. *The Downfall of Spain.* New York, 1971.

Wisan, Joseph E. *The Cuban Crisis as Reflected in the New York Press.* New York, 1935.

Woolf, Stuart, ed. *Nationalism in Europe, 1815 to the Present: A Reader.* London, 1996.

Young, Marilyn Blatt, ed. *American Expansionism: The Critical Issues.* Boston, 1973.

Zanetti Lecuona, Oscar. "Las relaciones comerciales hispano-cubanas en el siglo XIX." In *La ilusión de un imperio: las relaciones económicas hispano-cubanas en el siglo XIX,* edited by Salvador Palazón Ferrando and Candelaria Saiz Pastor, 95–117. Alicante, 1998.

Zanetti Lecuona, Oscar, and Alejandro García. *Sugar and Railroads: A Cuban History, 1837–1959.* Translated by Franklin W. Knight and Mary Todd. Chapel Hill, 1998.

Index

Sigsbee, Charles, 241–42

Slavery, 91; and cimarrones, 21, 73; abolition, 25–26

Spain: politics, 16, 18, 103–4; colonial administration in Cuba, 17, 18, 26; economy, 18, 104, 227–28; taxation of Cuba, 23; emigration to Cuba, 27, 40, 93; espionage, 82; militarism, 105–6; black legend, 218–19, 267; Liberal critique of Weyler, 233–34; and Spanish view of Americans, 254–55; and support for war with United States, 255–59; diplomatic isolation in 1898, 256

Spanish army: casualties, 9, 97, 128–29, 278; organization and personnel, 24, 43, 97; conditions and morale, 24, 75, 89, 98–102, 107–9, 115, 183, 258; strategy and tactics, 76, 78, 79, 80, 113–16, 131–32, 160–64; weaponry and supplies, 80, 130; political role in Spain, 103–6; attempts to reform, 106–7; training, 111–12; garrisons, 113–18; hospitals, 133–35; poor condition in 1898, 269–70, 275; poisoned by experience in Cuba, 286–87

Spanish navy, 83–84; failure to modernize, 261, 266–67; and jeune école, 262; torpedoes, 262–67

Suárez Inclán, Julián, 168–69

Suárez Valdés, Alvaro, 92; informally reconcentrates civilians, 205

Sugar: development in Cuba, 15–16; and slavery, 16, 20; beet, 26–27; planters, 59–60

Tamayo, Esteban, 168

Tampa, 13, 36, 82, 162

Taxation, 101; as cause of Cuban rebellion, 17, 23

Ten Years' War, 1, 3, 25, 31, 49, 57, 61, 70, 113, 120, 127–28, 155, 157, 180

Tobacco, 36, 161–63

Toral, José, 281–82

Total war: Cuban practice of, 57–68, 90–91, 125, 150–51, 200; and use of terror, 140, 147–48, 234; Weyler's strategy of, 163; in Pinar del Río, 198

Trochas, 157; Júcaro-Morón, 1, 24, 90, 116, 118–19, 167; Mariel-Majana, 167–68, 170, 174, 176, 180, 182, 184–85; reconstruction of, 188–89; becomes impassable, 191

Turno pacífico. See Spain: politics

United States: expansionism, 12, 245–49; relations with Cuba, 15, 19, 27–28; intervention in Cuba, 239, 244–45; deterioration of Cuban relations, 280

U.S. Army, 258–59; invasion force, 276

U.S. Navy, 260, 267

Veguitas, 73, 76

Venta de Pino, battle of, 62

Vietnam, 4, 11, 75, 155, 286

Volunteers, Cuban pro-Spanish, 9, 32–33, 93, 114, 118, 139–41, 148–49, 155, 168, 170; and control of Cienfuegos, 172

Weyler, Valeriano, 4, 109, 113, 151, 187; and reconcentration, 8; ignores use of mosquito netting, 76; youth, 153–54; contracts yellow fever, 154; in Carlist War, 156; in the Philippines, 157; arrival in Havana in 1896, 159; announces strategy, 160; brutality in Catalonia, 162; destroys tobacco and sugar industries, 162–63; reputation for cruelty, 164; energizes occupation forces, 165–66; survives Cuban assassination attempt, 173–74; dubbed General Almost Pacified, 189; poor at public relations, 219; accused of rape, 221; relieved of command, 234

Wheeler, Joseph, 277

Women and war, 142–43; and Amazon myth, 166
Woodford, Stewart L., 235, 253

Ya-lu, battle of, 262–63
Yara, Grito de, 24
Yellow fever. See Diseases: yellow fever
Yellow press, 219, 241–42

Zanjón, Peace of, 25, 57, 120, 157
Zaragoza, 31, 39; as model for Santiago, 257–58
Zayas, Bruno, 174